Tina Macaulay

WORKING WITH FAMILIES

WORKING WITH FAMILIES

Perspectives for Early Childhood Professionals

Rena Shimoni
Mount Royal College

Joanne Baxter
Mount Royal College

Addison
Wesley
Longman

Toronto

Canadian Cataloguing in Publication Data

Shimoni, Rena, 1948–
Working with families : perspectives for early childhood professionals

(Addison Wesley Longman series in early childhood education)
2nd ed.
Includes index.
ISBN 0-201-69781-5

1. Family social work. 2. Social work with children. 3. Family. I. Baxter, Joanne M. (Joanne Marlena), 1955– . II. Title. III. Series.

LB1139.23.S55 2001   362.8   C99-932924-3

ISBN 0-201-69781-5

Vice President, Editorial Director: Michael Young
Executive Editor: David Stover
Senior Marketing Manager: Sophia Fortier
Associate Editor: Susan Ratkaj
Production Editor: Joe Zingrone
Copy Editor: Ann McInnis
Production Coordinator: Peggy Brown
Page Layout: Heidi Palfrey
Art Director: Mary Opper
Interior Design: Dave McKay
Cover Design: Lisa Lapointe
Cover Image: PhotoDisc

3 4 5   05 04 03 02

Printed and bound in Canada.

Contents

About This Book

More often than not, people entering the early childhood field see children as the prime focus of their work. As they learn about their profession and begin to practise, they begin to realize that, in order to understand children, they need to understand the families of these children. Moreover, they learn that the well-being of children and the well-being of families are inextricably connected, and that early childhood professionals have an ethical responsibility to support families and promote their involvement in the care and education of their children. That being so, most training programs for early childhood professionals include at least one course on families. Scholars from many disciplines write about families—sociologists, psychologists, anthropologists, to name but a few—and each discipline enriches the knowledge base with its own particular perspective. After we had searched for a suitable text on families with an early childhood perspective, Addison Wesley Longman honoured us by requesting that we write such a text, focusing on practical issues that early childhood professionals would be interested in.

Both of us have come into the early childhood profession with a background in other "helping professions," psychology and social work. Both of us have practical experience working with families in a number of frameworks and have continued to be involved in the field as well as in the classroom. In the years that we have taught courses on the family, we have collected stories and anecdotes about the families of our students, who have repeatedly told us that they are different from "textbook" families. We hope that, in this book, we have combined our theoretical knowledge with our professional experience, and added to them the wisdom gained from listening to our students.

The book is divided into three parts. Part 1, "Understanding Families," provides the conceptual framework for understanding families. Part 2, "Facing Family Challenges," consists of ten chapters devoted to challenges families face today. Early childhood professionals are very likely, in the course of their career, to work with children who have dealt with a death in the family or a divorce. Many children are from single-parent families, families who live in poverty, or families in which one of the members has special needs. Understanding these families' challenges will help the early childhood professional offer support in a nonjudgmental and empathic manner. Finally, Part 3, "Working with Families," offers a framework for early childhood professionals to apply their understanding of family in their efforts to involve families in the care and education of the children. This begins with an overview of parental involvement from a theoretical perspective, then proceeds to consider practices with parents from a family-centred approach.

We hope that our readers will share our interest in and respect for the diversity among us that is rooted in the various cultures from which we come. Although in the last few years there has been improvement, much of what has been written about families in social-science textbooks has focused on White, middle-class, English-speaking North Americans. Sometimes, in an effort to portray people of different ethnic and cultural origins, writers relay information in a manner that may in fact reinforce stereotypes. We have attempted to portray diversity by including clips of interviews with many of our students. There is a wide range in age, social class, cultural, ethnic, and religious representation in these interviews. However, it must be remembered that the students are telling their own personal stories and speaking of their own personal beliefs and attitudes. Although they all recognize that their heritage has affected their beliefs, they do not necessarily represent a particular group or culture.

Our thanks are due to many people who contributed to our understanding of family. First and foremost, our own families—our mothers and fathers, siblings, and grandparents; our husbands, Dave Baxter and Yakhin Shimoni, and our daughters, Orit, Galit, and Tammy Shimoni, and Chelsea and Carissa Baxter. Our colleagues at Mount Royal College have, as always, offered support and ideas. Most of all, our students over the years have given us a window into the lives of many different kinds of families, so that we could enrich our understanding and sensitivity. To all, a warm thank-you. A well-deserved thank-you is also extended to the crew at Pearson Education Canada, for their encouragement and not so subtle prodding, but mostly for their faith in our ability. Lastly, though perhaps unconventionally, we want to thank each other. This is the second book that we have co-authored. We have gone through many stages of work together, and have experienced the excitement, disappointments, stresses, and ultimate satisfaction of arriving at a worthwhile final product. We have now been collaborating for many years, as co-teachers, co-authors, and friends, and hope that we will continue to do so for many years to come.

We would like to express our appreciation to Pearson Education Canada for inviting us to prepare the second edition of *Working with Families*. We have been delighted with the very positive feedback we have received about the book from students and instructors, and hope that the additions and changes we have made will meet the expectations of our readers. As with any revised edition, we have gone through the text and added newer references, and adapted sections that required change as new knowledge has emerged. In addition, we have added two new sections, based on feedback from reviewers. The most common requests were for a chapter on gay and lesbian parents and on adoptive families. We decided to combine these topics into one chapter, and view them from the perspective of fostering resilience in children. Another popular request was for a chapter on working with children and families of new Canadians who are immigrants and refugees. Authentic writing requires, in our view, that writers have direct experience with the subjects about which they write. Joanne has been actively involved in the reorganization of Children's Services and Supported Child Care in the Calgary region. This work has brought her in contact with the issues in the new chapters as she works closely with a broad range of children's services in the community. Rena has been a program developer and evaluator for a range of programs for new Canadian families through the Calgary Immigrant Aid Society. We hope that our experience in these realms brings life to these new chapters. As we are beginning to gain more experience in working with Aboriginal communities, we promise that, if a third edition comes to be, we will include a chapter on this topic. As well, a chapter would focus on parents who present special needs—parents with developmental delays, parents with addictions and parents coping with chronic physical or mental illnesses. As we said in the first edition, it is our students from whom we learn the most. As we continue to teach about families, we learn more and more about families from the stories our students tell us about their own lives, and about the lives of the families with whom they work.

part 1

Understanding Families

Part 1 provides a framework for understanding families. Chapter 1 discusses the concept of family and highlights diversity in today's families. In Chapter 2, we study changes that are occurring in the roles of family members. Chapter 3 discusses developmental transitions for children, parents, and the family unit.

These chapters will enhance readers' understanding of families in general. Most people view and make judgments about families based on their own experiences. They often view differences as undesirable or somehow wrong. However, every individual will have different experiences and expectations about families and how they should function. It is our intention that, as early childhood professionals read through these three chapters, they will reflect on their own families and their own experiences and become aware of how these have affected their lives as adults. In conjunction with the development of this self-awareness, we hope that caregivers will also reflect on the diversity that exists within and among families. In the end, they should come away with an increased awareness, understanding, and appreciation of the children and families with whom they work.

Defining and Describing Families

1

Objectives

- **To discuss the concept of family.**

- **To highlight the diversity in today's families.**

- **To discuss the relevance of the study of family for professionals who work with children.**

At a Grade 12 graduation ceremony, a five-member rock group provided musical entertainment. After an enthusiastic round of applause, the leader of the group bowed and said to the audience, "Now I'd like to introduce you to my family." While his parents in the audience were about to stand up proudly, the young man proceeded to introduce his fellow band members as his family. Proud as they were of their son, his parents still looked a trifle disappointed.

Why Study Family?

Each of us comes from a family of some sort, and many of us have already started or will go on to create our own families. Because of our experiences, the word "family" brings forth certain pictures and associations in our minds. Some of these pictures we will share in common with many other people; some of them will be unique to ourselves. Families are being defined and redefined continually, both by those who study people and society (such as psychologists and sociologists) and by those who influence laws and policies that affect families (such as spousal and child benefits, and maternity and paternity leave policies).

It is inevitable that professionals who work with young children also work with their families, be it directly or indirectly. Just as children in day care are affected by their families and have an influence on the dynamics of the day-care program, so the children return home from day care to influence and affect the dynamics of their families.

Working effectively with children and families requires an understanding and appreciation of families in all their diversity. We need to know what is happening to families in our society. Are North American families falling apart? Will the family, as some "prophets" claim (Kain, 1990), totally disintegrate as an institution, or is the institution called "family" simply undergoing healthy changes? Opponents of day care claim that a universal child-care policy undermines the family. Day-care advocates claim that quality day care in fact supports the family. Understanding the issues faced by North American families is essential for early childhood professionals who are committed to the well-being of children.

In any class of preschool children today, you are likely to find at least one child whose family is undergoing a divorce, in the process of becoming a blended family, or experiencing the hardships of unemployment or poverty. Data collected from the 1996 Census by Statistics Canada shows significant changes in the make-up of Canadian families since 1991. For example, in 1996, common-law and single-parent families made up 26 percent of Canadian families. Between 1991 and 1996, the rate of increase of common-law families was 16 times that of married couple families (*The Daily*, Tuesday, October 14, 1997). In some cases, early childhood professionals will have children who have witnessed or directly experienced violence and abuse. Professionals who work with children must understand how these phenomena affect the child, the parents, and the family unit. A first step in developing rapport with families is the ability to empathize—to be able to imagine what it feels like to be in another person's situation. Only with this understanding and empathy will early childhood professionals be able to support the children and, either directly or indirectly, the families they come from.

We are privileged to live in a multicultural society. Each cultural group brings with it its own traditions, beliefs, and values regarding childrearing and, either consciously or unconsciously, its own definition of the family. We can learn much from other cultures and thereby add to our understanding of children (and ourselves). We must be sensitive to cultural norms and rules if we want to ensure that children's experiences at day care or nursery school are not contrary to the beliefs and norms of their families. Yet it is vital not to stereotype cultural groups and to recognize the wide diversity that exists among families within the same cultural group. It is important to realize that culture and religion are often interpreted and reflected differently by each family and each family member. One way to avoid making stereotypical assumptions is to ask people directly about their beliefs, customs, and traditions. We have done this, and throughout the book we have provided examples to describe the perspectives of people from different countries and cultures and with different religious orientations. They do not speak as representatives of their ethnic group or culture, but rather as individuals whose ideas about families have been strongly (but not exclusively) influenced by their cultural heritage.

When good relationships exist between the families of the children in early childhood settings and the caregiver who works directly with those children, there is increased satisfaction at home and at the centre. Parents can be outspoken and effective advocates for day care, and in many ways they can provide as much support to the centre as the caregivers provide to the family. The children, as well, benefit from positive relations between staff and parents. There is much we can learn about families that will assist us in developing and maintaining positive relations with them.

One of the hallmarks of an effective early childhood professional is self-awareness. Over and over again, we learn that before we can be effective in helping others, we must have a good understanding of our self (Brammer, 1988). At the root of understanding ourselves is understanding the families we came from. Therefore, any study of the family has to involve some reflection on the way that this new knowledge "fits" with our own experience of family. We should gain a deeper understanding of what affected our own family as we were growing up, and this should help clarify our own values regarding family. This process, hopefully, will contribute to our personal as well as professional development.

Perspectives

Alemu Ayallel is a 40-year-old man who comes from Ethiopia. He describes himself as an Orthodox Christian.

"I arrived in Canada from Ethiopia in 1988. I am married and have one daughter, aged 7. I was unable to return to my country due to the political climate there. I had nowhere else to go; I either had to stay in Sudan in a refugee camp or come to a place where I could be accepted on a humanitarian basis. Fortunately, I had a cousin in Canada who could sponsor me. Because of the civil war in Ethiopia, my extended family has been affected by being dispersed to many places, and I don't even know where many of them are today, or if they are alive.

"I came from an old country with old traditions. In that culture, the mother's role is to nurture her children and stay at home. The father is the breadwinner; he is the guardian of the family, and the brother is socialized to become the father figure later on. He is given responsibility in the family.

"Grandparents are treated with a great deal of respect. If someone rejects or disrespects their grandparents, they would be considered an outsider by their community. Grandparents have the power and control in family decisions. The paternal grandparents have more influence than the maternal grandparents. While many marriages are arranged, not all are; however, the wife would need to be accepted by the husband's parents and extended family. Marriage in our country is not only a relationship between husband and wife, but a relationship between two sets of extended families. These relationships have a great influence on the married couple and, therefore, it is extremely important that the extended families accept each other.

"The traditional family life that I described above does not relate to all parts of my country. In many urban areas, the lifestyle is very different.

"The roles in my family here have changed somewhat. I now contribute to household chores, and my wife works outside the home, so there are two breadwinners. Decision making is mutual. I don't have a son, but if I did, I would try to treat him more on an equal basis than what has been traditional for me.

"I am quite comfortable with these changing values. I think that I would expect more discipline and respect for parents than is common today. I am uncomfortable with violence and open sexuality in the media. All these things I feel are disrespectful to the family. I believe that we are still far away from full acceptance and integration of people of colour in Canadian society, and I want to instill in my daughter a sense of pride in her roots and her heritage."

Personal Perceptions of Family

Our own definition of family is usually rooted in our own experience and is affected little by the latest sociological, psychological, and legal definitions. As professionals, however, it is important that we be aware of the current definitions and debates about what constitutes a family. This knowledge, combined with an awareness of our own beliefs and feelings about family, will enhance our ability to understand and work with families.

Definitions of Family

While probably few people in North America would disagree that a married couple living together with their biological children are a family, there is less consensus about other family constellations. Consider, for example, the following situations:

- If a couple has cohabited, had a child together, and then separated, are the parents and the child still considered a family?
- Is a cohabiting but unmarried heterosexual couple a family?
- Is a gay couple who live with the biological child of one of the partners a family?
- Is a child who was never formally adopted but has grown up with a couple and their biological children a member of that family?

The answer to some of these questions will be: It depends. It depends on whether one is considering the concept of family as it relates to the emotional bonds between members (for example, the rock group who considered themselves a family) or whether one is considering legal aspects of the definition (as they apply, for example, to benefits, parental leave policies, and other matters). The answer to these questions will in turn depend on the time and place they are asked. For example, gay couples can be legally married in some countries. Although gay couples are gradually gaining more acceptance in North American society, they still meet with much opposition. This becomes particularly evident in custody disputes, when the gay parent generally receives less support than the heterosexual parent (Fraser, Fish, & Mackenzie, 1995). Cohabiting couples were not legally accepted as families a decade ago, while today there is movement in that direction. This movement is reflected in changes in tax laws that give cohabiting couples the same benefits as married couples.

The complexity of some of these issues is illustrated in the following case.

Scenario

What Are the Criteria of Paternity?

Dominique is a 26-year-old woman who decided to raise a child on her own and became pregnant through artificial insemination. In the early months of her pregnancy she met and fell in love with Brian, who moved into her apartment a month before the baby was born. They were not legally married, although they made a serious commitment to staying together. Brian took an active role in caring for the baby for its first two months of life. Since Dominique wanted to return to work after six weeks, Brian applied for a paternity leave to enable him to stay home and care for the baby. Emotionally, he felt that he was the baby's father, though legally and biologically, he was not.

The response to Brian's request for a paternity leave will depend largely on how the person making the decision defines the concept of family. In fact, the way in which a society defines family will be the basis for many kinds of decisions that affect many different people. For example:

- How much will you pay in taxes?
- Will you get a student loan?
- Who is your legal heir?
- Who will be given custody of your children should you suddenly die?
- How big a social assistance cheque are you entitled to?
- Can you share your pension?

The answer to all these questions depends on official definitions of the family (Theilheimer, 1992).

Sociological Definitions of Family

Sociologists have tended to define families based on the function they fulfill in society, the primary function being the continuance of that society. So family has been defined as "whatever system a society uses to support and control human reproduction and sexual interaction" (Cox, 1987). Another definition states that family is a set of persons related to each other by blood, marriage, or adoption, and which constitutes a social system whose structure is specified by familial positions, and whose basic function in society is replacement (Cox, 1987). One leading sociologist has defined the family as "an institution found in several variant forms, that provides children with a legitimate position in society and with the nurturance that will enable them to function" (Duberman, 1977: 10).

An Inclusive Definition of Family

While similarities do exist in the way the family has been described, it is clear that there is no one "right" way of defining families, and that there is little probability that scholars will ever come to a consensus on the topic (Levin & Trost, 1992). However, it is important to have a working definition of the family that reflects the realities of life in North America, rather than one particular group's ideal. The Vanier Institute of the Family (Glossop, 1992) argues that families should be defined by what they do rather than what they look like (i.e., the emphasis is on function more than structure). In its definition, therefore, the Institute has attempted to be as inclusive as possible. Read the Institute's definition in the box on the next page and consider whether the above descriptions of diverse kinds of families would be included in it.

The fact that the Vanier Institute's definition does not require that each item apply to every family makes it more inclusive. Two people who live together by mutual consent, take care of each other, and show affection to each other could meet the requirements of this definition, as could the foster sisters described in the next scenario.

This brief overview of definitions of family helps us to understand the diversity that exists in perceptions of what a family is and should widen our own perspective. It is essential for societies to have a working definition of family to help guide social policies. Also, early childhood professionals working with families need to recognize the diversity of families and work towards an inclusive definition. We need, perhaps, to work harder at "embracing, encouraging, or supporting the many different kinds of families that exist today . . . (rather than) fighting over what constitutes a legitimate family" (Sweet, 1992).

> **The Vanier Institute of the Family's Working Definition of Family**
>
> Any combination of two or more persons who are bound together by ties of mutual consent, birth, and/or adoption/placement, and who, together, assume responsibilities for variant combinations of some of the following:
>
> - Physical maintenance and care of group members.
> - Addition of new members through procreation or adoption.
> - Socialization of children.
> - Social control of members.
> - Production, consumption, and distribution of goods and services.
> - Affective nurturance.
>
> Source: Vanier Institute of the Family, 1994.

Functions of Families

One perspective used to define the family is to focus on the role that it plays in society. This role is usually defined as replacing dying members of society by having children and socializing those children to be productive, contributing members of society. Many governments, for example, enthusiastically support families since they are seen as the best mechanism for keeping the population at desired levels. In Quebec, families are paid bonuses for having children, in addition to the federal family allowance program (Vanier Institute, 1994). This is not unusual in places where the population is decreasing. Families are the "mechanisms" for procreation and rearing future citizens, and therefore, in these cases, are supported by the government.

In our society, the limitations on the family in terms of childrearing or socialization are sometimes ambiguous because the family does not have exclusive jurisdiction over its children. Consider, for example, how much control the family has over its children compared with other institutions in society such as the judicial system and the schools. Some people believe that parents should be punished for their children's behaviour if it involves breaking the law. Others feel that parents cannot always be held responsible for their children's behaviour, and that the children should be directly accountable to society as a whole. Whose responsibility is it when children fail in school? Should the parents be responsible, or the society through its institution, the school? Should schools engage in sex education as a means of preventing teen pregnancies and sexually transmitted disease, or is sex education the exclusive domain of parents? These and other debates illustrate the sometimes hazy boundaries between family and society in matters of socialization.

Other functions of families have focused more on the needs of individual family members than on the role they play in society. These are discussed in terms of

a) meeting basic physiological needs such as food, water, and sex;

b) meeting safety needs;

c) meeting the need for love and belonging; and

d) meeting the need for self-esteem.

Families serve two purposes (Garanzini, 1995):

First, they provide children with an environment which helps them grow into productive and capable participants in the institutions which surround them. Second, they offer love and security in relationships which enable them to become loving persons. The first purpose of a family, then, is to help the child individuate, to give the child a sense of his or her capacity for autonomy and industry.... The second helps the child become a loving person by being the object of love and by witnessing the various aspects and hurdles involved in maintaining relationships of intimacy and dependency." (p. 16)

The definitions of family that focus on childrearing and social control are problematic because they exclude many people who would otherwise consider themselves families. For instance, all childless couples, married or unmarried, heterosexual or homosexual, would not meet the criteria of replacing dying members and socializing children. Many, however would fit the other criteria above.

Characteristics of Healthy Families

So far, the question "What is a family?" has been addressed and considered through different perspectives. We have been very neutral in these descriptions, and we have avoided making value judgments about what a "good family" is. This is a tricky question, and the answer we give to it is very much influenced by our own beliefs and values, and certainly affected by our cultural background. But tricky as the question may be, all professionals who work with families must ask themselves what they believe the components of a healthy family are, and they must combine their personal knowledge and beliefs with their professional knowledge about that subject. Below we consider some ideas about what constitutes a "healthy family," derived from Western psychology and sociology. It is important that these ideas be considered in light of the ideas about healthy families that stem from other cultures. Note that healthy families are described in terms of what happens within the family, rather than in terms of the structure of the family. That is, whether the family has a traditional structure (a married couple with children) or a very untraditional structure (even the rock group family described at the beginning of the chapter), these characteristics could apply.

Characteristics of Healthy Families

1. *Commitment.* Family members are committed to promoting each other's welfare and to investing time and energy in the family group.

2. *Appreciation.* Family members appreciate, support, and encourage each other.

3. *Effective communication patterns.* Family members spend time talking with each other and listening to each other. They solve problems effectively, and feel free to express ideas and emotions with each other.

4. *Spending time together.* Efforts are made to ensure that joint family times happen (meals, recreation, and chores). Time together is spent in "active interaction" (rather than in passive activities, such as watching television).

---

5. *Shared value system.* Family members share and base their actions on the same value system. This system could be based on religion, but this is not always the case.

6. *Coping with stress.* Families have to cope with stress. This includes being aware of the stressors that develop and working together to cope with these stressors.

7. *Balancing of needs.* A healthy family finds ways to balance the needs of the family as a group with the individual needs of its members. For example, while parents spend much time meeting the needs of their children, they also realize that they need to spend time together as a couple, and find time to develop their own interests as individuals. Also, parents understand that developing children need to spend time with peers, to make and have their own friends beyond the family.

This list is not definitive. It is provided as a framework for discussion. Some questions you may want to ask are:

- Does this list, or parts of it, relate to "real" or "ideal" families?
- Does this list, or parts of it, relate to all families, or is it culture biased?
- What would you add to this list, and why?
- What would you remove from this list, and why?
- Think of two or three families you know. Does the list above apply to them?

Diversity in North American Families

As you work out your own definition of family, consider the following scenario, in which a 22-year-old social work student tries to come to grips with what the word "family" has meant in her life.

Scenario

Who Is Family?

When I was a little girl, my parents took in two foster children for three years. They returned to their biological parents, but we remained very close. When we finished high school we got together again, and we have been sharing an apartment now for four years. We truly are a family.

Last month I got engaged. My fiancée immigrated to Canada a few years ago, and most of his extended family still lives in Greece. At our engagement party, I looked around the room at his wonderful family, with whom I couldn't communicate because I don't speak their language, and whose way of life seems so different from mine. These people, after the marriage, would become my family. Then I looked at my former foster sisters who have shared so much of my life and so many of my most intimate thoughts. It's amazing that these people are not really considered family.

Wylie (1992) reminds us that we need to include many kinds of families in our thinking. For example:

One's spouse and children: Often the spouse is not the biological parent of the children in the household, but is still considered "family."

A group of related people living in the same house: People can be related by a common interest, as well as by marriage or biology. Residents of a group home, or students who live together for economy's sake, often function as a family.

A group of related people, a tribe: Some people are related by a common cause, ranging from a political interest to a shared concern.

Co-vivants, common-law partnerships: These may be either a prelude to marriage or a substitute for marriage.

Very close friends: These include homosexual couples, both male and female, who live together, as well as people, same or opposite sex, who share accommodation and expenses to ease their finances.

Extended families: This refers to one or more nuclear families plus other family positions such as grandparents, uncles, and cousins.

Blended families: One or both of the partners has been married previously and has children from that marriage.

Scenario

Expect the Unexpected

A 4-year-old at a day-care centre was enthusiastically telling his caregiver that he was going to Vancouver to visit his uncle. The caregiver asked the child what they were going to do when they got there. "Oh," said the child, "I'm going to take him for a walk in his stroller." The caregiver smiled and said, "You mean that you are going to take your cousin for a walk in the stroller." "No, he's my uncle," said the child, as he strutted off to play. When the mother arrived to pick up her son, the caregiver related the conversation to her and said that perhaps the child was confused about the meaning of the words "uncle" and "cousin." The mother laughed and told the caregiver an enlightening story. "My mother died four years ago, and my 75-year-old father soon after remarried a woman much younger than himself, and they had a baby." This 1½-year-old baby was indeed the uncle of her 4-year-old son!

Clearly, in this scenario, the caregiver's perception of family had led her to believe that uncles are adults and cousins are children. Early childhood professionals working with families need to consider how their own upbringing has affected their images and perceptions of what constitutes a family.

Levin and Trost (1992) have devised a questionnaire that will help you analyze your ideas about what is and what is not a family. As you answer the questions with a "yes" or "no," think about why you answered the way you did.

Anna and Anders are a middle-aged married couple without children. Are they a family?

Bodil and Bertil are a married couple in their 30s; they have a 6-year-old son, Bengt. Are these three a family?

Cecilia is divorced and has a 10-year-old daughter, named Carin, and she lives with Carin. Are these two a family?

Carin's father, Curt, lives in the other end of the city. Are Carin and Curt a family? Are Cecilia and Curt a family?

Doris and David are Daniel's grandmother and grandfather. They do not live together with Daniel. Are these three a family?

Eva and Edvin are married and have a daughter, named Elisabeth. These three live together. Eva and Edvin have a son, Erik, who lives in another city. Are these four a family?

Fanny and Fredrik are married and have a son in his teens, Frans, who has a pal, Sven. All these four live together. Are these four a family?

Göran and Greta are in their 30s and have cohabited for three years. They have no children. Are they a family?

Hanna and Hakan are in their 30s and cohabit. They have a 6-year-old daughter, Hedvig. Are these three a family?

Ingemar and Inger have cohabited, but they are now separated. They have a 10-year-old son, Isak, who lives with Ingemar. Are these three a family?

Isak's mother, Inger, lives in the other end of the city. Are Inger and Isak a family?

Jan, Johanna, and Jesper are siblings, and they are all three around 30 years old. The three live together. Are these three a family?

Karl and Krister are in their 30s and cohabit. Neither of them has a child. Are these two men a family?

Lena and Lisa are both in their 30s and cohabit. Lisa has a 6-year-old daughter, Lotta. These three women live together. Are these three a family?

Mona and Martin are married and have a daughter, about 10 years old, Maria. Mona has a very good friend, with whom she can speak about everything. Are these four a family?

Participating in this exercise should help clarify some of the assumptions you have about the family: the importance of biological ties versus social ties, the importance of legal ties versus emotional ties, the influence of official policies, whether living together is an essential component, and the status of same-sex couples.

Source: Levin & Trost, 1992.

At the conclusion of this chapter there are a number of exercises that will help you reflect on how your own family has affected your perception of how families are defined. As early childhood professionals, however, it is important to understand families not only from our personal perspectives, but also from a more theoretical point of view.

Beyond defining families, however, it is helpful to have a conceptual model for understanding how families function as a unit, and as a unit within a society. For this reason, in the following section we will examine in detail two models that guide our work with families.

Models for Understanding Families

Many different theories about families have been formulated over time, each with its own particular view of how families work. Two approaches, or models, that will be considered in this book are the family systems approach and the ecological approach. Both of these approaches are highly relevant to working with families.

A Systems Approach to the Family

In the 1970s psychologists began to write about a model for understanding families that had direct implications for working with families. This has become known as the systems model; it is widely accepted in fields such as psychology and social work, and it provides the theoretical basis for much family therapy practice. It is becoming more and more common for early childhood professionals, rehabilitation practitioners, teachers, and nurses to view this model as meaningful and relevant to their work.

Most would agree that, when a group of people are connected together by family ties, what happens to one member of the family usually affects other members. Parents often bring home stresses from their work environment, and children pick up and often act out that tension. A situation as common as a child with a cold or ear infection often affects the entire family dynamic. If the parents are up with a sick child several nights in a row, their exhaustion may well influence their relations with each other, their relations with the other children in the family, and the siblings' relations with each other. Because family members function in this way as a unit composed of interacting members, psychologists began to think of families as "systems."

A system is any unit that consists of interacting parts, that is identifiable, and that is distinct from the environment in which it exists (Gillis et al., 1989). There is always a boundary that separates the system from the environment. Each part of the system is influenced by other parts, and together, these parts produce a whole—a system—that is larger than the sum of its interdependent parts (Goldenberg & Goldenberg, 1985). Just as people who are concerned about the environment talk about an ecosystem, in which what happens to one part (for example, using chemicals for weed control) eventually affects other parts of the system (the water supply), in the same way professionals who advocate a systems approach to family therapy see the members of a family as forming an interconnected whole.

While this interconnectedness may seem very obvious, considering the family as a system has not traditionally been part of working with families. It is still quite common for a child with behavioural problems to be seen by a therapist who has little or no contact with the parents. Teachers, as another example, will often have a conference with parents and expect them to carry out certain tasks with their children (such as homework) without attempting to gain an understanding of "the bigger picture" of how that family functions as a system.

Scenario

The Bigger Picture

The mother of a 5-year-old, developmentally delayed little boy was asked to carry out a "simple" behavioural program at home. The mother was to make sure that her son always made an attempt to communicate verbally before being given what he wanted. This seemed simple enough, and the caregiver wondered why the mother seemed reluctant to do this. She was unaware that the mother had two younger children, that she helped with her husband's business, and that she tried to care for her aged, chronically ill mother, all in addition to working part time. This simple request was not as simple as it had seemed.

Systems can be open or closed. An open system interacts with, affects, and is affected by the environment around it. A farm, for example, can be thought of as an open system. While all the components of a farm (the land, the people, the equipment) interact within the farm unit, the farm itself is also influenced by and influences the environment beyond its boundaries (weather conditions, the economy, consumer preferences).

A closed system, on the other hand, has few exchanges with its environment, operating almost completely within its own boundaries. Most prisons, especially those situated far from residential areas, and where inmates have almost no contact with the outside world, can be thought of as closed systems. Most systems are neither completely open nor closed, but lie somewhere in between.

Families, like all other systems, can be open or closed. A family system that is open is thought to be more flexible and adaptable to change, and a family system that is closed is thought to be less adaptable to change. Open family systems can react to and cope with changes, both positive and negative, more readily than closed family systems.

Understanding this concept about families can make early childhood professionals' interactions with different families a little easier. For example, closed families will be less likely to discuss their problems or concerns, or to look for outside sources of support. Families that are more open tend to discuss their concerns, and to elicit and utilize outside supports. The degree to which a family is open or closed will often be a prime consideration in determining how the caregiver will interact with the family.

Scenario

The Risks of Being Open

Verna and Amira are a gay couple who have lived together with Verna's daughter, Joanne, for more than five years. As Joanne began to approach her teen years, they were experiencing a fair bit of tension at home. Amira suggested that the three of them see a family counsellor. Verna replied that she was reluctant to do that, since it could be interpreted as an admission of failure. "I always feel," she said, "as if we are on trial, and if anything goes wrong I may lose custody of my daughter."

This scenario suggests that the degree to which a family is open or closed may be affected by factors outside the family, such as prejudice or preconceived ideas, as well as by internal factors.

Family Balance (Homeostasis)

All systems strive to maintain some kind of a balance. This striving towards balance is called homeostasis. The human body, for example, can be thought of as a system. This system strives to maintain a steady temperature. When the outdoor temperature is exceedingly hot, various mechanisms in the bodily system work towards maintaining a steady temperature (perspiration, respiration, etc.).

Likewise, it is thought that a family system finds ways to maintain its balance. An analogy to the example above would be the way various families "let off steam" to maintain balance when tension arises. Taking a vacation, with or without the children, could be seen as an attempt to maintain balance. Similarly, many families have developed ways of discussing and solving problems as a method of maintaining balance. However, sometimes less positive measures are employed to maintain family balance, and many of these do not even occur at a conscious level. Family therapists often relate anecdotes of how children become ill when tension develops between parents.

Scenario

A System out of Kilter

One therapist tells of a family in which the youngest son had a severe stutter. The parents had been experiencing serious marital problems, but decided to put their own problems aside in an effort to help their son. Due to the parents' efforts, the child received treatment and support and soon his symptoms almost disappeared. However, it seemed that as the son got better, the tension and conflict between the parents worsened. As the stress in the home increased, the boy's stuttering returned.

This scenario is not untypical. In some families, a child may function as a "stress barometer." As the stress rises, so does the incidence of behaviours such as stuttering, bed wetting, and nail biting.

If the parents do not have mechanisms in place to resolve their conflicts, the child's illness might be the only factor that can make them forget their own difficulties temporarily. The illness becomes a mechanism for maintaining balance in the family (Goldenberg & Goldenberg, 1985).

Although the family-systems model has been extremely useful in helping professionals understand the interconnectedness of family dynamics, it can lead to a "blame the parents" approach if understood only superficially or misunderstood. There are many reasons why a child may stutter, or have behavioural problems, and although in the scenario above the child's behaviour was an indication of stress between the parents, that may be only part of the picture. It is important to remember that many families do have healthy coping strategies for maintaining family balance.

Family Subsystems

Another important aspect of systems is that they can be divided into subsystems; in the case of the family, these would consist of smaller groupings of members within the family. The parents form both a marital and a parental subsystem, and the siblings form a subsystem as well. Sometimes other subsystems form, such as a mother–child or a father–child subsystem. It is important to understand how the subsystems interact with one another, but we should keep in mind that they may interact differently from family to family. For example, some families allow young children to sleep with their parents up until the age of 6 years. Other parents cringe at the thought of this since it contradicts the subsystems and boundaries that existed between them and their own parents.

The marital subsystem

The interaction between husband and wife or between partner and partner is referred to as the marital subsystem. (The term reflects the perhaps outdated notion that most partners are married!) Couples interact in a variety of ways and develop patterns of interacting with each other over time. Just ask any couple how having a child affected their relationship and their marital subsystem. Some parents will find their marital relationship constricted when children come along. Others may find children or the role of parenting to be a source of conflict that affects their relationship as partners. The response will be determined by many factors: their readiness to become parents, the health and personality of the child, and the support networks available to the family, to name but a few.

The parental subsystem

The parental subsystem consists of the interactions between the parents and the children. This relationship will grow and change over time as the child grows and as parents develop their parenting abilities. Again, these interactions will be influenced by many factors. These can include the parents' perceptions of gender role (Katzev, Warner, & Acoot, 1993; Goetting, 1986), their employment status, and the way their personalities interact with each other and with each of their children. Outside factors can also affect parental subsystems. For example, in many families today fathers have become the primary caregiver; sometimes this has happened by choice, and sometimes because of unemployment.

Sibling subsystems

Siblings often have a profound impact on each other. They often spend a great deal of time with each other and will develop unique ways of interacting. Siblings can be supportive of one another or be in conflict. The number of self-help books available to parents on dealing with sibling rivalry attests to the prominence of the sibling subsystem in families and to the potential for conflict there. On the other hand, siblings whose families are undergoing crises often find each other the only, or the most important, support network available. In fact, positive sibling relations have been identified as one of the most important variables related to longevity and a healthy old age (Peck, 1968).

Extended family subsystems

In spite of all the myths about the proverbial mother-in-law, extended family relationships can make a major contribution to the quality of life in many families (Turnbull & Turnbull, 1990). In times of stress or tragedy, extended family members are often major sources of support. Today, as we will discuss in the next chapter, grandparents are emerging as the heroes in many families, if only because they often take an active role in nurturing the children of working or single parents. Uncles, aunts, cousins, in-laws, all of these relatives can be part of extended family subsystems. These relationships can be supportive and nurturing or serve as a source of conflict and stress. The nature of these relations will depend on many factors, including geography, health, family history, and the personalities involved.

Boundaries

Families vary tremendously in the kinds of boundaries that exist between the subsystems. In some families, for example, financial matters are considered very private and discussed only within the marital (or partner) subsystem. In other families, the children are privy to much of what parents discuss. In some families, the house is arranged in terms of "children spaces" and "adult spaces"; in others, toys are found in all areas, including the living room. Some couples want to maintain distance from their own parents, as part of their need to become independent. For other new couples, parents are automatically included in the decisions they face.

There is no right or wrong way to establish boundaries between family subsystems, but it is generally considered healthy to have clearly identified (though not necessarily rigid) boundaries between them (Ward, 1994; McGoldrick, 1982). For example, when children understand the role that parents play and understand the marital relationship, they are less likely to try to interfere by "playing" one parent against the other. The child knows that this will not work. As another example, therapists tell us that getting along with in-laws is easier if clear boundaries are established. ("We would love to have you for dinner once a week, but when you drop in unexpectedly we find it a bit disruptive.") Sibling relationships are often better when there are clearly defined boundaries. One child does not take toys from another without asking, for example.

The relationship between family subsystems may also be influenced by culture. In some cultures there are very clear expectations for how to maintain relationships with parents, siblings, grandparents, and other extended family members.

Family Roles

While the family unit functions as a system, each member of that system has "official" and "unofficial" roles: mother, father, son, daughter, and grandparents, to name the most common. With each role comes expected, permitted, and forbidden behaviour. The role expectations come from societal norms, and are affected by age, gender, and personality (Goldenberg & Goldenberg, 1985). The next chapter will take a more in-depth look at the roles of mothers, fathers, grandparents, and siblings. It is important to stress here that our society today is undergoing a dramatic change in the traditional roles of parents and grandparents. Many fathers have been taking on much of the caring and nurturing role traditionally associated with mothers, and many mothers have become breadwinners. Social changes like the prevalence of single-parent and dual-income families have resulted in a rediscovering of the potential of grandparents as nurturers and providers of care and support to the family (Jendrek, 1993). A systems perspective highlights the impact that changing the role of any family member has on the entire family system.

Family Rules

Rules govern all systems, including the family. Some of these rules are very clear and some are not so clear. It may be clearly stated in some families, for example, that families will eat supper together, or that children are to tidy their rooms before they can watch television. Other rules may not be as clear, though they may be evident to an astute observer of families. The Goldenbergs (1985) give several examples of rules such as:

- "It's best to ask Mother for money after dinner when she is in a good mood."
- "Stay away from parents' bedroom Sunday morning; they like to be alone."
- "Parents can ask Jill but not John to help with the cooking."

Nobody talks about these informal rules in the family, but everyone seems to know them. Children's behaviour is certainly influenced by these rules. The first indication of this is often when the 4- or 5-year-old begins to play with other children in their homes and sees different things happening. Young children will often bring these examples home and make comparisons with their own family. For example, they might remark, "At Lindsay's house, her Dad cooks" or "Jill and her brother take baths together." When families experience conflict, a family counsellor or therapist might try to help the family understand how these "unstated rules" are affecting relationships.

Early childhood professionals working with families need to be sensitive to family rules, even though some may not be congruent with the professional's ideas about raising children. For example, in some families there is a clear division of sibling roles based on gender, and boys do not participate in activities such as housekeeping and playing with dolls.

Scenario

Not in Our Family

A father came to pick up his 4-year-old son from the day care. When he arrived, Jonathan was in the housekeeping corner dressed in a long yellow gown, a floppy hat, and high heels. The staff explained that Jonathan loved to pretend that he was a princess. Jonathan's father was extremely embarrassed. He reprimanded his son and the staff openly, saying that in his family men didn't dress like women and he did not want his son playing there again.

A more detailed discussion of how to approach these potential areas of conflict will be provided in Chapter 15. For the purpose of this discussion, it is important simply to understand that if we view the family as a system, attempting to influence a change in the behaviour patterns of one member can in fact have a much wider influence (both positive and negative) on the entire family.

The family-systems approach is broad and complex, and the purpose here has been to familiarize early childhood professionals with some of its key concepts, especially as they relate to professionals' work with children and families. Although early childhood professionals do not engage in family therapy, understanding some of these concepts will heighten their awareness of how they may, either inadvertently or on purpose, affect the family as a whole. This understanding may also give them a better idea of how to enhance their ability to work with parents and families.

The Ecological Approach

Just as a child is affected by the entire family system, so too are families affected by other systems with which they interact. They are affected by the neighbourhood in which they live, the workplace of the parents, the nature and scope of available support services (such as day-care centres, schools, and health and recreational facilities). These aspects of family life are affected, in turn, by the social policies and ideologies prevalent in our society. An ecological approach recognizes that all these (and many more) interrelated factors ultimately affect the way in which each child develops. An understanding of the ecological model can assist early childhood professionals to empathize with families and to understand better their role in supporting and helping families.

The conceptual foundation of the ecological model stems from the work of Urie Bronfenbrenner (1979, 1986) who outlined four basic structures—microsystem, mesosystem, exosystem, and macrosystem—in which relationships and interactions that affect human development take place (Berns, 1993). Garbarino (1982) has also described extensively how families are part of interlocking systems that influence each other.

The Microsystem

The microsystem consists of settings or environments with which the individual has direct and ongoing contact. The family, the school, and the peer group would be examples of microsystems with which the child interacts. Some authors (Berns, 1993) have argued that television is also an important microsystem in children's lives with the potential to affect development significantly. The workplace, place of worship, bowling club, golf course, or community centre would be examples of microsystems with which adults in the family may interact. The microsystems with which family members interact most directly affect their quality of life. A high quality day-care centre, a positive school environment, and a flexible and positive work environment directly affect the individuals who interact with those systems.

It is important to remember that microsystems will vary from person to person. For example, one single mother may have a network of friends with whom she interacts on a very regular basis. Another mother may not have such a network but may be very involved with her extended family and church.

The Mesosystem

The mesosystem consists of links and relationships between two or more of the microsystems with which the individual interacts. Examples of mesosystems would be the relationship between a family and the day-care centre, or the workplace and the day-care centre. These connections between microsystems can be weak or strong, positive or negative.

One can see how the mesosystem can affect the quality of life for a family. Suppose, for example, a mother has a highly paid job (a microsystem) that provides her with much personal satisfaction. She also has two children (another microsystem) and feels a deep commitment to their well-being. Her children are in a day-care centre (a third microsystem) that offers affordable quality care. This mother may not notice the links in this mesosystem (the relationship among the three microsystems) until her employer changes her work schedule to one that does not conform to the hours of the day-care centre. When this happens, her life changes dramatically, as do the lives of her children. Now the mother has to find and pay for extra child care, and make arrangements for transporting the children from setting to setting. The children feel the impact of the weak links in the mesosystem when they sense their mother's increased stress.

The Exosystem

The exosystem consists of the many structures in a society that affect people's lives even though they may have no direct contact with them. These include institutional and government decisions and policies, societal norms, and laws. Government decisions (e.g., who will receive day-care subsidies), policies set by school boards (e.g., age criteria for school entry), and policies of agencies like day-care centres (e.g., hours of operation) strongly influence families.

The ecological model describes the influence of different systems on each other as dynamic and reciprocal. This means that individuals or families can influence policies just as much as they are influenced by them. Consider the following example: A government decision (an exosystem) to reduce funding for services to children with special needs can affect many of the microsystems with which family members are involved. The schools (a microsystem) may have fewer resource teachers to help children with special needs, which may result in policies (an exosystem) that discourage the integration of children with special needs into the school system. These children will be in need of much family (microsystem) support. However, if the families of these children join forces together with the schools (forming a mesosystem), they may be able to advocate effectively enough to force the government to rethink its policy (the exosystem).

The Macrosystem

The macrosystem refers to the beliefs and values (i.e., the ideology) and lifestyles of the dominant culture and the subcultures within a society. Macrosystems are viewed as patterns or frameworks for exosystems, mesosystems, and microsystems (Berns, 1993). For example, policies made on the exosystem level (such as universal access to school) are based on shared assumptions and beliefs about the value of education in our society. Belief in democracy determines what laws are passed and what is taught in school, and this same belief gives the people the right to challenge laws and policies they do not like.

Canada and the United States contain many different subcultures, each of which encompasses different values. Sometimes the values of different macrosystems may be in conflict. Formulating policies and decision making become more difficult when a society encompasses so many different values. The macrosystem, like the micro-, meso-, and exosystems, is not static but changes in response to changes in the other systems. Not too long ago, for example, there was a widely shared belief in the "traditional family" in which fathers were the providers and mothers the childrearers. Today, this belief has been widely challenged and we have begun to see more and more opportunities for women in the work force.

If we return to the example used above about funding for children with special needs, we can see the interactive nature of all four systems. Legislation and policies in this regard are influenced by how people with special needs are valued in our society. If the belief is strong that, given the appropriate supports, people with handicapping conditions can develop to become fully participating members of society, it is more likely that policies will be established to ensure the required support. Furthermore, if the belief is strong that all people have a right to participate fully in society, provisions to ensure those rights will probably be legislated. Thus, when we consider the quality of life of a child who has special needs, we must consider microsystem factors such as his family and the school, mesosystem factors such as the relationship between his parents and the school and his parents and other community resources, exosystem factors such as policies regarding funding for resource teachers and aides in school, and macrosystem factors such as widely held attitudes towards people with disabilities.

If we consider the discussion of definitions of family that was presented at the beginning of this book, we can see how ideologies and values also influence the definition of a family. These definitions, in turn, influence the kind of policies that are developed. The policies tend to support some kinds of families more than others, which in turn affects family functioning and the functioning of all the individuals within that family.

Applying the Ecological Model

How does the ecological model relate to early childhood professionals? Its significance can be understood in a variety of ways. First, it helps us to see the child in a more holistic way, in the context of the environment that is affected by and affects the child. It helps us to understand the broad range of factors that directly and indirectly impact the child. The ecological model also provides insights into the relationship between the child, the family, and the day-care centre. Frequently parents are blamed for not providing the best environment possible in which to care for and nurture their child. Yet often the stressors (such as unemployment and poverty) that make positive parenting difficult stem from factors outside the family (in the exosystem or macrosystem).

Furthermore, the ecological model helps us see that what early childhood professionals can offer to children often depends on factors beyond the doors of the centre, such as laws, policies, and cultural values. Lastly, the ecological model suggests to early childhood professionals that promoting the well-being of children entails involvement on many levels: direct work with children, working with the families and other microsystems with which the child is involved, influencing policies and legislation that affect children and families, and helping to define the value that society places on children. The challenge for early childhood professionals is to identify within the different systems strategies for their work that are feasible and realistic given the limits of their time and professional qualifications.

Conclusion

It is important to gain an understanding of families as they exist in society today. Although the nature of families may vary in different eras and in different cultures, they almost universally have retained their prominence as a primary social unit. This chapter has attempted to outline some of the theoretical definitions and concepts of families to provide a framework for the information contained in the rest of this book. By being aware of how our own experience of families has affected our views, and by being aware of the need to learn more about the many different kinds of families that exist today, we will become more competent as professionals who work with children and families.

1. Levin and Trost (1992) have developed a simple method of helping people understand their perception of family by having them think about their own family. It is an interesting exercise and one worth trying.

   First, take a piece of paper and list the names of all the people that you consider to be in your family.

   Second, using cut-out triangles for males and circles for females, create a family map by sticking the cut-out shapes on a piece of paper in a way that represents an image of your family. Your diagram may look something like this:

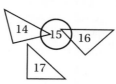

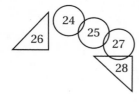

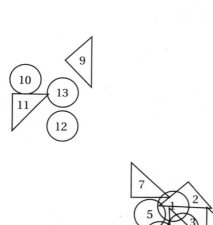

1. Woman/wife
2. Husband
3. Daughter from earlier marriage
4. Son
5. Stepdaughter
6 and 7. Parents
8. Brother
9. Ex-husband
10. Ex-husband's new partner
11 and 12. Ex-parents-in-law
13. Husband's ex-wife
14, 15, and 16. Husband's siblings and wife
17. Husband's father
18, 19, 20, 21, 22, and 23. Uncles and aunts
24, 25, 26, 27, and 28. Uncles, aunts, and cousins

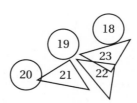

Third, look at your "family diagram" and consider the following questions:

- Do the distances between the shapes signify emotional distance (how close you feel), geographical distance (how far away these family members live), relational distance (how closely they are related, either biologically or through marriage), or some combination of these?

- Are households clustered together, or are nuclear family members grouped whether or not they live together?

- Who is included in your family, who is not included, and why?

- How would the family map have looked five years ago? What would have been different and why?

- How might the family map look five years in the future? What would be different and why?

- Would your parents or other family members view the family map differently? If so, why?

- How would an official, such as an immigration officer, a social assistance worker, or a personnel officer, view your family map? What would be the differences between the official's view and your own, and why?

This exercise should bring to light some of your perceptions about your own family and about families in general.

2. In this exercise, you will draw a *family map*. This will bring to light many factors that have had an impact on your own family, and will assist you in identifying the range of factors that have influenced your concept of family.

For this exercise you will need a large sheet of paper and markers. Use symbols or pictures, rather than words, to illustrate some of the most influential factors in shaping who you are today. You may include family members, friends, places of worship (church, synagogue, mosque, temple), activities, interests, travel, and any other factors that occur to you. Try to draw the symbols in order of importance, or in chronological order.

After you have completed your family map, compare it with others' maps, or reflect upon what you have drawn. Which factors were most prominent in your development?

How are the factors in your diagram interrelated? For example, some students recall that happy family memories are associated with holidays, leisure activities, or religious festivities. Unhappy memories may be associated with events such as a divorce or a death in the family. A consideration of the family map leads to an awareness of how factors outside the home, such as the nature of the community, influence the family.

3. One very simple but effective method for evoking thoughts about the family is simply to draw a picture of a family festive dinner. Include in the drawing an empty chair for family members who are not present. Notice the seating arrangements around the table. Who is sitting next to whom, and why? Who is not present, and why? Who is actively engaged in food preparation and distribution? A description of a family meal sometimes can tell us a great deal about family relationships and norms.

4. On a sheet of paper make columns listing the following relationships in your life: parents, siblings, extended family, friends, classmates or co-workers, and strangers. Then ask the question: Whom would you tell?

The list of questions should range from very personal (e.g., trouble in an intimate relationship) to quite superficial (e.g., a good book I have read). Compare your "who would I tell" chart with those of your fellow students and note similarities and differences. What does this tell you about your own family's rules and boundaries?

5. Identify some of the unwritten "boundaries" that your family has. Were these boundaries established by you, or "inherited" from parents or other family members? How have these boundaries affected your family relationships?

6. What were the spoken and unspoken rules in your family? How did you learn about the "unspoken" rules?

7. How do you think your views and experiences affect your work with families?

8. Describe a possible role of the early childhood professional that relates to the micro-, meso-, exo-, and macrosystem.

Family Members and Family Roles

chapter 2

Objectives

- To review some of the most important roles of family members.

- To discuss the impact of social trends on family life.

- To consider how family roles are interconnected in family systems.

One day Timothy, who was 5 years old, came home from his preschool with tears in his eyes. Brian, his father, paused in his lunch preparation to find out what was wrong with his son.

"They called me a sissy today," explained Timothy.

"Why do you think they did that?" asked Brian.

"Because I was pretend cooking."

"Who called you a sissy?" Brian continued to probe.

"Petey and Mark."

"Well," said Brian thoughtfully. "I cook—am I a sissy?"

"No, of course not, Daddy."

"And we are friends with both Mark and Petey's parents, and both of their dads cook sometimes. Are they sissies?"

"Daddy!! Of course not!!"

"So do you think that cooking makes you a sissy?"

"No—I guess not."

"So then, what will you say to them next time they do that?"

"I'll say that my daddy cooks and he's not a sissy and he's bigger than your daddy and can beat him up."

"Well," thought Brian to himself. "This is the 21st century and men's roles are changing. We are allowed to be in the kitchen as long as we can still beat other people up!"

Family Members and Roles

Commitment to children forms the very foundation of the early childhood profession. Our education and training prepare us to consider most circumstances from the child's perspective, that is, from the viewpoint of what is in the child's best interest. However, we are also aware that the child's well-being is inextricably connected to the well-being of the family as a unit and the subsystems within it. An understanding of the roles of some of the key players within the child's family system should assist us in interacting with them in a sensitive and empathic manner. It should also help us to broaden our understanding of the world of the child.

After completing the exercise on perceptions of family in the previous chapter, you probably realized that opinions regarding who is (and is not) considered a family member are quite diverse. A parent's partner, an aunt, uncle, cousin, or friend, a nanny or a care-giver may well be included in many families. As professionals working with young children, you may have the opportunity to interact with many people who are considered family, whether or not they conform to biological or legal definitions of family. Therefore, although the discussion in this chapter focuses on mothers, fathers, siblings, and grand-parents, it is important to be aware of the significance and role that other members of the child's extended family may have.

Mothers
The Role of the Mother

Although many people consider mothering to be "instinctual and natural," the roles moth-ers play have in fact changed over time and differ across cultures. The most central issue today concerning the role of mothers relates to employment. There have been significant changes in women's participation in the labour force from 22 percent in the 1940s to 57 percent in the 1990s (Cleveland & Krashinsky, 1998). The increase has been particularly noticeable among married women with preschool children. Barlow (1992), for example, points out that full-time mothering became a socially desirable phenomenon only in an affluent society in which families could thrive without mothers actively engaging in production (e.g., on the farm or in the factory). Poorer societies generally do not foster full-time mothering. Furthermore, historians have shown (Arnup, 1993) that full-time mother-ing was intentionally promoted when there were insufficient numbers of jobs available for the men, such as after World War II. When the soldiers returned home after the war, women who had been employed in factories were "encouraged" to return to the home. Again, the economic climate and availability of jobs influenced the role of mothers.

Today, we hear vocal advocates both for mothers staying home and for mothers working. Both sides can find research to back up their claim that "stay-at-home moms" have happier families, or vice versa (Baydar and Brooks-Gunn, 1995; Lowe-Vandell and Ramanan, 1995). The truth is that researchers are likely never to be able to agree which way is superior to the other, if only because too many factors come into play. Factors like the availability of quality child care, the existence of support networks, and the role the father plays in childrearing and household tasks will all affect how a working or nonwork-ing mother influences family life. Although strong feelings exist on both sides of the issue of working mothers, the fact remains that many families in North America depend on the mother's income to make ends meet.

Supermom

When I read some of the magazines, I get the impression that mothers are supposed to be these superbeings who rise at dawn to exercise, jump into the shower, and run downstairs to prepare a hot breakfast for their family. Then they put on their business suit, successfully finalize two or three business deals at work, and pick up their children from day care. On the way home, they lead a sing-along of "The Wheels on the Bus" as they battle the traffic. After serving a nutritious meal, engaging in quality time with their children, and then bathing and putting them to bed, these women miraculously transform themselves into loving and sexy wives before the evening ends.

For many women, the task of nurturing and rearing their children is the most fulfilling and rewarding experience they will have. Yet mothering in our society is not always easy, and the stress factors faced by mothers today affect the family as a unit and all the subsystems in the family. A phenomenon called "mother blaming" (Barlow, 1992; Caplan & Hall-McCorquodale, 1985) has become fairly prominent in our society over the past century. When a child has behavioural problems, or is experiencing difficulties in school, or even when an active child is disrupting a social event (Turecki & Tonner, 1989), the tendency is to look at the mother and wonder how adequate a parent she is. How many times have you seen a screaming toddler at the grocery checkout, and wondered why the mother could not control her child? If early childhood professionals understand how their own expectations of mothers have developed, and if they can gain some insight into the problems and pressures that mothers face in today's changing society, they may be better equipped to offer appropriate support to the entire family system.

Attitudes Towards Mothers

A simple word association exercise can be helpful in beginning the process of understanding the vast range of expectations (some positive and some negative) that society has of mothers. When our classes of early childhood students have been asked to write down quickly the first associations that come to mind when the word "mother" is mentioned, the blackboard quickly fills up with a wide range of adjectives: *loving, caring, nurturing, steadfast, nagging, cranky, always there*, and *never there* are but a few examples. Some students have considered their mothers their closest friends, while others would not even think of having an intimate conversation with their mothers.

Examine Your Attitudes

What do you think of mothers?

A. Complete the following sentences.

1. Mothers are _____.

2. Mothers should _____.

3. Mothers could _____.

B. Write the word "Mother" at the top of a blank sheet of paper and then fill the page with other words this term suggests to you.

Consider the results of both exercises. Are your feelings about mothers predominantly positive? Are they negative? Or are they mixed? How strongly do you think your attitudes towards other mothers have been determined by your relationship with your own mother?

Our concept of the roles and characteristics of mothers is shaped by many sources, and the nature of relationships between mothers and their children is extremely diverse.

Scenario

Take Nothing for Granted

A young caregiver worked in a day-care centre where her mother was the director. They had a very positive working and personal relationship. One afternoon a father came several minutes late to pick up his son. The young caregiver suggested that he recruit the boy's grandmother to pick him up on days he thought he might be late. The father shocked her by replying angrily, "I wouldn't trust my mother to take care of my son."

Early childhood professionals need to avoid making assumptions about family relationships that are based on their own experience.

Preparation for Motherhood

In previous times and in many other cultures today, by the time a woman becomes a mother she has participated in the care and nurturing of either younger siblings or babies of neighbors or extended family members. In North America, however, for many women, their own experience of childbirth is often the first time they have had contact with babies. Furthermore, it has been pointed out that there is a value conflict inherent in motherhood today. The school system, according to Kitzinger (1978), prepares young women to be successful members of society. That entails training them, from a very young age, to be task oriented—to establish time lines and schedules, to be precise, and to work hard towards a successful finished product. These are not necessarily the same skills required of mothers.

Scenario

The Best Laid Plans . . .

A 40-year-old woman who held a managerial position at a large institution had the first year of motherhood all planned out from two weeks after the baby was conceived. According to her plan, she would take a two-month maternity leave, after which the nanny (who had already been interviewed and hired) would begin. She had all her appointments scheduled for the next year based on her well-thought-out plan. Eight months after the birth of the baby, she met her friend in a park. "I thought you were going back to work!" the friend commented with surprise. The mother laughed and said, "I had everything all figured out, but I did not consider for a moment that the baby would not endorse my plans."

Motherhood doesn't neatly fit into a system of values that promotes high productivity and a fast pace. Mothers can't learn "perfect procedures" for childrearing because the child is constantly changing and developing. In motherhood, there is no "finished product" by which mothers can measure their success as there is in academic or business settings.

Role ambiguity

The role of mothers is changing and will continue to be influenced by social and economic factors beyond the control of the family. Personal and societal values are also reflected in attitudes towards mothers. In our diverse society there should be many possible ways to mother children. But sometimes this ambiguity or freedom of choice is associated with stress and feelings of guilt that impede enjoyment and fulfillment of the task. So, as well as juggling work, family, and childrearing, many mothers are struggling to sort out the very mixed messages they receive about what society expects of them. The images of women in the media rarely reflect the value of motherhood (except in advertisements about products directly associated with child care). Women are now expected to be successful at a full-time career and to be available to their children (and husbands) at all times as well. Society also demands that they be well groomed and slim and trim while they are accomplishing all this.

Scenario

Mixed Messages

I stayed home with my first baby until she was 4 years old. Wherever I went, people would ask me what I did. "I'm at home with my baby," was my reply. In so many words, the usual response was: "Is that all you are doing?"

When my second child was born, I went back to work after a six-month maternity leave and placed my child in a day-care centre. Now when people ask me what I do, I get a variety of responses that range from accusations of child neglect to pity for my child and myself. Talk about mixed messages.

As we will discuss in Chapter 15, early childhood professionals can sometimes inadvertently add to the stress and guilt felt by mothers. A study of the relationship between caregivers and parents (Shimoni, 1992) indicated that some caregivers felt quite strongly that mothers should be at home with their children unless they absolutely had to work. They grew especially angry when mothers left their children at the centre at times when they weren't actually at work (to do shopping or simply to rest at home). Feelings such as these will likely be conveyed to the parents in one way or another. One mother (Shimoni, unpublished data 1992) reported that, when she tried to discuss her son's problem behaviour, the caregiver stated outright that perhaps the solution would be to spend more time with her son.

On the other hand, early childhood professionals can also be instrumental in providing support and understanding. The first step in this direction is developing the ability to empathize with the problems and challenges that mothers face as they raise their children in a rapidly changing society.

Mothers and Experts

Scenario

Who Knows Best?

Before the birth of my first baby, I spent many hours talking with my grand-mother, who had nursed her children until they could walk. The expression on her face as she talked about her babies said more than any advice book could. Two months after my baby was born, I was visited by the community health nurse, who told me that I should begin the baby on solid foods. Reluctantly, I did as she said, and shortly after that my baby didn't want to nurse any more. Two and a half years later my second child was born. The same community health nurse visited, sat in the same chair as she had two years before, and with the same expert manner proceeded to tell me that solid food should not be introduced for several months, and that breast feeding was by far the preferable method.

Over the last century mothers have received an extraordinary amount of advice from experts (Wrigley, 1989). Over a span of just one decade, expert advice to parents can change several times, as the scenario above shows. One author (Barlow, 1992) describes how advice to a mother concerning feeding could change for each one of her four children. With the first baby, a mother could be told that children should finish all the carrots on their plates. When the second child was little, she could be told that children should be encouraged to eat, but not forced. Advice for the third child would likely be to provide the food, but not to encourage or discourage, so that the baby would learn to respond to his own inner signals. A few years later, with the birth of a fourth child, experts could be talking about using food as a sensory experience, and not be concerned about nutrition at all!

As professionals in early childhood development, we have come to appreciate the scientific knowledge available to help guide our interactions with children. But the examples above should make us humble. Every few years, as research and theories develop, new ideas emerge on the subject of what is best for children. Some of the practices that seemed unquestionably right are re-examined and reconsidered in light of new knowledge.

"Expert advice," whether it be in the form of books, magazine articles, or parenting classes, can sometimes undermine a mother's confidence and make her feel that she can never learn how to do things right. The author of a recent historical account of expert advice to mothers over this century concludes that "this barrage (of changing advice) from experts . . . has transformed women's experiences of pregnancy, birth, and mother-hood" and has led to "confusion and a sense of being manipulated by the experts" (Arnup, 1993). It might also be noted that many of the best known advice books for mothers were written by male doctors who had probably never spent an entire week at home as the exclusive caregiver of a child.

Our intention is not to belittle the importance of expertise about children gained from research and clinical experience. Experts from a variety of professions, including medicine, psychology, social work, and education, have provided parents with an abundance of knowledge concerning health and development matters. Today, however, many authorities on parent education are acknowledging the importance of parents' own expertise, and of working with them in a way that is collaborative and empowering. As one of the most prominent researchers in the area of parent education stated: "I want to move to an area where . . . parents' stories and parents' judgments are held as equally important as expert knowledge" (Powell, quoted in Shimoni, 1992).

Early childhood professionals possess a wealth of knowledge about children and are perceived by some (but not all) mothers as "experts." Hopefully, the understanding gained from reading this book will help caregivers find ways to share this knowledge with parents in a manner that is respectful and empowering.

Fathers

Couchman (1994) vividly describes how the father's experience at the time of a child's birth has changed in the last 25 years.

Scenario

Times Have Changed

"There I was in the delivery room. My newborn son resting in my arms. . . . The wrinkles and gurgles were familiar to me, but the surroundings and timing of the moment were new. Twenty years ago I had been in the same hospital to welcome the births of my elder son and daughter. I recall stepping out of the classic waiting room punctuated by pacing prospective fathers and clouded with the cigarette smoke of traditional fatherhood. The delivery room nurse summoned me to view my children before whisking them to the nursery. I was also routinely informed that my wife was all right and in an hour I could visit her . . . [This time] I found myself immediately thrust into an active role as father and husband. This experience was but the first of many changes to fatherhood which have occurred over 25 years."

Source: **Couchman, 1994: 4.**

The roles of and expectations for fathers have been changing drastically in our society. Many of today's fathers are moving closer to the current ideal of women and men being equal partners in childrearing. The move from the traditional image of the father as provider and disciplinarian, to the new image as equal partner in childrearing, has by no means been a smooth one (Glossop & Theilheimer, 1994). As with all family roles, the role of father is shaped by economic and social circumstances, as well as by personal values, beliefs, and personality. Early childhood professionals have traditionally had more contact with mothers than with fathers (Shimoni & Barlow, 1993). With changing family dynamics, it is important to understand how the changing roles of fathers may affect and be affected by the development of children, the family as a unit, and the systems (such as day care) that interface with families.

Until just over a decade ago, most of the research about the effects of fathers on the development of children focused on father absence rather than father presence (Shimoni, 1994). That is, psychologists looked for (and found) negative effects on children whose fathers were not a part of their lives (Wells & Rankin, 1991). Today, these ideas are mirrored by the media reports that link fatherless homes to crime, gangs, and drugs. Fathers are frequently criticized for their lack of participation in homemaking and child care; many claim that the messages that men receive about how they should act as parents are mixed and often explicitly hostile, and that there seems to be a polarized view of fathers in our society today (Skolnick, 1992). On the one hand, we have the image of the "good dad," the nurturing, caring, and committed father who, with the exception of breast feeding, has taken on all the tasks of childrearing with enjoyment and commitment. On the other hand, there are many fathers who avoid any responsibility for childrearing and domestic chores.

Historians have noted that, before the Industrial Revolution, fathers played an important role in the lives of their children (Couchman, 1994). Although mothers fed and cared for the infants and toddlers, fathers assumed responsibility for their moral education while the children were still quite young. Children (particularly sons) would work alongside their fathers in childhood and adolescence to learn their means of livelihood. As industrialization drew men out of the home and into the marketplace, their involvement with and influence on their children declined. While many men remained the disciplinarians, the hours spent away from the family resulted in emotional distance, and childrearing became the almost exclusive domain of women.

With the rapid social changes that have occurred in the last three decades, the role of father as the "provider" for children has changed. Perhaps the most noticeable change is the number of fathers who do not live with their children. American statistics reveal that at some point in their lives, almost half the children in the United States will live in homes without a father. Many fathers by choice or by decree are noncustodial fathers, and contact between children and noncustodial fathers is known to be minimal in most cases (Skolnick, 1992).

This view of the modern father is certainly incongruent with the old-fashioned image of "father as provider." Today, measures are being taken to force fathers to pay child support. While it may be possible to enforce the financial responsibilities of fatherhood, the emotional bond between children and their noncustodial fathers is much more difficult to guarantee.

As more and more women began to enter the work force (a trend that started in the 1960s), a concurrent transition in the role of fathers began (Glossop & Theilheimer, 1994). But that transition has been fraught with difficulties, both for those who are fathers and for those who are trying to understand the role of fathers in today's society.

Today, many fathers are involved in childrearing right from the beginning; they accompany their partners to childbirth preparation classes and participate in the birth experience. Psychologists have observed this trend of newly involved fathers, and have concluded happily that men indeed can, and do, engage in many of the activities of childrearing with as much success as women.

They can, for instance, soothe babies as capably as mothers, and they react to babies' signals as appropriately as mothers do. Yet psychological studies of father–child interaction point out that the way in which many fathers respond to and interact with children is different from that of mothers. Play with fathers seems more intense and "rough and tumble" than mother–child play (Lewis, 1987). Fathers tend to read and play less quietly with their tots than mothers; they are less likely to sing and talk to their children quietly, or to play at routine care times such as during diapering and bathing. Fathers tend to interact verbally with their children less than mothers do. It is interesting to note, however, that when fathers become primary caregivers, they tend to "act more as mothers do" (Lewis, 1987).

Psychologists have been trying to explain the effect that these different styles of interaction have on the children. Some have suggested that differences between mothering and fathering styles complement each other. For example, when a child is playing at a gym, the father is more likely to challenge the child "to climb to the top" while the mother will be warning the child to be careful. The balance between those two messages is considered important to the child. Other psychologists are hesitant to make too much of gender differences in parenting styles. We should be careful not to stereotype. Even though some studies have shown that mothers and fathers often behave differently, we need not assume that this is inevitable.

Many fathers (and mothers) ponder the question "What is a good father?" Fathers draw on their own childhood experiences to help them answer this question. Sometimes their own father provided a role model they wish to emulate. Many fathers, however, want to be very unlike their own fathers, particularly when it comes to expressing affection towards their children. Phil Donahue, a well-known talk show host, was quoted as saying "I honestly thought that being a father meant giving presents at Christmas and birthdays, occasionally changing diapers, occasionally spanking, and occasionally babysitting for the little woman's night out" (Decoste, 1994).

Since there are no "recipes" for good fathering, families have to evolve their own patterns and norms. In some senses, society has had a hand in influencing the image of the good father, especially through the portraits conveyed by television, newspaper and magazine articles, and advertising. Some fathers complain that the image of a good dad really means that dad is a good "mom."

Scenario

Congratulations, Dad!

My husband and I and our two daughters, aged 8 months and 4 years, were dining out at a family restaurant. The children were seated between us in order that we both could assist with the meal. Since I was preoccupied with the baby, who required more help, I began to eat only as the others were finishing. My husband took the 4-year-old to the washroom and returned with a washcloth for the baby's face. Several people in the restaurant commented on what a good father he was. Why do you think nobody congratulated me on being a good mother when we both were actively involved in parenting?

The experience of the woman who related the above scenario mirrors that of many families where childrearing responsibilities are divided. The father is viewed as almost a saint for participating at all, while the mother's contribution is taken for granted.

Many fathers claim that caring for their children is the most rewarding and enriching experience of their lives. Relating to their children on a deeply emotional level "liberates" men from the restraining stereotype of males. Indeed, many men who derive great pleasure from the cuddles, kisses, and diaper changing have no memories of physical contact with their own fathers other than a handshake.

Some fathers participate more in the upbringing of their children out of a sense of fairness to their partners who are working. For them, child care may be more of a task. Some fathers who spend many hours a day alone with the children while their wives work refer to themselves as the "babysitter" (Glossop and Theilheimer, 1994). This conveys the sense that they are helping their wives, rather than taking a primary role in nurturing their children.

Fathers sometimes care for their children because they feel pressured to do so by their partners. Sometimes social situations outside the home determine the degree of parenting a father will assume. For example, if the father is unemployed and the mother has a job, the father will take over child care during the day, often not by choice. The director of a service for immigrants to Canada reported that this is the case with many families who have come from Third World countries (Ksienski, 1994). The mother works outside the home (often caring for other people's children), and the father cares for their children at home. For many families, this role reversal is quite difficult.

We must not forget, however, that many men, including young men, still prefer the traditional role of father as provider. These fathers feel that by working hard to earn a good living for their families, they are making a positive contribution to their children's lives (Lupri, 1991). In fact, recently a support group was formed by men who want to maintain and promote this traditional role, but who feel that society is pressuring them to change.

It has been suggested (Lupri, 1991) that, in spite of the media pictures of the new involved dads, change is not occurring as rapidly as it seems. In fact, it appears that married men's participation in household tasks has only increased 6 percent in 20 years. In the majority of families, the mother is still the primary caregiver and the one on whom both the joys and burdens of childrearing fall (Decoste, 1994). It looks as though we can continue to assume that women will, by and large, remain a constant in this society as the primary caregivers for their children. Men's opportunities, choices, and personal preferences vary considerably, and it is therefore unlikely that a single "ideal" father model will emerge in the near future (Robinson & Barrett, 1986). In this respect, sociologists inform us that we should expect fatherhood roles to range between the traditional "provider" role and what they refer to as the "emerging androgynous role," where men perform all the tasks of childrearing traditionally associated with the mothers (Lupri, 1991).

Supporting Fathers

In spite of the increasing number of manuals, advice books, and television shows about fathering, many men still feel that they are relatively unsupported. Some complain of "the mothering double standard"—although women complain that men do not participate enough in childrearing, they themselves are hesitant to "let go" and allow men to take part. Mothers learn at an early age that childrearing is their domain, and feel obligated to train their partners to do it the "right" way. Sometimes they feel that the training isn't worth the trouble. While we must be careful not to generalize and blame mothers for the lack of father involvement, this may be a factor in some families. In cases where this is so, mothers can be encouraged to give fathers more opportunities alone with the children, to acknowledge the differences in parenting styles, and to build fathers' confidence by repressing the urge to "check up on" or "correct" them.

Outside the immediate family, fathers can be supported by more public acknowledgment of their childrearing role, and this could be reflected in paternal leave policies and informal support at the work place. Many fathers have admitted that they are ashamed to tell anyone they are missing work for reasons associated with their children.

Scenario

White Lies

When my two children were young, I helped out quite a bit. I would chauffeur them to their ballet lessons, take them to the doctor, dentist, and orthodontist, and often stay home with them when they were sick. Looking back on that time now, I realize how many times I told "white lies" to my boss and my co-worker. Any excuse for absence was better than actually admitting that I was busy with my kids.

Fathers have as much of a right as mothers to take time off work to attend to family matters, yet many feel that they will be penalized by their employers for doing so.

Early childhood professionals can assist fathers by ensuring that they are addressing them as well as mothers in their efforts to work with parents. In addition, it might be appropriate to offer fathers special programs, where they will have the opportunity to mix with and learn from other fathers.

Perhaps it is most important, however, that we discard the tendency to divide all fathers into polarities, seeing them either as "bad fathers" or "superfathers." We all have different ideas concerning the role (real and ideal) of fathers, and we must not let our personal views interfere with our acceptance of the diverse nature of fathering styles with which we come in contact. Our own acceptance of the diversity in fathering styles and roles may help family members be more accepting of each other, if that is appropriate, or support each other as they attempt to alter their roles and lifestyles.

How Can Society Support Active Fathering?

1. *Supportive workplace policies.* Such policies as flexible working arrangements, family leave, employee assistance programs, day-care programs or referrals, teleconferencing to reduce travel, options for working at home, and making information available on family topics can all help fathers to take a more active role in childrearing. Small things like the availability of telephones for workers to call their children after school can also make a big difference.

2. *Women's expectations.* If women expect men to play a bigger part in child-rearing, men will often take the cue.

3. *Role models.* If men see other men taking child care and domestic responsibilities seriously, they will find it easier to do themselves.

4. *Promotion.* We need to share success stories of active fathers and make them part of the culture at work and in the community.

5. *Education of the next generation.* Children must be taught that men can be active parents. Girls and women must learn that women do not have a monopoly on domestic duties.

6. *Government policy.* Men and women must receive equal benefits that recognize their family responsibilities.

7. *Value of "women's work."* Unless we value the domestic and caregiving work that women have traditionally performed, few men will want to take it on. This applies equally to paid and unpaid work.

8. *Public education.* Public attitudes can change. Conferences, media coverage, advertising, and continuing education are tools that can help change attitudes.

Source: Glossop & Theilheimer, 1994: 11. Reproduced with permission of the Vanier Institute of the Family.

Siblings

The majority of children in North America grow up with at least one sibling. Through the period of childhood, it is likely that siblings spend more time together than with their parents or with friends. Although conflicts are inevitable among siblings, sometimes the relationship is characterized by warmth, affection, and mutual support, while in other families jealousy and rivalry extend into the adult years.

Parents can play a vital role in fostering healthy sibling relationships; sometimes, however, we tend simplistically to blame the parents when siblings do not get along. In reality, many factors will affect how siblings relate to one another. The gender of the siblings, the spacing between them, the temperament and personalities of both parents and children, and external factors all come into play. Although sibling relations have been increasingly studied in recent years (Dunn, 1992), there is still much that needs to be learned. One factor that has received a great deal of attention and excited much controversy is the influence that birth order has on a child's personality.

Birth Order

It has often been said that the order in which children are born (referred to as birth order) has a very strong influence on their development. This belief is so strong among both psychologists and lay people that one often hears children being described as "the typical first-born" or of having "a middle child syndrome."

The first-born child is often thought of as a perfectionist and an ambitious high achiever. Since first-born children have no siblings to act as models, they have to look up to and learn from their parents. Parents have more time for their first child, so their influence upon them is thought to be stronger than on subsequent children.

The middle children are thought to be secretive and rebellious, but more social than the first-born. They are considered to be more socially competent with peers than first-born children, and their success with peers is somehow connected to their need to make up for the lack of parental attention through companionship with other children.

The last-born is often thought to be a charmer. By the time the third child is born, parents are thought to have relaxed their expectations, and to prefer to pamper rather than discipline (Harrigan, 1992).

This belief in the influence of birth order on personality development has become prevalent in some sectors. Some psychologists are also firm believers in the importance of birth order, while others reject it as a popular notion with little hard evidence to substantiate it (Harrigan, 1992).

It is true that the research on birth order is not at all conclusive and sometimes contradictory. Some studies do show that first-borns seem to have higher IQs and achieve more in school and in careers (Dunn, 1992). These statistical differences, however, are quite small. Today, researchers are suggesting that the total number of children in the family, and whether it is a one- or two-parent family, seem to have more effect on IQ than birth order does (Dunn, 1992). Large families and single-parent families often suffer more stress and are likely to be poorer than smaller, two-parent families, and these factors seem to be more influential than birth order.

Personality differences according to birth order may be explained by the difference in the way parents treat first- and later-born children. The oldest child is the only one who for a time doesn't have to share his or her parents. Although this point has not been considered in the research, it could well be that the high achievement of first-born children is promoted by their attempts to please their parents and regain that "special place" that they had before their younger sibling was born. Even with the birth of a new baby, many parents maintain an especially intense relationship with the first-born. They have higher expectations of the first child, and place more pressure on him or her for achievement and responsibility. Parents also generally interfere more in the lives of their first-born children.

Aside from differences in IQ and achievement, researchers have not been able to demonstrate clearly the effects of birth order on personality and behaviour. The effect of birth order on outgoingness, risk taking, self-esteem, guilt, autonomy, political views, and psychological problems has been studied with little success in finding clear-cut answers.

The only child has earned a negative reputation in our folklore, and is often considered to be spoiled and inconsiderate, lacking in self-control, more dependent on parents, and more self-centred than are children with siblings. However, the research seems to indicate that, although only children may be like first-borns in IQ and achievement, the negative traits mentioned are not necessarily associated in reality with being an only child.

One small study does suggest that only children are less autonomous than first-born children. The authors suggest that this may be because the process of separating from parents involves aggression towards them. When there are no sibling relationships for "back-up," children may fear this individuation process (Byrd, DeRosa, & Craig, 1995). Another study contradicts this by concluding that only children tend to be more autonomous than children who have siblings (Mellor, 1995). Since family size is decreasing and more parents are having only one child, researchers will have ample opportunity to devote more study to the nature of parent–child relationships in single-child families.

The problem with birth-order theory is that the development of children is influenced by so many different factors: gender, age spacing, peer and school experiences, accidents, illnesses, random events, and economic factors all play a role in shaping siblings' development. In addition, it is now well established that many aspects of a child's temperament (extroversion or shyness, low or high activity level, etc.) are evident at birth and fairly consistent over the entire life span. The baby's temperament influences how parents interact with him or her (Turecki & Tonner, 1989) and probably also how he or she will interact with siblings. For example, a child who is highly active and noisy, and who finds it difficult to adapt to new situations (both of these characteristics relate to temperamental traits, which will be described further in Chapter 8), is likely to require more parental attention than a quiet child who adapts easily, regardless of the birth order. This factor needs to receive more consideration.

Studies of sibling interactions and birth order have, however, given us information that is essential for understanding family dynamics. Dunn (1992) has highlighted how children, from a very young age, are extremely sensitive to the way in which their parents interact with siblings. She tells the story of a shy, insecure 30-month-old child who watched his mother interact with his lively 14-month-old sister, who had grabbed a forbidden object from a counter, despite being told not to. The mother affectionately commented on the little sister's actions, calling her a "determined little devil." The little boy sadly commented, "I am not a determined little devil." Apparently, young children watch the interactions of their parents with their siblings "like hawks" (Leder, 1993), and the greater the difference in maternal attention and affection, the more hostility and conflict there is between the siblings.

Parents' Role in Facilitating Healthy Sibling Relations

Unfortunately, there are no simple formulas to help parents foster good relations among siblings, in spite of the number of advice books available on the topic. Certainly, it is thought important to help older siblings adjust to the birth of a new baby in the family by ensuring that they feel important (giving them tasks to do, or preparing a snack for the older child to eat when the mother is breast-feeding the baby). While these strategies can be important, they are only a small factor in ongoing sibling relations.

Parents sometimes feel that they must treat all their siblings in the same way, but this is probably impossible to do when the children have sharply different personalities. One sibling, for example, might need a lot of support and coaching in school work, while the other manages independently. Yet the latter may feel jealous of the attention received by the former. These problems are often exacerbated when one of the siblings has special needs.

Rather than attempting to treat each child in the same way, it might be more helpful to focus on family communication. Children who grow up in families in which they feel free to discuss their emotions, including the common feeling of being treated unfairly, may be less likely to suffer from the jealousy and rivalry that plague the relations of so many brothers and sisters. Although we still have much to learn about the ways brothers and sisters influence each other's lives, it is clear that the impact of growing up in a family with other children is very potent indeed, and that the sibling family subsystem can be one of the few constants in a rapidly changing society.

Handling Sibling Rivalry

1. Keep in mind that most siblings fight a good deal of the time. It is quite normal behaviour.

2. Make a rule that they cannot call names or hurt each other physically, and if they seem about to do that, separate them.

3. Do not become their judge and jury; help them work it out. Try to keep in mind all the times that they play together nicely.

4. Try not to pay too much attention to fighting siblings, since this may result in even more fighting.

5. As a parent, perhaps your best and surest recipe for peace of mind is to expect considerable conflict between your children, appreciate its normalness, and do what you can to manage it. But keep in mind that fighting and squabbling are for many children a way of life. They enjoy it. Even the very young child tends to have a strong sense of self-preservation. Most could avoid a major part of their fighting if they wanted to.

The advice to parents in the box above reflects norms and expectations regarding conflict, sibling relations, and parent–child relations. Early childhood professionals need to view this advice with caution and sensitivity. For example, does it take cultural differences into consideration? Early childhood professionals are aware of the vital role played by adults in modelling desired behaviour for children and in mediating conflict situations when children do not have the skills required to do this on their own. The suggestions above do not reflect this aspect of adult–child relations. Finally, it is important to ask whether conflict and squabbling are normal or whether this idea is peculiar to our culture. Some parents may want to raise their children with values that encourage mutual respect, sharing, and compromise, and conflict may be considered "normal" only because it is deemed so by the predominant culture.

Jan is a 29-year-old college student and the mother of a 2-year-old daughter. She comes from St. Lucia, which she left at the age of 8. Jan's mother moved from St. Lucia to Toronto in 1968 with the hope of getting settled in Canada and then sending for her two daughters so they could have a better life and education in their new home. From the age of 2 until the age of 8, Jan lived with her grandmother and sister in St. Lucia.

"My grandmother was very strict. We were brought up with the expectation of proper behaviour at all times, and especially that we would show respect to our elders. Because my sister was four years older than I, I was expected to respect her as well and do what she said. My older sister, as in many West Indian families, was expected to look after me when Gramma was busy. And I was expected to do as my sister said. Gramma was from the old school, a devout Catholic, who stressed the importance of self-discipline and study.

"I don't remember my grandmother expressing affection readily. She seemed more concerned about raising us as proper young ladies. When I was 8, we moved to Canada to join my mother. The pattern of interaction between myself and my sister stayed the same throughout my childhood. My mother was a single working mother who relied on my sister's help in raising me and maintaining the household. Even today, all these years later, when I talk about my parents, I really am referring to my sister and my mother. Having lived in Canada for most of my life, I think that if I have two children, I will want their relationship to be different. I would not want my older child to have the responsibility of raising her younger sibling, and I would want a more equal relationship between the siblings than I had with my sister.

"I obviously have been influenced by Canadian culture in terms of what I want for my children. However, when I look back on my childhood and think of the adult I am today, I see how valuable it was for me to have respect for older family members. That seems to be lacking in North America today, and in my view this is a loss of a valuable aspect of family life."

Grandparents

For many people, the word "grandparent" evokes idyllic pictures of a little old lady with grey hair fixed in a bun and an apron, retrieving a baking tin full of cookies from the oven, while her kindly husband is working in the garden. For others, it evokes a picture of frail and elderly people dependent on a young family for assistance and support. The fact is, though, that fairy-tale images rarely reflect the realities of our society, and these are no exception.

In the United States today, 3.2 million children are known to be cared for by their grandparents. In addition, millions of grandparents in the United States and Canada care for young children on a part-time basis, many of those children coming from single-parent families. Grandparents have been referred to as "silent saviors," "who have stepped in to . . . rescue children from faltering families, drugs, abuse, and violent crime" (Creighton, 1991).

Other grandparents may be "embarking on a second or third career, or off on exotic cruises" (Taitz, 1990). As older people's health and life expectancy have increased, grandparents are gradually becoming recognized as a vital force in the family system, a force that warrants much more consideration than it has received to date.

In one early childhood class on the family, students were asked to identify the most constant relationship in their life. Many students named their grandparents, and talked about their appreciation of the love and support their parents' parents showed them, often in much more positive terms than they used when discussing their own parents.

Cheriline, a Native social work student, had the following to say about her grandmother.

Scenario

The Contribution of Elders

On my reserve the grandmothers raise the children. I never would have been able to look after my kids without my mother's help. She didn't only look after my children, she brought up her sister's children too. But, you know, life on the reserve is changing as well. Some of our elders are beginning to realize that they want their freedom as well. Our traditions are changing, just like the rest of the world.

The grandparent role, like all family roles, is affected by cultural norms and expectations. Some research from the United States indicates that grandparents in African-American, Asian-American, Italian-American, and Latino families are more involved with their grandchildren than grandparents in other groups. Another study suggests that Mexican grandparents in the United States may be less involved with their grandchildren. However, this can be explained by geographic distances between them due to migration (Hogan, Eggebeen, & Clogg, 1993) and can be contrasted to the 67 percent of Native American elderly who care for at least one grandchild and who live within five miles of their kin (National Indian Council on Aging, 1981). Native American grandchildren often spend periods of time with their grandparents so that they can be taught the Native way of life (Weibel-Orlando, 1990). Many native families may be experiencing adjustments due to the influence of residential schools on family life.

While culture seems to play an important role in determining the role of grandparents, there is likely almost as much diversity within each ethnic group as there is across ethnic groups. This is even apparent within families, as a Jewish student related.

Scenario

Differences Within Families

My grandmother on my father's side came to Canada from Poland. She spoke Yiddish, was the best cook in the entire world, and fit practically all the stereotyped notions of the typical Jewish grandmother, or "Bubby." I loved going to her house for Sabbath and holiday meals; she and my grandfather kept Jewish tradition alive in my family. My mother's mother was a professional woman. She hardly ever cooked, and in her free time played bridge, golfed, and read. She would take us out for dinner, and even sometimes on trips. But there was nothing "traditional" about this grandmother—she was a very modern woman.

Grandparents can affect the family system in a number of positive ways. They can provide a sense of history and continuity to a family in a rapidly changing world (Cooksey 1991). Grandparents can also give their grandchildren "a sense of the life cycle," and children who have contact with their grandparents over the years may develop a realistic and less frightening perception of aging.

Grandparents' contribution to the children in the family can be quite simple: they can provide children with a lot of love, without the stresses and tensions that are sometimes involved in parent–child relations (Taitz, 1990).

Many factors will influence the relationship between grandparents and grandchildren: geography, personalities, and the nature of the relationship between the parents and the grandparents. Although grandparents can be heroes to their grandchildren, it is not uncommon for conflicts to arise between the parents and the grandparents. Sometimes, the conflicts may be related to the fact that childrearing norms have changed considerably over the years, and what is now accepted as positive parenting may seem like "spoiling" to grandparents. On the other hand, sometimes grandparents glean so much enjoyment from being with their grandchildren without having to worry about discipline, that parents claim that they are spoiling the children. Often, when grandparents are involved in the rearing of their grandchildren, roles and family boundaries may be confused. This might be especially problematic in single-parent families where the grandmother lives with her daughter and grandchildren, and where the mother has to balance the responsibilities of being a daughter and a mother at the same time.

It is clear that grandparents play a vital role in the lives of many families, and for many this is a positive experience. However, as a society, we have tended to ignore the importance of their role. We need to learn more about "who makes up the grandparent population in all its diversity of age, gender, and ethnicity" (Aldous, 1995). Early childhood professionals must not ignore grandparents, as they have sometimes tended to do (Ward, 1994). Grandparents may also require information and support, since much has changed since they were parents. They may need information about their right of access to their grandchildren, and they may need some encouragement and support in working out old conflicts with their own children so that they will be welcome to share in the joys and challenges of raising their children's children.

Conclusion

We have attempted in this chapter to provide a brief overview of some of the key family roles. In North American society, there is a considerable degree of diversity in the way in which mothers, fathers, siblings, and grandparents perform their roles. Some of this diversity is related to culture and ethnicity. Social, economic, and geographic factors will also influence the way in which family members relate to each other and their expectations of each other. Understanding and appreciating this diversity will assist early childhood professionals in their work with families.

Exercises

1. Think of some "expert advice" you have been given, or ask a new mother about any advice she has been given from professional sources. Discuss whether you (or the mother) took the advice, whether or not it was helpful, and how you or the mother would change the advice given based on your/her experience.

2. Interview some mothers and fathers and ask them about the challenges and problems they face as parents raising children in today's society.

3. Compare the problems, joys, and challenges of parenting today with parenting a generation ago.

4. Discuss what you think you will be like as a grandparent, and how similar or different this will be from your grandparents.

Family Transitions

chapter 3

Objectives

- To examine the stages of family development.
- To understand the stages of parenthood.
- To review the stages of psychosocial development.
- To examine the ways in which the development of individuals, parents, and the family interact.
- To understand the stressors and joys associated with transitions.
- To highlight the role of the early childhood professional in supporting families through transitions.

A young teacher recounted her daughter's first morning at school. "Tammy and I were so excited about the first day of school. I was excited about the new possibilities for her learning, and for me, it represented a new stage in our relationship and in my parenting abilities. I could now help her to explore, to learn, and to interpret the new parts of her world just waiting to be discovered. We arrived to find many other parents and children, all suitably attired for the first day of school. Some children looked excited, others looked apprehensive, and some looked scared. After the introductions were complete and the children made their way to their new classrooms and new teachers, all of the parents left. I was amazed at the number of parents outside in tears because the first day of school signified that their 'babies' had grown up and didn't need them any more. They felt that this new world of school, teachers, and classmates was overwhelming, frightening, and certainly not to be greeted with the same enthusiasm and excitement that my daughter and I had felt on that morning."

Individuals, couples, and the family unit experience many changes in their lives and their relationships. Many of these transitions are developmental; that is, they are considered natural and somewhat predictable. Changes in marital relationships, changes in family composition including the birth of a baby or the departure of a grown child, changes in children as they develop, and the concomitant changes in parenting and in the family itself are all inevitable over time (Kalmuss & Seltzer, 1989).

Some transitions result in a change of roles. For example, the roles of husband and wife will be modified when they become parents. This may, in turn, cause changes in interactional patterns; husbands and wives may interact differently with each other when they are parents (Olson, Lavee, & McCubbin, 1988). As the above scenario indicates, these transitions may be seen as interesting, challenging, and exciting by some, while others may consider change to be stressful. In fact, this scenario is a good illustration of the fact that the same event may affect different people in very different ways.

Much of this book looks at transitions that occur in families. A divorce, or a sudden death, or the blending of families all can be seen as transitions. This chapter will examine transitions that are associated not with exceptional circumstances but rather with normal development. We will discuss family life cycles, parent development, and child development separately, and then consider how the interactions among these transitions influence each family in a unique fashion. The examples presented at the end of the chapter demonstrate how various developmental transitions in individuals and families can interact with and affect each other.

Family Development

Early childhood professionals have a broad understanding of children's stages of development. Families change and grow over time, just as each individual member changes and grows. Some of these changes are predictable. Family life will change drastically, for instance, with the arrival of a new baby, and it will change again when children grow up and leave home. Other transitions are more subtle and recognized only in retrospect or upon reflection.

Scenario

It's Hard to Keep Up

The mother of a teenage boy was having some difficulties with his behaviour. There was a growing feeling of tension in the family, and the parents noticed that they were quarrelling much more often, both between themselves and with their son. As a result, they decided to attend a series of parenting seminars. After listening to hours of advice and reading volumes of material, the mother commented that parenting was hard work. "We just got the knack of being parents to a new baby and he turned into a toddler. By the time we figured out what to do with him at that stage, he turned into a sweet, lovable 3-year-old. Things changed again when he started having playmates and going to school, and my husband and I actually managed to remember that we had a relationship. It seems like we just figure out what it is we should be doing and he changes again."

This scenario illustrates quite normal developmental changes in the child along with the required adaptation in parenting abilities and the resulting changes in the marital subsystem and the entire family unit. The concept of family *life cycles* or stages of family development gained recognition in the 1970s. Sociologists and psychologists began to study how families came together, developed, and adapted over time and in relation to the changes occurring in their lives (e.g., marriage, children). The theories emphasized typical phases or stages along with tasks and reactions common to each. Some parents, for example, remember their child's infancy as a time of joy and happiness, whereas others remember anxiety, exhaustion, and apprehension. For some parents, the "empty nest" years are a time of loneliness, whereas other parents thrive on their new-found independence and opportunities for self-discovery.

Our theoretical understanding of family development has been based on information primarily from "traditional" families. As well, theorists have tended to give little consideration to cultural, ethnic, or religious influences. More recently, researchers have attempted to consider family development in different family structures such as blended families (Carter & McGoldrick, 1989; Carter & McGoldrick, 1980) and families undergoing a divorce (Carter & McGoldrick, 1980). These fields of research are still in the preliminary stages of development, and as more work is done in them, our knowledge base will expand. However, in spite of these limitations, professionals have relied heavily on family development theories to aid their understanding of families and guide their practice. They have divided the "typical" family life cycle into seven stages:

- beginnings (coming together as a couple),
- the arrival of children,
- the family with young children,
- the family with school-age children,
- the family with adolescents,
- the family with older children (launching period), and
- the family in later life.

Following, we consider each of these stages of the family life cycle in turn.

Beginnings

The description of family life cycles typically begins with courtship and the development of a relationship that subsequently leads to marriage (Carter & McGoldrick, 1980). Involvement with the new person and developing the relationship become top priorities in both partners' lives. This period is a time of exploration, discovery, excitement, and happiness. Sometimes, adjustments may have to be made to include the new spouse in family and friendships that already exist (Carter & McGoldrick, 1989). This integration can happen very easily if the new person is welcomed into the family and friendship circles, but in other cases the introductions may be challenging and stressful. Another potential source of stress may be the difficulty of defining boundaries between the family of origin and the new family.

The Arrival of Children

For many people, the birth of the first child signifies the true beginning of the family (Carter & McGoldrick, 1989). Becoming parents is considered one of the most significant transitions in the family life cycle (Pittman, Wright, & Lloyd, 1989). This social transition involves reorganization in many areas of the new parents' lives and creates both stresses and rewards (Belsky, Lang, & Rovine, 1985). Parents report satisfaction from having another person to love, from observing their children develop, and from the settling effects on the family's lifestyle (Pittman, Wright, & Lloyd, 1989). Stress may stem from the multiple roles now required (e.g., wife and mother) and from the demands of caring for a new baby. These demands may interfere with the amount and quality of interaction the partners have with each other and with their extended families and friends (Pittman, Wright, & Lloyd, 1989).

In addition to the roles of husband and wife, the roles of mother and father must be negotiated and defined. This process may require some adjustments, and again relationships outside the new family may need to be changed. For example, when couples are part of a social circle that does not include children, they may lose some of their old friends and develop new friends with a common interest—children. New parents may seek more contact with family members as a means of support that may not have been desired previously.

The stage of becoming new parents requires change and adaptation in all aspects of life—in finances, in social lives, in sex lives, and in routines such as sleep and eating (Brooks, 1991; Belsky, Lang, & Rovine, 1985). Sometimes there is a decline in marital satisfaction during the period when all these factors are changing (Bernstein, 1993). For example, joint activities no longer consist of dining out or going to the theatre; instead they are restricted to the home and to daily chores like cleaning and laundry. All leisure time is centred around the baby. Couples are, in effect, making two adjustments—to the new baby and, once again, to each other (Brooks, 1991).

This change in focus may lead to feelings of stress and ambivalence about the new baby or about the couple's relationship. In this respect, change and the resulting stress appear to be greater for wives than for husbands (Belsky, Lang, & Rovine, 1985). Women undoubtedly experience more changes when they become parents, including a greater loss of freedom and having less time for themselves. For some, "the ambivalent feelings they experience towards the parenting role can result in a decrease in self-esteem" (Pittman, Wright, & Lloyd, 1989: 269). The following scenario attests to these ambivalent feelings.

Scenario

The Most Stressful Period

An elementary school teacher finally became a mother after many years of trying to get pregnant. Years later, asked to share her memories of being a new mother, she said, "I always considered myself an easygoing, competent person, but then this baby came along and shattered my image of myself. My baby cried all of the time unless I held her. Some days I was lucky to get showered and dressed before my husband got home. Then, he would look at me as if to say, "Is that all you did today?" Our relationship seemed different because I don't think he liked this new woman who nagged and watched him all the time to make sure he got it right. All my friends remember their babies with such joy, but it really was the most stressful and most unhappy period in my life.

Women often consider having children to be central to their marriage, and parenthood is more important to their self-concept than it is to that of men (Pittman, Wright, & Lloyd, 1989). When, however, there is a sharing of parenting and parenting roles, marital satisfaction is often enhanced (Brooks, 1991; Belsky, Lang, & Rovine, 1985).

The Family with Young Children

During this stage of family life, the relationship between the couple often continues to change. In "traditional" families, the mother becomes preoccupied with the needs of the children and home, while the father becomes increasingly absorbed in work or in meeting his family's economic needs. Tension between the couple can result from misunderstanding each other's roles. For example, the mother might interpret her husband's preoccupation with work as disinterest in the family, while the father may perceive her total involvement with the children as disinterest in his work and undervaluing his contribution to the family. There is often little time for the couple to relate to each other or to focus on matters other than the children. This stage of development, when children are little, is a very stressful and demanding period of time.

Couples with young children typically experience more interpersonal conflict and role strain, partially due to the high level of interference from the children (Pittman, Wright, & Lloyd, 1989; Olson, Lavee, & McCubbin, 1988). Divorce rates are at their peak during this stage (Peck & Manocherian, 1989; Richardson, 1988).

Many of the stresses of childrearing described above have been associated with families where the father is employed and the mother stays at home with the children. Families in which both parents work would undoubtedly experience many of the same stresses plus the additional stresses associated with the wife's working and with finding and maintaining child care (Cleveland & Krashinsky, 1998; Scarr, Phillips, & McCartney, 1995; Eshleman & Wilson, 1995). Cleveland & Krashinsky (1998) suggest that parents of preschool children may have difficulty locating and maintaining quality child care for several reasons. Young families may have inadequate incomes or be in a situation where financial resources are too limited or spread out to afford high quality care. Parents may have difficulty determining the quality of care their child receives or caregivers may attempt to conceal information (Lamb, 1998). Lastly, there may be a number of priorities parents/families must balance—the cost of care, convenience of child care arrangements, flexibility of child care, feelings of the child, need to be with friends or within the community for school entry along with apparent quality of care. Sometimes this

> *"Hidden action" compounds the problem. Knowing that parents are anxious to have higher quality care, but that quality is hard to judge, many caregivers will masquerade as good quality even if they are not. This may be particularly a problem in child-care centres, where parents may judge quality by the brightness and cheerfulness of the centre. These characteristics are obvious, and therefore easy to judge, but the fundamental determinants are the number and abilities of the staff, the quality of the programming, etc., which are more difficult to observe and judge. . . . there may be lots of mediocre child care masquerading as good quality. (p. 37)*

Thus, this phase of the life cycle may pose a myriad of choices and potential stresses for families that may impact child development. Family life cycles literature has not incorporated all of these factors, but more information and data are slowly becoming available. Current research suggests that, in many families where the mother works full time, the majority of childrearing and homemaking tasks still fall primarily on women, and that this often causes conflict and tension (Scarr, Phillips, & McCartney, 1995).

The Family with School-Age Children

The next stage of family development occurs when children grow old enough to attend school. Again, in traditional families, some mothers may be pleased with this change since it leaves them more time for themselves. Full-time mothers may also feel less needed and look to other means of gaining satisfaction such as part-time work and school or volunteer activities. While this may enrich the mother's life, it sometimes leads to conflict with the father or is perceived by him as yet another way for the woman to distance herself from her marriage. At this stage, husbands are often entirely preoccupied with their career, trying to ensure that they can continue to meet their family's needs.

The Family with Adolescent Children

The stage in which families have adolescent children is often described as a time when everyone seems to be very busy, with little time to connect with each other. Teenagers are typically involved in their own lives and peer groups, fathers continue to work hard to establish themselves in their careers, and mothers have likely developed many interests outside the home or may be re-establishing themselves in their careers. This level of engagement outside the home can leave little opportunity for communication. In addition, parents need to make adjustments in their relationship with their children to allow for their teenagers' new-found sense of independence (Carter & McGoldrick, 1980).

Stresses in parenting during this stage tend to affect the mother's self-esteem more adversely than the father's. Issues of control, privacy, and independence are most prominent at this time, along with mounting worries (Pittman, Wright, & Lloyd, 1989). Some studies report this stage to be the least satisfying for parents (Goetting, 1986). At the same time, parents may also need to become more involved with their own aging parents and a new set of concerns may be added to the family dynamic (Carter & McGoldrick, 1989; Carter & McGoldrick, 1980).

The Family with Older Children

The final two stages of the family life cycle involve families with older children. The first of these stages is the so-called launching period (Carter & McGoldrick, 1989), when children move on and the couple find themselves alone in their "empty nest." Once again, the marital relationship becomes the central focus. This time can be very exciting and rejuvenating for the relationship, or couples may come to realize that they have nothing in common anymore. In addition, parents need to realign their relationships with their grown-up children, which may include additional relationships associated with grandchildren and in-laws if the children leave home and get married. When adult children remain at home, adjustment may involve revising norms and expectations and examining patterns of relating to each other.

The Family in Later Life

The last stage in the family life cycle is that of later life, when parents attempt to maintain relationships with their children and their children's new families. As well, parents are dealing with their own issues associated with getting older and all its concomitant changes, and the loss of significant roles.

Family Development in Nontraditional Families

If we look at the families around us today, it may seem that few of them fit exactly into the above description of family life stages. Couples who are not married have children, and many families now are headed by a single parent. Blended families may be a union of people in very different stages of individual and family development. And without a doubt, many more families today include women who, through choice or necessity, work while their children are young. The challenges faced by a family in which both parents work usually differ considerably from those in a family where one parent stays home (Eshleman & Wilson, 1995). Certainly, changing economic and social forces influence family development. Today, many middle-aged men are not coping with career ladders and job stress, if only because unemployment has deprived them of any career at all. Many families postpone childbearing for many years so that their careers, finances, and personal relationships are solidified before children arrive. Couples who have chosen to have children later in life may have had time to establish themselves as individuals and establish relationships in their lives. They either find themselves ready to nurture their children when they do come, or experience difficulties with the disruption of established routines (Brooks, 1991).

Scenario

An Abbreviated Visit

Remeiko and her husband, Frank, were visiting friends with their 16-month-old daughter, Masami. Their friends did not have children and had a house full of beautiful but fragile objects. It seemed like every two minutes, one of them would have to jump up and rescue a china figurine, cup, or saucer from the coffee table. To have even the shortest conversation without being constantly disrupted was impossible. After a very short visit, Remeiko apologized to her friend and the young family departed. On their way home, the exasperated parents burst into laughter as Frank remarked: "I'm glad we had ten years of conversation before Masami was born, because I don't think we'll ever finish a conversation again."

When life doesn't unfold in the expected order or pattern, individual family members may experience stress and uncertainty.

Scenario

Empty Nest or Revolving Door?

A 45-year-old woman stated that she had read a lot about the empty nest syndrome as her children got older. "I wondered what life would be like without my two teenage children at home. Was I ever surprised to find out that the empty nest has turned into a revolving door. My son is 26 years old and has never left home. He is unemployed and cannot afford to move out. My daughter's marriage broke up, so she and my 3-year-old granddaughter now live with me. My nest isn't empty at all—it's bulging at the seams."

Blended families are becoming very common in North America. The coming together of two families, each of which may be at a different stage of development, can result in a highly complex transitional period, which is quite different from any experienced by the traditional family. The Goldenbergs (1994: 148) briefly illustrate the number of stages and processes that can be involved in a second marriage:

> Husbands and wives may be simultaneously biological parents and step-parents. . . . With remarriage, a man must cope with the complexities of not only being a part of an old family life cycle and perhaps an old marital cycle with an ex-wife, but also beginning a new marital cycle and complicated new family cycle with a step-parent–stepchild relationship (and possibly the relationship with a child of this new marriage as well).

Family Development Theory: A Multicultural Perspective

A final reservation about family life development theory is its relevance across different cultures. Cultural norms, beliefs, and traditions all have an impact on the kind of challenges posed by transitions during the family life cycle, as well as on the adjustments made to those transitions. Yehudit, a mature early childhood student, made the following observations after a class discussion on family development.

Scenario

Not Like in the Book

I was married at the age of 17, immediately upon completion of high school. The marriage was arranged; I had not met my husband before our engagement was formally announced. Birth control is not practised in my culture since the primary purpose of marriage is procreation. I had five beautiful children by the time I was 25. We didn't spend years discovering each other or defining and negotiating roles, as they are dictated by our religious belief. We did not consider children an adjustment—they were a blessing. We have a happy family life but not like the one in the book.

The Importance of Understanding Family Life Development

Even though the body of knowledge about family development needs to be expanded in terms of nontraditional families and in terms of multiculturalism, it constitutes an important knowledge base for early childhood and other helping professions. First, from a historical perspective, it is important for us to understand how our ideas about families have evolved. Second, family development theories suggest to us that many of the problems faced by families as they enter and emerge from transitional periods are normal. Many families derive comfort from this realization. Third, if family members are aware of the potential stressors associated with impending transitions, they can prepare for them. For example, couples expecting a baby may discuss how they will share the responsibility, or how they may try to reserve some time to share together alone. A mother who has stayed home to rear her children can begin to think about and plan for the changes that will occur when her children grow up. She may consider retraining for employment or furthering her education, for example.

Every family passes through life's transitions in its own unique way. A stressful transition for one family can be a joyous one for another. The age and developmental stages of each family member, their inner and outer resources, and economic and cultural factors all play a role in family development. Family members often learn about transitions from older family members or from friends, and sharing these experiences can be extremely helpful. The theoretical knowledge available about family development is an additional source of information that can be useful to families and to professionals who work with them.

Transitions in Parenting

Parenting involves a "continuing series of interactions between parent and child—a process that changes both" (Brooks, 1991: 2). Parenting also involves transition and changes in every aspect of life—money, sex, sleep, meals, and social life. These changes may occur easily and be welcomed by parents or may cause stress and conflict. Galinsky (1981) describes six stages of parenthood, which we will now discuss in turn:

- image making,
- nurturing,
- authority,
- interpretation,
- interdependence, and
- departure.

Image Making

At this time, when parents are preparing for birth and parenthood, they are creating images of their baby and images of themselves as parents. This stage is marked by anticipation, excitement, and, perhaps, some concerns (GAP, 1973). Images may be affected by the prospective parents' own childhood experiences, by their background and circumstances (including whether or not the pregnancy was planned), and by whether the pregnancy is the mother's first.

Nurturing

With the arrival of the new baby, parents, for the first time, can compare the images of their baby and themselves as parents to the real experience. As the parents' attachment to the infant grows, they change their priorities, their roles, and their relationships (GAP, 1973). For instance, the primary emotional attachment changes from the exclusive bond between the couple to include the child, and the roles of mother and father are added to the roles of husband and wife.

Authority

The next challenge for parents is establishing and exerting their authority over their children. Parents need to determine the scope of authority and establish order and structure in the family (Berns, 1993). They also need to learn how to communicate with their children and with each other about the children; parents must discuss and decide upon discipline practices and use them consistently. Many parents discipline their children in a manner that resembles their own upbringing, while others try to incorporate a style of discipline that they have learned through books or parenting classes. When partners have very different views on discipline, conflicts may arise. Child development specialists point out that consistent patterns of discipline are important to a child. Because most children have an inherent need for parental approval, they need to know what is expected of them. Inconsistent demands for discipline can therefore contribute to feelings of insecurity (Eshleman & Wilson, 1995).

Interpretation

During the school years, children become more skilled and independent. The parents' role is to interpret the world to the child. Parents teach manners and behaviours, and help the child understand and abide by authority figures outside the family, such as teachers. In this process, the child gains knowledge and develops skills and values. At the same time, parents are clarifying their values and ideas about parenting, and re-evaluating their childrearing practices in relation to the child's new independence and skills (Berns, 1993).

Interdependence

Adolescence raises concerns about authority and communication all over again. Often set patterns of communication and discipline no longer seem effective. New issues, such as sexuality, independence, and peer influences become relevant. Teens are involved in forming their own identity and they are engrossed in the process of understanding and differentiating which areas of authority should rest with the parent, and over which areas they should have control (Berns, 1993). Parents not only have to deal with these issues, but also are reflecting on their own identity as parents and how they measure up to the standards they have set for themselves.

Departure

When children leave "the nest" and enter society, parents must prepare for, adapt to, and accept the child's separateness and individuality. This stage marks the end of active parenting (GAP, 1973), so it serves as a time when parents are able to examine their performance and have time to redefine their identity as a couple once again.

When adult children do not leave home, this "incompletely launched" young adult sometimes represents a failure for parents (Skolnick, 1992). With adult children at home, family rules often have to be renegotiated and new patterns of communication established.

Change Is Difficult

When my children were growing up, we believed that as parents the best gift we could give them was an education. To that end, we made few demands on them at home, as long as they devoted their time to study. They were responsible for cleaning their own rooms, and we had a rotation system for the dishes. After my daughter graduated from college and got a job, I noticed that I was feeling some resentment towards her. After a moment of reflection, I realized that we were both women who worked full time, but I was the one who still felt obligated to run the household and prepare the meals. Changing old patterns is not easy, but we now have a more equitable arrangement. My daughter still doesn't cook, but she does take me out for dinner once a week.

The stages of parenthood described above are subject to the same reservations as those mentioned in the previous section. Social, economic, and cultural factors, as well as individual differences and the degree and kind of support available, all play a role in the way parenthood is experienced. This model of parent development focuses on the challenges inherent in parenthood and is a reminder that childrearing entails parent development as well as child development. The transitions noted here may be anticipated and subtle, or they may cause tension for the family members involved. An awareness of the stages and an understanding of the changes that accompany these transitions will be helpful to professionals whose work involves supporting families.

Theories of Individual Development

Early childhood professionals are well aware of the developmental milestones of young children across all areas of development. Through their ongoing interactions with the children in their care, they watch each child's development unfold in a unique manner. At the same time, they see children learn about themselves and the world around them and develop skills in a predictable sequence. This knowledge of child development helps them understand and support children. In this section we will consider aspects of development that may assist adults in understanding young children and in understanding how they may view situations they are in. Accordingly, we may then use this information to assist children in coping. We will consider three aspects. The first will be to consider psychosocial development across the age span as described by Erik Erikson (1963). Following this, a discussion of cognitive development and attachment, both of which focus on the early years, will provide a foundation for understanding. This understanding will be fundamental to the following chapters where we consider the many issues families may face and how children may perceive them. We now have a considerable body of knowledge about development across the human life span (Erikson, 1963; Havinghurst, 1972; Peck, 1968; Gould, 1988; Gilligan, 1982). These theories require constant updating as life expectancy is extended, social norms are altered, and other societal changes occur. The theorist best known for his study of psychosocial development is Erik Erikson (1963), who identified eight major stages in life and the tasks that require resolution in each stage. While Erikson's theory is not free of culture and gender bias (Gilligan, 1982) it has been one of the cornerstones of human development theory for many years (Barrett et al., 1995).

Stages of Psychosocial Development

1. Trust vs. Mistrust
2. Autonomy vs. Shame or doubt
3. Initiative vs. Guilt
4. Industry vs. Inferiority
5. Identity vs. Role confusion
6. Intimacy vs. Isolation
7. Generativity vs. Stagnation
8. Ego-integrity vs. Despair

Source: Erikson, 1963.

Infancy—Trust vs. Mistrust

According to Erikson, an infant's first developmental task is to acquire a sense of trust. This trust is the foundation upon which further emotional development builds. A child's sense of trust in the world is fostered when his needs are promptly responded to. Crying is the baby's primary method of communicating, and if his attempts to communicate are ignored, either consistently or randomly, he may find it more difficult to learn to trust the people around him.

Scenario

Like Mother, Like Son

Brian and Belinda were new parents. Taryn was a content baby and cried very little. When she did cry, Belinda would pick her up and check that everything was all right. Taryn usually stopped crying as soon as Belinda picked her up. One day, when the baby was fussier than usual, Brian remarked, "See, you've already spoiled her by picking her up all of the time. My mother let us cry for short periods during the day to make sure that none of us were spoiled, and we should do the same."

This is one specific example of where the child's task of developing a sense of trust can become a contentious issue. Some people believe that babies must learn to settle themselves and learn to put themselves to sleep. Others believe that the child must be responded to in order to foster his sense of trust and security. Balancing these two ideas can be difficult.

Toddlerhood—Autonomy vs. Shame or Doubt

The second stage of psychosocial development is autonomy or independence. Autonomy is often referred to as the "no, no," "mine," and "me do" stage typical of toddlers, who generally want to do some things on their own (Barrett et al., 1995). Anyone who has witnessed the temper tantrum of a toddler in a shopping mall should be able to recognize this stage. Toddlers have a strong drive to be independent but don't have the language or social skills required to manage the task completely. In addition, they are extremely reluctant to accept help. They often get frustrated and are, in turn, often very frustrating for their parents. Sometimes parents misunderstand the behaviour of their toddler, thinking that he or she is just being stubborn or behaving in a certain way to get attention. Yet toddlers need the understanding and support, along with patience and good humour of their parents to help them master their developmental tasks. If toddlers feel they can master important tasks such as feeding themselves or making choices, they will develop feelings of autonomy. If they fail, they will feel shame and doubt, especially when their parents demonstrate frustration or disappointment (Barrett et al., 1995).

Scenario

A Toddler's Behaviour

At an annual picnic hosted by a day-care centre, the children were playing on the grass with a variety of toys. One 20-month-old little boy was busily snatching toys from the other children, declaring "mine, mine." His mother was embarrassed by the behaviour and reprimanded him. The caregiver approached her, and the mother confided that being a single working mom was difficult. She had been promoted recently, and this left her even less time to interact with Teddy. "It sure shows in his behaviour," she said. The caregiver listened sensitively and then explained to the mother that Teddy's behaviour was normal for his age. "Toddlers," she said, "go through a stage of thinking that everything is theirs before they can learn to share." After she gave the mother a few tips for avoiding conflict with toddlers, the mother stated, "This won't make him any easier to live with, but at least I can stop feeling guilty about my parenting."

This example demonstrates that very normal behaviour for a particular stage of development can be misunderstood and evoke strong emotions in the parents.

Preschool Age—Initiative vs. Guilt

As the child develops independence and leaves the toddlerhood period, he or she moves to the stage referred to as initiative, which spans the remainder of the preschool years (Erikson, 1963). During this time, the child wants to create, discover, explore, and try everything at least once! Creating crafts with paper, glue, paints, and sparkles becomes a favorite pastime of the preschool child. Children at this age begin to take the initiative and make decisions on their own, and they crave the company of other children so that they may share in their creative endeavours.

For many parents, preschool children seem easier than infants and toddlers as long as they are kept busy and active. Children need many opportunities to create and explore, and they want to know that their work is appreciated by adults.

A Lasting Friendship

My closest friendships developed when Sandra was in preschool. We were new in the neighborhood and really didn't know anybody at all. Three or four times a week, Sandra would want to play with Julie after school. At first, I would just drop her off, and gradually her mother and I started having coffee together while the children were playing. Then we got together on weekends and our husbands got acquainted as well. Our friendship grew and lasted many years.

Sandra's developmental need was to make friends with children of the same age. We see how this need inadvertently affected the whole family. When the child is able to initiate new relationships, she will develop confidence in her abilities. If, however, the child is discouraged or punished, she will not continue to display initiative and may experience feelings of guilt.

School-Age Children—Industry vs. Inferiority

This stage relates primarily to children's school functioning, but it is relevant to the child within the family as well. During this stage, children are industrious. They want to be involved in projects and in creating, but unlike in the previous stage, completion and the final product are important. The child wants to be involved in meaningful, real-life tasks such as learning to read or write or helping with household chores. When the child is successful in developing ideas and following through to the end product, and is successful in mastering new skills, a sense of industry will prevail. When these attempts are marked by failure, the child will develop a sense of inferiority, which may be generalized (e.g., "I'm no good at school") or specific (e.g., "I can't draw", "I am not an athlete").

Failure

In an introductory early childhood education class, students were engaged in an assignment that required them to draw and be creative. When it was over and we were evaluating the activity, one student remarked, "I hated this; I can't draw. My teachers never displayed any of my art work at school." The same sentiment was echoed by several of her classmates. Another student added, "It's just like me—I have always hated music from the time I was in Grade 4 and the choir teacher told me to just mouth the words."

From their comments, it was clear that these students' failures in school had led to feelings of incompetence or inferiority in certain areas that lasted long beyond the school years. The family will play a role in providing successful learning opportunities and also in supporting children in their school experiences.

Adolescence—Identity vs. Role Confusion

The next stage is associated with adolescence. During this time, adolescents are attempting to determine who they are, what they stand for, and where they are heading. They review their history and then try out new possibilities and new roles in preparation for adult life. This stage is frequently very confusing and fraught with tension for children and parents alike (Goetting, 1986). Through the course of development in this stage, adolescents need to establish a strong sense of identity. In order to do this, they often feel the need to break away from the traditions and expectations of the family, and to "try on" new ways. This often results in conflicts with parents and other authority figures. Failure to resolve the crises associated with the formulation of an identity results in role confusion—a sense of uncertainty about "who am I?" Other related issues and concerns such as sexuality and peer influences can also affect families.

Perspectives

Mark is a 32-year-old social work student at a community college. He comes from a blended family. His father was a Black American who immigrated to Canada as a child. His biological mother was from the Cree Nation in Manitoba. Mark, his two brothers, and his stepsister and stepbrother were raised by his Danish stepmother and his father. Mark described his transition to adolescence and his later development in the following words.

"When I was about 13, we had a family reunion with my stepmother's family in another province. I asked if I could stay at home with friends. In a way I wanted to test my parents to see whether they really wanted me to be part of this family. They let me stay, and I interpreted this as quite a devastating rejection. I really did not feel part of the family anymore, and I remember quite desperately seeking out a group with whom I could identify and feel as if I belonged. The group I felt comfortable with at that time was basically a bunch of kids in trouble. Drinking, smoking, drugs, and vandalism were the norms for this group. This rebellious stage lasted for two years. I still lived at my family's house, but I didn't feel or act as part of the family. Although my parents didn't understand (and I never told them) why I had emotionally 'left' the family, they put up with me. My father tried to influence my behaviour (for example, we had arguments about my smoking), but he was unsuccessful.

"After two years (at the age of 15), I left home and continued to get into trouble until about the age of 17. I lived with friends, on the street, or with anyone who would take me in. At age 17, I sought out my biological mother. She was very happy to have me, although I was not very easy to like at the time. I blamed her for a lot of my problems and acted as if she owed me a great deal. I found out that my mother had left me as a baby because of a serious and chronic problem with alcohol. When we were reunited, I had an addiction problem with drugs, and she still was an alcoholic. We lived together for a couple of chaotic years.

"My addiction led me to trouble with the law, armed robbery, and a three-year jail sentence. The only support that I had through that period was my mother, since my father and I terminated our contact while I was with my mother. At the age of 21, I was released from jail, still with an addiction problem, and still on a path to self-destruction. My father died when I was 23. I became suicidal, and I blamed it on my mother. This situation continued for approximately three years. When I was 25, my stepmother died of an accidental overdose. Finally, I realized that I badly needed help.

"I entered a recovery program, during which my relationship with my mother changed somewhat. She realized how badly I needed help but couldn't help her own addiction. A crucial part of my recovery was realizing the need for reconnecting with my Native roots. I had been ashamed of them previously, probably due to my mother's experience. I sought contact with Native people and immersed myself in Native culture. I attended a Native educational program to upgrade my education and complete my high school diploma. It is interesting that while I strongly identified with the Native community, my mother remained alienated from it. Unfortunately, she died a year ago from an alcohol-related illness.

"At the age of 30, I entered the social work program. I am still very involved with the Native community, want to continue with university, and hope to work in community development with the Native community. The transition from childhood to adulthood and the development of a strong sense of self was a long process for me. The most important learning for me during those stormy transition years was that each person, as he approaches adulthood, needs to make his own choices in life."

Young Adulthood—Intimacy vs. Isolation

Once the young adult has developed a clear sense of identity, he or she is ready to enter into an intimate relationship with another person. Intimacy involves commitment and closeness to another person, and may be more easily achieved when both persons have a developed sense of self, of who they are and what they want. When intimacy does not develop, isolation and loneliness may result.

Middle Adulthood—Generativity vs. Stagnation

Adulthood is marked by the striving to reach social and professional acceptance (Barrett et al., 1995). Adults need to feel that they have contributed to the world either by raising children or by having successful careers. Often, they direct considerable energy towards maintaining the sense that they have contributed to the next generation, that they will leave someone or something behind them when they die. When the adult is not involved in such activities, there is a tendency towards stagnation, which may in turn lead to living in the past, when the person was more successful.

As parents pass through the stage of middle adulthood, their parenting skills will probably be affected. Ongoing parenting and career development will both occur during this period. Parents will likely be heavily involved and invested in these activities as a means of increasing their generativity.

Later Adulthood—Ego-Integrity vs. Despair

The last stage is the culmination of all the previous stages. The adult attempts to make sense of his or her life and to see it as in some way meaningful. As adults review their lives, they may feel satisfied and prepared to meet the challenges of growing old and dealing with the prospect of death, or they may feel despair, helplessness, and a fear of dying. Families will certainly be affected as older family members go through this stage.

We need to remember that the tasks described above in each stage are never completely accomplished and may carry over to later stages. People whose early childhood experiences have not been conducive to establishing trust may have difficulty with trust later on in life. But positive experiences with relationships later on in life can often compensate for earlier experiences. Similarly, positive experiences early on in life cannot completely immunize people from the effects of persistent stressors and crises later on. Development is a complex phenomenon and any attempt to predict its course with accuracy is open to many pitfalls. However, understanding the challenges typical of different life stages can enhance our ability to consider people's behaviour in a positive light, to empathize, and to offer support. For example, we can help parents understand that the toddler is not trying to frustrate the mother—he is exercising his independence—or that the young adolescent's perceived negativism towards her family is often temporary and an expression of her need to find out who she is, separate and apart from her parents. Understanding aspects of the development of the individual child may help parents to understand why their child behaves in certain ways. In turn, this knowledge may lead to less stress and more effective parenting. Early childhood professionals can play a major role in providing parents with information related to all areas of development.

This review has focused exclusively on psychosocial development to illustrate how development, across the life span, may influence the child or family. It is important to remember that development occurs across all areas of development simultaneously—physically, emotionally, in language, cognition, etc. We will now consider two other aspects of development in the early years—cognitive development and the development of attachment. This brief review will provide a broader understanding of how developmental issues may affect the family, but will also form the foundation for the discussion of issues affecting children and families in the impending chapters. Understanding how children may perceive and respond to situations affecting them will assist early childhood professionals in helping young children to cope.

Development in the Early Years

Developmental research over the years has provided us with many insights into how children grow and change, but also offers some insights into how children may view and interpret the events of their lives. Recent research on brain development has provided new insights into the development of emotional and relationship abilities and how these may be impacted by events within the family in the early years. We will now consider how the young child may attempt to understand their world, beginning with cognitive development and followed by considering how attachment and emotional development may be impacted by events in the early years. This review will assist adults in understanding how children may interpret and understand their world and how caregivers may support them.

Infants

Very young children are considered to be in the stage of sensorimotor development (Piaget, 1972). That is to say that sensory experiences and motor experiences form the basis of how children learn about themselves and their world. In this stage, children may be affected by events within the family because of changes in their environments or how the individuals in their environment care for them. The child may not be able to comprehend or hold the memory of a traumatic situation, for example, divorce or death, at this age. However, the child may be affected by the reaction of adults caring for them (e.g., lack of consistency in care, lack of nurturing). In addition, there may be consequences in terms of attachment or emotional development. Attachment will be considered later.

Preschool-Age Children

Preschool-age children are in Piaget's stage of pre-operational development (Piaget, 1972). Several key characteristics of how children think during this stage will help us to understand how they may view events that occur within their families.

The pre-operational stage marks the beginning of representational thought—the children can use symbols in language and in play. Accordingly, pretend play begins (and develops through this stage) and rapid growth and development in language occur. Children have many experiences behind them and have developed a solid foundation of motor skills and are ready, able, and keen to learn more about their world and to understand their world. They are curious and are active thinkers. They begin to solve problems by using thought pattern rather than physically acting on objects, as they did in the previous stage. In regard to this problem solving, children exhibit similar kinds of thinking patterns. They tend to deal with one variable at a time (e.g., Daddy left because I didn't clean my toys). They tend to be cause and effect focused (e.g., this happened because of that) and they tend to be egocentric in their perspective (e.g., this occurred because of me) and unable to take the perspective of others. When put together, this may lead to preschool children assuming fault (e.g., it's my fault that I am adopted) and forming inaccurate perceptions of situations. In addition to this, adults often avoid providing accurate or detailed information to children since they believe that the child will not understand complex situations (such as why he has two mothers instead of a mommy and a daddy). When the very typical preschool child continues to ask questions and ask for clarification over and over, the adults' belief that the child does not understand is reinforced. Children require this type of repetition to learn. They ask questions over and over, seeking reassurance. In addition, they may incorporate elements of the family situation into their play, e.g., playing out the funeral. This is how the child comes to learn, to understand the complexities of their world and events of their lives.

At the same time, the child who is actively acquiring language abilities may not have the words to express feelings or ensure understanding. This, too, may lead the adult to believe that the child does not understand or is not experiencing strong emotions. Children often display short sadness spans in that they do not hold sad feelings over extended periods of time as adults do. When the child feels sad for a time, then resumes play, the parent may again conclude that the child doesn't experience similar feelings or does not understand.

At this age, children have difficulty separating fantasy from reality and may experience fears or nightmares that are very real to them. Unusual circumstances at home combined with the lack of information or feelings of insecurity may cause children to develop intense fears, e.g., fears that Mommy will leave like Daddy. Adults need to be mindful of this and realize that children's fears are real. Generally, adults need to ensure that children receive information, that they are listened to and that their feelings are acknowledged and respected.

School-Age Children

School-age children continue to be curious and actively involved in understanding their world. They, too, are likely to want to try to understand and make sense of situations that occur. School-age children are better able to work with more than one variable so to consider the many factors in a situation. They can better take the perspective of others and understand how someone else may be feeling or see both sides of the story. However, they may have difficulty understanding all the dynamics of a situation: they still blame themselves and may develop fears based on reality (e.g., Who will love me? Who will take care of me? Will Mommy leave me, too?). Although they may need less repetition to understand, they still need access to the information and someone to listen. Children at this age may still be developing abilities to cope.

We have seen that children's perceptions and interpretations of life events may affect their understanding and, perhaps, their behaviour. When parents and caregivers understand how children view the world, they may be more willing to provide suitable information in assisting the child to cope.

Attachment

Attachment (Bowlby, 1969, 1951; Ainsworth, 1969) is the process of developing a trusting bond and relationship with a significant other over the first three years of life. Typically, this relationship occurs with a primary caregiver, usually the mother. New research is focusing on the child's ability to form multiple attachments that involve the significant others in the child's life (e.g., fathers, caregivers). Attachment develops when the child lives in a predictable, nurturing environment where their needs are met. Understanding attachment and emotional development may assist parents and caregivers in providing children with what is most needed in the early years and to understand the consequences when warm, stimulating environments are not available. Having a secure attachment is one of the best indicators of children's ability to cope with stress (Steinhauer, 1998). Children with a secure attachment have developed a sense of trust. Based on this trust, they have the capacity for empathy and an expectation that they can count on others in times of trouble. This secure attachment also provides children with the knowledge and confidence to explore the world, to develop the ability to soothe themselves and is a major source of self-esteem. Attachment helps to lay the foundation necessary for cognitive development.

Healthy attachment can be harmed when the child's needs are not met consistently by a warm and nurturing person. Because this relationship serves as the foundation for future intimate relationships, it may be relevant throughout the person's life. Conditions that may put the child at risk include neglect, abuse, sudden separation, drug and alcohol abuse before and after birth, frequent foster placements or abandonment (Karen, 1994). When any one of these conditions exist, the child's ability to form a trusting bond may be hampered. This lack of trust may generate feelings of aloneness, pervasive anger and a need of control. Children with severe attachment problems may be superficially charming and engaging, demanding and clingy. They ask questions persistently, are indiscriminately affectionate with strangers, are destructive to self and others, and demonstrate poor impulse control and poor peer relations (Egeland & Farber, 1984; Karen, 1994). Many of these behaviours are controlling in that they are effective at keeping the parent or caregiver actively engaged, while at the same time, maintaining a safe distance. These feelings may lead to increased frustration and interfere with the child's relationships in all aspects.

It is now well known that the first three years of life are critical to brain development such as abilities related to emotional development. Steinhauer (1998) suggests that the first years of life are a sensitive period for the development of emotional abilities such as the regulation of emotions. This includes the capacity to inhibit strong feelings of rage or anxiety. Around the age of three, children should have developed the ability to soothe themselves and to modulate strong feelings. If the child does not have a nurturing and stimulating environment, the ability to regulate emotions may be compromised and they may experience long-term effects on development and behaviour.

This brief overview of cognitive development and attachment is intended to provide some insight into how children may perceive events and how they may be affected. There are many other facets of development and factors that may also play a role. Adults—parents and caregivers alike—who understand children's reactions from a developmental perspective are more likely to provide children with what they need in the present to develop an understanding, as well as in the future to ensure continued development.

The Interaction of Developmental Cycles

The development of the child, of parenting skills, and of the family does not occur in isolation. Parents are learning about the child and their own parenting abilities "on the job," so to speak, as changes and transitions occur. At the same time that parents may be adjusting to the birth of a child, they may also be dealing with their own developmental tasks, such as establishing themselves in a career. While they are trying to strengthen and develop the intimate bond between themselves, the attachment needs of their first child may seem to interfere.

As a family progresses through the different stages in the life cycle, there may be times when the developmental needs of the family unit, the parents, and the children seem to fit together well. For example, a couple who have a firmly established relationship and are settled in their careers may be able to respond with more ease to the demands of a developing toddler. On the other hand, if young parents are struggling with their own identity issues, meeting the demands of their own relationship and those of parenting may be more difficult.

The two examples below highlight the interaction between different developmental patterns and the needs associated with each.

Example 1

A single teenage mother with a newborn baby moves back home with her mother.

Family Life Cycle Tasks

Teen Mom
- unattached young adult
  - develop peer relations
  - differentiate self from family
- arrival of children
  - assume parenting role
  - realign relationships to include parenting and grandparenting

---

Teen's Mom	
• family with adolescents	– shift parent-child relationship to permit more independence – refocus on marital relationship and career

Parenting Tasks

Teen Mom	
• nurturing	– challenge of attachment – concern with demands of infant – relationship among family members may change

Teen's Mom	
• interdependent	– authority and communication issues – development of new relationship with child – increased independence – assessment of own identity as a parent

Developmental Tasks

Baby	
• trust vs. mistrust	– requires stable, consistent, and nurturing environment – depends totally on caregivers

Teen Mom	
• identity vs. role confusion	– needs to sort out her identity – deals with peer influence

Teen's Mom	
• generativity vs. stagnation	– wants to contribute to the next generation – pursues generativity at work

As we consider the different developmental stages of each family member, potential sources of stress become clear. The teen is dealing with issues of independence, while her situation calls for increased dependence on her family. As she is sorting out her own identity, how have the physical changes associated with pregnancy affected her? How will her new role of mother interact with her other roles? Likewise, her mother may be at a stage when she wants to devote her energies to her career, and is now faced with a long-term commitment to her daughter and grandchild. The baby's key needs are for stability and consistency. How will these needs be met, given the multiple transitions that all the family members are experiencing?

Example 2

A working couple in their late 30s have a 4-year-old and a toddler. The husband's parents are elderly and will probably need nursing care in the near future.

Family Life Cycle

Parents	
• family with young children	– adjust marital relationship to make room for children

	- assume parenting roles
	- realign relationships to include parenting and grandparenting roles
Grandparents • family in later life	- maintain functioning in face of deterioration - deal with losses - prepare for death - make room for emerging role of middle generation

Parenting Tasks

Parents • authority	- establish rules, authority - learn to communicate with their children and with each other about their children - begin to form self-concepts
Grandparents • departure	- adapt to and accept child's separateness and individuality - examine successes and failures - redefine identity as a couple

Developmental Tasks

Toddler • autonomy vs. shame	- exerts need for independence and decision making - resists accepting help
Four-Year-Old • initiative vs. guilt	- wants to do, to create - seeks peer relations
Parents • generativity vs. stagnation	- want to contribute to the next generation and career work - strive for acceptance
Grandparents • ego-integrity vs. despair	- make sense of own lives - cope with changes due to aging and impending death

Again, we see family members dealing with multiple transitions in their lives. The parents need to allow the older child to take initiative, while at the same time ensuring that the toddler is safe and realizes that the same opportunities are not available to him at his age. They are simultaneously struggling to meet the needs of their new family and their marriage and to cope with the needs of their aging parents. Without considering any other factors, the multiple transitions occurring here may contribute significantly to family stress.

Conclusion

This chapter has focused on the transitions that are common within a family over its life span. As children grow and develop, so do parents in terms of their parenting skills. Family development implies change over time (Pittman, Wright, & Lloyd, 1989; Olson, Lavee, & McCubbin, 1988). Families inevitably change with the major additions, departures, or modifications of roles (Aldous & Klein, 1988). These transitions produce varied reactions within different families. Early childhood professionals who are aware of the nature of transitions may be better able to provide resources and support families as necessary.

Exercises

1. Interview a couple with young children. Ask them how their relationship changed and grew when children came along. Take notes and write up a brief report after the interview.

2. Interview a single parent of a young child. Ask how his or her life has changed in response to the growing and developing child. Write a brief report afterwards.

3. Interview your own parents. Question them on how your own family developed. Ask them how they changed as parents over the years. List the ideas or concepts relevant to your family history.

4. Interview couples with children other than their own biological children. How did their relationship change and develop? Write a brief report outlining their responses.

5. Compare the responses in the four brief reports you have written. Write a final report summarizing your findings and answering the following questions:

   - How did the family life cycle differ for the four parent groups you interviewed?

   - What similarities did you note in these four families?

   - What can you conclude about the family life cycle after considering these similarities and differences?

part 2

Facing Family Challenges

In most day-care centres today, you will find children whose families are facing particular challenges. Research suggests that some high-risk children may develop difficulties due to living in these environments; however, many become competent, healthy adults. In the past, the focus was on dealing with the problems associated with adversity. Our focus will be on *understanding* these difficulties—the causes or correlated factors, and the effects on children, on parents, and on the family as a system.

Part 2 will examine the various issues that families may face, although all families will not face every one of them or be affected by them in the same way. Each chapter will explore a different issue in detail, outlining the adult's and child's view of the situation and closing with practical ideas that caregivers may use to support the child, the parent, and the family as a whole. It is essential that early childhood professionals become aware of the potential risks that families *may* face so that they are better prepared to support families as needed. It is essential to realize that these are *risks;* they may not affect families, nor affect families in the same way. Topics include divorce, blended families, death in the family, poverty, single parenting, teen parenting, violence and abuse in families, the child with special needs, adoption, same-sex parenting, and immigrant families. We hope that, as caregivers learn more about these issues, they will develop an understanding of the challenges faced by children and their parents. This understanding should in turn form the foundation of support offered in a nonjudgmental and empathic manner.

chapter 4

Divorce

Objectives

- **To understand the prevalence of divorce.**
- **To understand the potential impact of divorce on the child and family.**
- **To understand the factors that influence adjustment to divorce.**
- **To examine attitudes towards divorce.**
- **To discuss ways that the early childhood professional can support children and their families who have experienced a divorce.**

> When Karen's mother brought her to day care one Friday morning, the woman was clutching an infant car seat and overnight bag in her arms. "We just finalized our separation arrangement," said the mother matter-of-factly. "Please make sure that her dad remembers the car seat. He doesn't have one for his car and he'll need it." Linda, the caregiver, sighed and thought to herself, "I knew that something was going on at home because Karen has not been her usual happy self, but I had no idea that this is what it was."

Divorce and separation have become substantially more prevalent in North American society over the last two decades (Peck & Manocherian, 1989). Ruggles (1997) cites the rise of female labour force participation and the decrease in farm employment as two factors which are closely associated with this increased prevalence. It is estimated that, in the foreseeable future, approximately 50 to 60 percent of marriages will end in divorce (Eshleman & Wilson, 1995; Peck & Manocherian, 1989; Vanier Institute of the Family, 1994). Conway (1995) predicts one in two marriages will end in divorce in the 1990s. Although recent statistical trends suggest that the divorce rate in Canada has stabilized (McCloskey, 1997), approximately two out of five children will see their parents separate and subsequently experience the consequences of such a family disruption (Furstenberg & Teitler, 1994). Bearing this statistic in mind, we will discuss the various aspects of divorce, how it will affect the young child's perceptions and feelings, and how it will affect the relationship between the children and their parents. Lastly, we will discuss how the early childhood professional might provide support to children and families who are experiencing a divorce.

Divorce

Even though divorce and separation are much more prevalent today than in the past, children and adults alike often consider it to be a tragedy, a crisis, something that happens "only to other people," and something that disrupts their whole world (Richardson, 1988). Divorce continues to be consistently rated as the second most stressful life event after the death of a loved one (Peck & Manocherian, 1989; Kitson et al., 1989). It is a multi-level crisis that may be experienced emotionally, socially, and financially, and that can have a devastating effect on the parent–child relationship (Ward, 1994). Along with this, there may be a series of immediate "transitional crises" (Ward, 1994: 178) during which a number of significant changes are made. Everyone involved is forced to make emotional and practical lifestyle adjustments that can further contribute to the stress of the divorce itself. There is as yet no normal or easy way to divorce, so couples may feel inexperienced and isolated as they make their way through the process. All parties should realize from the start that periods of crisis and stress will occur and, in fact, will likely reoccur over long periods of time.

More recent literature suggests that attitudes towards divorce appear to be changing, with a trend towards approval (Eshleman & Wilson, 1995). More people are coming to believe that divorce is the best solution when marital difficulties cannot be overcome. Divorce is now being seen as an escape from an unhappy marriage rather than a personal failure. This trend is supported by the evidence that divorce is permitted in almost every nation of the world. However, even though attitudes may be changing, we must remember that divorce is still a stressful event for anyone who experiences it.

Divorce is a process that begins and ends at different times for parents and children (Wallerstein, 1991; Brooks, 1987). For example, the parents may have accepted the idea that their marriage is over and may have made plans to separate long before they inform the children. The parents in this case may be near the end of the process, while it is just beginning for the children. On the other hand, when parents have been arguing and fighting over long periods of time, the child may have been wishing for the fighting to stop or for a separation to occur. When the announcement is finally made, the child is more than prepared. In this case, the child may be at the end of the cycle while the parents might be at the beginning. It is important to realize that people may be at different levels of awareness and acceptance. It may be helpful to remind parents of this, if, for example, they don't understand why their preschooler is not yet sleeping through the night or is showing signs of anger many months after the divorce.

Divorce is a disorganizing process that extends over years and has lasting effects (Jaffe, 1991; Hetherington et al., 1982; Richardson, 1988; Wallerstein, 1991; Skolnick, 1992). Many adults may recover after two or three years. However, two to three years in the life of a young child may have much more of an impact on that child's development.

Divorce involves a major restructuring of the child's world view (Richardson, 1988). In the eyes of the preschool child, the world consists almost entirely of the family, and now that family, as the child has known it from birth, ceases to exist. The child must adapt to living with one parent rather than two. The child may experience a sense of abandonment by the parent who is not living at home. There may also be tensions associated with building a relationship with a "weekend parent." This visiting relationship will usually be an unfamiliar experience for both the parent and the child. Because of the frequent disruptions—the repeated need to say goodbye to each other just when they are renewing their relationship—hostility may develop on both sides. Also, there will likely be a substantial decline in the child's standard of living (Hetherington et al., 1995), as we will discuss later in this chapter. All of these factors will prove to be of major significance, not just in the present but also in the future, especially when such children begin to establish relationships of their own.

Effects of Divorce on Children

Studies suggest that younger children suffer more short-term difficulties and behavioural outbursts and that behavioural problems will be noticeable at the time of the divorce rather than surfacing later (Wallerstein & Kelly, 1980). Young children with little or no memory of "family" prior to the divorce seem to have the easiest time adjusting (Wallerstein, 1984). It also appears that boys have more difficulty coping with divorce than girls do (Peck & Manocherian, 1989; Ward, 1994). Typically, when there is family stress, as in divorce, boys seem to be more vulnerable (Galinsky, 1986). Skolnick (1992) reported that, five years following the divorce, more boys were still preoccupied and upset about it than girls were. It may be that girls internalize their feelings while boys externalize them so that they are more noticeable (Furstenberg & Teitler, 1994). However, other studies have indicated that boys may experience more difficulties in the short term, while girls experience coping difficulties later in development, particularly when they reach adulthood (Ward, 1994; Wallerstein, 1991; Furstenberg & Teitler, 1994). Although more studies need to be done to enhance our understanding of children's responses to divorce, the research has consistently pointed to certain typical effects that divorce has on the children involved.

Divorce has been associated with poor academic achievement, behavioural difficulty, poor self-esteem, and difficult social relations (Eshleman & Wilson, 1995; Amato, 1993). It creates a sense of loss and failure, and it marks the beginning of a difficult period of transition for the child (Skeen & McKendry, 1980). The magnitude of the effects appear to be related to the child's temperament and personality, the quality of the parental relationships prior to the divorce, the adjustment by the custodial parent, and the parents' post-separation relationship (Jaffe, 1991).

There is, in fact, great diversity in children's reactions to divorce (Hetherington et al., 1995). Some will react with behavioural outbursts, anger, resentment, and confusion. On the other hand, sometimes divorce will remove the child from stressful relationships, thereby enhancing his or her competence (Hetherington et al., 1995). A child who generally adapts to new situations with ease will likely have an easier time adjusting to the divorce than one who seems to need regularity and consistency and has trouble adapting to new situations. A child who has witnessed severe conflict between parents over a brief period prior to the divorce may experience the divorce quite differently from one whose parents gradually grew apart and agreed to terminate the marriage. Similarly, a child whose parents continue to demonstrate their love, commitment, and involvement with their children, and who relate to one another respectfully, will experience divorce differently from one whose parents are involved in bitter post-divorce conflict.

Factors Affecting Adjustment to Divorce

Several factors have been identified that may affect both the adults' and the child's understanding of and adjustment to divorce. Every child will not react in precisely the same way following a divorce. Throughout the divorce process, both adults and children experience emotional highs and lows that often resurface and intensify when a new crisis or transition occurs.

Scenario

Missing the Father

Marcy had been divorced for two years. She had a well-paying job and had managed relatively well with her two children, aged 4 and 6 years. By the second summer after the divorce, she felt that she was ready to take her children on a vacation. In a holiday mood, they drove to their favorite campsite and began to set up camp. As she unpacked their camping equipment, she suddenly realized that the task of setting up the tent was all hers. As she tried to ready herself for this task, her 6-year-old noticed the look of despair on her face. "Daddy always did this part, didn't he?"

The length of time that situations like the one described above continue, and the intensity of the mood swings involved, will vary from person to person. But professionals need to be aware that strain does manifest itself long after the actual decision to separate or divorce is made and may in fact intensify over time rather than diminish.

The Amount of Conflict

The amount of conflict that exists in the marriage is one factor to consider when gauging the child's emotional adjustment (Hetherington et al., 1995; Ward, 1994; Skeen & McKendry, 1980). Conflict may exist either prior to the separation or after the separation occurs. When the child has been living in an environment with a high degree of conflict and much fighting, he or she may be better off living with one stable parent than living with two parents who are constantly embroiled in conflict (Eshleman & Wilson, 1995; Richardson, 1988). Parental conflict and displays of hostility are more often associated with poor adjustment than the fact of the parental separation itself (Jaffe, 1991). Neglect of the child's physical and emotional needs is more common when parents feel trapped (Skolnick, 1992).

Circumstances may also exist where conflict escalates only after the separation or during the divorce process as the parents attempt to divide their belongings and decide on custodial arrangements. The children then become central to the conflict, whereas previously the parents attempted not to involve them in their problems. At this stage, children may be forced into the difficult position of having to take sides (Amato, 1993). Several studies support the view that the level of conflict is the key factor in the child's adjustment to the divorce (Peck & Manocherian, 1989; Richardson, 1988; Wallerstein, 1991; Furstenberg & Teitler, 1994). Post-divorce conflict may lead to chronic strain on the children (Amato, 1993). The chances of an easy adjustment can only be hindered when the children become the focal point of the conflict in a custody battle. This scenario is particularly difficult for the child, and it seems inevitably to work against the best interests of the child (Skolnick, 1992).

Changes in Relationships After Divorce

The number and nature of relationship changes that may occur for a particular child as a result of separation and divorce also affect that child's ultimate adjustment to the divorce (Peck & Manocherian, 1989). It is very rare that separation and divorce result in the change of just one relationship, that between the parent and child. For example, the loss of the father may lead to changes in the standard of living. The mother may need to go back to work, leading to the need for day care and leaving the mother with less time for the child. Other relationship changes within the family may also occur. For example, the child may not continue to live with his or her siblings, and contact with grandparents, aunts, uncles, and cousins may lessen. If the divorce necessitates a change of residence, then friends, day care, school, and lifestyle may also change. The child may lose a pet with a change of residence. The more changes that children encounter, the more new factors they must learn to cope with (Stolberg et al., 1987) and the more disorganizing the entire process will likely be (Hetherington et al., 1995; Furstenberg & Teitler, 1994).

In addition, during the process of separation and divorce, children may feel estranged from one or both parents and other people (e.g., not seeing or interacting with grandparents, etc.). Along with this, it is not uncommon that few people outside the family may know about the situation. This may cause stress for the child (e.g., who can I tell, what do I say?) and may leave the child with few supports available (Garanzini, 1995).

Economic Factors

The most problematic and enduring change for mothers and their children is the decline in economic conditions (Skolnick, 1992; Galarneau & Sturrock, 1997). Divorced women with children continue to be disadvantaged (Eshleman & Wilson, 1995; Furstenberg & Teitler, 1994). One likely reason is the difficulty for mothers with children, especially preschool children, to find and maintain employment. This problem may be compounded by the fact that earnings for women continue to be lower in most occupations and that child support payments from fathers are sometimes irregular (Eshleman & Wilson, 1995). Withholding child support payments may be associated with the ongoing conflict between spouses and the frequency of visits from the noncustodial parent. Financial support is more likely when the spouses have a workable relationship and fathers have greater economic resources at their disposal (Furstenberg & Teitler, 1994). In the end, the child's nutritional and health needs may be affected. In addition, resources may not be available to provide the child with the educational materials, such as books, required to foster academic success (Amato, 1993).

Families living in poverty are more likely to divorce and to have difficulties in adjustment, partly because they experience more stressful lives generally (Kitson et al., 1989).

Father Absence

Many studies have focused on the father's absence and the effects it has on children after a divorce. For example, it was thought that children raised in father-absent homes experienced higher levels of school failure, delinquency, and promiscuity (Furstenberg & Teitler, 1994; Richardson, 1988). However, more recent research has indicated that the father's presence is but one of a number of factors that change for the child when divorce occurs (Hetherington et al., 1995). It is the multiplicity and interaction of factors that may contribute to difficulties—not just one dimension.

It must be recognized that, in many divorce settlements, mothers are granted custody and fathers become the noncustodial parent (Furstenberg & Teitler, 1994; Umberson & Williams, 1993). This new arrangement requires the changing of roles and functions for all concerned and may be extremely difficult. For men, divorce may lead to a sense of loss and failure, both as a husband and as a father. Over time, fathers may have a diminishing incentive to maintain a relationship and support. For example, both fathers and children may have to re-form their relationship on the basis of weekend visits, there may be continued stress in always having to say goodbye, and conflicts may increase if spouses disagree about the children's upbringing and parental visits. Fathers who were the decision makers within the marriage may experience a sense of loss of control over their children after divorce. Children may be confused by different rules and standards, different ways of interacting, new people who become involved in relationships with either parent, etc. All of these factors may have negative implications for the relationship with the child (Umberson & Williams, 1993).

Availability of Both Parents

A related factor that is important in the child's adjustment is the availability of both parents (Peck & Manocherian, 1989). The literature suggests that the noncustodial parent decreases involvement over time and that the custodial parent is often employed, which limits the time available for the children. The custodial parent may also be experiencing high levels of stress, which may further impair the relationship with the child (Jaffe, 1991). Is the child able to see each parent frequently and openly? Is the child able to be honest with each parent? Although one or both parents may physically be there, are they available for their child to talk to, to listen to, or is only one parent available emotionally for the child? The literature indicates that consistent visits by the noncustodial parent are critical if the child is to learn how to cope after the divorce (Kurtz, 1994). Furthermore, children need and desire an ongoing relationship with both parents and often are dissatisfied with the traditional access arrangements, which may allow them to spend only every second weekend with the noncustodial parent (Peck & Manocherian, 1989).

Responsibilities

Another factor related to the impact of divorce is the number of responsibilities that the remaining family members must assume in the absence of the one parent (Skeen & McKendry, 1980). When the responsibilities are too great, the child may become resentful. For example, the reaction might be "If Dad were still here, I wouldn't have to take out the garbage or mow the lawn." Or, "If Mom were still here, we wouldn't have to go to the babysitter's all the time." On the other hand, when the level of responsibility is appropriate to the child's age, the child may feel more competent and more positive about the experience (Skeen & McKendry, 1980). For example, "I'm Mommy's little helper." Or, "Daddy and I make supper together."

Custody Arrangements

Until the middle of the nineteenth century, fathers were automatically awarded custody of children after a divorce because children were considered the property of their fathers (Jaffe, 1991). Later, mothers were generally awarded custody because it was believed that they were more nurturing; fathers were given custody only when they were able to prove that mothers were somehow unfit (Jaffe, 1991). There is now a variety of options or trends associated with custody arrangements. It is still relatively common in North American cultures that the mother gets custody of the children. This arrangement continues to account for 73 percent of custody settlements (Eshleman & Wilson, 1995). Baker (1997) argues that the practice of awarding custody and child support remains closely tied to traditional gender roles and labour force gender inequality. However, this practice is being met with increasing opposition from many fathers who want to continue their parental role and spend more time with their children. The most popular arrangement, whereby mothers maintain custody during the week and children spend alternating weekends with fathers, often presents difficulties. It may lead to the perception that father has the "easier" role, since he does not need to place any demands on the children over the weekend, and their time can be spent having fun. Mothers, on the other hand, find it difficult to spend quality time with their children during the busy weekdays when other chores and responsibilities vie for their attention. Children also report that these arrangements are not satisfying and that they are difficult to maintain (Richardson, 1988).

One current option that divorced couples are turning to is a form of joint-custody arrangement where both can be equal partners in parenting. Joint legal custody refers to shared responsibility for decision making in regard to the children (Eshleman & Wilson, 1995). However, in an environment of hostility and conflict, these arrangements are often difficult to implement (Richardson, 1988). Court decisions in favour of joint custody are limited in their effectiveness unless the parents have worked out a solution on their own and have demonstrated that they can cooperate. Because there have been so few of these arrangements, there is limited evidence of how they actually work (Hetherington et al., 1995; Richardson, 1988).

Another option currently being tried is joint physical custody, where children spend one week at their father's house then one week at their mother's house. Although this may offer the best solution for the parents, it can be very difficult for young children to understand and make the necessary adjustments. The children will have to contend with two different homes and with two different sets of rules, expectations, and routines. Just as they become accustomed to one, it will be time to change to another. Also, if parents live in different neighbourhoods, children lose a sense of continuity with their friends and neighbourhood activities. The day-to-day problems of keeping track of their belongings and other aspects of their life lead most children to think of one place as home, as their permanent residence (Skolnick, 1992). When children are alternating between two homes in this manner, the day-care centre might be the most consistent environment in their lives.

Given the difficulties inherent in divorce and in finding a solution that will work best for all parties involved, the most common basis for determining custody arrangements has been called "the best interest of the child" principle (Richardson, 1988). This process includes consideration of the parents' wishes, the expressed wishes of the child, the child's relationship with both parents, the length of time in residential custody with the one parent, the child's adjustment during the separation period, and both the financial and emotional ability of either parent to provide for the child's needs (Skolnick, 1992). Any past history of neglect, abuse, or addictions may also be relevant in determining custodial arrangements. Needless to say, custodial arrangements are by their nature controversial. The bottom line is that long-term legal battles full of conflict are ultimately not in the best interest of the child (Skolnick, 1992). According to McKenzie and Guberman (1997) there are many emerging programs in Canada for divorcing parents that focus on the interests of children. However, most programs are still small and voluntary with a limited number of participants.

In summary, there are many factors that influence the child's eventual adjustment to divorce. The child must cope with the accumulation and interaction of many stressors at the same time (Hetherington et al., 1995). When there are a greater number of stressors, poor coping mechanisms, and few resources, the child is more at risk for serious adjustment difficulties (Jaffe, 1991).

The Child's Perception of Divorce

The infant or toddler may not react to the separation or divorce itself simply because of their level of cognitive development (Peck & Manocherian, 1989). That is, the infant will not comprehend the changes that have occurred. The infant or toddler may, however, react to any change in the quality of caregiving from the mother. For example, since the mother is preoccupied with her own stresses related to the divorce, she may be less attentive to the child's needs. The child may cry more, want more cuddling, or change eating and sleeping patterns as a consequence of this change in the mother. The child's attachment to the departing parent may be at risk. In situations where the father is the nonresidential parent, it is he who frequently feels excluded and, as a result, decreases contact over time (Peck & Manocherian, 1989). The baby then is more reluctant to spend time with the father, who seems more and more like a stranger. This reaction may, in effect, create even more distress as the mother feels more burdened and the father feels even more excluded and more inadequate.

The toddler may be just as affected as the infant by the change in caregiving from a distressed or resentful parent. Toddlers may not yet have the time concepts to realize that Daddy has been gone for a long time; thus their reactions will be similar to those of the younger child. However, since toddlers are moving from the developmental stage of acquiring trust or security to independence, this transition may be threatened as they experience a loss of security in their world (Peck & Manocherian, 1989; Skeen & McKendry, 1980). Autonomy and independence may be much more difficult for the child and parent to achieve in these circumstances.

The preschool-age child has developed a fairly clear idea of his own family, and a divorce is disruptive because it destroys that concept. This is a devastating event for young children, because they do not yet have the cognitive or language capacity to understand this kind of change fully. For example, the child may ask, "How long will Daddy be gone?" or "What do you mean that Daddy is gone?" Regressions to earlier forms of behaviour are common (Richardson, 1988; Jaffe, 1991). These include crying, clinging, separation anxiety, bedwetting, or needing a soother, bottle, or blanket again (Peck & Manocherian, 1989; Richardson, 1988). Preschool children who see the world from their own perspective, and who therefore have difficulty separating reality from their own thoughts, are highly likely to experience guilt, confusion, and self-blame (Amato, 1993; Peck & Manocherian, 1989). For example, a little girl may tell herself, "If I am a good girl, Mommy will come back." It is common for young children to have fantasies of their parents or families reuniting (Hetherington et al., 1995). Children often think that the parent left because they were bad (Jaffe, 1991). There may also be an increase in fears that the child exhibits (Richardson, 1988). When divorce occurs, it is not uncommon that classic childhood fears become more pronounced because the home base is no longer secure for the child (Schneider, 1998). For instance, the child may demonstrate an intense fear reaction when Mom leaves for the day and experience a much more difficult separation than earlier. Fear of abandonment by adults, leading to clinging, is common in young children (Schneider, 1998; Skolnick, 1992; Skeen & McKendry, 1980). Children may sometimes interpret the loss of a parent through divorce or death as rejection (Stolberg et al., 1987). While acknowledging the confusion that preschool children experience, Hetherington (1995) suggests that their cognitive immaturity may actually be beneficial over time since they tend to forget the conflict and their own feelings about it rather quickly.

Children between the ages of 5 and 7 are considered to be more vulnerable (Wallerstein, 1991) because they understand more about the implications of divorce but do not yet have ways to cope or a means of arranging activities that give them some relief (Kurtz, 1994). Children at this age may feel sad, deprived, angry, and lonely, and they may be more demanding or disobedient (Skeen & McKendry, 1980; Jaffe, 1991). Often, they may experience fears (Farrell, 1989) including the fear of abandonment or loss of love. These fears, combined with the child's level of reasoning, may lead to what adults perceive as strange ideas. For example, the child may reason that "Mommy loved Daddy and Mommy loved me. Now Mommy doesn't love Daddy, so maybe Mommy doesn't love me either." Although adults may not understand this fear, it may be very real for the child.

Preschool and school-age children are likely to view divorce from their egocentric point of view (Amato, 1993) and, therefore, believe that they are to blame, (Kurtz, 1994). (For example, "I should have cleaned my room better" or "If I didn't fight with my brother, this wouldn't have happened.") In addition, since children often are not provided with all the details or given all the information about the divorce, they attempt to make up their own understanding of it by piecing together bits of information. (Consider the case of the 4-year-old who explained that Daddy's feet were too long for the bed and so he had to find a new one, or that of the 6-year-old who believed that Mom and Dad were allergic to each other because they both said the other made them sick.) Sometimes adults are puzzled by the child's understanding or conceptualization of this situation, but it is important to remember the child's developmental stage and reasoning abilities. Helping the child to understand and cope with the divorce requires seeing the situation from the child's perspective, bearing in mind how the child thinks and feels at different developmental stages, and providing him or her with age-appropriate information (Skeen & McKendry, 1980).

Grieving the Loss

Since divorce constitutes a devastating loss for the child, adjusting to a divorce may be similar to the grief process experienced after a death (Richardson, 1988; Ward, 1994; Kitson et al., 1989). The child may deny that the parent is gone forever and maintain that the separation is temporary. He or she may experience anger at one or both parents and then may attempt to bargain to get the parents back together. The child may exhibit sadness or depression followed by adjustment. Not all children will react in the same way, and often many of these emotions do not last for long periods of time (e.g., the child is sad until he or she needs a peanut-butter sandwich). The importance of these emotions, however, should be recognized and not be minimized merely because they are short-lived. On the other hand, the child may feel a recurring sense of loss because the "departed" parent still comes by. Each time the child sees the father, feelings of anger, bitterness, and loss are renewed (Ward, 1994). In summary, the child may experience one or a range of emotions that may last for a long time or be short-lived. No matter how long they last, though, these feelings have a powerful impact on the child.

The Impact of Divorce on Parenting

Divorce is considered to be a crisis or tragedy in the lives of many adults. Generally, the mental and physical health of divorced adults is at greater risk than that of their single, widowed, or married peers. Men tend to exhibit more symptoms of distress (Skolnick, 1992). Parenting is affected in a number of ways. Parents are likely dealing with feelings of failure, loss, guilt, loneliness, depression, and helplessness (Peck & Manocherian, 1989). A study by Amato (1993) revealed that divorced mothers generally have less social support, are more anxious and angry, show less affection to their children, communicate less, and punish more. It is clear that emotions can interfere with parenting (Skeen & McKendry, 1980).

Children commonly report that their parents were less available and less supportive during the divorce (Jaffe, 1991). Because parents are enmeshed in their own problems and need for support, the needs of their children are sometimes forgotten, and it becomes increasingly more difficult to provide a consistent environment for them (Peck & Manocherian, 1989). Due to the crisis, parents may be unable to respond to the emotional needs of their children (Ward, 1994). Several studies have noted that the quality of the mother–child relationship is more likely to suffer because of her personal emotional needs at the time, her anxieties associated with being single, and her self-involvement (Hetherington et al., 1995). The mother's relationship with the father is bound to deteriorate over time as he becomes more absent and more detached (Skeen & McKendry, 1980). All of these effects on the adult have corresponding effects on the children and on parenting.

What Happens to Parenting?

Often, as both parents become immersed in their own situations and the wide range of emotions involved, the first and most significant result is that the amount and quality of communication between the parents and children will decline (Amato, 1993; Skeen & McKendry, 1980). This effect is due partly to the parents' inability to verbalize their feelings and thoughts to the young child in a way that the child will understand. How do you explain love, infidelity, or a change of heart in terms that a child will understand, when these things are difficult even for adults to grasp? This feeling of helplessness often leads to less and less communication because the parents automatically assume the young child won't understand, or because they feel that it is crucial for young children to be protected from the crueler aspects of life. Very few children have reported that there was a sympathetic parent or adult available to them during the process of divorce (Jaffe, 1991).

It is important, however, to realize that the young child does usually know that something is going on and often thinks that since no one will talk about it, then it must be *really* bad. If we also consider the child's way of thinking (i.e., the egocentric thinking, the self-blame, and the guilt) and the disproportionate fears that children often have, we realize that the child may perceive the situation to be much worse than it actually is.

In the period of transition after a divorce, parents of preschool children are often much less effective and consistent in their discipline, communicate less well, and hold changing expectations for their child's behaviour (Hetherington et al., 1995; Skeen & McKendry, 1980). When the parents feel able to cope, they are attentive to the needs of the child (e.g., "It's time to take a bath" or "Tidy up your toys" or "Eat all of your supper"). When the parent is in a period of emotional upheaval, these day-to-day activities may not be completed. It is also common for the remaining parent to spend extended periods of time alone or on the telephone, and for the children to be left to fend for themselves or shuffled from babysitter to babysitter.

As parents experience a range of emotions, they may respond to their children in inconsistent ways. There may be times when they make few demands for appropriate behaviour, while at other times their expectations are very high. These conditions may alternate without the child understanding the cues that govern the particular situation. For example, one request for a bottle may be met with a quick response while the next is met with reprimands (e.g., "You're too old for a bottle" or "Stop acting like a baby" or "Daddy doesn't like babies"). The child begins to fear that there will be a negative reaction every time he or she approaches the parent, and communication again is diminished. Although these things do happen in all families, it is likely that they happen more frequently when a family is experiencing high levels of stress, as in a divorce.

The last factor to consider is that, under the demands of the situation, the parent may actually lose the ability to listen to the child. This failure is partly the result of the parent's self-preoccupation, but it also stems partly from the child's cognitive representation of the situation. Children ask the same question over and over (e.g., "When will Daddy come home?") in an attempt to increase their understanding of the situation (i.e., "Never is a long time; it's more than one sleep"). The child also puts together pieces of information in ways that seem incomprehensible to adults, which further reinforces their belief that the child cannot grasp even the least complex aspects of the situation. Children may express strange ideas (e.g., "You were angry and yelled at Daddy and he had to leave, so if you get angry with me, I'll have to leave too") or may begin to play out the happenings at home (e.g., the fights, the threats, the separation). Sometimes, children direct their anger at the custodial parent (e.g., "I hate you" or "You can't make hamburgers like Mom" or "I like Dad's stories better"). The parents may think their child's coping mechanisms are inappropriate or indicate a lack of acceptance rather than try to understand how children think and express themselves.

Supporting Families

We will now consider how professionals can deal with the children in their care whose parents are divorced and how they may help the parents to understand the child's point of view. Early childhood professionals can provide a great deal of direct support to the child and either direct or indirect support to the parent.

Examine Your Attitudes

- Do you think children are better off with one parent than with two that fight?
- Is divorce always traumatic for children?
- In your opinion, can children ever get over the divorce of their parents?
- Can divorcing parents keep the interests of their children in focus?
- Do you think parents use children as pawns in divorce?
- Should custody always be awarded to mothers?
- Can divorce have positive effects for children and families?
- Do you believe that parents should sacrifice their personal happiness and gratification to keep the family together?

As professionals whose primary concern is for the well-being of the children in our care, we sometimes find it difficult not to feel angry when we see children deeply distressed because their parents have decided to divorce (Farrell, 1989). These feelings may be exacerbated if the divorce brings forth associations from our own lives, rekindling memories we find painful. If, for example, your father abandoned your family for another relationship, there may be some carry-over of personal resentment to the present situation. On the other hand, your parents' divorce may have been a relief for you. If this sort of memory interferes, you may not be as aware of the impact of divorce on the child in your care.

Scenario

Personal Experiences Can Affect Our Sensitivity

Dianne was a caregiver in a playroom of 5-year-olds. Her earliest memories were of her mother and father fighting constantly. Often, her mother was physically abused. When her mother decided to leave, the fighting and beatings stopped. Dianne felt a sense of relief and thought that divorce was a good thing. So when 5-year-old Jessica was sad because her daddy left, Dianne tried to explain that this was good and that her life would be much better now. Jessica felt otherwise and stopped talking about her feelings about the divorce. Because the circumstances were entirely different, Dianne's personal experience interfered with her ability to respond to the child with sensitivity.

Sometimes religious or cultural values prohibit divorce. And sometimes, even when we have the most liberal views, seeing the child suffer can encourage us to view the parents as selfish.

A Caregiver's Perspective

Shauna, a caregiver at a day-care centre, admitted she had negative feelings for Bernice's parents. Bernice was a well-behaved, happy child until her parents separated. They arrived at a joint-custody agreement that meant Bernice spent one week at Mom's and then one week at Dad's. Both parents felt that this was the best possible arrangement for all concerned. Shauna saw Bernice every day of the week and had a different impression. On Monday and Tuesday, Bernice was unsettled and cried at transitions and any change in plans for the day. Wednesday and Thursday, she was more settled and calm, but by Friday, she was anxious, clingy, and unsettled again. Perhaps the weekends were fine for the parents, but Shauna indicated that she was lucky to have one or two good days a week with Bernice.

While there is no easy way to overcome these feelings, it is important to recognize and be aware of them. Some reminders to ourselves may be helpful:

1. Remember that there are two sides to every story and that you may not be hearing the whole story. The family is a complex system and many factors may lead to divorce. Although painful, the divorce may very well be in the best interest of the whole family.

2. Never take sides. You may have heard one partner's version, but this may vary substantially from the other's. As a professional, you must remain concerned about the child's best interest without becoming involved in the parents' conflict. This is not always as easy as it seems, especially when the parents appear to be using the child as a pawn in the divorce settlement. Approach the situation with the best interest of the child in mind and reserve judgement.

3. Examine your own beliefs and attitudes towards divorce and how these will translate into interactions with the young children and families with whom you work. Try to remember that divorce can have positive effects, especially for families in which divorce may represent an escape from an abusive situation or an opportunity for a second chance (Eshleman & Wilson, 1995). When this is the case, divorce can provide the opportunity for growth for all family members, including the children. Early childhood professionals must then be available to children and families to capitalize on such opportunities as they become evident.

Perspectives

Lea is a 44-year-old divorced mother of two children, Rebecca, aged 9, and Grant, aged 5. Lea was recently talking about her divorce with several of her colleagues.

"I grew up in a small town in Saskatchewan in a strict Catholic home. I went to convent schools for all my education and our family was very religious at home. I left for Saskatoon to continue my university education. I worked very hard at my studies and then later at my teaching career. Consequently, I did not marry until later in life. I met Pascal, who was also a teacher and devout Catholic, at a church fundraiser. We were both very actively involved in the church, and our love grew from there. We married when I was 33 and he was 37 years old.

"I think we both realized that our marriage was in trouble when I was expecting our second child. I was having a difficult pregnancy, and Pascal was not as supportive as when our daughter was born. We had a major argument the day I arrived home with Grant, and I remember thinking, 'What am I going to do?' Divorce was just not something that we could consider—the Church forbids it, and my parents have been married 44 years and Pascal's parents were married 46 years before his father died.

"I stuck it out—I think we both stuck it out because we felt that we had no options. I tried seeing a counsellor, who suggested joint sessions, but Pascal figured that I had the problem, not him, so I didn't continue.

"Last year, things became unbearable. I knew that Pascal was seeing another woman, although he denied it. I finally broke down and issued him an ultimatum—either me or her. To my utter surprise, he chose her and left.

"I can't say that I'm proud of my behaviour over this last year. I have been mean, vindictive, have used the kids to get at him, and have blamed all of our problems on him. Needless to say, he also blamed all of our problems on me. Now that the air has had time to clear, I know why I did what I did. First, I was hurt and I wanted him to be hurt too. But I also realize that my Catholic upbringing played a role. Divorce was not allowed, so I could not let the problems be my fault—if the breakup was his fault, then it was his sin and I did not need to feel guilt. I did feel guilt, and some of my behaviour was a result of it too, I guess. I blamed him for everything, everything was his fault, he was always the bad guy so that I could carry on with a clear conscience. I realize that much of my behaviour was influenced by my traditional religious and family beliefs."

Working with the Child

Lack of stability typifies the life of a child whose parents are in the process of divorce. Therefore, the early childhood professional must try to maintain as stable an environment as possible (Skeen & McKendry, 1980). This may be the only stability the child has in his or her life during this difficult period (Garanzini, 1995). If circumstances permit, it may prove beneficial to have a primary caregiver assigned to the child to ensure this constancy. It is important to maintain consistent expectations for the child, to maintain firm yet reasonable limits, and to try not to overprotect or to indulge the child. Although it is true that the child may need more attention and affection, consistent limits will usually be helpful. For example, the child cannot come to believe that it is okay to hit or act out frustration or to expect extra privileges because of what is happening at home. Nevertheless, these feelings of anger and frustration must still be acknowledged and validated.

Children need to be listened to in an honest and nonjudgmental way. They may need to say that they hate their mom without fear of reprisal. In such a case, reflecting the child's feelings may be helpful (Kurtz, 1994). When the child asserts, "I hate Mom," the responsive caregiver can say, "You are feeling pretty angry at your mom, right?" Listening to the child can provide the professional with some insight into what might be happening at home so that further support can be offered. Listening in this way includes observing what the child does in interactions with other children, with adults, and with toys.

It may be possible to help children of divorced parents gain an understanding of their situation both cognitively and emotionally (Kurtz, 1994). Give the child information through discussion, by reading stories or sharing information—other children may have had similar experiences. Recognize that children may experience a variety of emotions and may need to grieve the loss of a parent or of their family. Provide them with opportunities to work through their feelings. This means allowing each child some time to spend alone, providing them with a variety of activities like art, play-dough, physical activity, or dramatic play to work through their feelings (Skeen & McKendry, 1980).

Supporting Families

Divorced parents may create difficulties for early childhood professionals (Farrell, 1989). Parents may disagree about what is best for the child or may try to use the caregiver's comments against one another, thus putting the caregiver in the middle of conflict. Parents may be preoccupied with their conflicts and not communicate with professionals or the child. They may be too overwhelmed by the situation to support their child, to meet their child's needs, or to recognize achievements or milestones important to the child (Farrell, 1989).

There is much that the early childhood professional can do to help families experiencing a crisis such as divorce. However, it is important to realize that every family will differ vastly in the kind of help it wants or is able to receive. Timing may be a critical factor. If parents, for example, are experiencing intense emotional turmoil, this may not be the most appropriate time to supply information about how to talk to the child. Although parents may find being informed about their children's possible reactions to be helpful, they will also find information difficult to digest or use under conditions of duress. It may be best to pass along this information at another time, but soon enough to prepare the residential parent for the child's "I hate you" screams when they come.

Bearing in mind the vast individual differences among parents in their need for and ability to act upon information, the following suggestions are cautiously offered. Early childhood professionals may provide parents with much support during this difficult time in their lives (Kurtz, 1994). At the minimum, this may consist of the parents feeling confident that their child's needs will continue to be met at the day-care centre or day home. Sometimes just acknowledging the possibility of positive parent–caregiver communication will smooth the way for such communication to occur. When the parent trusts the caregiver, it is likely that communication will be enhanced. It is not uncommon for the caregiver to be certain that something is happening at home but not actually be told anything until much later, usually when raising a concern about the child's behaviour (see the opening vignette of this chapter). All parents are different; some are very open and willing to divulge all information, while others believe that divorce is a private issue. These feelings must be respected and deferred to in future communications. Early childhood professionals must convey to parents that their place is not to judge but to offer support.

Early childhood professionals need to be sure that clear boundaries are established when working with families experiencing a divorce. While they possess a firm foundation of knowledge concerning children, and some knowledge about families and family dynamics, they must also be prepared to acknowledge the limits of their expertise. Early childhood professionals are not marriage counsellors and must be careful about which aspects of the divorce they discuss with parents. They need to understand these boundaries and know when to refer the parent to appropriate community resources.

The following scenario demonstrates how one caregiver offered support within the context of appropriate professional boundaries.

Scenario

Dealing with a Distraught Parent

Mrs. Kortright approached Guadelupe, the caregiver, at the end of the day. She had tears in her eyes and seemed to be on the verge of sobbing. "Everything seems to be falling apart," she said. "My ex-husband disappeared two weeks after the divorce. Shanda [her 3-year-old daughter] wets her bed every night and then can't get back to sleep. Steven [her 9-year-old son] has been called to the principal's office three times this week for fighting with the other children. I feel like I'm going to collapse."

The caregiver responded with empathy, acknowledging that there were a seemingly endless number of pressures that Mrs. Kortright had to face. "Perhaps I can assist you by offering some ideas that may help you and Shanda through this difficult time. It is often helpful in times of crisis to have contact with a trained counsellor who specializes in helping families cope with divorce. I know that things may seem overwhelming now. Would you like me to give you the names and phone numbers of some counsellors? Their services are offered on a sliding fee scale, so cost should not be a concern. Also, I know that a counsellor will be available immediately. We will continue to do all we can at the centre to help Shanda through this difficult period."

Note that the caregiver responded with nonjudgmental support and empathy, outlined clearly the boundaries of her professional expertise (i.e., the preschool child), and referred the mother to more appropriate resources that she had checked out ahead of time. She also reassured the mother that her child would continue to be cared for at the centre.

Early childhood professionals must be very careful not to take sides with one parent against the other. Parents embroiled in custody disputes may attempt to put the caregiver in a difficult position by using comments made against the other parent in court. Caregivers must recognize this possibility and attempt to remain neutral.

Scenario

In the Middle of a Custody Dispute

Beth's parents were embroiled in an 18-month divorce proceeding. Beth lived with her mother, saw her father every other weekend, and spent weekdays in the day-care centre. When Pete picked Beth up, he would ask how her week had gone, what times she had arrived, and what times she was picked up. When Karen picked her up after these weekends, she would ask the caregiver if Beth's clothes were clean, if she was tired, and if she had been fed properly. The caregiver assumed that the parents merely wanted to know about Beth and that she should be providing them with information about Beth and how she spent her days. When the lawyers for both parents later called the caregiver to ask for more details about how the other parent was caring for Beth and her needs, the caregiver felt as though she had been set up and put into the middle of a custody dispute she did not want to be a part of.

Caregivers need to be aware that this may occur and be prepared to deal with it.

Scenario

Refer Parents' Questions to a Neutral Person

A noncustodial father asked his 20-month-old son's caregiver for a record of what time his son was being picked up daily. He stated that he wanted to be sure that the days were not too long, because his shift-work schedule would allow for an earlier pick-up time. The caregiver knew that this was a source of conflict between the parents, so she suggested that he discuss the matter with the director. The director explained that this was an issue that probably needed to be worked out with the parents' lawyers, but that she and her staff would be pleased to share any information on how the child was doing or behaving while in the centre.

Although the parent may not be pleased with such a response, the caregiver and director were able to remain neutral while still providing necessary information about the child. Caregivers should keep their director or supervisor updated in cases like this so that an informed neutral person is available if needed. They may also want to discuss potential situations, such as the scenarios provided above, to ensure that they will know in advance how to deal with future situations.

Early childhood professionals should have the expertise to explain to parents how their children may be perceiving the divorce and to prepare them for reactions or behaviours their children may exhibit. Such behaviour may include, for example, more crying, more of a need for cuddling, more resistance, giving strange explanations, and asking constant questions. Children may also play out the divorce or give mothers and fathers two separate houses at the housekeeping centre. Assure parents that their children need to be listened to and suggest trying to talk about what is happening in their family and home. Parents should also try to prepare the child for impending changes by, for example, providing them with plans for visiting the nonresidential parent (Peck & Manocherian, 1989). It may also be helpful to encourage parents to talk openly to their children to reassure them that the divorce is not their fault and that both parents still love them. The early childhood professional may assist the parents by giving them simple words or explanations that the child may understand, by providing them with books or videos to promote discussion, and by providing concrete activities that may enhance planning (e.g., "You will see Daddy in four sleeps"). Make sure that the parents understand that children also grieve and that they need to grieve and express their anger. Children may ask the same questions over and over (when is Daddy coming back?) and although this may be difficult, parents need to provide answers and reassurance (Daddy still loves you). Children need to feel safe and for this reason they need time to adjust to the situation emotionally.

The child's need for stability becomes apparent when transitions occur from one situation to another. Both parents and caregivers may have to be more aware of the need to warn the child in advance. Although it seems odd, caregivers may want to let the children know when they are moving to another group of children or making a transition to a new playroom at the end of the year, so that the children do not come to think that everyone leaves them.

Resources may be useful for both the child and parent. Books such as *Mom's House, Dad's House* (Isolina, 1980) can be instrumental in helping the parent to promote discussion with the child or in helping the child to realize that divorce is a normal experience for many families. Parents can be referred to local social agencies that may provide emotional support for them or for their children. Awareness of the resources available in your community will be most helpful to families in this time of need.

How You Can Support Families That Have Experienced a Divorce

1. Be aware that the day-care centre may be the most constant factor in the child's life. Maintain consistency in caregivers, settings, expectations, and routine as much as possible.

2. Listen to the child. Be nonjudgmental and help the child to express feelings and questions openly.

3. Share developmentally appropriate information about divorce with the child.

4. Provide the child with opportunities and play experiences for self-expression, e.g., play-dough, art, physical activity, dramatic play, or a place to be alone.

5. Be respectful of the parents in their crisis and attempt to support them.

6. Establish clear boundaries with parents.

7. Provide resources and referrals for families as requested.

8. Encourage the parents' understanding of their child's reactions. Encourage parents to talk openly with the child about divorce, to discuss feelings and impending changes or plans.

Conclusion

Although, for some families, divorce can proceed smoothly, for many it is a time of crisis for both adults and children (Peck & Manocherian, 1989). Parents may be experiencing their own loss and associated pain, while the children are suffering the loss of the familiar family structure and secure home base (Schneider, 1998; Amato, 1993). This change may include the permanent loss of one parent and, at least temporarily, a lessening of the availability of the remaining parent. Communication can easily break down because parents become involved in their own concerns, but also because they may think that their children are incapable of understanding or that they need to be protected from the harsher realities of life. Early childhood professionals can play a key role by maintaining a safe and stable environment for the child, one where it is okay to talk and express feelings. They can also help by providing parents with the support and information that they may be ready to hear (Amato, 1993). Empathic and knowledgeable professionals can offer stability and support during this difficult time for both the child and parent.

Exercises

1. Role-play or consider your responses to the following situations. (Caregivers may not be confronted with any or all of these, but a thoughtful response to any unexpected situation may cause less stress and conflict than making an inappropriate response on the spot.)

a) One parent asks you for information about the other parent.

b) The custodial parent puts you in the position of telling the noncustodial parent that the weekend visit has been cancelled.

c) The parent wants to tell you everything about the divorce.

d) The child refuses to go home with Mom. He says he hates her because she made Daddy go away.

e) The father is attacking the quality of care at the day-care centre. You find out that if Dad has custody, the child will stay at home with a full-time nanny. If Mom has custody, full-time day-care will be required.

f) The mother lies to the child and says, "Daddy isn't here because he didn't want to see you this weekend."

g) The parent tells you that what happens at home is none of your business.

2. Check community resources for those that deal with divorce—support groups for parents, programs for children. These will vary from community to community, so it may be useful to know in advance what is available.

3. Check your local library and bookstore for books pertaining to divorce. Are there any that you would want to recommend for parents? Are there any that would help parents to understand divorce better from the child's perspective? Is there a book that might stimulate conversations about divorce with the child? Would this book be appropriate for parents to share with their children?

Blended Families

chapter 5

Objectives

- To consider the challenges involved when new families are formed.

- To discuss children's feelings about becoming part of a blended family.

- To discuss parents' reactions to their children during the blending process.

- To discuss the role of the early childhood professional in supporting parents and children.

Frank, a 50-year-old man who had been divorced for 15 years and whose children were grown up, made the following comment shortly after his marriage to Margaret, a 42-year-old woman who had a 5-year-old son. Margaret and Jordan had moved into Frank's condominium while they were all waiting to buy a new house. "When I came home from work the other day, I tripped over Jordan's toys as I entered the front door. Jordan heard the beginning of a string of profanities, which I controlled as soon as I realized that I was not alone in the house! I guess there are a lot of things that I'm going to have to get used to, not the least of which is having to share my living room with a 5-year-old and his toys!"

Remarriage and the creation of a blended family represents a major transition in the lives of all concerned. As divorce rates have increased, so have remarriage rates (Dolny, 1996). The practice has become much more common among younger people with children (Eshleman & Wilson, 1995; De'Ath, 1996). It has been estimated that 70–85 percent of adults who divorce will remarry (Garanzini, 1995). The perception of stepfamilies as incomplete or inferior institutions can be attributed to the idealization of the nuclear family as a cultural norm. This view is reinforced by labels, stereotypes, myths, and media representations that portray stepfamilies in a negative manner. The adjustment to a parent's remarriage appears to take longer for children to make than the adjustment to divorce (Hetherington et al., 1995). This adjustment is often complicated by the fact that, as a society, we do not yet have norms or realistic expectations for how this type of family should operate or for how the new roles and relationships should be defined (Ihinger-Tallman & Kay, 1997). Stepfamilies always face the threat of instability, but especially in the first few years. Lack of support from society may be a contributing factor (Rutter, 1995). Researchers have noted that there is a lack of quality assistance available for remarriage and stepfamily preparation, and that few family professionals have been trained for working with stepfamilies (Kaplan & Hennon, 1992; Goldenberg & Goldenberg, 1994). Recently, there has been less of a tendency to consider stepfamilies nontraditional, atypical, or pathological in nature.

Many terms are used to describe what results when previously distinct families come together—reconstituted, blended, or stepfamilies, "the Brady Bunch," or "Yours, Mine, and Ours," to name a few. Some of these terms seem to carry with them negative implications. "Step-parents" may bring forth images of Cinderella's wicked stepmother; indeed, some authors have commented on the need to overcome the stepmother myth (Skeen, Robinson, & Flake-Hobson, 1984; Dainton, 1995). Ward (1994) agrees that the term "step" implies that the new family is not a real family or is less than whole (Garanzini, 1995)! The term "blended" has been used since it seems to capture the tasks of families to blend old and new ways with new expectations and approaches (Garanzini, 1995). The term "blended" has been criticized for implying a closer bond, or more integration, than often occurs. For example, in the vignette that opens this chapter, Frank's older children may not really "blend" or develop a close bond with their young stepbrother (or blended brother), and this may be perfectly appropriate for this particular family. Some parents do not take on maternal or paternal roles with their spouse's children, especially when the children are older. The children themselves may substitute the term "aunt" for that of "mother" in such a case (Hetherington et al., 1995).

The term "remarried families" may be less laden with meanings and expectations, although in some cases this union may not be a remarriage for one of the spouses. Interestingly, Ward (1994) points out that the Stepfamily Association of America, the largest support group for stepfamilies, still uses the term "step." New families often begin by using this term but may eventually drop it, perhaps indicating a successful integration of the family unit. Since there appears to be such great variability in the terms used, we have decided to use the terms interchangeably in this chapter. We bring this to our reader's attention if only because it seems that the language reflects a certain ambivalence in our society concerning this particular family structure. It might be useful for professionals who come in contact with stepfamilies to view their concerns as typical transitional items, rather than insurmountable problems (Cobia, 1996).

There is great variability in the makeup and structure of blended families. In some of these families, both spouses will have children from previous marriages; in others, only one will have children. As well, new children may be added after the remarriage, or the new couple may have no children together. In some cases, one of the spouses has never been married before and thus has no experience with young children (Hetherington et al., 1995). Thus, the experiences of stepfamilies may be very different because of the great variation in structure that exists among them.

When two families join together to form a new family, the end result is often a positive one. Remarriage can offer each spouse emotional and financial security, another adult to share parenting duties, intimacy and sexual satisfaction, and the happiness that comes from having a successful relationship (Brooks, 1987). For all these reasons, the task of parenting itself may seem easier, partly because step-parents may enrich the child's life and provide an extra measure of emotional security. After divorce or single parenthood, this may be perceived as a welcome relief. However, most step-parents will attest to periods of friction and doubt with their stepchildren. They will also point out the need for patience and support from within the family and for external support as well. In this chapter, we will consider the challenges facing blended families, both from the adult's and the child's perspective, and the role of the early childhood professional in supporting families in this major transition period. Such a discussion is timely, since it has been estimated that the blended family would outnumber all other types of families by the year 2000 (Rutter, 1995).

Challenges for Stepfamilies

Stepfamilies face many challenges in the context of the couple relationship, in the new parent–child relationship, and in extended family systems. Other challenges may be related to previous family histories. These various challenges will be explored in more detail.

Myths About Step-Parents

One of the co-authors of this book tells the following story about her daughter.

Scenario

The Evil Stepmother

One day I was driving in the car with my 4-year-old daughter. She repeatedly asked to have the window wipers turned on, even though it was not raining. After I refused her request for the third time, she stated that if I did not turn on the wipers, I would be a stepmother. My daughter has never met a stepmother and does not understand what one is, but she obviously has her own idea of what a stepmother must be like.

We can assume that her perceptions have been shaped by stories or television, and that if she were to become part of a blended family, that perception would have an impact on the development of her relationship with a new stepmother.

Misconceptions or myths about step-parents abound. Stepmothers are thought to be mean, evil, and manipulative (as in Cinderella or Snow White). The stepfather is sometimes viewed as a molester. Add to this the multitude of stories about the vindictive ex-wife and the absentee biological father and it becomes obvious how our culture burdens a stepfamily from the moment it is formed (Rutter, 1995).

Several authors (Ward, 1994; Zastrow & Kirst-Ashman, 1994) have described three additional myths about stepfamilies. The first is that "step is less" (Wald, 1981). This myth entails the belief that a nonbiological or step-parent can never love a child as much as a biological parent. On the other hand, some people believe in the myth that blended families will have "instant love" for each other (Dainton, 1995). They assume that stepmothers will immediately love their new children and that the children will automatically love the new parent. Because of this instant love, mothering will come easily (Dainton, 1995). Images of instant love or of one big happy family (Ward, 1994) are difficult to live up to. Finally, there is sometimes the belief that the new parent will "fix everything." For the child who has had an absent father, or for the child who has experienced parental conflict prior to divorce, the hope is often that the new step-parent will be the "rescuer," who will undo the damage done in prior relationships. Obviously, this is an unrealistic expectation.

One last myth has surfaced out of society's beliefs about single-parent families. The remarriage is seen as a way to rehabilitate the single-parent family (Erera & Fredriksen, 1999). This view may lead to the development of unrealistic expectations in that it is expected that they will behave like first-married families. When this does not happen instantly, families may feel that they have failed or are inadequate.

Roles and Expectations

While hopefully we are moving away from the concept of "the wicked stepmother," we still lack a clear idea of the new roles that parents take on in a blended family situation. Sometimes step-parents are seen as "mature friends" for the children of their spouses, who play with the children but do not participate in discipline or in making major decisions. However, in a shared household (as in the scenario at the beginning of the chapter), this role may be difficult to maintain. Is the new parent to become a partial replacement for a noncustodial parent? If so, in what aspects of parenthood should the step-parent engage—financial commitment, discipline, or recreational activities?

One must also consider how the step-parent is viewed by the wider, extended family system. Is the new spouse considered a friend or the person who broke up the family? Based on these perceptions, the roles and expectations will vary tremendously. According to Ahrons and Rodgers (1987), Fine et al. (1997), and Haberstroh et al. (1998), stepfamily members often bring conflicting role expectations into the new family unit due to their different experiences and family histories. These expectations usually involve how they think people in different family roles (husband, wife, brothers, and sisters) should or should not think, feel, and behave. Often these differing expectations are not recognized until after some conflict has occurred (Kaplan & Hennon, 1992).

Complexity of the Family Structure

Along with redefining roles and re-establishing role expectations, the coming together of two families enhances the complexity of the family system, partially because of the number of people involved (Brooks, 1987). Blended families typically experience "boundary ambiguity" (Eshleman & Wilson, 1995: 495). This term refers to the uncertainty of who is part of the family and how the roles and relationships are to be defined. Simple questions come up, such as: Are the parents of the step-parent to be thought of as "grandparents"? What kind of a relationship will develop between siblings, stepsiblings, and new siblings who arrive after the remarriage? How do children distinguish between roles and relationships with their "dad" and their "stepdad"? Are there guidelines available for how to be a step-parent? The following incident occurred in one blended family.

When Stepchildren Are Treated Differently

Sam and Marina married when Marina's two daughters were aged 14 and 16. A year after their marriage, they had a son, Steven. When Steven was 2, Sam's mother invited the family to a Christmas dinner. As the gifts were opened, Steven gasped with delight when he opened his generous gift from his grandmother. The step-granddaughters attempted to hide their hurt feelings when they opened their token gifts. In discussing this later with a family counsellor, the two girls were embarrassed about their reactions. "We know that she is not our 'real' grandmother," said the 19-year-old, "and it is very childish of me to feel hurt. But it's kind of hard being 'family' but not really part of the family."

This scenario is one of many that exemplify the complexity and confusion that are often part of consolidating new family relationships. It is important to remember that there are usually many more people involved in a blended family than in a traditional family (Hetherington et al., 1995). For example, there may be ex-spouses, ex–in-laws, as well as an assortment of cousins, uncles, and aunts (Zastrow & Kirst-Ashman, 1994). When roles and relationships become more complex, adjustment for each family member becomes more difficult (Hetherington et al., 1995). In families with many members or where new children are born into the marriage, the adjustment period may last longer. Involvement with step-grandparents is most intense when there are no biological grandchildren, grandparents live close by, and the children are young. Children usually differentiate between natural and step-grandparents (Hetherington et al., 1995). These members of the extended families have been humorously referred to as the "supporting cast" of the new marriage (Zastrow & Kirst-Ashman, 1994). The relationships involved can indeed offer the new family much support, or they can be a complicating factor.

A further complication is that this new blended family is made up of two families with very different histories and traditions (Goldenberg & Goldenberg, 1994). Little things, like how birthdays are celebrated or which holidays will now be celebrated when two cultures join, may cause confusion. Families may be at very different stages in the life cycle. One parent may have adolescent children and be dealing with the associated concerns and parenting issues, while the other spouse brings an infant or toddler into the remarriage, introducing a completely different life cycle into the blend. All of these factors add complexity and perhaps play a role in adjustment of all family members.

The Couple Subsystem

A new intimate relationship is usually a source of joy to both partners. As they begin to explore the physical and emotional aspects of their new relationship, they can be hampered by the presence of young children. This may be more of an issue in stepfamilies where the parent–child relationship existed only with one partner prior to the couple's relationship (Eshleman & Wilson, 1995; Brooks, 1987) or where that relationship was exceptionally strong (Hetherington et al., 1995).

Adjusting to the Presence of Young Children in a Remarriage

A single mother with a 4-year-old daughter had been involved with a young man for a few months when they decided to marry. He had not been previously married, and had become very fond of the young girl. When they decided that the three of them would go on a honeymoon together, it did at times seem strange to the young man to hear his future stepdaughter discuss her honeymoon plans with her friends.

Sometimes the step-parent may feel that his or her needs come second to the needs of the partner's biological children. On the other hand, the relationship between the couple is legally binding, as in any marriage, but there is no such binding relationship between the step-parent and stepchildren. For example, few states and provinces have legislation obligating step-parents to support stepchildren, especially after a divorce (Eshleman & Wilson, 1995).

The new couple may become absorbed in their new relationship and become distracted or have less time available for the children (Rutter, 1995). Supervision and discipline may suffer as adults become involved with each other and cement their relationship.

Some studies have suggested higher levels of tension and disagreement in remarried couples than in first marriages (Eshleman & Wilson, 1995). There are usually qualitative differences between the parent–child and step-parent–child relationships. Children are dependent upon their parents, and their love is typically unconditional (Eshleman & Wilson, 1995). The developing relationship between adults is very different. When not all needs can be met at the same time, it can be helpful to prioritize, taking into account the long- and short-term consequences of these decisions for all family members.

Planning the Marriage

For most people, the decision to remarry involves much thought and planning. Sometimes, however, the needs of the children involved are given less consideration than the needs of the adults (Garanzini, 1995; Hetherington et al., 1995). The timing of the introduction of the new friend and future partner to the child, the nature and boundaries of the relationship between the child and new partner, and the amount of time given for the relationship to evolve before marriage are all factors that will have considerable importance for the child.

Stepfathers seem to have an easier time adjusting to stepchildren than do stepmothers (Larson, Golz, & Hobart, 1994), and several reasons have been put forth to explain this. First, divorced mothers usually have custody of the children, so the future stepfather has the opportunity to develop a relationship with the children during the courtship period. On the other hand, the future stepmother has fewer opportunities to develop a relationship with her partner's children, who likely reside with their mother. Secondly, the burden of step-parenting tends to fall on the woman's shoulders. More cooking, cleaning, and household organization is required when more children are added to the home, and men do not always increase their share of housework even when their children visit (Ambert, 1990). Something that further complicates the process for stepmothers is the belief that women will automatically love their new children so mothering should come easily (Dainton, 1995).

Planning the blending process by taking into account these potential difficulties might serve to reduce their intensity. For example, steps can be taken to foster the development of the relationship between the step-parent and children before the marriage, and agreements regarding household task-sharing can be discussed during this preliminary stage.

Planning and communication between the new partners and their children is thought to ease the transition to the blending of families (Brooks, 1987; Kaplan & Hennon, 1992; Kheshgi-Genovese & Genovese, 1997). However, sometimes even with the best of intentions, these processes do not occur and many remarrying couples do not discuss parenting issues beforehand (Ganong & Coleman, 1985). Sometimes the parents become so involved in the happiness of their new relationship that they may be unaware of the doubts or hesitations of their children. Sometimes the parent who has struggled with the social and economic burdens of single parenthood may be so relieved at the idea of remarriage that she or he may not want to come to terms with the potential problems of "blending."

One newly remarried parent confided: "I read all the books, and I knew all the 'recipes' for successful blending. Then I did everything practically the opposite of what I had planned to do." Experts often forget that emotions do sometimes interfere with the implementation of their advice or that advice may not be available until it is too late. When conflicts appear, parents may encounter feelings of guilt ("Why did I do this?"), self-blame ("It's my fault that everyone is so unhappy!"), helplessness ("How can I get everyone to live happily together?"), or confusion ("If they liked each other before we were married, why are they now at each other's throats?"). Children's reactions to the new situation, which we will discuss in the next section, can increase these feelings, thereby putting further stress on the marriage and on the task of parenting.

Children's Reactions

Divorce and remarriage both put children at risk for developing social, psychological, behavioural, and school problems (Hetherington et al., 1995). Children in blended families are more likely to be described as aggressive and noncompliant, to display acting-out behaviour, to be disruptive in social relationships, and to have adjustment difficulties. Behavioural problems are often prominent in the early months after the remarriage, when the family is consolidating. Problems tend to subside over the next two years as communication and discipline are established (Garanzini, 1995). On the other hand, some writers suggest that behavioural problems may result from reduced involvement with the noncustodial parent, common after remarriage, and may not be a result of the remarriage per se (Hetherington et al., 1995).

It is sometimes the case, however, that both divorce and remarriage will remove children from stressful, conflict-ridden family situations and serve to provide them with new resources. These conditions may help to enhance the child's development. Hetherington et al. (1995) suggested that blended families have high rates of healthy children, and further, that the children may be more resilient. When remarriage occurs when children are young, there is a greater potential for adjustment (Rutter, 1995). Younger children eventually are able to form a relationship with a step-parent and accept that person in a parenting role. However, at the same time, it has been suggested that preschool children are often ignored through the process of divorce and remarriage since it is believed the young child cannot comprehend (Garanzini, 1995). Older children, particularly those in early adolescence, have more difficulty with this and are more likely to question or confront aspects of roles and functions that the younger child would not (Hetherington et al., 1995). Adjustment is generally more difficult with older children, particularly adolescents (Rutter, 1995). Some studies suggest that this difficulty is associated with increased risk of delinquency, beginning by the age of fourteen, among boys with preadolescence experiences of stepfamilies (Coughlin and Vuchinich, 1996).

Children's reactions to this transition will, as with other major life changes, be related to their own developmental level and their ability to comprehend. Their responses will be influenced by the way in which they are prepared for the event, by their experiences prior to the blending of families, and by the number of changes that accompany the remarriage. Besides adjusting to a new parent, children also have to adjust to new rules, new traditions, new extended families, new siblings, and a new way of life. This may be further complicated by a move, by a change in day care or school, and by new neighbours and friends (Goldenberg & Goldenberg, 1994). All of this can be somewhat overwhelming for the child (Sprujit & de Goede, 1997).

A stepfamily typically comes together after a loss, either through divorce or death (Rutter, 1995; Goldenberg & Goldenberg, 1994). Children need to grieve this loss and to bid goodbye to the dreams they carried about their first family. This is sometimes referred to as the early stage in the development of blended families and can last two years or more (Garanzini, 1995). Remarriage may shatter their fantasy that their original family will reunite or their parents will reconcile (Goldenberg & Goldenberg, 1994). Children may lose their status as the oldest child, the baby, or the only child when other children enter the stepfamily. They may also lose a valued role with their biological parent. For example, a mother and daughter may have had a close relationship where they confided in each other about everything, which may be lost within the new stepfamily.

The early stage involves coping with loss of the old family. During this time, a new co-parenting style must emerge while all family members need to accept the new family dynamics and feel comfortable in both houses. The middle stage represents a time of adjustment and rebuilding. An understanding and appreciation of the new family, and the way each parent behaves, develops during this period. The later stage involves the continued reorganization of rules and boundaries as all family members, particularly children, grow and develop.

Several factors seem to influence the intensity of the effects of remarriage on children. First, continued involvement of the noncustodial parent in the life of the child seems to be important, particularly for children aged 9 to 13 (Hetherington et al., 1995). Second, it seems easier for children to make the adjustment to stepfamilies when they have spent less time in a single-parent home (Montgomery & Anderson, 1992). Third, a number of studies have found gender differences to be a significant factor (Hetherington et al., 1995; Clingempeel, Brand, & Levoli, 1984; Needle, Su, & Doherty, 1990). Consistently, the literature suggests that boys will adjust to remarriage easier than girls. After two years, boys typically showed no more aggressive or noncompliant behaviour than boys from non-divorced homes. Girls' behaviour, on the other hand, improved less steadily over time (Garanzini, 1995). Reasons for this are unclear, but it is thought that girls would be more likely to take on more responsibilities following the divorce, and they may therefore feel threatened and resentful when replaced by a new partner (Larson, Golz, & Hobart, 1995). In addition, boys may benefit from more time and involvement from stepfathers.

Long-term adjustment is related to the personality of the child, the number of new stresses encountered by the child, the quality of the new blended family's home environment, and the resources available to support the child (Hetherington et al., 1995).

Loi came to the United States from Hong Kong to do doctoral studies in biology. She was 33 years old and had never been married. Six months after her arrival in the United States, she presented a paper at a national scientific conference, where she met Philip. Philip was a single father who had three sons, aged 6, 11, and 15. Loi and Philip began dating and fell deeply in love. Several months after they met, Loi was invited to spend a weekend with Philip and his sons.

"I remember how strange it felt walking into the house—hockey sticks, basketballs, everything seemed so very male. Phil kept his house immaculately clean, but there didn't seem to be anything soft or feminine in it. We continued dating, and it became clearer to us that we wanted to spend the rest of our lives together. 'But how will I blend?' I remember thinking—the challenge of blending a female into a very male household, blending Chinese culture with Philip's culture, and forming some kind of a relationship with the three boys.

"The two older boys remembered their mother and still felt very attached to her. The youngest boy, Mark, had been brought up by Phil and his two older brothers and didn't remember his mother very well. We started the blending process very gradually. I would visit once a week and spend quite a bit of time with Mark. When I was a little girl, I had a huge selection of miniature statues from all over the world. Each week I brought a statue and told Mark the story of how and where I got the statue, and he would help me find a place for it on the shelf. This became a weekly ritual that we both looked forward to. By the time I moved into the house, most of my collection already lived there.

"Phil's oldest son tried to ignore me as much as possible, and I didn't want to pressure him. You can't force someone to like you. I wouldn't put up with rudeness, but I accepted his cold shoulder. The middle son was more ambivalent. Sometimes he would get very close to me, and then, perhaps feeling guilty, he would seem almost hostile.

"Although I didn't really like the decor of the house, I made only minor changes for the first while. I changed the furniture in our bedroom, and we converted the spare room into a study-guest room, which definitely had a Chinese flair. The one thing I was sure no one would object to was some good Chinese cooking. They all seemed to enjoy the meals that I would occasionally prepare. But I might have been too hopeful. One day when I had just finished preparing a grand meal, the boys came down, looked at the table, and groaned, 'Dad, what's wrong with hamburgers? Have you forgotten that we like hamburgers?'

"Sometimes I felt that I was under a lot of pressure. I had to adapt to a new household and a new country. It felt sometimes like I was the only one who was trying to compromise. Many things felt strange to me. The informality of the relations between parents and children here often seemed to me a lack of respect. I sometimes wavered between telling myself that I needed to adapt to American ways and thinking that it wouldn't hurt these boys to learn a bit about how children should behave according to my culture.

"We have been married for three years now, and the blending process that began six years ago is still continuing. I feel that I have been successful in establishing a warm relationship with Mark; he feels like a son to me. I was very happy when we all went to Hong Kong for a long visit last summer. It was so important for me that Phil and the boys experience the world in which I grew up. Both of the older boys left home after high school, and there is still some ambivalence in our relationship. But they are busy establishing their own lives now and hopefully, as the years go by and they get married and have children, we will have more opportunities to share our lives."

Obstacles in Step-Parent–Child Relations

The establishment of the step-parent–child relationship can be challenging, and several obstacles appear to be common.

Discipline and Childrearing Issues

The development of a bond between a step-parent and the children can be hampered by a number of factors. The one most often discussed (Brooks, 1987; Zastrow & Kirst-Ashman, 1994; Ward, 1994) centres around discipline. Discipline and childrearing issues are often the primary source of disagreement between remarried spouses (Eshleman & Wilson, 1995). Often, approaches to discipline are not discussed during the courtship, and differences may become apparent only afterwards, when conflicts arise. When there are discrepancies in approaches, the parent–child relationship may suffer (e.g., "Why did you let him do that to me?"). The emerging step-parent–child relationship may also be put at risk and the spousal relationship may feel considerable strain.

When the new parent undertakes the role of disciplining and guiding the children, it is sometimes a matter of trial and error. While all parents make "mistakes," a step-parent does not have the long-standing bond of unconditional love that forms over the years between parents and children. While the biological mother may overreact to a cup of spilled milk and speak harshly to her daughter, an apology and a cuddle might set things straight. However, if the step-parent overreacts to the same incident, it is harder afterwards to resolve the hurt feelings (Hetherington et al., 1995).

Because of these difficulties, new step-parents typically shy away from involvement in discipline, especially in the early stages of remarriage (Brooks, 1987). Sometimes they may become too authoritarian, expecting the child to obey simply because that is the expectation. Both stepmothers and stepfathers tend to take a less active role in parenting than the biological parents do (Hetherington et al., 1995). Although stepmothers are more active than stepfathers, they may be expected to act as the family conflict resolvers with stepchildren and they may have some difficulty with that role (Ahrons & Wallisch, 1987). Some studies suggest that stepmothers are more likely to experience difficulty in raising stepchildren (McDonald & DeMaris, 1996). Another reason why discipline problems are common in stepfamilies is the guilt often felt by the noncustodial parents. When, for example, the father's noncustodial children come for the weekend, his guilt over leaving them and spending more time with his stepchildren may well result in failure to discipline appropriately or consistently (Fowler, 1993).

Divided Loyalties

In many cases new step-parents, usually stepfathers, will have children of their own who live with their ex-spouse. It is not uncommon in such a case for guilty feelings towards the biological children to interfere with the development of positive relations with the stepchildren. In families where the children of both marriages reside together, jealousy and rivalries between the stepchildren are not uncommon. A new stepmother who tries to establish a bond with her stepchildren may feel disloyal to her own children. A stepfather may need to decrease involvement with his biological children in order to make his new marriage and stepfamily work. Stepmothers often feel caught between the love for their husbands and guilt for remarrying against their children's wishes (Giles-Sims & Crosbie-Burnet, 1989). Not surprisingly, women seem to be more deeply upset about stepfamily problems than are men (Fowler, 1993; Benokraitis, 1993). It is not uncommon for all the members of newly reconstituted families to feel pulled in many different directions.

Just as the parents may feel torn between bonds of loyalty with various members of the new family, children, too, often experience this dilemma (Goldenberg & Goldenberg, 1994). This concept of loyalty is particularly strong with school-age children (Garanzini, 1995). Attachment to the step-parent may cause the children to feel disloyal to their biological parent. A simple issue such as what to call the new father can be a source of major concern and trigger many emotions. When the new step-parent assumes a role in discipline and guidance, children may feel that compliance involves disloyalty to their biological parent. It is difficult for children to ascertain where their loyalties should lie or how to divide those loyalties among all of the players.

In addition, trends seem to indicate that noncustodial, biological parents become less involved with their children, especially after a remarriage (Eshleman & Wilson, 1995). It has been suggested that almost half of children of divorce have had no contact with one parent in the last five years (Garanzini, 1995). The effects of this decreased involvement are similar to those experienced after the divorce but may be further complicated and produce additional stress for the child in a blended family situation. If animosity is carried over from the former marriage, the situation becomes more complicated and entangled for the child. In situations where the relationship does continue with the biological parent, the children will need to learn to live in two houses with different rules and parenting styles (Goldenberg & Goldenberg, 1994). In either event, complications and stress may be the end result for the child. In addition, it has been suggested that adjustment to remarriage will be facilitated by access to both parents (Garanzini, 1995).

Sexuality

Scenario

Will Affection Be Misinterpreted as Sexual Abuse?

A newly remarried mother of a 4-year-old girl was talking to a family counsellor about how her husband seemed to be unresponsive to the child. Upon further investigation, it became apparent that the new stepfather was deeply concerned about any intimacy with this young girl being perceived as sexual abuse. "If I cuddle her on my lap before bedtime and kiss her goodnight, how will this be viewed? And if a hug and cuddle are okay at the age of 4, are they at the age of 5, 6, and 7?"

This man's anxiety was well founded. There is a higher incidence of sexual abuse in step-families than in biological families (Eshleman & Wilson, 1995; Brooks, 1987), although there are fewer cases when the children are young (Hetherington et al., 1995). This may be a result of ambiguities in roles and relationships and in assessing appropriate boundaries in these new relationships. While the vast majority of step-parents are not abusers, fears surrounding this sensitive, seldomly discussed issue can impede the development of affectionate relations. Certainly it is also true that, as children grow older, stepsiblings can be attracted to each other and will need guidance and protection in this regard. Stepfamilies that include adolescents may need to consider this issue prior to moving in together (Hetherington et al., 1995).

Finances

While the blending of families often results in improved living conditions (Hetherington et al., 1995), money can become a source of conflict in some cases (Brooks, 1987). Some studies have suggested that financial strains are more frequent in remarried couples (Eshleman & Wilson, 1995). Typically, financial matters are more complicated with issues such as support payments to children to be resolved. And since there are no norms regarding the obligation of step-parents to offer financial support to stepchildren, problems deciding who pays for what often arise. These problems are more likely to occur when the children get older and questions arise such as who will pay for college education. However, there are many expenses involved in the rearing of young children, and issues of financial responsibility need to be carefully worked out.

Idealized Images

Children often idealize the parent who no longer lives with them. Although this is more likely to occur after the death of a parent, it does happen after divorce as well. When the shadow of an "ideal" real parent looms large, it is difficult for the child to form an attachment to the step-parent. "Mommy would never get mad at me for doing that" or "My real daddy always played with me after supper" are difficult ideals for the new step-parent to live up to.

It is not uncommon for children to be jealous of their parent's affection for the new partner and new stepsiblings. Children may view the new adult as a threat to their established parent–child relationship (Hetherington et al., 1995). This may be more pronounced for the only child of a formerly single parent, who may not be used to sharing parental attention with anyone and may have had a special relationship with that parent (e.g., "You used to tell me everything; now you only ever talk to him"). When we bear in mind that the parents may be very involved in their own relationship, it is understandable that the child may feel left out and jealous.

Supporting Blended Families

Sometimes children who are in the process of blending into a new family are undergoing so many changes in their lives that the day care or preschool becomes a secure haven for them. Recognizing this and providing the child with security and support may be the most important way in which early childhood professionals can assist blending families

(Hetherington et al., 1995). Structured, predictable environments may offer much-needed stability at a time of major changes at home. It may be especially beneficial to provide the child with a primary caregiver, if possible. The constant reassurance of having a caring and trusted adult with whom the child feels secure can play a strong role in providing that extra bit of support that the child may require at this time of transition.

Empathizing with the tensions that the family may experience is an essential component of supporting families. Our attitudes and beliefs about step-parenting will affect our ability to empathize and offer the necessary support.

Erera & Fredriksen (1999) suggest that stepfamilies often do not have strong support systems within the community because they do not wish to bring attention to their step-status and because they have become more accepted within society. Although the desire to not stand out or be labelled was true several decades ago when remarriage rates and acceptance rates were lower, this legacy has led to stepfamilies feeling isolated.

Check the following "Examine Your Attitudes" box to see whether any of the myths about blended families mentioned earlier in this chapter may influence your thinking. It would also be a useful exercise to think of how you would address the step-parent in a letter or in a face-to-face exchange. In this way, you may be better able to empathize with any feelings of awkwardness the stepchild is experiencing.

Examine Your Attitudes

- Do you view the step-parent as the "wicked stepmother(father)" or as a "white knight" who rescues the stepchildren from an uncomfortable situation?

- Do you think that mothering comes naturally to women and that there will be "instant love" between a stepmother and her stepchildren?

- Is a stepfamily something less in your view than a "real family"?

- Do you believe that a stepfamily is automatically a better situation for children than a single-parent family?

- Do you think blending is an easy process that just naturally happens when people love each other?

Sharing Information with Parents

Bearing in mind our hesitations about giving advice, we still believe there are times when providing parents with information can be very helpful. The three major issues most likely to be raised in a blended family are (a) establishing discipline and parental authority for children, (b) forming a strong marital relationship, and (c) developing ongoing arrangements with the noncustodial parent. Functioning in stepfamilies may be improved when parents know which problems are common to other stepfamilies and which are temporary, and when they understand that integration into a stepfamily takes time (Rutter, 1995). Early childhood professionals may be able to provide this type of support and information. It is important that the information shared not be interpreted as criticism of the parents or as an expectation that they will implement the advice. We must also bear in mind that the advice we have to give is tentative, since we too have much to learn about what works and what does not. In addition, we must remember that blended families form a diverse population; therefore, not all suggestions will be appropriate to all families.

New Territory

A review of the challenges and problems involved in the blending of families should not be interpreted as a warning never to remarry. Many authorities claim that stepfamilies can be as happy as first marriages (Coleman & Ganong, 1991). We have a lot to learn about how different kinds of reconstituted families work out ways to face their challenges and become "real" families in ways that may be quite different from that of the biological nuclear family.

Scenario

Different Family Backgrounds

Charlene and Lauren were talking in the back seat of the car. Lauren was explaining that she was going to spend part of the summer with her real mom and Bill, her new stepfather. She would see her old stepfather and stepbrother for a week, then spend the rest of the summer with her real dad, her step-mother, and her children. Charlene had trouble following the conversation and attempted to gain an understanding by describing her family with her one dad and one mom. Lauren sat for a minute and then stated, "That means you only get one birthday present from your mom and dad. Wow, that's too bad."

This conversation between children from very different families shows that, once they grow accustomed to them, children often accept their lives as being normal or typical. Lauren was shocked by the news that her friend would only get one present because she had only one set of parents. Caregivers can help children to appreciate differences in household styles and routines. Helping children to recognize and appreciate the differences in routines, expectations, roles and other aspects of family life may help the child to adjust to blending.

Hetherington (1995) suggests that stepfamilies need to give up the fantasy image of the happy, nuclear family in order to adjust. When they let go of this ideal, they will become more flexible, more realistic and better able to cope. They may need to establish more flexible boundaries with the many people involved with the blended family, including the noncustodial parents, rather than closing in like the nuclear family.

Some step-parents might appreciate being reminded that, just as they are exploring the new territory of a remarriage and blended family, so is society at large only beginning to learn about this increasingly common phenomenon. Stepfamilies need basic information about what to expect (Rutter, 1995). They will gradually learn what works for them and what doesn't and then be able to establish their own expectations.

Erera & Fredriksen (1999) suggest that both families bring their own habits, routines and connections. In the early stages, stepfamilies are typically made of two subsystems—the "absorbing" or "veteran" family members and the "newcomer(s)" (p. 264). Eventually, the subsystems become less distinct, but this does take time.

Time

Sometimes step-parents feel very pressured to "make it work," and they become frustrated when the bond between themselves and their stepchildren does not develop as well or as rapidly as they hoped. They may find it helpful to be reassured that these relationships often take time. Emotional attachments between the step-parent and child may take longer to develop because this relationship is not binding as the marriage is and because integration into a family can take time (Goldenberg & Goldenberg, 1994). Women are often surprised and upset when they don't instantly love their partner's children (Dainton, 1995). Children may need some time to adjust to all the changes and to the new parent. Step-parents cannot be expected to like or love their stepchildren automatically and, likewise, demands cannot be placed on children to accept or love their new parent (Hetherington et al., 1995). Loyalty or love cannot be forced. Research has shown that stepfamilies take on average approximately five years to integrate as a family (Hetherington et al., 1995).

There is another time factor involved in the relationship of the parents. It is important for a newly married couple with children to have time alone together. Early childhood professionals can help alleviate parental guilt by demonstrating an understanding of their need to be alone and by helping them to explain this to their children.

Permission

We described earlier the problem of divided loyalties that many children experience during the transition to a new family structure. Children may not be comfortable calling the new parent "Mom" or "Dad," but they may be more comfortable with first names or an original title. One early childhood student told her class that she was called "Mom Number Two" for many years after she became a step-parent. Another said that she was called "New Mom."

It may in fact be easier for children to adjust to the new situation if the adults in their lives give them explicit verbal "permission" to maintain their loyalty to their biological parent. Communication between early childhood professionals and parents can ensure that children's decisions about how they refer to their biological and step-parents are reinforced both at home and in the centre.

Communication

Studies have indicated that major improvements take place in behaviour, child adjustment, and self-esteem when communication occurs between step-parents and the children (Rutter, 1995). Just as the adults in the new relationship need to clarify their roles and expectations, these matters have to be clearly communicated to the child. Sometimes caregivers can help parents formulate these role clarifications in simple language, at the child's level of comprehension. "When Mommy is not home, John will give you supper. If you don't want to finish all your food, you don't have to. You can have a snack later when Mommy gets home. When Mommy's away, John will be in charge."

Enjoy

With all the new arrangements and attempts to blend, families sometimes lose sight of the joy of being together. Joint fun activities can go a long way in assisting the development of positive relationships. Caregivers may be able to suggest day-care activities or community events for families to participate in. Sometimes a gentle reminder and permission to let go and laugh can be very helpful.

Adjusting Expectations

A child in the nursery school was having a difficult time getting used to living with his new father. His mother had remarried four months previously, and this new dad had never been married or had children. One of the first activities they participated in as a family was a picnic at the nursery school. After the evening, the parents remarked that this event had been special because it was the first they had enjoyed as a family, and because the father was finally able to see what other 3- and 4-year-old children were like. After this, he could readjust his expectations for his son's behaviour.

Establishing New Family Traditions

Family traditions and rituals can be seen as binding agents that help hold families together (Visher & Visher, 1989). Newly reconstituted families can be encouraged to develop new family traditions to replace the ones that the members may have left behind or to adapt rituals and traditions from the previous household. These could be as simple as the stepfather making a pancake breakfast each Sunday or the family enjoying a video evening every Saturday. They could also involve more elaborate events like celebrating the anniversary of the family's move to their new home. Establishing these traditions can add to children's sense of security and identification with the new family.

Sometimes newly remarried parents suffer from "superparent" syndrome. They may feel that the world (and their children's teachers) is judging them, and that it is important to demonstrate that all is well. An empathic caregiver somehow gets the message across that parents will not be judged, and that the door is open to discuss issues that concern their child. If parents express concerns that go beyond the professional boundaries of the caregiver, then they should be referred to community resources such as support groups for stepfamilies or family counselling agencies. Caregivers may also be able to suggest books for children or adults that may be helpful. When parents understand that early childhood professionals can be counted on to listen and, if necessary, to provide resources, then the adjustment of both children and parents to their newly blended family can be greatly facilitated.

Conclusion

Each stepfamily is different from every other one and each faces many challenges. Families may include different people from various extended families, each with their own histories. There may also be complicating factors such as the need to deal with noncustodial parents. Stepfamilies are still subject to societal pressure, as is evident in the many myths that still exist about stepfamilies and in the common belief that the most successful stepfamilies are those that most closely resemble the nuclear family. The mere fact that these myths are so commonplace puts an enormous amount of stress on the blended family. However, the literature suggests that, over time, children do adjust and that stepfamilies do integrate successfully (Hetherington et al., 1995). When families understand the problems they may have to deal with and they know about the support systems available, adjustment is more likely. Early childhood professionals can play an important role in providing information and support to the children and the parents of blended families.

Exercises

1. List some of the challenges a new blended family might face. Discuss strategies that might help the family to overcome these challenges.

2. What beliefs do you hold about blended families? Try to identify how you might have acquired those beliefs. How might your particular beliefs hinder you in providing appropriate care for the children of blended families?

3. How would you explain blended families to a group of young children all of whom come from nuclear families?

4. Check out community resources and support groups that relate to blended families. Which would you feel comfortable in recommending to parents? Under which circumstances?

5. Check your library for books pertaining to blended families. Make a list of those that would be appropriate for children and those that would be beneficial for their parents.

6. Review the books in your centre. How many of these show blended families to be as normal as two-parent nuclear families?

7. Consider ways that non-custodial parents may stay involved in the child's life. Is this possible? desirable? Discuss.

Single Parents

chapter 6

Objectives

- **To clarify attitudes towards single-parent families.**
- **To discuss the implications of single parenting for adults and children.**
- **To consider the role of the early childhood professional in supporting single-parent families.**

> A young single father made every attempt to attend preschool events with his 4-year-old son, Rahim. He regularly acted as a classroom volunteer and never missed a parent function. At the final wind-up party, the preschool teacher kept telling the children to show their moms this, or get their moms to help them with that. Jokingly, the single father would yell out each time "And dad!" The last straw came when the teacher gave each child a year scrapbook and said, "Show this to your mom!" When she presented Rahim's book, he threw it down and began to wail for his mother. "Why can't she be here, I hate her!" he cried. At this point, the caregiver realized what she had done but it was too late. A very angry father gathered his son and his belongings and left.

Profile of Single-Parent Families

Single parenthood is a reality today, with the result that many children attending day care only one parent at home. Approximately one in five families with children are single-parent families (Vanier Institute, 1994). The majority of these, approximately 80 percent, are single-mother families, yet the number of single-father families is growing as well (Skolnick, 1992; Gringlas & Weintraub, 1995). As of the 1996 Census, there were 1.1 million single-parent families in Canada. Since 1991, they have increased at four times the rate of husband-wife families. Single-parent families headed by women continued to outnumber those headed by men by more than four to one (Statistics Canada, 1997).

Today, being a part of a single-parent family at some point in life is statistically as common as being in a two-parent family. It is estimated that 40 to 50 percent of children will live in single-parent families for at least a brief period in their childhood (Vanier Institute, 1994; Gringlas & Weintraub, 1995). Yet the lingering attitude prevails that single parenthood is somehow not normal.

Although we tend to lump all single parents together as a group, they are in fact a very diverse population, often more different than alike (Okun, 1996). There are many routes to becoming a single parent. In today's society, divorce is the major cause of lone parenthood; a generation ago, it was the death of a spouse. Until recently, it was generally thought that single parents were predominantly teen parents, but this too appears to be changing (Gringlas & Weintraub, 1995). There has been a dramatic increase in the number of older women choosing single motherhood as an option (Mattes, 1994). This has been most common among mid-30s, educated, professional, White women. The majority of single-parent families consist of women with their children (Gringlas & Weintraub, 1995; Skolnick, 1992). For this reason, much less is known about the growing numbers of single parents who are fathers. In the United States, Hispanic and African-American groups have higher rates of single parents than the population at large (Skolnick, 1992).

The financial and social circumstances of single-parent families vary as well. Many single parents are women who are struggling to make ends meet financially and who are stuck in low-paying jobs that grant little satisfaction. On the other hand, some single mothers are fortunate to have high-paying jobs and interesting careers. Some single parents live with and receive emotional support from their extended families, while others live alone with their children and feel socially isolated. Some children of lone parents have ongoing positive contact with the nonresidential parent. In other cases, especially where there is continued animosity between the parents, children have little or no contact with their noncustodial parent. Some lone parents may be living with partners who are actively involved with the children, and some may live alone. All of these differences, in addition to family background, personality, and coping styles, will have an impact on how single-parent families function and how the children in those families develop.

Effects on Children

It is difficult to determine what effects living with a single parent may have on children, since any effects may be complicated by the factors of separation, divorce, and the absence of the noncustodial parent (Jaffe, 1991; Nissivoccia, 1997). It is important to be aware that the reason for the single-parent family poses a different reality for the child and may impact children in different ways. For example, single-parent families due to death face different issues than do single parent families by choice, divorce, or military service. Different issues are involved if remarriage is pending. In fact, most of the literature is based on studies from father-absent homes, where the interaction of a number of variables may not have been fully considered. Difficulties associated with increased stress, a lower standard of living, and fewer social resources may complicate our understanding. Children from single-parent homes have been characterized as more dependent, less compliant, more antisocial, and more likely to experience difficulties at school and to have psychological concerns (Ward, 1994; Mattes, 1994; Bank et al., 1993). A recent study found that differences in behaviour, social competence, and academic success were also present in single-parent families where there had not been a divorce or disruption

(Gringlas & Weintraub, 1995). Studies show that teachers expect more behavioural problems from children in single-parent families (Skolnick, 1992). Ongoing stress within the home appears to be the most influential factor relating to these concerns. Again, it is critical to remember that father absence may be only one factor of many that this family or child is dealing with.

Although there is sparse data to date, there are indications that single-parent families headed by fathers are often more financially secure and children are better disciplined (Garanzini, 1995). Fathers also felt less sure of their ability to meet the emotional needs of the child.

On the other hand, children in single-parent families typically have more responsibilities placed upon them. These additional duties may lead either to an increase in self-esteem, when children feel that they are making positive contributions, or to resentment, if children perceive these additional duties as unfair.

During the preschool years and beyond, it is not unusual for single-parent children to fantasize about having another parent or having a "dad" (Brooks, 1987). When the parent begins to date, however, children often display ambivalent reactions. They may be concerned that this new person will take the parent's time and affection away from them, they may feel threatened and attempt to sabotage the relationship, or they may easily accept the parent's need for adult companionship and affection.

Attitudes Towards Single Parents

Single parents have often found themselves socially stigmatized. Because the literature grew out of concerns of mental health professionals, there has been a tendency to focus on the "dysfunctional" aspects of such families (Garanzini, 1995). Single-parent families tend to hold a marginal position in society, partly because of their economic status but also because of the couple-centred view that society continues to hold (Hardey & Crow, 1991). For instance, one man in his fifties told an early childhood class that his birth certificate classified him as a "bastard" since his father was not named. Although the birth certificate was written half a century ago, it serves for this man as a constant reminder of society's views.

This stigma may still hold in parts of society today. Not too long ago, terms such as "illegitimate children" and "children from broken homes" were used in reference to children being raised by single parents. The normal or traditional family was one in which the parents were married and residing together. The term "illegitimate" implied that it was immoral to have a child out of wedlock. Families in which the mother and father did not reside together were referred to as broken, implying that they were in need of fixing (Ward, 1994). The only kind of lone parents that seemed to escape moral judgement was widows and widowers. In spite of statistics that indicate that single parenthood is a very prevalent family structure, we still see writers today refer to two-parent families as "intact" families. This subtly implies that one-parent families are not altogether acceptable. Many single parents feel that although their families may be different in structure from society's concept of a normal family, they are still just as intact and acceptable. Society clings to this concept of a normal family, despite the decreasing gap between the number of lone parents and the number of two-parent families.

Many single parents have said that they are tired of being blamed for many of society's ills. Single parenthood is often discussed in the same context as the "break-up of the family," that is, as one of the great ills of modern society. Some feel that their parenthood is constantly scrutinized and criticized. As one single mother said: "All parents lose their patience with their children sometimes, but when I do, people shake their heads and look at my children with pity. They probably think I abuse them."

Changes in attitudes towards single parents *are* occurring, however, in part because of the increased number of divorces and separations, which in turn result in more single-parent families. For example, one study found that the amount of interaction with single-parent families for college students who lived with their biological parents predicted more positive attitudes (Burke, 1996). In addition, the number of women who have chosen to have children on their own has also increased. Social programs and benefits have been established to support single parents and their families. We are living in changing times and must realize that the alternative types of families may soon be more common than the traditional form. We must also be aware that children may be just as healthy when raised in nontraditional types of families (Mattes, 1994).

Abandoning Our Preconceived Ideas

Considerable debate continues, both on local and national levels, about what kind of family is best for rearing children (Bird & Sporakowski, 1994). Nuclear families have had their share of problems—especially with child abuse and domestic violence—and many adults have expressed discontent with their own experiences in so-called "normal" families (Collins, 1991). Different points of view, each of them backed up by research, are held by politicians, religious leaders, and lawyers at custody hearings (Bird & Sporakowski, 1994). The attention devoted to U.S. vice-president Dan Quayle's condemnation of the television character Murphy Brown (a single mother by choice) is itself a testament to the controversy surrounding this topic (Mattes, 1994). However, as the discussion in this chapter should make clear, it is unlikely that research alone will ever provide us with very clear-cut answers about the superiority of one kind of family structure over another, if only because it is impossible to isolate all of the interrelated factors affecting family units. In addition, values often play too strong a role in both the formulation of research questions and the interpretation of research results.

For all these reasons, early childhood professionals might be better advised to shift the focus from asking which form of family is better to understanding the facts at hand. In addition, early childhood professionals may play a role in assisting families to adapt. To put it very simply, these facts tell us that single parenting is a common social reality today. Therefore, the debate about whether two-parent families are "better" for children may not be relevant. Research suggests that the level of stability within the home and the absence of conflict together influence children's adjustment more than the number of parents (Mattes, 1994; Hetherington et al., 1995). In fact, it has been suggested that in many cases children in single-parent homes may get more individual attention than in two-parent families (Scarr, 1984). What is most relevant is that single-parent families do exist, and that parents raising children alone may share common difficulties. These difficulties may include technical problems such as finding medical care when a child is sick, paying for babysitters, or simply in arranging for an evening out with other adults.

Early childhood professionals can play a more supportive role with single-parent families, as they will with any other kind of family, if they develop an understanding of some of the issues faced by single-parent families today.

The Challenges of Single Parenthood

While the diversity among the single-parent population makes it difficult to generalize about them, there do seem to be some specific challenges associated with single parenthood that are worth considering for the early childhood professional. Care must be taken not to make assumptions, while at the same time one must be sensitive to some of the areas in which support and understanding might be welcome. Although many parents indicate that single parenting presents no special problems, many others report they do indeed face a considerable number of challenges.

The Economics of Single Parenting

Canadian and American statistics on poverty lead to the inescapable conclusion that single parenthood and poverty very often go hand in hand. Single-mother families account for a significant number of people living in poverty (Ward, 1994; Vanier Institute, 1994; Skolnick, 1992). Although social supports are available, being a single parent can be a great financial burden (Goldenberg et al., 1992; Jaffe, 1991). Studies show that, in Canada, single parents (along with the elderly) make longer-termed use of welfare than any other group (Cragg, 1996). Since we will deal with the problems of poverty in Chapter 9, it should be sufficient here to note that we should be aware of and sensitive to the financial burdens that complicate the lives of many single parents.

Economic hardship leads to a variety of other problems. Low-income families typically do not own homes and are therefore more likely to be tenants or homeless (Crow & Hardey, 1991). This problem is often compounded by the fact that today's homes are built and marketed for the two-earner household (Bourianova, 1996). Poor housing may lead to less than desirable living conditions, constant moving, or poor health for parents and children over the long term (Hardey & Crow, 1991). The lack of quality child care that is also affordable and flexible may present a number of problems. It is likely that educational opportunities for children and leisure activities for the family as a whole may be hampered as well. It has been suggested that a change in financial status may trigger a change in self-esteem (Garanzini, 1995).

Barriers to Employment

Working becomes a necessity in single-parent families; however, many single mothers with preschool-aged children are not able to work because of the needs of their children. A recent study found multiple barriers to employment of single parents, particularly single mothers, including issues of self-esteem and job readiness following a divorce, ambivalent social attitudes about women's role in the labour force, and sexual harassment in the workplace (Huth, 1998). Research has shown that the majority of single mothers would work if quality, accessible day care was available (Hardey & Glover, 1991; Simons, 1996; Benzeval, 1998). Working mothers with school-age children are constrained by school hours and school holidays. The choices of day-care facilities may be limited by income (Hardey & Glover, 1991), and such a large portion of the single parent's income may be used for child care that there is little left over for anything other than the most basic neccessities (Jaffe, 1991).

Many single mothers still face barriers of discrimination in the labour force. Often, they have no choice but to work in low-paying, insecure, and unstable jobs with fewer opportunities for promotion (Skolnick, 1992; Hardey & Glover, 1991). Job opportunities may be restricted for single mothers due to their limited, inflexible hours and their inability to work overtime. Many employers continue to think of women as unreliable employees who are working only for a second income (Ward, 1994). Even lone parents with good incomes will experience more economic strife than their counterparts who are married and either in a two-income household or not burdened by child-care costs because one parent is at home. Because of employment and child-care conditions, the only alternative for many single mothers is social assistance, in which benefits typically do not provide an adequate standard of living and come with a stigma attached. The majority of single mothers, however, do choose work over welfare, and, contrary to the popular myth, research indicates that the majority of them are employed (Skolnick, 1992).

Stress

Being a single mother can present many challenges. In Chapter 2 on family roles we looked at the "supermom" syndrome, the pressure that many women feel to have successful careers while at the same time being excellent homemakers and childrearers. Many single mothers experience this kind of pressure, but they also talk about an additional factor. The single parent takes on the roles of both parents and needs to shift from one to the other as the situation warrants (Brooks, 1987). This requires patience and flexibility and may lead to role overload. As one single mother noted, "It's as if there is this obligation upon me to be a better mother than a mother in a two-parent family, since I am also expected to be the father. I am the breadwinner, I do the nurturing, I am in charge of the household and finances, and I do a lot of the kinds of things that are normally associated with fathers, like sports and special outings."

We should not assume, however, that every aspect of single motherhood is negative. In fact, some single mothers report they have fewer time pressures than their married counterparts because they do not have to deal with demands from the spouse (Skolnick, 1992). Many single mothers enjoy control over resources, a greater sense of autonomy, freedom from marital conflicts, and a general sense of well-being. Thus, some single mothers may be better off even though they are poorer (Hardey & Crow, 1991). Shaw (1991) describes single mothers as having more independence, confidence, and self-esteem than married mothers, as well as improved parenting abilities.

Although the majority of single parents are still women (Skolnick, 1992), more men are assuming the role of single father. Approximately 18 percent of single-parent families in Canada are now headed by single fathers (Eshleman & Wilson, 1995), and the number is increasing as more fathers seek custody of their children after divorce. Many of the concerns and challenges faced by single fathers are similar to those faced by single mothers. Although single-father families are much less likely to live in poverty since the fathers tend to be more educated and better employed, many single fathers feel more social stigma attaches to them than to women in similar circumstances. Many single fathers report that they feel they are able to provide both the daily care and affection required to "mother" and that they feel close to their children (Eshleman & Wilson, 1995). However, some studies have indicated that abuse is commonly higher in single-father homes, particularly where poverty is a factor, which suggests that a high level of stress can be associated with single-parent homes whether they are headed by a man or a woman (Jaffe, 1991).

Ron is a 24-year-old single father. He recently attended a parent night at his children's day-care centre and discussed his experiences as a single father in the 1990s.

"I come from a military family. My father was a commander in the Canadian Armed Forces, and he raised me and my two brothers in the 'army ways'—lots of discipline and a firm hand. My mother died when I was 11 years old, and it was really hard for all of us, especially my dad, who wasn't really good at talking about things that were bothering him. He never changed at home; he was still the boss, the disciplinarian, the commander.

"I joined the army as soon as I finished high school, just like my two brothers. It wasn't something we thought about; we just did it; it was expected. I got married and we had two children; Amy was 13 months old when Andrew was born. I was a father just like my father—I set out the rules and was the commander at home. When the children got older, I decided to quit the army because it was too hard to balance work with my family life—the army is kind of like that. I quit and became a firefighter, which gave me more time at home. I don't really know what happened, but six months after that major change in my life, my wife decided that this was not the life for her and left me with a 3-year-old and a 2-year-old. I have never felt so scared and so alone in my whole life, and I had nobody that I could talk to about being a father. My dad and brothers didn't understand, my guy friends were not used to sharing stories about bedtime routines and sick children, and single mothers were a bit unsure about this single father. I thought I knew what being a father was all about—I'd done it for three years and had a strong role model in my own father—but I had no idea how to be a mother.

"One of the first things that I did was to quit my job, since it is hard to be a single parent working shift work. I found a job in an office—not what I want to do forever, but at least it's easier to manage a home life. I had to put the children into day care.

"When we started at the day care, I was very quiet and very cautious. I really felt that I had to do it all. I didn't tell them very much and tried to pretend that our lives were normal. When the staff would ask questions or offer suggestions, I would get really bent out of shape. I remember once coming to pick Amy up at the end of the day. She was excited because her caregiver had french-braided her hair with ribbons. I was so angry because I saw this as a slap in the face—you can't do this, so we will. I blew up at Sally, the caregiver. She was shocked at my reaction and explained that all the staff try to spend individual time with each child. Today, Amy got up early from nap, and they had lots of time to spend together and play with her hair. It took me a long time, and other incidents like this, to realize that I couldn't do it all, and I needed other people to help. Their mom was not coming back and finding a new mom was not a solution, and Sally was trying to give Amy the things that she needed, that I didn't have time for.

"Things are getting easier. Being a single parent will always be hard, but at least now I have some people that I can count on, and I don't feel so alone and so scared—that's enough for now."

Social Support

Social difficulties can manifest themselves in two ways. Many single parents cite loneliness as a major concern (Garanzini, 1995; Ward, 1994), especially if their situation represents a change from their former couple-centred lifestyle (French, 1991). Loneliness may come from not having a partner in a society where couples are the norm (Shaw, 1991). This may be the result of having few social opportunities. It is difficult to meet potential partners when you are busy attending to the needs of your children. Social activities often have to be curtailed as a result of economic hardship, and child-care arrangements may also play a role in preventing leisure activity. Social support has been identified as a significant alleviator of the stress many single parents experience (Cheung and Liu, 1997).

The second social aspect that often causes concern for single parents is emotional support. Emotional and social isolation are still cited as having a significant impact on the well-being of children and their single parents (Gringlas & Weintraub, 1995). When single parents have good informal social networks for emotional support, child care, and financial assistance, their adaptation and experiences as single parents are more positive (Goldenberg et al., 1992). In one survey, single parents listed arranging child care for social activities and taking complete responsibility for child care in general as the two most challenging aspects of lone parenthood (City of Calgary, 1985). These two challenges accounted for more than 50 percent of the difficulties that lone parents mentioned. This is due, in part, to the lack of informal social supports available, and to the enormous responsibility of parenting in general.

Some single parents have a tendency, however, to become too dependent upon informal supports and then to have to deal with constant interference from family and friends. Dependence on family or friends can be another source of strain. In addition, lone parents also report that they have difficulty depending on these supports for long-term arrangements. In such circumstances, feelings of isolation or loneliness are increased to the point where single parents need to reach out for support from social agencies.

Once again, in describing the difficulties faced by many single parents, we must be careful not to stereotype or to paint too bleak a picture. Given the demands of parenting and work, most single mothers feel competent and satisfied (Skolnick, 1992). African-American single mothers consistently report more satisfaction because of the availability of the extended family for support. Extended families often facilitate the mother's adjustment, increase the quality of child care, enhance parenting, and provide social interaction opportunities and emotional support.

Single fathers report that even less social support may be available to them, as the following scenario suggests.

Scenario

No Support for Single Fathers

Jack is a single father of two children—Jillian is 3 years old and James is 18 months. Jack tells two stories that exemplify his experiences as a single father.

Whenever Jack is out with his children and they are upset, crying or dirty, people repeatedly remark, "Where's their mom?" or "Your mommy will take care of you." He says that this happens so often that it clearly demonstrates society's views of fathers in general and single fathers in particular.

Soon after Jack's wife left, he knew that he needed help and someone to talk to about parenting. He did manage to find a local support group for single parents, but when he walked into the first meeting, all of the single mothers stopped talking. He joined the group but said, "I felt so uncomfortable and it was so obvious that they were all uncomfortable, that I left at the break." Next, he tried a men's support group, but his concerns about parenting were a foreign issue to this group. "The bottom line," he said, "was that I just didn't fit anywhere and I am truly on my own."

Time

Many parents talk about the need for having time for themselves. This may involve time to develop and foster intimate relationships with a partner, to pursue their own interests, or just to relax. Although this is a yearned-for luxury among most parents, those who live without partners often find it even more difficult to get some time away from their children. "I can't call a babysitter if I just want to go for a walk for 15 minutes, and the extra cost of babysitters makes going out for an evening or weekend something I very rarely do," said one single mother.

Childrearing

Single-parent families are often characterized by lack of discipline or consistent control (Brooks, 1987). Several studies have suggested that single mothers are less effective in discipline, are more negative in their comments, give more commands, and are more hostile and dominating (Bank et al., 1993). Single mothers have also been found more demanding and critical of their children than are married mothers (Jaffe, 1991). Poor single-parent families seem more likely to experience violence and abuse within the home (Bank et al., 1993; Jaffe, 1991). Ineffective discipline may result from the increased level of stress that is common in single-parent homes, combined with social and financial pressures (Gringlas & Weintraub, 1995). It may be difficult for the lone parent to discipline the children without the ongoing support of the other parent, or the custodial parent's efforts may be undermined by arrangements at the noncustodial parent's house (e.g., "Daddy doesn't make me do that!"). Recent studies suggest that the parenting abilities and attitudes of single parents may not differ from those of married parents to the extent that was previously believed (Austin et al., 1997). Single parents who have social and emotional support find it easier to deal with authority issues in a consistent manner.

Different Gender Role Models

We often assume that children need parenting from both genders. This assumption is reflected in the fact that single mothers still experience more difficulties with authority in relation to their sons (Skolnick, 1992). Children's problems in single-parent families have been attributed to the lack of attention, stimulation, and modelling that occur when the second parent is unavailable (Gringlas & Weintraub, 1995). Girls, it is thought, need to learn about being feminine from their mothers, and about how to establish relationships and to feel comfortable with the opposite sex from their fathers (Mattes, 1994). Similarly, boys need to learn about being masculine by modelling themselves on their fathers, and about how to establish positive relations with the opposite sex through their relationships with their mothers.

These assumptions are being challenged today as gender roles are becoming blurred. As women are engaging in career activities that formerly fell within the exclusive domain of men, many men are taking on traditional female roles associated with nurturing and homemaking. The gender role model may be less significant than is often assumed. Regardless of gender, in a family where two parents are present, children have the opportunity to observe different ways of communicating, solving problems, and resolving conflicts. They might also be exposed to a more diverse range of interests and talents than when in a single-parent household. Therefore, some single parents do wish that their children had other close adults in their life as models and support. The feeling that the responsibilities of parenting are easier if shared by two is succinctly expressed by Clarke-Stewart (1989: 71): "One parent can model only one gender role, give only so many hugs, offer so much discipline, and earn so much money."

The Role of the Early Childhood Professional
Clarifying Attitudes and Values

Perhaps the first step in providing support is to maintain a nonjudgmental approach. The way you answer the questions in the "Examine Your Attitudes" box should reveal how you, as a caregiver, will interact with single parents and their children.

Examine Your Attitudes

- Do you think a single mother or father can do an adequate job of parenting?
- Do you feel the child of single parents is missing something?
- Does the language you use reflect your knowledge of single-parent families? (For example, the teacher in the vignette at the beginning of the chapter did not demonstrate an awareness that there are single-father families.)
- What social stigma do you attach to single parents?

Supporting Families

Providing support to single parents and their children should not be very different from supporting any other family. It is critical to remember, though, that single-parent families may be facing the challenges of parenting in conjunction with additional stresses brought on by the absence of one parent. Three dimensions appear to be important for single parent family adjustment (Garanzini, 1995). The first is the presence of resources within the family including the parents' abilities along with the presence of authority and communication. Environmental stress is the second. This might include pressures outside the family (e.g., illness, transitions). The last is the availability of social networks to the family. Such stresses may include child-care responsibilities, lack of role models, and economic need. Single parents facing economic pressure will appreciate sensitivity on the part of caregivers when asking for extra fees for special events or for special equipment for the children. All parents who find the task of juggling jobs and family life difficult will appreciate being understood by the caregivers. No family likes to feel that their parenting is being scrutinized and criticized by caregivers, but single parents who are sensitive about being socially stigmatized may react a little more defensively. Staff members need to bear this in mind and take care not to offend, either in words or actions.

Any efforts to eliminate the stigma associated with single parents, by seeing them as competent and their children as typical, will go a long way in supporting lone-parent families. Recognizing that additional stresses may be present, and that extra support may be needed, is an important step in this process, but single parents should not feel they are being singled out or pitied. This support may come from the day-care centre, for example, by arranging flexible hours or by organizing parent involvement activities to accommodate single-parent families. Sometimes referring single parents to professionals can help link them to formal and informal community networks, such as support groups or short-stay relief homes.

Supporting Children

Scenario

Choose Your Words Carefully

A caregiver gave her group of 5-year-old children instructions for making Father's Day gifts. At one table, the children asked Amanda who she was making her gift for, because her father lived far away. Amanda did not participate in the activity. At another table, Lisa stated that she was making her gift for her grandfather, because he took care of her when her mother worked at night. Her peers told her that she could not do this, because this craft was for fathers.

In this case, the feelings of specific children could have been protected, and the understanding of all children enhanced, if the caregiver had been more careful with the words she used with the children. Explaining that the craft was for a special person would have helped include all of the children in the activity.

Single parents and their children will appreciate efforts to treat their family structure as normal. This normalization occurs when toys, books, and stories in the day-care centre reflect single families as intact and typical. When stories are read in which only traditional nuclear families appear, caregivers can use the moment to explain that families are different and then encourage discussion, if this is warranted. Sensitive early childhood professionals should think carefully about events that are likely to make the child of a single parent feel left out. Mother's Day and Father's Day are just two examples.

Supporting children may also involve helping them to understand the various types of families and providing a range of experiences for them to think about. For example, the caregiver could provide books about different types of families or stories that feature male role models. Showing sensitivity in day-to-day activities may be the best starting point for developing a base of support.

Conclusion

Single-parent families are becoming more and more common in today's society, but they still face many challenges. Challenges may come from the stigma attached to them by society, from increased stress, or from poor economic conditions. All single-parent families are different—they have each taken their own path and encountered different combinations of difficulties and challenges. Single-parent families need to be recognized as "normal" and as having the potential to raise healthy and well-adjusted children. Like all families, they may at times require support. The early childhood professional can play a supportive role by being aware of their strengths and difficulties and by maintaining a nonjudgmental attitude.

Exercises

1. Interview three single fathers and three single mothers. Ask them about the joys and the challenges of being a single parent and about the support networks available to them. Record their responses, and then compare them. Were there significant differences in the responses you received? To what do you attribute these differences?

2. Review the books in your day-care centre. How many of these reflect the single-parent family as "normal," compared with the images presented of two-parent families?

3. Check local community resources for support groups that may be available to single-parent families. Will the needs of single fathers be accommodated in these groups?

4. Are the policies and activities in your centre sensitive to the needs of single-parent families?

Teenage Parents

chapter 7

Objectives

- **To examine the social factors related to teen parents.**
- **To examine attitudes towards teen parents.**
- **To discuss the risks to the teen parent and child.**
- **To discuss the role of professionals in supporting teen parents.**

> I resent being singled out as a bad mother. I had my first baby before I turned 16, and my second child two years later. My children have always been well cared for, and they are just as well adjusted as any of the other children I see around me!
>
> (An early childhood student who was a teen mom.)

The above comment came from a student who had sat quietly through a lecture on the sociology of teen parents. She felt that the lecturer had dealt with the subject in a very judgmental fashion, particularly when he outlined the risks faced by the babies of teen mothers. In fact, many early childhood students have commented on the negative tone associated with the study of teen parents, claiming that they have teenage friends who are marvelous parents. Many young mothers do, in fact, face the challenge of rearing their children with commitment, courage, and determination, and they have very positive relationships with their children. They face the same risks and challenges that all parents face. The availability of psychological and social supports appears to play a major role in the success of teenage parents (Kurtz & Derevensky, 1994; Luster et al., 1996).

Yet, as we will discuss in this chapter, teen parents do face a number of challenges, and research indicates there are a number of very real risks to the children of teen parents. As we learn about these risks, we must keep in mind that, despite the existence of common challenges, teenage mothers exhibit a broad range of parenting behaviours and abilities (Whiteside-Mansell et al., 1996).

As early childhood professionals who work with families, we should be aware of the special challenges and risks facing any particular population. Perhaps our first concern should be to determine what risks to the baby are associated with teenage pregnancy, and how these risks can be reduced. Since we know that the well-being of the family and the child are inextricably connected, we also should be concerned with the potential risks faced by the mother. Will she be able to complete her schooling or participate in job training, or is she likely to be on welfare? Does becoming pregnant as a teen affect one's chances for a stable marriage? What is the likelihood of a second pregnancy? How does having a baby affect the young mother's own personal development?

In the following discussion of teen parents, while we will bring to light some of the difficulties faced by young families, our main objective will be to enhance our ability to provide appropriate support when needed, rather than to single anyone out for judgment. It is our contention that caregivers may be better able to anticipate and support the needs of teen parents if early childhood professionals are aware and informed. It is important to use this information sensitively, and not to stereotype or jump to conclusions. This chapter will begin with a review of the prevalence, risks, and challenges of teen parenthood, and then look at the role of the early childhood professional in supporting these families. We avoid stereotyping by reminding ourselves that whatever we have learned from research only informs us of general probabilities. It does not predict anything for an individual.

The Prevalence of Teen Pregnancies

The media often refer to teen pregnancies as an epidemic in our society (Jaffe, 1991). They are seen as a "serious social problem facing the nation, and shared across racial, geographic, and economic boundaries" (Skolnick, 1992: 162). It is estimated that in the United States a million babies are born to teen mothers every year (Kurtz & Derevensky, 1994; Suri, 1994; Jaffe, 1991). These statistics need to be considered in context; the figure of "one million babies" includes children of married 18- and 19-year-olds (Skolnick, 1992; Eby & Donovan, 1995). These children may have been planned for within a marriage. In Canada in 1990, there were approximately 20,000 births to unmarried women under the age of 20, 239 of whom were under age 15 (Larson, Golz, & Hobart, 1994). There is a decline in teen parenting in both the United States and Canada since the 1970s, which may be a result of the increasing number of adolescent abortions (Suri, 1994). Despite this decline, teenage parenthood remains a vital social concern today (Barnett, 1997). The statistics do not tell us whether young people chose to have babies at an early age, whether the father is involved in the choice, or whether the pregnancies are unplanned. It is important to realize that there are many routes to becoming a teen parent.

Causes of Teen Pregnancy

Why do teens become pregnant? First and obviously, many teens in North America are sexually active (Kurtz & Derevensky, 1994). Adolescents typically use contraceptives inconsistently and inefficiently, and this leads to the majority of teenage pregnancies. Few teens consciously plan to start a family, although the majority become committed to motherhood as time progresses (Kurtz & Derevensky, 1994; Coley & Chase-Lansdale, 1998). On the other hand, Skolnick (1992) has suggested that teens, especially those living in poverty, might drift into pregnancy and parenthood not out of choice, but because of limited alternatives in life. It is believed that, in these cases, pregnancies are planned and actively desired because the teen wants someone to love and someone to love her, and that she will usually be committed to caring for the baby (Kurtz & Derevensky, 1994; Jaffe, 1991). Approximately two-thirds of all pregnant teens will carry on with the pregnancy and only 4 percent will choose to put their babies up for adoption (Kurtz & Derevensky, 1994; Suri, 1994; Jaffe, 1991). We do know that teen pregnancies occur much more often in families that are poor (Skolnick, 1992), and, in Black families, one in ten female teens will give birth (Eby & Donovan, 1995; Luker, 1997). Middle-class teens are more likely to prevent early childbirth through the use of contraceptives and abortions than are those from families that are economically less advantaged (Eby & Donovan, 1995). Teens are often encouraged to consider abortion as an alternative (Eby & Donovan, 1995).

The Risks of Teen Pregnancy

Risks Associated with Teen Pregnancies

- Teen parents are often poor.
- Teen parents often do not complete their education.
- Teen parents are likely to be single parents or have marital difficulties.
- Teen parents have limited knowledge about childrearing.

In this book, we look at some of the risks associated with raising families, such as poverty and single parenthood. Stevens (1991) has pointed out that children of teenage parents face the same risks as many children, but they usually face more of them at a time. That is, teen parents are more likely to be poor when they become pregnant and to remain economically disadvantaged (Trent & Harlan, 1994). For example, Gleason et al. (1998) found that teenage mothers in American inner cities are dependent on welfare for longer periods of time, and have higher recidivism rates than other groups of women receiving welfare. A large percentage of teen parents will come to rely on social assistance within four years of the child's birth (Eby & Donovan, 1994). The dependency engendered by public assistance, high rates of unemployment, and poverty often continues for years (Trent & Harlan, 1994). Many teen parents experience academic difficulties before their pregnancy, are likely to drop out of school, and will remain uneducated for the rest of their lives (Kurtz & Derevensky, 1994). Teen mothers who finish their education report receiving ongoing family support and support from role models (usually teachers) and are also self-motivated to complete school (Kurtz & Derevensky, 1994). Lacking high school diplomas and work experience leads the teen to remain in poverty or on welfare (Jaffe, 1991). Factors such as resistance to school, the demands of parenthood, and concerns about money, safety, and childcare increase the likelihood that these circumstances will remain unchanged. Statistically, teen parents are likely to be single parents or experience marital difficulties (Trent & Harlan, 1994; Suri, 1994; Kurtz & Derevensky, 1994). Women who have babies when they are teens are also more likely to divorce or not marry than other women. Adolescent parents typically have limited knowledge about childrearing and have fewer support networks available to them (Trent & Harlan, 1994).

Few North American teenagers have grown up in large, extended families where the opportunity exists to learn about babies from siblings, cousins, aunts, or grandmothers. It is no wonder, then, that teens would have little or no idea about a baby's needs and the associated responsibilities. Being a teen, pregnant, and single is generally not viewed as a positive development, and for this reason, it is not surprising that few support networks exist for teen parents.

Physical Risks Associated with Teen Pregnancy

The risk of complications in pregnancy is four to five times higher for teen mothers than for older women. These risks include toxemia, premature birth, lower birth weight, and other physical and mental problems (Jaffe, 1991). There are long-term consequences associated with these risks. Premature and low birth-weight babies tend to be more difficult to care for than full-term babies and those of average weight (Eby & Donovan, 1994). They tend to cry more, have irregular schedules, and develop more slowly (Kurtz & Derevensky, 1994). This can have an impact on the developing relationship between parent and child. When a mother is very young and inexperienced, the risk of neglect and abuse may be heightened under these circumstances (Kurtz & Derevensky, 1994; Jaffe, 1991), leading in turn to permanent disabilities. As we will discuss in Chapter 8, a child born with physical and mental disabilities, or one who develops them in infancy, can be a life-long source of stress for families.

The birth problems associated with teen parents can stem from a number of factors. Sometimes teen parents do not know or admit to being pregnant until the pregnancy is very visible, in other words, well into the second trimester. It is well known that development of the fetus during the first three months can easily be affected by poor nutrition, smoking, and drug or alcohol abuse (Barrett et al., 1995). Because many teens are already involved with substance abuse, the problems associated with it are more commonly found in teen pregnancies than in those among the population at large. Many teen mothers are unaware of these risks, and therefore substance abuse, as well as other dangerous behaviour, continues during pregnancy. Some pregnant teens will continue drug and alcohol abuse even when they are aware of the risks to their baby. Some teens will not know of their pregnancy until the fetus has already been exposed to risks, so even if they do stop, these habits may have already caused damage to their baby.

Added to this, maternal stress is thought to have an effect on the unborn child. Teens, because of their situation, will not only experience the normal stress associated with pregnancy, but may also experience tension with their parents, boyfriends, and peers, in addition to the added stress of having to make difficult decisions for their future. All of these factors suggest that teen pregnancy presents serious risks for both teen parents and their children.

The Teen Mother

When considering how the birth of a child might affect a 13-, 14- or 15-year-old adolescent, it is helpful to consider the adolescent from a developmental perspective and also to think about the nature of the changes taking place at that period of life. It is said that teen mothers face three crises simultaneously (Kurtz & Derevensky, 1994). The first is the crisis of identity versus role diffusion (Erikson, 1963). At the same time puberty, the second crisis, is taking place, complicated by pregnancy. The third crisis is caused by the physical, emotional, and temporal demands of the new maternal role. Let us consider each of these crises in more detail.

The Identity Crisis

Adolescence in North America is usually a time when young people try to establish their individual identity. This process is referred to as identity versus role confusion or diffusion (Erikson, 1963). Teens reflect on their own past, on who they are in the present, and on who they may turn out to be in the future. A sense of identity involves first of all a sense of independence from parents. Adolescents attempt to inform parents, in many different ways, that they are grown up and autonomous. This assertion often puts teens in conflict with their parents. In the quest for independence, adolescents tend to be very responsive to their social environments. Peers are probably more important and more influential during the teenage years than in any other stage of life.

As part of their development, teens begin to experiment with abstract thinking and to learn to deal with their emotions. They are in the process of learning to foresee the consequences of their actions and plan accordingly. Young teens may not have the capability to understand the risks associated with sexual activity (Suri, 1994).

It is said that adolescents tend to overdifferentiate feelings in the process of learning (Honig, 1984). They often feel very strongly that they are completely alone. They believe that they are unique and special; they often feel that they are invulnerable to danger, and therefore engage in risk-taking behaviour (Jaffe, 1991). This explains, in part, why providing high-school students with facts about the dangers of drinking and driving and unprotected sex is usually an insufficient strategy for prevention. Many teens simply do not believe that these things can happen to them. This emotional and psychological immaturity can also lead to a lack of understanding of the real nature of motherhood.

Scenario

Some Teenage Misconceptions

A junior high school counsellor had been talking to a 14-year-old student about her pregnancy, stressing that she should take care of herself and the developing baby, and that she should begin making plans for the future. One day, they were discussing the option of adoption and the teen agreed to consider this over the weekend. She returned the following Monday and excitedly announced that everything was okay—her friend's mother had a stroller that she could use. For this reason, they did not need to discuss options or future plans anymore.

In another case, a social worker was attempting to help a pregnant 15-year-old consider some of her options. "Do you really think you can look after a baby?" she asked. "I know it will be hard in the beginning," replied the young mother-to-be, "but after a couple of years, it will be able to look after itself."

Puberty Complicated by Pregnancy

During her pregnancy, the teen is also dealing with issues associated with puberty, including hormonal changes, body changes, and the formulation of a sexual identity. Many parents joke about the hours that teenage girls spend gazing at themselves in the mirror. This preoccupation with the body and body image is part of the growing-up process. The teen mother has the added burden of dealing with changes to her body and body image, and hormonal changes associated with her pregnancy.

Bearing in mind the developmental tasks facing adolescents, how might a pregnancy affect the teen's development? Becoming a parent will very likely make the quest for individual identity exceedingly difficult, since the teen's world is changing so rapidly, and plans for the future are at least temporarily interrupted. Just at the point when teens are attempting to become independent, the pregnancy often puts them in a position where they are forced to depend on their parents for increased financial and emotional support. The physical changes that occur throughout the pregnancy can also be quite difficult for teenage mothers, since they complicate their attempts to define their sexual identity and sense of self. Recent studies suggest the existence of a relationship between teenage parenthood and low self-esteem, drug use, and assaultive behaviour. Some authors point to evidence of an increased incidence of childhood sexual and physical abuse among teenage parents (Herrenkohl et al., 1998).

Demands of the Maternal Role on the Teen Parent

One of the most difficult consequences of teen pregnancy is the alienation from family and friends typically experienced (Kurtz & Derevensky, 1994). To put it simply, the teen often loses her peer group. Her needs and life are so different from those of her old friends that they no longer associate with her. When the baby is born, child-care duties, time demands, and limited finances can interfere with her social life and lead to feelings of isolation. Finding a new peer group is not always easy.

Scenario

Loss of the Peer Group

A child-care centre in a high-school program had been established and running for several years. The program offered many resources and supports for teen mothers. A new teen mother started to bring her 5-month-old son to the child-care centre. From the beginning, she was cold and aloof towards the other mothers, because she considered them to be "sluts," and she was not about to associate with that type of girl. It had never occurred to her that her old friends rejected her for the same reason.

Since there seems to be some conflict between the developmental tasks of adolescence and the tasks of being a parent, some experts have expressed the concern that the personal development of teen mothers is often placed on hold (Honig, 1984). This may have severe negative impacts on the teen on a long-term basis (e.g., social isolation, interrupted education, and welfare dependency). All of these factors may result in lower self-esteem, which in turn can negatively influence their ability to be competent parents.

The Mother–Infant Relationship

The very nature of adolescence, combined with the physical, social, and economic stressors associated with pregnancy and childbirth, is thought to pose a risk to the parenting abilities of teens. Although teen parents are characterized as caring, they are typically not competent as parents (Jaffe, 1991). Teen parents may have less patience, be less sensitive to the child's needs, and be less emotionally involved than more mature adult parents. Teens appear to have unrealistic expectations of development for their babies (Honig, 1984). On the one hand, they may expect some skills to emerge earlier than they do; for example, they may be impatient for the baby to begin walking, self-feeding, and toileting. On the other hand, they are often unaware of the need for language or cognitive stimulation, for close attachment to the mother, and for praise and encouragement (Kurtz & Derevensky, 1994). The teen mother may not provide the stimulation required for all areas of development or may not realize the child's need for a close attachment, thus demanding independence earlier. Teen parents are also less likely to be aware of the baby's nutritional requirements than the more mature parent.

Scenario

Misreading the Baby's Needs

Fifteen-year-old Jenny frequently took her 12-week-old son Dylan to McDonald's with her friends, and reported that Dylan loved McRibs. When the child-care staff questioned her, she pointed out that the ribs were big enough that he wouldn't choke on them, and hard enough that they wouldn't break into pieces. From her perspective, she had considered the baby's needs. The staff at Dylan's child-care centre were having a difficult time convincing her that the baby was not ready for spicy barbecue sauce. When the baby turned his nose up at pablum, Jenny felt her choice of food was reinforced. "See," she said, "he likes barbecue sauce!"

There is some evidence that babies of teen mothers tend to lag behind the development of babies of older mothers. Studies suggest that children of teen mothers exhibit academic delays, delays in development, and behavioural and emotional problems (Eby & Donovan, 1994; Suri, 1994). This could be due to both the prenatal factors discussed earlier and parenting.

What About Teen Fathers?

So far we have discussed teenage mothers and their babies, and have not referred to the young fathers of these infants. The truth is that only recently has the role of the teenage father been given much consideration. Teenage males are often pleased when their girlfriends get pregnant (Jaffe, 1991). They want a baby just as much as the teenage mother, and usually for the same reasons. The baby may be their first real possession, and caring for him or her may represent a real accomplishment for both teens. The baby may also represent someone to love and to give them love. Unfortunately, like teenage mothers, teenage fathers often have unrealistic expectations about support, and this is one reason males are likely to give up involvement with the baby soon after birth (Kurtz & Derevensky, 1994). In some cases, support from teenage fathers decreases as their children age from infants to toddlers, and as the relationship with the mother becomes more distant (Rangarajan & Gleason, 1998). It is also common for teenage males to be shut out of the decision in the case of abortion or adoption. Even though teen mothers often desire the support of the fathers, few are allowed to participate, and minimal expectations exist for their involvement. Recent studies indicate that the father's education and employment status has a positive influence on the level of economic support provided to the mother, but does not strongly affect the degree of social support provided (Rangarajan & Gleason, 1998). Where the teen father *is* involved, this support may assist teen mothers in their adaptation (Kurtz & Derevensky, 1994).

The Family Dynamics of Teen Pregnancy

Although news of a teen pregnancy often causes much distress in a family, the extended family is often the most crucial and indeed the only means of support for the young mother and her baby. Most teen parents live with their parents or relatives until the child is 3 years old (Kurtz & Derevensky, 1994). The role of the child's maternal grandparents has been shown to be a positive factor both for the teen mother and for the development of the child. Grandparents often provide the new family with financial, technical, and emotional support. This often coincides with some conflict, since teens have to accept their increased dependence, and their parents have to learn how to be supportive without taking over.

Scenario

The Grandmother-to-Be Confronts Her Emotions

Leila was a 38-year-old woman who recently found out that her 16-year-old daughter was pregnant. "First," she said, "I was in total shock. How could this happen? Then I had to work through a vast range of emotions. I felt guilty. Maybe if I had been a better mother and a bit stricter, this wouldn't have happened. Then I felt intense anger at my daughter and her boyfriend. How could they do this to me? I felt so betrayed. I had trusted her and she broke that trust. When my emotions calmed, I realized that I really wanted to put aside some of my other goals for a while and devote the next few years to giving this child and my daughter the best start possible."

Sometimes, grandparents can become so involved in their new role that the teen parent is not allowed to experience all aspects of parenting. For example, if grandparents are "built-in babysitters," the teen never has to worry about child care. When grandparents pay expenses for the teen and the baby, the teen may not come to understand financial responsibility. Often, the extended family needs to walk a very fine line by being supportive while at the same time letting the teen parent take responsibility and experience parenthood fully.

Perspectives

Carlos is a social worker in his early 50s. He came to Canada as a refugee from El Salvador in 1984, with his wife, Rosa, two sons, aged 11 and 12, and a daughter, aged 7. Both Carlos and Rosa were teachers in El Salvador. Once they settled in Canada, Carlos felt that he could be more effective helping immigrants, so he retrained and has been a social worker for several years.

"When we left our home and came to Canada, my main goal was that my children complete their education, be healthy, happy, and contributing members of Canada, while at the same time maintaining a strong sense of identification with their Spanish culture. Religion does not play a big role in our lives, but the beliefs are there in the background. My children all attended a Catholic school.

"When my son was 19 and a student at college, he fell in love with a 16-year-old girl from El Salvador. Although we had hoped that he would concentrate fully on his studies, we noticed that he seemed sad and withdrawn and seemed to be avoiding us. One day, my daughter heard from some friends that he was planning to get married. We were absolutely shocked, because he had not said a word about this to us. Normally, we talked a lot; we had a good relationship with lots of communication between us. Shortly after that he came to us and said, 'Dad, Mom, I need to talk to you... You'll be very angry with me. My girlfriend is pregnant.' Our first response to him was 'We are here to help you.' 'Are you planning to get married?' and 'What about finances?' were some of the questions we had. At that time he answered that he didn't think they should get married, because neither of them had any money.

"We decided to speak with his girlfriend's mother, and we all came to the conclusion that it was probably best for them not to marry, and for the girl to live with her mother until they had finished school. We would help them financially, if necessary, and of course my son wanted to be involved with the baby. But marriage just didn't seem feasible. However, the next time we saw each other, my son told me that they had decided to marry. We think that his girlfriend's mother was desperate to see her daughter settled and officially part of our family, as she herself had not really integrated into Canadian life and hoped to return to El Salvador, confident that her daughter would be taken care of by us. Part of me felt that I was losing my son, and not to the best of circumstances. It was quite sad.

"We held a family meeting. I said that we need, as parents, to support our children. We don't want our grandchild to suffer. The young couple was very emotional, and many tears were shed.

"They got married, with my son still in college and my new daughter-in-law at a high school for pregnant teens. Our biggest concern was that he stay in school. After all we had been through, the thought of our son ending up uneducated and employed in some menial job was hard to bear. With some social assistance and a summer job, they managed to get an apartment in a municipal housing project, and six months after their marriage Juan Carlos was born.

"My wife gave up her part-time job to look after the baby while my daughter-in-law finished high school and my son attended college. Maybe it's a cultural bias, but we feel that babies should be looked after by loving family members. We both love the baby dearly, but Rosa at times felt burdened by the responsibility. My daughter-in-law loves her baby, but we worried that at times she seemed a bit careless, about food or other matters. You can understand that—she is a young girl; she wants to go to parties and be like her friends. It must be quite a conflict for her. I think she regrets being in this situation, having such a big commitment. I believe that my son is a caring and responsible father and very proud of his little boy. He is working and studying full time but tries to spend as much time as possible with the baby. He is still very connected to us. He calls or visits almost every day. Their marriage seems to be okay—they seem to love each other. I sometimes suspect that my son is being manipulated a bit, but that might be a biased perspective.

"Two years have passed now; my son is almost finished his education, and my daughter-in-law has completed high school. We feel now that it is time to pull back a bit. Rosa wants to have some time to herself again. I hope that soon my son will get a good job. We have been giving them financial support up to now, and that has been a bit of a strain. We have worked hard for many years and want to be able to think about our retirement. We also hope to return to El Salvador for a period of time so that I can spend some time with my own parents before they die. I think it will be a bit hard for them—finding care for the baby, and so forth.

"My son and daughter-in-law's unplanned pregnancy changed all of our lives. It has not been an easy time for us. But always our first thought has been 'We must do what is best for the child.' We must support our children so that they can be good parents."

Supporting Teen Parents and Their Families

In order to work effectively with young parents, as with the members of any population, it is important that early childhood professionals consider their own beliefs and responses. On a professional level, an effort must be made to avoid being judgmental and to determine the areas where support can be provided. Moral convictions about premarital sex and other religious and culturally based beliefs make it difficult for some of us to accept teen parents in an objective fashion. In addition, there seems to be a general tendency to view teenagers as irresponsible, rowdy, and generally quite disagreeable. It is common for high-school and college students to report incidents where they were wrongly accused of shoplifting or of other misdemeanours simply, they think, because they were young.

Scenario

What Are Your Feelings About Teen Mothers?

After seeing a film about a 14-year-old new mother who was having trouble keeping her patience with a cranky baby, students were asked to jot down some of their feelings. Some said they felt felt sorry for the young mother and her baby; others were honest enough to admit that they felt quite angry. Why didn't she use birth control in the first place? Didn't she know that having a baby was not going to be like playing with a doll? Another student, a teen mother herself, said that she remembered feeling the frustration expressed by the mother in the film, but reminded the class that any mother, regardless of age, might feel frustrated with a baby who cries incessantly.

It is often assumed that children born to teen parents are unwanted and are largely the result of a mistake or promiscuous sexual behaviour. "Really? How could she? How could she not know to take precautions? How stupid!"—these are comments commonly made about the teen mother. This lack of understanding of teen parents and their particular situation can lead to the teen feeling isolated, as if she were an outcast. Sometimes these feelings result in teens making unfortunate decisions about their babies.

Scenario

A Mother's Defensiveness

Because of the increasing prevalence of child abuse, hospital emergency staff and medical staff in clinics have been trained to look for and investigate any signs of abuse. A teen mother was told by the day-care staff that her 8-month-old daughter had a slight temperature that should be monitored, and that the baby should be taken to the emergency clinic if his fever worsened. The young mother avoided going to the clinic for two days. When she returned to the child care with her baby on the third day, he was very ill. The caregiver asked her why she had not followed the staff's advice and gone to the clinic. The mother finally admitted that she hated going to emergency clinics because the staff there always assumed that she was not a good mother and that whatever was wrong with her baby was her fault. The caregiver realized how difficult it must have been for this young mother to deal with such a situation, so she accompanied her to the clinic to provide support.

This scenario shows that, despite the positive intention of the professionals, their attitudes and response to the mother made her feel angry and defensive. It is likely that she had been exposed to these negative attitudes and statements before, and the latest instance only served as yet another affirmation that she was a bad mother.

Examine Your Attitudes

- Do you lose your temper when you see a teen mother failing to control her child? Or do you think, "Any Mom would have her hands full with a baby like that!"

- Do you tend to think you could do a better job of parenting than the teen mothers you know?

- If you are religious, does your religion emphasize that it is morally wrong to have premarital sex and children out of wedlock? Or does it stress that we should never judge our fellow human beings harshly?

- Do you get along with teens in general, or do you find them too rowdy and irresponsible?

- Do you think the babies of teen parents are most often the result of (a) an accident, (b) simple ignorance, or (c) deliberate planning? Would your answer be different if you were asked the same question about adult parents?

- Consider the situation where a baby is born to a 15-year-old girl who is also poor and has dropped out of high school. Do you think the baby would be better off being put up for adoption and raised by relatively affluent parents? Or should the child remain with its natural mother in spite of any hardships involved?

Methods of Support

Supporting teen parents can best be viewed from the ecological perspective (see Chapter 1). Although caregivers will work primarily and directly with the teen mother and her child, other systems such as the extended family, peer group, schools, and employers all need to be considered in supporting the teen. After examining their personal beliefs about teens and teen parents, caregivers should become knowledgeable about the stressors and risks facing these families, and support them when required, but always in a nonjudgmental fashion. This means first, not making assumptions, and second, recognizing the strength and potential in young mothers as well as the difficulties that they may face. It is particularly important to ensure that the young parent does not sense any disapproval on the part of the professional. Be aware that society's most effective response to the problem of teen pregnancy is still to advocate prevention in terms of birth control, abstinence, and better educational programs (Kurtz & Derevensky, 1994), and to reduce conditions of poverty.

Providing the babies of teen parents with nurturing, responsible, and stimulating care while the young mother completes her schooling can enhance the life chances of both the baby and the mother (Kurtz & Derevensky, 1994). Early childhood professionals can give demonstrations of appropriate care and invite the young parents to spend time at the centre to provide them with an opportunity to observe and learn. Extra care needs to be taken to help the young parents feel at ease and to reassure them that they are not being constantly observed and judged. Young parents may benefit from information about development, discipline, health, and nutrition, as long as the information is transmitted in a manner that is not threatening or that contributes to defensiveness. Research has indicated that social support is necessary but that it must promote the positive development of the teen along with providing models of appropriate childrearing approaches (Kurtz & Derevensky, 1994).

Today, many programs are available in the United States and Canada that provide teen parents with an opportunity to continue their education while learning to be effective parents (Kurtz & Derevensky, 1994). These programs combine social, psychological, and educational support for the teen mother, her baby, the teen father, and the extended family as well. This support may include on-site day cares, flexibility in hours and requirements, child-care classes, child-development classes, prenatal care, social workers, counsellors, and so on. All professionals in such programs work together with the teen. These comprehensive programs are thought to be effective in promoting the well-being of both the young mother and the baby, and even in decreasing the likelihood of another pregnancy during the teenage years. Professionals committed to the well-being of children might wish to lobby for the establishment of such programs in their community.

Supporting the Child

Attendance at a high-quality child-care centre could offset some of the risks for children whose young parents need time to develop their parenting skills. A good child-care centre can ensure adequate nutrition and can also monitor the health and development of the children in its care. A child's ongoing interaction with caregivers in the context of a secure and responsive environment can facilitate the cognitive, language, motor, emotional, and social development of the child. Such care is important for all children; however, if the young age of the parent and accompanying social conditions have a negative impact on parenting, the importance of the highest quality of care is accentuated.

Conclusion

In essence, the needs of teen parents for information, support, and guidance are not very different from those of other parents. What is most important is the ability of the early childhood professional to understand the challenges faced by the teen mother and the developmental tasks of adolescence, and to offer support and assistance in an accepting, nonjudgmental, and nonthreatening fashion.

Exercises

1. Reflect on your own level of maturity at the ages of 13, 15, and 18. In what ways would you have been ready to become a parent, and in what ways would your level of development have hindered your ability to parent? How typical do you think you were at those ages?

2. Draw up a list of your preconceived ideas about teenage parents. After you have done so, ask yourself if these ideas could also apply to the following: new parents, parents over the age of 40, parents who are poor, or parents who are experiencing family problems. Can you identify a pattern of stereotyping in your attitudes towards parents?

3. Check community resources to find those that may be used to support teen parents and their children.

4. Check your local library and bookstore to find out which books may be helpful to teen parents in raising their children.

Children with Special Needs

chapter 8

Objectives

- To understand the reactions of parents who discover that their child has special needs.

- To understand how parents' reactions affect their interactions with their child who has special needs.

- To understand how the family system and all its members are affected by the special needs of a family member.

- To understand the role of the early childhood professional in supporting families with a child who has special needs.

A support group for parents whose children had Down syndrome invited an early childhood educator to speak at an information session called "Choosing Quality Day Care." The speaker described all the important components of a high-quality centre. At the end of the session, one parent approached the speaker and remarked angrily, "You didn't even talk about children with Down syndrome." The speaker replied that certainly parents in this group would need to examine the additional aspects of a program related to the special needs of their children, but that it was important to remember that their children, like all children, required a caring and responsive social environment, a developmentally appropriate physical setting, and nutritious meals and snacks. "Sometimes," the speaker added, "we focus exclusively on meeting the 'special needs' and don't pay enough attention to the aspects of a program that are crucial to all the children."

Another parent was listening thoughtfully to the discussion. She commented: "A year ago I would have been just as angry, because I could only see how my child was different from all the other children. I know that Marcy will always have special needs, but I've learned that children with disabilities must be viewed first and foremost as children."

All expectant parents look forward to the birth of a normal and healthy baby. When a child's health or development is impaired, families often enter a period of intense crisis, which is followed by a lengthy and difficult process of adjustment. The scenario above describes two parents who are in different stages in the process of adjusting to the birth of a child with special needs.

From a family-systems perspective, we can see how the characteristics of the child can evoke intense emotional responses in the parents that could potentially interfere with the developing relationship between them. If this situation remains unresolved for an extended period of time, it can pose risks to the development of the child and the siblings and to the stability of the family unit.

The ecological perspective helps us understand how attitudes towards children with disabilities, legislation protecting their rights, and the extent and quality of both formal and informal support networks can either help or hinder the parents' ability to raise a child who has special needs. Early childhood professionals can fulfill a vital role in facilitating the family's adjustment to the special needs of their child and can also help enhance their ability to provide for the child's optimal development. In order to do that, they need to understand the profound effect that the special needs of a child can have on the family. They also need to be sensitive to the initial and ongoing reactions of parents during the process of adjustment, and they should be aware of the challenges faced by all families whose children have special needs.

Defining Special Needs

The term "special needs" is sometimes confusing, because every child has unique and special qualities that are often identified as needs. Some people prefer to use the term "exceptional children" (Neisworth & Bagnato, 1986; Hallahan & Kauffman, 1994), "developmentally delayed," "handicapped," or "atypical." Professionals debate both the advantages and disadvantages of using any label at all to describe children, as well as the pros and cons of each particular label.

We use the term "children with special needs" in this book for two reasons. First, this is the term most commonly used in the early childhood literature. Second, we know that some children require extra support in order to be able to develop their abilities to the maximum. The term "special needs" can apply to all children who need extra support whether or not they are exceptional or have a particular disability.

Special needs are usually described in terms of atypical development. For example, cognitive development may be delayed (or accelerated, as with gifted children). The special needs may relate to physical development, with atypical motor development (such as cerebral palsy), or sensory development (such as visual or hearing impairments). The special needs of some children relate to the social–emotional domain. Examples of this would be emotional or behavioural problems, or disorders such as autism. Some children have special needs in the area of language, resulting in delayed speech or a stutter. Special needs may also be due to chronic conditions, such as epilepsy, diabetes, or severe allergies.

We will consider special needs in the broadest sense of the term, that is, as they relate to any child who presents specific concerns to his or her parents, and who requires extra support in order to integrate successfully into educational programs. Often, special needs are diagnosed at birth. Other kinds of special needs are identified only later in the child's development. In most settings, an official diagnosis (usually given by medical doctors) is required in order to qualify for professional or financial assistance for the child and family.

There are many children, however, who although not officially labelled as having "special needs," still warrant special consideration. For example, some children are extremely challenging for parents to raise due to a special combination of temperamental traits. These children have been called many things, ranging from hyperactive children to children with behavioural problems to simply "difficult children."

The notion of the "difficult child" stems from the work of Thomas and Chess (1977), who describe a number of traits or characteristics that people seem to be born with and that remain fairly consistent over time. Examples of such traits are *activity level* (some people seem to need to be in constant motion; others are content to sit still), *adaptability* (some people adjust easily to new situations; others find change difficult), and *regularity* (some people have very regular sleeping and eating patterns, while others seem to thrive on an irregular schedule). A child, for example, who is very active, who does not adapt easily to new situations, who does not establish eating and sleeping routines, and who gets fussy when exposed to different textures or sounds may pose difficulties for parents. This is particularly true if the parents' own temperaments are very different from that of their child (Turecki & Tonner, 1989). Although these children are completely "normal," the fact that parents find them difficult to raise can put them and their families at risk.

Reactions of Parents

The reaction of parents to the news that their child has special needs has been compared to the grief cycle experienced after a death. Parents struggle to cope with the loss of their "wished for" or normal child (Simeonsson & Simeonsson, 1993; Turnbull & Turnbull, 1990).

Early childhood professionals who have learned to accept and respect the uniqueness of each child sometimes have difficulty understanding the intensity and duration of parents' responses. Each family is unique in terms of their coping styles and their inner and outer resources. However, there is some commonality in the way in which families experience the grief cycle, and understanding this may assist in appreciating the parents' point of view and in empathizing with the emotion displayed. It must be remembered, however, that people do not generally progress through the stages described below in this particular order.

Understanding the Grief Cycle

Shock

Often parents are completely unprepared for the birth of a child with special needs. The possibility is usually not considered, mentioned, or discussed among couples during the pregnancy, and it is usually avoided in childbirth preparation classes. When it does occur, almost all parents react with shock (Tomlinson, 1986). The parents may experience emotions such as numbness (the inability to feel anything at all) and denial (thinking that the doctor cannot be right; there must be a mistake).

Guilt and shame

Many myths about children and adults with special needs exist in society today. Although these myths have been proven to be untrue, they continue to influence people's views. For example, a belief stemming from the 1940s was that a child's disability was somehow the parents' fault. In the case of psychological or psychiatric disorders, there has been a tendency among professionals to blame mothers.

Some religions can reinforce parents' guilt or shame by teaching that a disability is a consequence of the "sins of the father." Although it has been demonstrated that these ideas are, for the most part, false, the beliefs are still harboured (Paul, Porter, & Falk, 1993). Thus, when parents receive the news of the disabling condition, they must question whether they hold these beliefs and attitudes themselves and learn to deal with their feelings of guilt and shame. The fact that some disabilities are linked to heredity or the parents' state of health at conception and during pregnancy can reinforce the sense of shame and guilt.

A period of intense emotions

Following the first stage of shock and denial, there is a period of intense emotions including confusion, depression, loneliness, anxiety, guilt, and anger (Quine & Pahl, 1987). These emotions can be very strong and are often directed at a wide range of people (e.g., guilt can be directed at oneself; anger might be directed at the spouse, the doctor, or God). Parents often attempt to bargain with God or the doctor as their way of dealing with or denying the diagnosis.

These intense emotional responses of the parents can affect their ability to interact with the child. We know, for instance, that parents who are depressed will interact less with their children. In addition, the baby, due to his or her disability, may have a reduced ability to interact or to give parents positive feedback. Sometimes, initial contact between baby and parents is limited because the baby is in an incubator, is attached to feeding tubes or other equipment, or simply does not respond well to cuddling. This lack of rewarding and positive interactions could hamper the bonding and attachment process. In addition, if the baby is ill, sometimes parents restrain themselves from becoming attached, fearing that the baby may not live. Given the importance of bonding and attachment to the social development of all children, the effects of these initial reactions can be significant in the long term.

While it is important to be sensitive to the intensity and potential risks involved in these initial phases of the grieving process, it is just as important to note that most parents do manage to move beyond these stages (usually with a few setbacks) to stages of adjustment and acceptance.

Adaptation and reorganization

When the intense feelings begin to subside, the stage of adaptation begins; during this period, the parents usually feel better able to care for the child. This leads to the last stage, reorganization (Turnbull & Turnbull, 1990), when the parents reach a positive, long-term acceptance of their child's condition. This stage is marked by the parents' attempts to find suitable services and to organize their lives with their child's disability in mind. Seligman (1991) talks about this stage as one of realistic acceptance in which parents love their children despite their disabilities but would still prefer, if they could choose, for the child not to be disabled.

Parents vary in the intensity and duration of their grief as well as the order in which they experience their reactions. The emotions experienced may intensify or change over time. In our society, for example, it is expected that "good" parents will do everything possible to help their child (Seligman, 1991). At the beginning, many parents relentlessly seek a cure for their child's problem. When it becomes apparent that there is no such "miracle" solution, parents often try to provide their child with a series of educational opportunities—they will teach this child everything he or she needs to know. When parents stop shopping for a cure or if they begin to think that teaching is of little value, they often feel that they have lost control over their child's life, that they are powerless, without a plan. Usually in time, families reach a stage where they no longer hope for miracles or that they can make the problem go away, but feel that they can help the child develop to the best of his or her ability.

Factors That Affect the Grief Cycle

The parents' adjustment may depend on a number of factors, such as the presence or absence of support, the reaction from others, and the parents' religious and cultural beliefs (Smith, 1993; Turnbull & Turnbull, 1990).

Breaking the news

Adjustment may depend partly upon when and how parents are told of the disability (Quine & Pahl, 1987). The birth of a baby with a disability is often perceived as a "failure" for the parents and for the doctors as well (Paul, Porter, & Falk, 1993). It seems as though there is an unwritten rule that if you do everything that the doctor says, all will be well. When this does not occur, the medical profession is often at a loss. Sometimes their reaction is to delay informing the parents until they are sure of the diagnosis (Quine & Pahl, 1987). Sometimes they think they are helping by putting the new mother in a room by herself so she can have extended visiting hours and time alone to deal with the situation. From the parents' point of view, though, this can lead to feelings of suspicion and isolation (Seligman, 1991).

Scenario

Ignored at the Hospital

A mother was in a private room with her newborn baby who had been diagnosed as having Down syndrome. Due to concerns for their health, the mother and child stayed in hospital for four days. The mother reported that she was left pretty much to herself. She would wander the hallways and was in and out of the nursery, where she frequently heard nurses exclaim, "What a cute baby. Isn't he adorable?" She realized that no one had commented on her own baby until she was leaving, when the receptionist took notice and told her how sweet her new baby was. This lack of interaction with medical professionals was so noticeable that it had a significant effect on this new mother.

As the above scenario makes clear, the attitudes of the doctors, nurses, and other professionals involved can provide the parents with hope, or they can be subtly discouraging. Sensitive professionals can assess a parent's need for support and information; and although they cannot (and should not try to) diminish the parents' sorrow, they can facilitate the adjustment process.

Delayed diagnosis

Children may be diagnosed with difficulties immediately after birth or a traumatic event (e.g., head injury), or the diagnosis may be delayed (Brillhart, 1988). When the diagnosis is not immediate, the parent is usually the first to notice something is wrong with the baby's development. Anxiety often increases as parents read more books about development, as they attempt to compare their child to others of the same age, and as they discuss development with their family doctor. When this continues for a lengthy period of time, parents often report a feeling of relief upon hearing the diagnosis (Turnbull & Turnbull, 1990). They feel that their concerns have finally been heard and their suspicions confirmed. This sense of relief is usually short-lived, though, as the parents adjust to the reality of the situation and as the quest for more information and services begins in earnest.

Religious and cultural beliefs

Earlier we suggested that some religious beliefs can reinforce a sense of guilt or blame. However, many parents have attested to the critical role their religious beliefs have had in helping them accept their child. Below is an example of how one parent's religious beliefs affected her adjustment to the birth of a child with special needs.

Scenario

Religious Beliefs as a Factor in Acceptance

Ann was raised as a Christian and was very devoted to her religion. Her third son was born with severe developmental delays and major health problems. He was in intensive care for three months before he was physically well enough to go home. Ann seemed to deal with her son's condition extremely well. She did not appear shocked, deny the condition, exhibit anger, or blame others or herself. When questioned by the early intervention worker, Ann explained that in her religion, a handicapped child was considered a gift. She believed that God had chosen her and her husband as special parents because he felt that they were able to cope with the child. Her beliefs helped her and her family to make the transition directly to acceptance.

Ongoing Adjustment Throughout the Life Cycle

It may be useful for professionals to realize that the grief cycle discussed earlier may repeat itself at different developmental or family life-cycle stages. Although parents may have apparently adjusted to the diagnosis of their newborn child with special needs, they may re-experience strong feelings of grief or crisis at transition times, as when the child reaches the age to begin school (Simeonsson & Simeonsson, 1993). In the same way, as families progress through different stages, the transition from one stage to another may once again remind the parent of the child's special needs. For instance, while other children become more independent and attend functions outside the home during their early school years, the child with special needs does not become involved in these activities. These transitions in development or family life cycles may either produce a mild reminder of their child's needs or launch the parents back into the emotional ups and downs of the grief cycle as they learn to cope with the difficulties and realities that each new stage will bring.

As the child grows older, the family realizes again what a serious, long-term commitment they have made to daily care, and they have to learn again about what social resources are available and about the best ways to advocate for their child. Parents may be at a stage in their own lives when their friends are beginning to experience the freedom that comes with having older children. Even though the child with special needs may be the same age, he or she may not be able to get around without supervision or help. Again, the parents are likely to feel tied down and somehow restricted by their child's needs. Throughout the life cycle, parents are reminded of their child's disability, of their long-term commitment, and of the lack of support, such as respite care or babysitting, that is available to families with children like theirs.

The Impact on the Family System

As we have seen, parents of young children with special needs are confronted with many stresses and strains at a time that is likely to be very emotional for everyone involved. The birth of a child with special needs can change families dramatically. Parents are in a position of exploring new territory and facing unforeseen challenges, while coping with physical, financial, and emotional challenges (MacAuley, 1996). Sometimes, these stresses can affect the entire family, in what has been referred to as the ripple effect (Turecki & Tonner, 1989) or the domino effect. These effects are evident in both the long and short term functioning of the family (Hendler, 1997). We must be aware that families who have a child with special needs are likely to deal with more stress on an ongoing basis than most families (Simeonsson & Simeonsson, 1993). Consequently, these families are likely to be at greater risk for marital difficulties (Friedrich, Cohen, & Wilturner, 1987), and the mothers are more likely to be subject to depression (Gallagher, 1993). It has been reported that there is a disproportionately high number of children with special needs living with emotional, verbal, and physical abuse, and neglect (Blickstead, 1996; MacAuley, 1996). There is also a greater sense of disruption in family life (Gallagher, 1993). Stress is increased when there is ambiguity or uncertainty in the diagnosis, and stress is also related to the severity of disability and whether the responsibility (or blame) is placed on a particular family member (Brillhart, 1988; Tomlinson, 1986). Let us then examine how the different subsystems in a family might be affected by the presence of a child with special needs or behavioural challenges.

The Parental Subsystem

We have described the intense emotional responses experienced by the parents of children with special needs and how the bonding and attachment process may be affected. In North American culture, where mothers still carry the major responsibility for raising children, they are also most often blamed when things go wrong (McGoldrick, 1982). When a child throws a tantrum at the supermarket checkout counter, most people still think, "Why can't that mother control her child in public?" Many mothers believe that they should have the ability to raise and parent their children. They also believe that they should love and like their children. When the child exhibits difficult behaviour, the mother is left questioning her abilities, her intentions, and her effectiveness. It is not uncommon for mothers to feel emotions such as guilt, isolation, depression, embarrassment, or denial. A mother may overprotect her child or become overinvolved as a means of ensuring that the child is successful. As time passes, her self-esteem and image of herself as a mother can be eroded (Turecki & Tonner, 1989).

Often mothers have difficulty interacting with the child consistently and effectively because they do not understand the child's behaviour and may inappropriately ascribe motives to that behaviour (e.g., "He is doing that to bug me; my child hates me") (Turecki & Tonner, 1989).

Misinterpreting Behaviour

At a preschool picnic, Monica was trying to get her 2½-year-old son ready to leave. She had given several warnings that they were getting ready to go. When she finally called him to go, he screamed and ran off in the other direction. She waited for several minutes then called again. He looked at her and followed a group of children in the other direction. She called again and he screamed back "No!" The mother attempted twice more before the caregiver approached. "See," she said, "he hates me."

Ineffective or inconsistent discipline may result from such a failure to understand a child's behaviour. One day the mother may be restrictive; the next day she may be too tired to argue, so she allows the child to run freely. She may then attempt to regain control by using harsher discipline techniques, which can make the behaviour worse. Unfortunately, punishment often seems to be effective immediately, and this reinforces the parent's decision to use it. Usually, however, punishment is effective only in the short term because the child has not learned a better way to behave. This vicious cycle of control and behaviour leads to the lowering of self-esteem for both the child and mother. Breaking out of this cycle can be a very difficult process (Turecki & Tonner, 1989).

In traditional families, the father may either present the solution for breaking out of the leniency/punishment cycle, or he may contribute to its continuation. Father may arrive home at the end of the day to provide Mom with a welcome respite and help re-establish her authority, or he may not understand why the child acts the way he does or why the mother reacts the way she does. His questioning of her actions may be interpreted as criticism or as a lack of confidence in her parenting techniques.

The father may be put unwillingly into the role of the disciplinarian (e.g., "Wait until your father gets home!") or left out of the parenting process altogether because he does not agree with the mother. She may sense this lack of support or feel jealous because he has a conflict-free relationship with the child. He, on the other hand, may feel that he is not permitted to be part of the parenting routine and may spend more time away from home to avoid further conflicts.

Although we have been speaking of the traditional family, the same effects can be seen in all families. Two working parents, a single parent, or a noncustodial parent will also experience this additional stress within their family unit. These parents may also find themselves without any supports to provide them with a much-needed respite or to restore balance within the household.

The Marital Subsystem

The stresses involved in raising a child with special needs can put a great deal of strain on the marriage. The husband may feel left out of the relationship with the child and even perhaps of the marital relationship since the mother may be too exhausted for intimacy with him. She may direct some of her intense and negative feelings towards her husband—feelings of anger, anxiety, or resentment. The husband often responds by pulling away and decreasing his involvement in child care, which intensifies the mother's frustration and leads to an even wider rift between the parents. If the rift grows wide enough, it may lead to a breakdown of the marriage. In fact, divorce continues to be disproportionately high in families with a child who has special needs (Gallagher, 1993; Turnbull & Turnbull, 1990). It is important to remember that this is not always the case (Friedrich, Cohen, & Wilturner, 1987), and that some families report feelings of renewed closeness after the birth of a child with special needs (Turnbull & Turnbull, 1990).

The Sibling Subsystem

The siblings may also be affected by the child with special needs. An example of the variation in effects on siblings can be seen in the work of Wolf et al. (1998). The researchers found that siblings of children with Pervasive Development Disorders often feel that they are favoured by their parents over their special needs siblings, while siblings of children with Down Syndrome may feel that their special needs sibling is preferred. One or both parents may have less time for their other children and may place higher expectations on them. These expectations may be in the form of day-to-day responsibilities or in expectations that they will achieve goals that their sibling with special needs is not able to attain. Siblings may find it difficult to talk about the situation or even to gain clarification about the disability (e.g., "Why is he like that? Is it contagious? Was it my fault?"). Later in life, siblings report either that the experience was positive and that it made them more accepting, tolerant, and understanding, or that they experience feelings such as shame, guilt, resentment, and jealousy. This difference in feelings can be attributed to several factors including attitudes of the parents, supports available to all family members, religion, culture, family cohesiveness, and severity of the disability (Turnbull & Turnbull, 1990).

Scenario

Doing Chores

Two students in a rehabilitation studies class were comparing their siblings with special needs. Nina explained that her severely mentally challenged sister was always treated as a member of the family. She had her own chores to do, which were well within her capabilities—she set and cleared the table, and she loaded and unloaded the dishwasher daily. Even though she had special needs, there were expectations for her, just as for anyone else in the family. June recalled that her asthmatic brother was treated very differently. Since no one was sure when he would have an attack, he was never expected to help out around the house, and his sisters did all of his chores for him. Their mom woke him, prepared his meals, and protected him from the other children. As the two were talking, their lasting impressions of their siblings and the effects on them and their families became very clear. While Nina was quite accepting, June was resentful of her brother's needs and of the effect they had on her.

Siblings may also be affected by the presence of the child who is difficult to manage or requires a lot of parental time and attention. Either parent or both of them may have less time to spend with the siblings; for this reason, the brothers and sisters may come to resent the difficult child for the attention taken away from themselves, resulting in jealousy or competition. Siblings could decide that the way to get attention is either to be perfect or to get into trouble as well. These reactions can lead to further difficulties within the family.

Examples like those in the scenario above illustrate the domino or ripple effect, whereby one source of stress ends up affecting the entire family. The child with special needs presents a situation with different tasks, responsibilities, and emotions for each family member. The emotions felt by the primary caregiver in learning to cope may affect the interactions with the child with special needs, the spouse, and eventually other children within the family. Sometimes the ripple effects are even felt beyond the nuclear family, reaching the extended family and friendship networks as well (Turecki & Tonner, 1989). Despite the greater degree of stress that is associated with parenting an exceptional child, recent research suggests that many parents today show resilience in adjusting to the presence of a child with special needs in their family (Sanders & Morgan, 1997).

Challenges for Families Who Have a Child with Special Needs

In addition to coping with their own grief and with the stressors within the family unit, families who have a child with special needs often encounter difficulties in their interactions with "the outside world." These difficulties usually relate to common prejudices in our society about people with special needs. Sometimes parents are faced with very negative and insensitive beliefs about people who have disabilities.

Scenario

Ignorant Remarks

The parents of a 5-year-old little boy with severe mental and physical challenges worked very closely with the child-care staff in an attempt to get Donny ready for school. Since he was noticeably cross-eyed, staff recommended that the parents have his eyes examined. Donny's parents made an appointment, but returned from it absolutely devastated. The optometrist had matter-of-factly stated that since correction of the child's eyes would make no difference to "his condition," why would they want to spend the money?

Incidents such as these reflect a fairly widespread attitude that parents of children with special needs come up against all too often. In some cases, the negative attitudes may be less blatant, but parents still find themselves interacting with people who have very unclear expectations about the potential of children with disabilities.

These negative attitudes are usually based on ignorance, and the ignorance is usually a result of the fact that many people have limited interactions with people who have special needs. Therefore, they do not know what to expect or what potential a particular child may have in the future. This is surprisingly true of some medical professionals as well (Seligman, 1991).

Lack of Information Among Doctors

A young mother had just given birth to a baby with Down syndrome in a hospital. First the obstetrician came to deliver the news. This visit was followed by one from the family doctor and a pediatrician, who both described the child as a person who would grow physically to a normal size but would always have the mind of a 2-year-old.

Although this scenario occurred 15 years ago, it is not untypical of statements made today. In fact, Quine and Pahl (1987) have noted that parents continue to express dissatisfaction over the ways that medical staff communicate with them. The kind of conversation illustrated above could be extremely frightening for parents who have had little contact with people who have special needs. Furthermore, it is often very difficult to ascertain at an early stage what the full potential of any child will be. Although professionals should not be unrealistically optimistic, they should also not err on the side of pessimism.

Interaction with Professionals

One of the most stressful factors reported by parents of children with special needs is the necessity for increased interaction with professionals (Smith, 1993; Pizzo, 1993; Turnbull & Turnbull, 1990). Parents who have had little contact with professionals may suddenly be required to deal with doctors, nurses, dietitians, physiotherapists, speech therapists, psychologists, and social workers. What makes these interactions so difficult is that the parent usually has a strong emotional reaction, while the professional normally does not.

Many parents interacting with medical professionals have reported that they feel a loss of control over their child's life and treatment (Seligman, 1991; Clawson & Bigsby, 1997), and that they feel disempowered by their constant struggle (Pizzo, 1993). This was even more common in the past, when families were made completely dependent upon professionals (Gallagher, 1993; Pizzo, 1993). Parents may attempt to challenge a professional's authority, but this is a very difficult task indeed. Parents and professionals, especially medical professionals, often operate at different status levels, which in itself commonly makes interaction and communication difficult. This situation may require the parents to learn a new set of skills to get information and to act as advocates on behalf of their child. Parents may also be in situations where they do not understand the terminology or jargon or where there are conflicting messages presented by different professionals. Typically, each professional focuses primarily on a particular aspect of the child's development (e.g., the physiotherapist is concerned with physical abilities, the speech therapist with speech development); sometimes, the "whole child" is forgotten.

Conflicting Advice from Professionals

Jan was the mother of a 2-year-old girl with cerebral palsy who attended a hospital-based early intervention program. The program included a speech therapist, physiotherapist, and social worker who all provided guidance and direction to the mother. The physiotherapist explained the absolute necessity of the mother completing range-of-motion exercises daily and of changing Kaitlin's position regularly. The speech therapist explained that Kaitlin was at the developmental stage when hearing speech and having many opportunities to communicate with her mother would be crucial to her development of language skills. The social worker closed by explaining that it was important for Jan to plan time off from her caretaking duties, and that she should not become overinvolved in Kaitlin's care. Needless to say, Jan felt a little confused by the end of the session.

This sort of confusion can be further complicated by the rapid turnover of professionals that sometimes occurs. One social worker may be replaced by another as the child grows older or other professionals may be transferred or promoted. Each new professional represents a new challenge for the parents and the child, and these continual changes can be extremely stressful.

Interaction with professionals often involves interaction with social agencies that provide specific care and assistance to children with special needs. Unlike systems for normally developing children (e.g., playschool or the public school system), there is a range of services for exceptional children, each with its own criteria for admittance and subsequent service. These criteria may be based on age, developmental level, severity of the disability, type of disability, proof of disability, and income. Parents must acquaint themselves with all of the services that exist and with each particular set of rules if they wish to gain access to the services. Whenever parents request something a little different for their child, such as inclusion in the neighbourhood school, their communication and advocacy skills will be truly tested.

Thus, although the involvement of professionals from many different disciplines is sometimes warranted, the truth is that more is not necessarily better (Simeonsson & Simeonsson, 1993). Traditionally, professionals and services have attempted to deal with each and every concern or problem, but this approach has proved to be stressful for both the child and the family. Professionals need to recognize this fact and attempt to provide support based on the needs and desires of each individual family. Professionals should also try to remember that families with children who have special needs have many other interests and concerns. For this reason, it is important to treat the family as a unit rather than to single out or focus exclusively on the child with special needs (Simeonsson & Simeonsson, 1993). Appropriate support from professionals can be very helpful to parents of children with special needs (Bennett et al., 1996).

Jody is now a single parent of two boys—12-year-old Ryan and 13-year-old Xenon. She works as a full-time college instructor.

Jody and John adopted a child who, at 3 weeks, had major heart surgery to correct a congenital heart defect. At that time, the doctor told them that these children may develop on "both sides of normal," but that Xenon's progress was excellent thus far. In addition to the surgery, he was on Phenobarb for a period of time to control seizures and had serious respiratory problems, with the possibility of cystic fibrosis. The list of medical conditions seemed to go on forever: auditory discrimination problems, memory problems, visual motor problems, mild myopia, poor tooth enamel, bowel and bladder problems, and asthma. If you were to meet Xenon, you would think that he looks just like everyone else, but when all these "little" problems are added together, he has definite special needs. The frustrating part is that each problem is treated by a different doctor, specialist, or teacher, who does not know about or think about the other problems. So, one medication will treat one set of symptoms but cause an unpleasant interaction with another medication or affect his behaviour in some way that causes difficulties at school or in learning.

"As a parent, I always feel that I walk a fine line about what to tell to whom. On the one hand, I don't want him singled out as the child with special needs, but I also don't want him to be labelled as lazy or having a bad attitude because people don't understand that, because of his medical problems, his performance can't always be optimal.

"Xenon always has been, and still is, in a regular school with supports. So far, the schools and teachers have been great in meeting his particular needs, but sometimes they don't realize the impact that some of their statements, although likely quite innocent, have on Xenon or myself. For example, one teacher explained to me that completing a certain assignment should be easy because 'even Xenon can do it.' I think I know what she meant, but Xenon was devastated by her comments and so was I, knowing how hard he tries to get things done. On one occasion, when Xenon was left behind on a class outing due to health concerns, he thought he wasn't allowed to go because he had been bad. It took a lot of convincing by myself and the teacher to reassure him that this was not true.

"Maybe my experiences have made me a little oversensitive, or maybe, because I know Xenon, a kind, gentle, caring, whole person, I am a little more sensitive about what people say. Anyways, I hope that all the professionals and specialists that come into contact with Xenon see him for the person that he is, not today's problem or symptom."

Unrealistic expectations placed on parents

In the last two decades, professionals have made great strides in the treatment and education of children with special needs. They have learned through research and practice that therapy initiated in the early years is the most effective in treating the disability as well as in preventing secondary problems that may be a result of the disability.

In addition, a number of earlier research studies led to the belief that the parent should be the child's primary teacher, and this became the cornerstone in many early intervention programs (Katz, 1980). Many models of intervention were developed where the professional would "teach" the parents to carry out a wide range of exercises and individualized programs with their child. Sometimes this put tremendous strain on families. Parents were instructed to teach their child at every possible moment, to have a wide assortment of professionals into their homes, and always to have the best interest of the child in mind. With all of these expectations placed on parents, some began to wonder when they would be able to relax and "just be a parent." When would they have time to cuddle and spoil their baby rather than always being the teacher and therapist? These expectations put additional pressures on the families of children with special needs. On top of all the other emotional stresses, the expectation that the parent be available for constant teaching may have placed excessive demands on parents.

Because of these difficulties, the early intervention movement has attempted to rethink the demands placed on parents by incorporating the family-systems approach into their practice with families (Turnbull & Turnbull, 1990; Gavidia-Payne & Stoneman, 1997).

Work and Parenting Children with Special Needs

Many parents face challenges in attempting to maintain employment and family responsibilities. When the family includes a child with special needs, there may be additional challenges in terms of extra expenses, changes in employment income, and stresses due to inadequate child care and supports in the community and workplace (Hope Irwin & Lero, n.d.).

In the report *In Our Way: Child Care Barriers to Full Workforce Participation Experienced by Children with Special Needs* (Hope Irwin & Lero, n.d.) it was found that a significant number of parents were unemployed or worked fewer hours in order to meet the demands of their children with special needs. Typically, mothers' employment was affected. Moreover, 88 percent of parents said they felt tired and overloaded, and 90 percent said they were stressed about balancing work and family obligations. A major cause of stress was the lack of access to appropriate, affordable licensed child care (p. 3).

Supporting Families with a Special-Needs or Difficult Child

Family is important to all children. The presence of a supportive family will undoubtedly be a major influence in the life of the child with special needs. The child may require additional support from his or her family in daily routines and in developing new abilities. In addition, the child with special needs may be ridiculed and teased by other children in school and on the playground. A strong family unit provides the child with a solid foundation to face present and future challenges.

We will examine how caregivers may support families that include a child with special needs. By attempting to understand and empathize with what families may be experiencing and feeling, caregivers may be better able to provide assistance. Their role may be twofold. The first role lies in helping the family to recognize that the child may have special needs. Through their studies of child development and experience with groups of children in the early years, early childhood professionals are often in a position to recognize a developmental or behavioural problem (Kaiser & Rasminsky, 1993).

Second, the early childhood professional can offer support to the family members as they come to cope with this reality in their lives, and they can also help the family in their continual struggle to maximize opportunities for their child.

Changing times have altered the role of early childhood professionals who work with parents of special-needs children. It was generally believed for many years that problems could be eliminated by direct and early intervention with the child (Gallagher, 1993). Thus, it was thought that working with the child in a certain program would be sufficient to deal with that child's special needs. More recently, it has become evident that families need to be considered as a unit, and that early childhood professionals may play a valuable role in attempting to facilitate the strengthening of families and in developing support networks (Gallagher, 1993; Simeonsson & Simeonsson, 1993; Turnbull & Turnbull, 1990). Family-focused programs serve to ensure that the child with the disability is not seen in isolation but as part of the whole family. Programs serve to strengthen the whole family (MacAuley, 1996). When early childhood professionals are sensitive to a family's particular needs and provide appropriate support, the family develops a sense of control and empowerment over its world (Heath, 1994; Pizzo, 1993; Gallagher, 1993).

Examine Your Attitudes

Myths abound about children with special needs. It is also true that negative attitudes—fear, prejudice, and dislike—often influence people's reactions to the parents and siblings of these children.

As you ask yourself each of the following questions, consider it again for a person with one of the following challenges: cognitive, physical, visual, hearing, and mental health.

- Do you think people with special needs cannot learn, or do they learn in different ways and at different rates than other people?

- Do you believe that people with special needs contribute to society, or are they unproductive members who sap medical and financial resources while contributing nothing themselves?

- Should people with special needs be educated together in special classrooms, or is it better to "mainstream" them?

- Is it true that parents are always directly responsible for their children's behaviour? Is bad behaviour the result of parents' failure to discipline their children?

- Have you found that parents of special-needs children are reluctant to work with professionals? If so, have you discovered a reason for this reluctance?

- Would you work with a staff person who had special needs in your day-care centre? Would you expect as much from him or her as from the other staff members?

Identifying Special Needs

When the early childhood professional suspects that a particular child may have special needs, the most difficult task will be in sharing this information with the parents (Abbott & Gold, 1991). Many staff members feel anxious about facing parents in this situation.

Early childhood professionals may first want to collect and document examples rather than making their suspicions known to parents with little supporting information. Discussing observations clearly and honestly face-to-face is often a better approach than discussing them over the telephone or using jargon that parents may not understand (Kaiser & Rasminsky, 1993). Often, talking to parents can be easier when there is a sharing of information (e.g., "What have you noticed? How does he do this at home?"). Early childhood professionals should be prepared to share ideas and resources with parents. For instance, they can help parents decide what the next step will be, or they can provide a list of potential services to consider. Bearing in mind the stages of shock, denial, and intense feelings referred to earlier in the chapter, caregivers should also expect the parents to react intensely, sometimes with anger and vociferous denials (Abbott & Gold, 1991). Being prepared for such emotions may help in dealing with them.

FAS/FAE

Fetal alcohol syndrome (FAS) and Fetal alcohol effects (FAE) are two terms that are becoming more commonly known and better understood. Children with FAS and FAE have alternatively been labelled behaviour problems, emotional problems, learning disabilities, or attention deficit disorder. However, there is a constellation of difficulties associated with FAS and, to a lesser degree, FAE. These concerns include developmental delays, along with emotional and behavioural concerns including difficulty attending to task, difficulty in peer interactions, difficulty following directions, and difficulty following rules and routines. Children with FAS typically have particular facial features, which become more distinguished with age, along with particular growth patterns.

Children with FAS and FAE can present challenges in the playroom. They require extra personnel and resources to assist in meeting the child's special needs.

Families with children who have FAS also often present particular challenges. It may be difficult for natural parents to come to terms with having a child with FAS. Parents may be unwilling to discuss the child's concerns or deal with problems due to the nature of the syndrome. Many children with FAS live in adoptive and foster care settings. This, in and of itself, may present challenges to the child and family. Parents may experience negative emotions in dealing with the realization that this foster or adoptive child has lifelong difficulties. Issues surrounding attachment may result. Other parents are prepared to deal with the situation and readily work with early childhood professionals to locate and access the appropriate resources.

It is important for caregivers to understand the difficulties associated with FAS or FAE along with the particular family dynamics that may result. FAS has become a focal area of study in many provinces and states, therefore much more information on the syndrome and strategies for caring for children are becoming available to parents and caregivers alike. Caregivers may wish to search out potential sources of information to ensure that they are able to meet the challenges that children with FAS and their families may present in group care settings.

Providing Ongoing Support

Once the diagnosis has been made and the reality of the special needs or behavioural concern is evident, parents may require support on an ongoing basis. Early childhood professionals may assist parents in many ways. First, caregivers can share information regularly with parents. This means not just giving parents information about what the child is doing, but also asking the parent to share their information. Parents know the child from a different perspective, one that caregivers rarely get to see. Be sure that parents hear positive things about their child along with the not-so-pleasant details. In the busy activity of the day, it is easy to overlook the positive aspects of the child's development and remember only the difficulties presented. Parents need to hear about both, and if they are having difficulty coping, it may be beneficial for them to hear more positive than negative statements.

Interpreting Information

The early childhood professional may play a role in helping parents to interpret information. For instance, parents may be unable to ask the specialist or therapist for an explanation of terms because the professionals are too busy or because the parents feel awkward admitting that they do not understand the terminology used. In this case, providing information in understandable terms and in relation to this particular child may be of real benefit to the family. If the caregiver, however, is unable to understand and interpret the information, he or she can still play a valued role in helping parents to get the correct information (e.g., by giving them reading material or the number of another professional to call). This may be the first step in helping the family to build a support network.

Scenario

Difficult Terminology

Tony's mother was invited to a case conference with the speech therapist, physiotherapist, Grade 1 teacher, and psychologist. She asked if Tony's caregiver from the day-care centre would come along because she felt intimidated by all of these people. The conference began with each professional providing the most recent assessment results. The speech therapist talked about Tony's "inability to form fricatives and his lack of occlusion." The physiotherapist described his "poor motor control in the prone and supine position and total lack of balance and coordination." At this point, the mother left the room in tears. When the caregiver found her in the bathroom, she stated that she understood two things very clearly. First, her son was not capable of doing anything. Second, she was too stupid to understand what it was exactly that he could not do.

The caregiver may support the family by providing or interpreting information whenever possible. She may also escort the parents to meetings and help them listen and ask appropriate questions. Or, she may simply listen to the parents and act as a "sounding board" as they determine their course of action. When early childhood professionals establish a good working relation with parents, the particular course of action can be worked out together.

Sharing Coping Strategies

Caregivers can also play a role in making parents aware of ways to deal with difficult behaviour. Role modelling of effective strategies may be beneficial to parents. For example, the early childhood professional may be of benefit in intervening and breaking the cycle of negative reactions with a temperamentally difficult child simply by giving the child time to settle down when the child and parent are embroiled in a conflict.

Scenario

Establishing New Routines

A caregiver observed that each morning when Shane came in, his mother was usually in a rush. She would carry him in, help him remove his clothing, and then he would cry and cling. She would react with harsh statements, and he would cling more. It did not take him long to work himself into a real emotional outburst. Whenever the caregiver attempted to intervene, both the mother and Shane would get upset. Finally, the caregiver realized that she needed to intercept the situation before it occurred. The next morning, she arranged with the other staff in the playroom to wait for Shane at the door. The moment Shane walked in, she greeted the two by saying, "Good morning. I know that your mommy is in a hurry. I'll take you from here, so let's give her a big hug and kiss goodbye and say, 'Have a good day at work, Mom.'" There were hugs, kisses, and a cheery goodbye. The next day, the same routine was repeated. By the third day, a new morning routine was in place.

Early childhood professionals need to be cautious when they report their own "successes" with the child, since the parent may interpret this to mean that they are a failure in parenting. For example, when the caregiver adamantly declares that this child is never a problem, that he always acts like a complete angel, the parents may question their own abilities and wonder why the child is always a problem for them. In fact, caregivers may provide tremendous support by simply assuring the parent that the situation is not their fault and that their children are "normal," albeit difficult to handle (Heath, 1994).

Sharing Information

Scenario

Benefits of a Nonjudgmental Attitude

Ann was a 33-year-old mother of two boys and had returned to college to earn her diploma in early childhood education. In a class on working with families, the topic of temperamentally difficult children was being discussed. She remained quiet throughout the class and when it was done, she approached the instructor to thank her. Ann's eldest son had many difficult traits, and this was the first time that someone had ever said that his problems were not her fault. She continued by telling the instructor that not everyone openly accused her of being at the root of her son's behavioural problems, but she could tell what people were thinking by the way they said things or the advice that they gave her.

Sharing information about the problems typical of children who are difficult or have special needs may be the first step in helping families cope. It is usually a tremendous relief for them to realize that it is not their fault, that they are not bad parents. The change in this attitude may provide the impetus to change the parents' reactions to the child. Often, it is not necessary for the child's behaviour to change; rather, everyone involved learns to deal with the behaviour. For example, if the child does not cope well when tired, every effort can be made to begin bedtime routines long before tiredness sets in. The child who does not adapt well to new settings may require more time and patience on the part of the parent and caregiver and will also appreciate warnings that activities are about to change. Changes in the parents' reactions may thus serve as a catalyst for the child's behaviour to improve.

Respecting the Family's Needs

It is important for early childhood professionals to remember that each family they deal with has a life extending beyond the child with special needs or difficult behaviour. So much of the family's time and effort will be expended in caring for the child that other needs and perspectives may be neglected. Early childhood professionals can easily fall into this trap themselves by urging parents to try a new idea or carry out a program at home.

If early childhood professionals will consider the entire family unit, they may be able to support the family in such a way as to benefit the family as a whole. For example, providing information about accessible activities in the community may give the whole family the chance to do something together. This may also help each family member feel part of a "normal" family and give them a chance to relax and enjoy recreational activities together. Such interaction can help strengthen the family (Turnbull & Turnbull, 1990).

Providing Emotional Support

Early childhood professionals may also play a role in providing families with emotional support. Families will experience many different emotions and cope in many different ways. The early childhood professional may be able to provide different perspectives, approaches, or resources for families to consider. Sometimes parents simply need to have their feelings validated or be given permission to feel angry or disappointed. Providing emotional support requires understanding that each family will respond to circumstances in a unique way and will have different strengths and different needs.

Helping Families Access Resources

Parents of children who are difficult or have special needs often benefit from support groups that consist of parents in similar circumstances (Seligman, 1991). In a survey by the Canadian Association of Family Resources Programs in 1994, it was found that many parents of children with special needs are providing support to other parents already. Professionals, however, can play a fundamental role by offering leadership, support and practical assistance (e.g., contacting or notifying parents, providing meeting space, liaison with medical services). In this way, parents can share their fears and experiences, and they can offer each other support and encouragement. Parents share a great deal with other parents. Parents may need reassurance about parenting decisions they make. They may require specialized information and advocacy skills. These specialized needs can often be met effectively by other parents of children with special needs as they experience similar needs (MacAuley, 1996). Knowing about support groups and providing this information to parents may be most helpful.

Scenario

The Usefulness of Support Groups

A mother with a successful professional career had adopted two young children. The older child was 2 when the second baby arrived. It soon became apparent that the second child had severe special needs. The mother experienced a range of emotions, but felt that, since she was highly trained and skilled, she should be able to cope. When the child was 2, the child-care staff told the mother about a meeting where diet and nutrition for preschool children was the topic of discussion. Understanding her reluctance to seek support, they did not emphasize that the presentation was for parents of children with special needs, nor did they coerce her into attending. The mother decided to attend because her daughter experienced extreme feeding difficulties. After the meeting, she met other parents who had children with similar disabilities. They shared hopes, disappointments, and practical ideas. This was the first time that this mother had been involved with other parents in similar situations, and she found that it was truly beneficial for her.

Be aware, however, that support groups may not be a good alternative for all parents (Turnbull & Turnbull, 1990). For example, a mother with a severely mentally and physically disabled baby was encouraged to join a local Moms and Tots program that met one morning a week. When she finally decided to attend, she was depressed to see how advanced the other babies were. Some of them were younger than her 15-month-old son and were doing things that he could not yet do. She stated that the experience was so depressing that she never returned and would never join another parent group. Parents are probably the best judges of the appropriateness of support groups for themselves. Eary childhood professionals can provide parents with information about support groups, then leave the decision whether to participate to the parents.

Advocacy and Education

The ecological approach reminds us that, for a child with special needs to develop optimally, factors beyond the child and the immediate family must be considered. These factors include attitudes in our society towards people with special needs, legislation that protects the rights of people with special needs, and the kinds of support services available to children and families.

Early childhood professionals may find it necessary to educate and to advocate on behalf of children with special needs. This can happen in a number of ways. It may involve demonstrating to other children how to interact or play with the child who has special needs, and establishing norms of acceptance and equity for all children within early childhood programs. Caregivers may also play a role in helping parents become effective advocates, or may be involved in direct advocacy activities such as writing letters to the press or to politicians, making presentations, or providing information. Self help groups should not be taken over by professionals. Instead professionals can assist by providing leadership and support autonomy. Professionals need to consider how to empower parents, what supports may be useful, and how parents can be assisted to help themselves and each other (Blickstead, 1996). Through advocacy and education, early childhood professionals can contribute to the well-being of children with special needs by promoting their acceptance and inclusion in all aspects of society.

Conclusion

Working with families that have a child who is difficult to raise, has a particular disability, or has chronic health problems will pose particular challenges for early childhood professionals. Interaction and helping strategies need to take all family members into consideration. Early childhood professionals need to be aware that although parents may be suffering their own type of grief, even many years after the diagnosis, most parents' love for and commitment to their children help them overcome many obstacles. Caregivers should work collaboratively with parents and remember that parents are often best able to articulate the needs of their children (Porter et al., 1996). Extra understanding and appreciation of their struggles is always warranted.

Although the strategies for working with parents discussed in the final portion of the book will be just as relevant for these families, early childhood professionals may be required to search for resources, services, and information suitable to a particular child's and family's needs. It is important to remember that the child with special needs or behavioural concerns is part of a family and to consider and support that family whenever possible.

Exercises

1. Review the following case study and discuss how you would present your information and concerns to the parent involved. Role-play this situation with a partner who can respond as a parent might. Have one person observe the role-playing to provide feedback regarding your role.

   Case Study
   Rhanda came to your centre at the age of 3 months. She was a very easygoing child who demanded little attention. As she grew older, she was quite content amusing herself with toys and activity centres and with watching the other children play. You noticed that she was usually the last child in the playgroup to achieve milestones, such as rolling over or sitting up, but she still did progress. Over time, more things became noticeable. At 16 months, she was just beginning to walk, relying far more on crawling. She seemed to be quieter and not playing with sounds and words as much as she used to. Sometimes, it seemed as if she did not hear people calling her or was oblivious to noises in the room.

2. Check your community centres and local government offices to determine what types of resources exist for children with special needs and their families. Determine whether the resources are run by parents or professionals (i.e., parents may want a support group of parents rather than adding more professionals to their list). Check to see if all the resources can provide support to children with special needs (e.g., a local

Big Brother program might not accept children with special needs; a support group for difficult teens might not deal with children labelled as having behavioural problems). Keep your list updated so that you are prepared should a parent request information.

3. Role-play the following situations or discuss them with a classmate or colleague. It might be helpful to write out a list of possible responses beforehand.

    a) You want to discuss a child's development with her parents because you believe that the child is not progressing like the other children in your group.

    b) A parent arrives after a case conference at the hospital and yells at you for not providing adequate information to her and adequate programming for her child.

    c) A physiotherapist has just asked you to develop and implement a program with one of the children in your care that will take "only" 45 minutes three times a day. The parent cannot understand why this would be a problem.

4. You have just found out that, due to funding cutbacks, the support services for the integration of children with special needs in schools have been eliminated. Write a letter to the editor of the local newspaper explaining how these cuts may affect children and their families.

Families and chapter 9
Poverty

Objectives

- **To examine the factors associated with poverty.**

- **To examine the effects of poverty on families.**

- **To examine values and beliefs regarding poverty and the poor.**

- **To discuss the role of the early childhood professional in supporting children and families who are poor, including the homeless.**

> When my husband and I first split up, I talked to my kids about the changes that were going to occur. Sandra would no longer be able to wear the same kind of jeans as some of her friends, and we probably wouldn't be able to afford many after-school activities. I would no longer be able to chauffeur the kids, because I would not have a car. My daughter asked, "Does that mean we are poor now?" I answered, "Maybe, in a way, but it doesn't matter because we have each other." That was four years ago. Now, it is no longer a matter of doing without the extras—now I can't even manage to buy the basic necessities. Now when my children ask me if we are very poor, I say, "Yes." But I can't say it doesn't matter anymore. It does matter. It matters a great deal.

Being poor affects every aspect of family life and every family member. It may mean getting food at a food bank, eating dog food to survive, or not having running water or heating. Being poor often means having only worn-out and inappropriate clothing. For many, being poor may result in homelessness and moving from shelter to shelter. Often poverty results in feelings of powerlessness, shame, isolation, helplessness, and hopelessness. Poverty is a fact of life for many Canadian and American families. It can have such an astounding effect on family life as a whole, and on the growth and development of children, that all professionals concerned about the well-being of children must be committed to addressing the problems of poverty.

To be born poor is to face a greater likelihood of ill health in infancy, in childhood and throughout your adult life. To be born poor is to face a lesser likelihood that you will finish high school; lesser still that you will attend university. To be born poor is to face a greater likelihood that you will be judged as delinquent in adolescence and, if so, a greater likelihood that you will be sent to a "correctional institution." To be born poor is to have the deck stacked against you at birth, to find life an uphill struggle ever after. (Standing Senate Committee, 1991, p. 74)

What Is Poverty?

Discussions of the poor often lead to heated debates about what constitutes poverty. We hear stories of times gone by when there was barely enough food on the table, clothing was mended and handed down from sibling to sibling and family to family, and brothers and sisters had to share a bed at night. The stories of bygone days continue: "We all worked hard, didn't feel sorry for ourselves, and shared the little that we had. We didn't think about being poor."

Does "poor" simply mean not having enough money to meet survival needs (food, clothing, and shelter), or does it mean not having enough money left *after* meeting basic survival needs to participate in a lifestyle that is viewed as "average" or "normal" in our society? The answer to that question is that both are important measurements of poverty. Poverty has both an *absolute* significance (i.e., there is not enough money for food) and a *relative* significance (i.e., there is not enough money to live as most Americans or Canadians do).

In Canada, the average household spends 38.5 percent of its total income on basic necessities. If a family spends more than 58.5 percent of its total income on necessities, they are defined as poor (Larson, Goltz, & Hobart, 1994).

Statistics Canada reported 1.5 million children lived in poverty in 1996, an increase of 60 percent since 1989 (Ross, 1998). Ross (1996) suggests what this really means must be evaluated. Statistics typically used involve meeting the basics of food and shelter, however participating fully in Canadian or American society requires more than this. It is dependent upon access to good pre- and post-natal health care, positive parenting, quality child care experiences, access to quality education, recreational and community opportunities, along with a safe environment.

Attitudes Towards the Poor

Scenario

Students' Attitudes

A class of early childhood students were asked whether they thought that people who lived on social assistance wasted taxpayers' money by drinking, playing bingo, and passing the days watching soap operas. The instructor thought that the students would get angry at her for stereotyping this population, but to her surprise, at least half the class nodded their heads in agreement. She now starts every new class with the same question, and each time receives similar responses from the class. The instructor has realized that teaching facts about poverty is not enough. The assumptions and value judgments made about the poor have to be addressed as well.

One of the basic principles of North American society is that of equal opportunity. Underlying this principle is the belief that, with hard work and effort, anyone can achieve success (Ross, 1996; Skolnick, 1992). This belief has been a strong motivator in our culture, and many will attest to its truth.

Perhaps because of this shared belief, many people who have never been poor feel at least a twinge of resentment towards poor people. "If only they worked harder or wasted less money, they would be able to make ends meet," some people say. This feeling is sometimes stronger among people who began their lives in poverty and through hard work have managed to overcome many obstacles to become successful. "If I did it, why can't they?" they wonder. When children arrive at the day-care centre or school without having had breakfast, all too often a bit of resentment towards the parents emerges. "Don't they care about their children? If they didn't waste all their money, the children would not have to come to school hungry."

Another offshoot of the belief in equal opportunity is the idea that people who are poor haven't tried hard enough and only have themselves to blame. The poor are often described as passive, unable to delay gratification, and believing in luck rather than hard work. These beliefs may reflect society's refusal to admit that there is a genuine lack of opportunity and control in the world of the poor (Skolnick, 1992). Negative attitudes towards the poor persist despite the best efforts of Canadians and Americans, collectively and as individuals, to address the problems of poverty.

Myths Surrounding Poverty

A number of myths are often associated with negative attitudes towards any group of people. A myth in this sense is a widely held belief that is accepted uncritically, even when much evidence to the contrary exists. The prevalence of these myths has in fact interfered with government policy initiatives that have the potential to alleviate some of the problems of poverty.

The first myth centres on what we might call the self-sufficient family. If we truly believe that "each family is on its own," then we have no responsibility to help others. Yet in our society no family is completely independent, and families who lack the means to acquire their basic needs must rely on others for help. Ross (1998) suggests that the growing movement in North America towards privatizing services and responsibility has put a greater emphasis on self-sufficiency onto individual families.

The second myth assumes that families who seek help are incompetent. Underlying this idea are stereotyped notions that the poor are lacking in motivation, or "deficient" in personal qualities or values. We think: "There must be something wrong with those people," rather than thinking that there may be something wrong with the economics or organization of our society. Yet many factors beyond individual control, such as unemployment, a slowdown in economic growth, and a shift to high technology jobs (Chafel, 1990), result in poverty for many families.

When the rate of poverty is disproportionately high among members of a particular ethnic group, such as Aboriginals or Blacks, the tendency to blame poverty on the poor tends to increase (Skolnick, 1992). Those who believe in this myth often neglect to take into account that a large segment of the poor do in fact work full time. In the United States, it is estimated that there are approximately six million working poor; in Canada, 27 percent of poor families are working poor (Ward, 1994). We must remember that a full-time job at minimum wage will not keep a family from poverty.

The third myth that affects the poor in our society is the belief that public assistance condones failure, or takes away from people the will to be self-sufficient. We are constantly reading about "welfare bums" who would rather be on welfare than work. This generalization simply does not apply to many people who require financial assistance. It has been noted that most welfare recipients are willing to work when jobs and job training are available (Gringlas & Weintraub, 1995). One study demonstrated that approximately three-quarters of mothers on welfare would prefer to work, and one-half of them were able to be self-sufficient when the opportunity was provided (Gringlas & Weintraub, 1995).

Many people are familiar with the concept referred to as "the welfare trap." People on welfare cannot receive continued assistance (such as medical coverage or child care) if they find work. Often, however, the low-paying job leaves the family with fewer resources than they had while they were on welfare (Card & Robins, 1996). Parents whose first goal is to protect and provide for their children often reluctantly choose to stay on welfare rather than become part of the unprotected group of working poor. The following scenario exemplifies this dilemma.

Scenario

Retraining or Regressing?

A single mother with three children, aged 1, 3, and 5 years, had been receiving social assistance for a number of years. When she became aware that the assistance included a retraining program, she eagerly signed up for the early childhood education program at a community college. She graduated, got a job, but quit after three months. Her net income, taking into account her child-care expenses, clothing, and commuting costs, was about the same as what she had received on social assistance. More important to her, she was away from her own young children for most of the day, caring for other people's children and coming home extremely tired and stressed. The bottom line for this woman was that she and her children were better off on social assistance.

Early childhood professionals will inevitably come into contact with children whose families are struggling with poverty. If you have an attitude of resentment or blame towards poor people, you will have to overcome that before you can hope to work effectively with these children and their families. The next step will be to educate yourself about poverty in our society, and understand the effects that poverty has on families and children. The third step is to learn more about your role, as an early childhood professional, in working with families and children who are poor.

Perspectives

Jean Swanson works at End Legislated Poverty in Vancouver, Canada. End Legislated Poverty is concerned that the discrimination against poor people in our society is increasing, and that politicians and the media are contributing to this discrimination by the way in which they discuss poverty.

The phrases that are used to discuss welfare and unemployment insurance all seem to imply that low-income people themselves, not the lack of jobs or decent wages, are the cause of poverty. Swanson calls this phenomenon "newspeak," a term coined by George Orwell in his novel 1984. Here are her explanations of some of the common newspeak phrases:

Incentive to work/disincentive to work: The repeated sentiment that "welfare is a disincentive to work" suggests that people would rather collect welfare than work at paid jobs. This is not the case. Increasing minimum wage would eliminate any "disincentive to work."

Active, not passive, social programs: This phrase implies that existing programs keep people lazing about, doing nothing, and suggests that training and prodding people to get off welfare will create jobs for them to take.

Hand up, not hand out: This term comes from the United States and lately has been used more and more by Canadian social policy makers. It implies that social programs always keep people from getting work, and that counselling, teaching money management skills, and training people for low-paid jobs will get them off welfare. In reality, the only thing that will really accomplish that goal is decent jobs and decent wages.

Discouraging dependence: This term implies that welfare and UI create people who are "dependent" like children. Dependence, a term often used in relation to addicts, implies that there is something inherently wrong with people who require assistance. We hardly ever hear the term "dependence" used to describe how affluent people depend on their incomes to maintain a comfortable lifestyle.

Breaking the cycle of poverty: Lurking behind this phrase is the theory that children are taught to be poor by poor adults. Note that no one is exhorted to "break the cycle of wealth" where rich people pass on their wealth to their children, perpetuating inequality of income distribution.

Self-esteem: This phrase is bandied about in sentences such as "People need work to build self-esteem." It implies that a single parent must build her self-esteem by working at a low-wage, exploitative job rather than by staying home to raise her children to be good citizens.

Truly needy: This phrase is used to justify cutting universal programs or programs for the "merely needy." It implies, for example, that people on unemployment insurance, who may get more than people on welfare, should have to give up the UI so that the government can cut the deficit and maintain payments to the "truly needy." Lost in the dialogue is the status of the "truly greedy" who, one assumes, continue on with their tax breaks and incentives to accumulate more wealth.

Training for the jobs of the future: This phrase implies that, if only we get ourselves trained in computer programming, we could get off welfare. But training does not create jobs, and most available jobs are low paid.

Poverty culture: Again, this implies that poor people like to be poor and should get counselling from middle-class professionals who can help them choose another "culture," presumably one that supplies more money.

Jean Swanson reminds professionals who may be working with poor people to be careful not to be influenced by this discriminatory and misleading language. There is a need to remind people that the vast majority of poor people are poor because they are in low-paying jobs, or because there are not jobs available, rather than because of any flaw in their character.

Source: **Swanson,** n.d.

Who Are the Poor?

Lochead & Shillington (1996) have found a diversity in the profile of poverty in Canada. Yet certain groups of Canadians seem to be at higher risk for living in poverty.

Children

Children make up the largest single group of poor people in Canada—more than 1.5 million (Ross, 1998; Ward, 1994) or one in five children (Kelly & Ramsey, 1991). In the United States, 23 percent of children under the age of 3 are from poor families. Childhood poverty among aboriginal peoples may be as high as 50 percent (Dooley, 1994). Aboriginal children are four times more likely to experience hunger (Turner, 1998). The overall rate for poverty decreased slightly in the 1980s, while the rate for childhood poverty actually increased (Vanier Institute, 1994). Childhood poverty has subsequently decreased, but this is a result of a decline in the birth rate—there are simply fewer children than in the late 1980s (Dooley, 1994; Picot & Myles, 1996). Most poor children are from single-parent homes (Vanier Institute, 1990). Long-term poverty in families with children has increased significantly and is concentrated in large inner-city neighbourhoods where most people are young and unskilled (Kelly & Ramsey, 1991). Both of these conditions present risks for the young child.

Racial and Ethnic Groups

African Americans and Puerto Ricans are much more likely to live in poverty in the United States (Huston, McLoyd, & Garcia Coll, 1994). In addition, they are more likely to experience persistent poverty and to live in run-down, isolated urban neighbourhoods. For many Black Americans, poverty is the rule, not the exception (Duncan, Brooks-Gunn, & Klebanov, 1994), and poverty among Blacks is three to four times higher than among Whites (Garret, Ng'andu, & Ferron, 1994). Minority women, especially Puerto Ricans and Blacks, are more often represented as poor than their male counterparts are; however, their level of poverty may not be as high because they benefit from child-care arrangements through extended families (Starrels, Bould, & Nicholas, 1994). In Canada, similar statistics exist for Aboriginals (Turner, 1998; Ryerse, 1991).

Gender and Poverty

The relationship between gender and poverty has been established for some time now (Dooley, 1994; Chekki, 1998). Single-mother families are five times more likely to live in poverty than dual-parent families. This has been true since the 1970s (Garret, Ng'andu, & Ferron, 1994). Women have higher rates of poverty since they are still unlikely to have wage parity with men and are concentrated in low-paying jobs. Even when women are employed, they are likely still to be poor. Recent studies suggest that a large number of women with post-secondary education and completed degrees continued to live in poverty and experience hunger (Turner, 1998). Women are more often single parents with custody of their children and more often adolescent parents (Starrels, Bould, & Nicholas, 1994). In addition, there is often little support from absent fathers. All of these factors, along with a dependency on social assistance, have led to what is now known as the "feminization of poverty" (Eshleman & Wilson, 1995). Women cannot always escape poverty through remarriage, since many dual-parent families live in poverty (Starrels, Bould, & Nicholas, 1994).

Location

Chekki (1998) notes that, in recent years, the number of poor in Canadian cities has been dramatically increasing. Most studies suggest that poverty is higher in urban areas, especially in those areas referred to as the urban ghettos. Most hungry children live in large urban areas where there are 500,000 or more people (Turner, 1998). Poverty in urban ghettos is associated with a number of high-risk factors. The population of urban ghettos is seen as an underclass characterized by continual poverty, welfare dependency, joblessness, crime, and substance abuse (Eshleman & Wilson, 1995). The population most commonly associated with urban ghettos has been Black unwed mothers; however, White unwed mothers appear to be joining this group (Turner, 1998; Bogert, 1995).

Although the urban ghettos have received the majority of media attention, poverty rates are higher for nonurban families who are typically White, married-couple families where one or both parents work (Garret, Ng'andu, & Ferron, 1994). These families have been the hardest hit by recession and changes in employment patterns and are ineligible for government assistance. They continue, however, to struggle to maintain a quality of life for their families.

Effects of Poverty

Poverty is a complex, multidimensional phenomenon with a wide variety of effects. Bronfenbrenner's (1979) ecological model is useful for considering the context in which poverty exists. Poverty has profound effects on the home environment, family structure, and parenting. It is known that poor families are at risk for physical, health, and psychological difficulties (Huston, McLoyd, & Garcia Coll, 1994). Concerns go beyond the immediate home environment and extend to neighbourhoods, schools, and child care (Philips et al., 1994; Huston, McLoyd, & Garcia Coll, 1994). We will now consider some of the consequences of poverty that may affect children and their families.

Social Networks

People living in poverty, including single mothers, typically have difficulty developing and maintaining effective social networks (Garret, Ng'andu, & Ferron, 1994). Therefore, poverty is often accompanied by social isolation. The higher rates of child abuse associated with poverty often result from stress in the family that is compounded by having few social networks and being socially isolated (Hashima & Amato, 1994). In addition, poor parents are often unable to pay for services that would decrease parental strain. Poverty and lack of social support can result in parents being less nurturing and supportive and using inconsistent discipline. This in turn leads to children experiencing higher rates of abuse (Hashima & Amato, 1994). When families have people they can call on for informal support, especially in crises, there is usually a reduction in the stress of parenting and parents display more supportive behaviour (Hashima & Amato, 1994). Among minorities, families often adapt to poverty by utilizing extended families and social supports and thus decrease their level of stress (Garret, Ng'andu, & Ferron, 1994).

Reduced Opportunity

Generally speaking, children who are poor live in poor neighbourhoods. Growing up in a poor neighbourhood can reduce a child's chances for success in later life. One reason for this is the type of socialization to which children are subjected. Children typically encounter less encouragement to achieve academic success or to modify their behaviour to agree with social norms; at the same time, they are often socialized to be more physically aggressive (Duncan, Brooks-Gunn, & Klebanov, 1994). Another serious concern is the consistently lower quality of child care available to low-income families (Ross, 1998; Duncan, Brooks-Gunn, & Klebanov, 1994; Phillips et al., 1994). Although it has been repeatedly demonstrated that high-quality programs can alleviate the negative consequences of poverty, most programs in low-income areas are characterized by higher child–staff ratios, larger group size, less teacher training, and high staff turnover. Children in higher-income families continue to be cared for by better-trained, stable, and better-compensated caregivers using more developmentally appropriate practices (Phillips et al., 1994). In addition, poverty often leads to decreased opportunities for recreational and cultural experiences which may have long term consequences on development (Ross, 1998).

Effects of Poverty on Parents

When we try to understand the effects of being poor on mothers, it is difficult to distinguish the stresses of poverty from the stresses of single parenthood because the two are so often connected. Several studies have shown that single parents who are economically disadvantaged tend to have higher rates of depression, anxiety, low self-esteem, and dissatisfaction with their lives (Eshleman & Wilson, 1995). Maternal poverty is also associated with stress, poor nutrition, and poor prenatal care that often results in low-birth-weight babies. Some writers have characterized single mothers as providing developmentally inappropriate stimulation and as authoritative, punitive, and unsupportive (Garret, Ng'andu, & Ferron, 1994; Hashima & Amato, 1994). It is difficult to determine if poverty, single parenthood, the effects of divorce, or an interaction of all these factors produces these effects on parents.

Unemployment and Parenting

Although many families who face poverty are working families, the adults in many poor families (approximately 70 percent in Canada) are unemployed (Larson, Goltz, & Hobart, 1994). Unemployment has social and emotional consequences for all members of the family that add to the stresses of poverty.

To begin with, unemployment often is a blow to self-esteem. Men tend to blame themselves, and they tend to be blamed by other family members. The unemployed man's presence in the home all day can cause strain for the entire family. He may be used to being the authority figure, the disciplinarian, and he may go to extremes to maintain this role with his wife and children. In addition, he may be used to being the breadwinner, and the loss of this traditional role will increase the strain he feels (Garret, Ng'andu, & Ferron, 1994). As a result, he is likely to use more punitive measures with his children in instances he likely would have ignored when he was employed. Rates of alcoholism, suicide, psychiatric problems, and domestic abuse traditionally rise in communities when unemployment rates rise (Skolnick, 1992). These correlations have been found to span sex, age, and cultural groups.

Effects of Poverty on Children

There is a body of statistical evidence growing in Canada as a result of the National Longitudinal Survey of Children and Youth and the National Population Health Survey that examine the link between family income and the well-being of children. There appears to be compelling evidence that family income has a major effect on the child's well-being. Associations between income and measures including poor health and delayed vocabulary have been consistently high. Children living in poverty are less likely to participate in organized sports activities and experience fewer family and social relationships (Ross, 1998).

Children are poor because their parents are poor. When employment or income is unavailable or irregular, food, clothing, shelter, and other essentials are also unavailable and irregular. As a result, children can develop a pervasive sense of insecurity (Eshleman & Wilson, 1995).

Children growing up in poor families face many other risks. We know that a healthy baby gets a good start in life. However, as mentioned earlier, when a mother is poor, she may be less likely to eat properly during pregnancy, to attend to her own health concerns, and to receive consistent prenatal care (Garret, Ng'andu, & Ferron, 1994). These factors are associated with lower birth weight, higher infant mortality, and more birth defects (Ryerse, 1991). Early deprivation resulting from poverty has long-lasting effects on the physical and mental health of children (Phillips et al., 1994). Children living in poverty are more likely to suffer from inadequate nutrition, physical illness, and emotional and psychiatric problems than children living in better-off homes (Offord, 1991; Beiser, 1998). Poverty in childhood is associated with a decline in imaginative ability, low motivation for educational or vocational achievement, low self-esteem, short attention span, a feeling of being externally controlled, and poor language use (Schorr & Schorr, 1988).

Children growing up in poor families are much more likely to suffer interruptions or delays in learning and are thus more likely to fail or drop out of school. Overcrowding, hunger, lack of space to do homework, stress, and illness all may contribute to school failure (Offord, 1991; Ross, Scott & Kelly, 1996). Poor children often feel uncomfortable in school because of hunger, shabby clothing, or their lack of money for school outings (Ryerse, 1991). They may also need to work to help support the family (Eshleman & Wilson, 1995), or they may have to take on housekeeping and babysitting tasks at home while their parents work. For these reasons, few remain in school beyond the legal age limits. We often see the cycle of children of poor parents dropping out of school and having limited opportunities for employment. Thus these young people join the ranks of the unemployed or the working poor just as their parents did before them. Limited opportunities are also often associated with teen pregnancies (Skolnik, 1992), and in these cases the poverty often extends to the next generation (Duncan, Brooks-Gunn, & Klebanov, 1994).

Homelessness

While homeless people face many of the same risks and consequences as other poor people, educators are becoming increasingly aware of the devastation to family life that is caused by homelessness. Life tends to be unstable and irregular for families living in poverty, which all too often leads to homelessness for families with young children.

In the early 1980s, most homeless people were men. Today, women with children under 5 years of age make up 30 percent of the homeless population (DeAngelis, 1995). About half of these women belong to ethnic minorities, and many of them have been severely abused. There are also large numbers of homeless women who have chosen to turn their children over to their extended family or to social agencies. It appears that poverty, not mental illness or abuse, is the chief reason for the increase in homelessness (DeAngelis, 1995).

Homelessness can only be described as an immense trauma that leads to the disruption of social networks, family roles and routines, and emotional stability. Homeless children, for example, report significantly less peer support than do children who have a home (DeAngelis, 1995). Homelessness is also associated with high anxiety about the future and, often, with fear of violence and death (DeAngelis, 1995).

At any age, being homeless shakes the very foundations of life (Klein, Bittel, & Molnar, 1993), but for younger children, homelessness is particularly disruptive. If we consider the developmental needs of young children and the importance of security and consistency in building trust and autonomy, it is clear that the instability of homelessness can be highly detrimental to development. Indeed, studies of homeless children have demonstrated that they are more likely to suffer poor health and developmental and behavioural problems (DeAngelis, 1995). These problems include short attention spans, speech delays, sleep disorders, aggressive behaviour, and awkward motor control (Klein, Bittel, & Molnar, 1993). In short, homelessness not only deprives a child of a decent quality of life, but also of most of his future opportunities.

The role fathers play in this situation has been relatively unexplored. This is probably largely because fathers quite simply tend not to be involved once they have left their wife and children. Also, many shelters have policies preventing involvement by men because of concerns about privacy and violence. The presence and involvement of fathers may also jeopardize mothers' financial benefits (DeAngelis, 1995).

Short-Term or Long-Term Poverty?

It makes sense to assume that the longer the time people spend in poverty, the more serious will be the risks to their families and children.

The majority of poor people are poor for intermittent periods (Skolnick, 1992; Eshleman & Wilson, 1995). Many children may find themselves living in poverty at least once during their childhood. Persistent poverty, however, causes more concerns. Low intellectual achievement, behavioural problems, social and emotional problems, and reduced motivation are consistently associated with living in poverty for a lengthy period of time (Huston, McLoyd, & Garcia Coll, 1994). One factor that may mediate the effects of poverty is the mother's behaviour. If the mother's ability to cope has not been affected by poverty, she may be more able to create an environment in which fewer effects on the child will be evident (Duncan, Brooks-Gunn, & Klebanov, 1994). Also, it has been found that when family income improves, parents do use the resources to improve the child's quality of life (Garret, Ng'andu, & Ferron, 1994).

Reducing Poverty

In the past, the poor were at the mercy of their families, communities, or charities for assistance. Since about the time of World War I, however, governments in the West have taken various steps to address the problem of poverty.

In North America, poverty was "discovered" (that is, there was widespread acceptance of the need to address poverty) in the 1960s (Huston, McLoyd, & Garcia Coll, 1994). The War on Poverty in the United States then began on two fronts. The first focused on welfare reform; the belief was that an increase in family income would solve the problem of poverty (Phillips et al., 1994; Schorr & Schorr, 1988). It soon became clear, however, that issues such as minimum wage and partial assistance to the working poor needed to be considered in addition to welfare payments. In this respect, it is crucial to remember that public assistance programs *can* help families cope with difficulties and *can* protect children from the harsh realities of poverty until their families are able to return to being self-sufficient (Chafel, 1990).

The other strategy in the War on Poverty was the funding of social programs that were aimed at reducing both the immediate and long-term effects of poverty and at preventing "cycles of poverty" from occurring. Examples included programs designed to reduce the number of teen pregnancies, to improve prenatal care, and to provide health care, family support, and compensatory education programs. Some of these programs have accomplished much in demonstrating how the lives of children can be positively affected by intervention. The success of Project Head Start, for one, has been testimony to this (Schorr & Schorr, 1988).

Campaign 2000

In Canada, there has been an erosion of programs and supports for women and children. Campaign 2000 was established to ensure the implementation of a House of Commons resolution to eliminate child poverty by the year 2000. The goals are as follows:

1. Raise and protect the basic living standards of families across Canada so that no child ever lives in poverty.

2. Ensure the availability of adequate housing as an inherent right of all Canadian children.

3. Create, build and strengthen family support and community-based support to empower families to provide the best possible care for their children.

4. Improve the life chances of all children in Canada to fulfill their potential, so that they become responsible and contributing members of Canadian society.

Source: Popham, 1992.

The chief problem with social programs that are intended to alleviate poverty is that they are paid for by taxpayers' dollars. Many people are disinclined to support these programs because they think they are a waste of money. Yet three decades of research in the United States has shown quite dramatically that high-quality programs for families with young children can have dramatic positive effects (Phillips et al., 1994; Schorr & Schorr, 1988;

Weikart, 1989; Chafel, 1990). A long-term study of the Perry Preschool Project in Ypsilanti, Michigan, focused on Black children from disadvantaged homes. These children participated in special programs that combined quality preschool education with parent-involvement programs. Twenty years later, the children who participated continued to do better in school, have better jobs, and be more self-sufficient than their peers who did not attend the programs. There was a consistent improvement throughout school years along with lower delinquency rates, lower teenage pregnancy rates, and decreased dependency on welfare (Weikart, 1989). The conclusion seems to be that while good quality programs are expensive, they save money in the long run. Not only are these programs a long-term social investment, they are also a prime means of ameliorating conditions for the poor (Weikart, 1989). Similar economic analyses have been conducted in Canada, also suggesting a two-to-one return on resources invested in the development of young children (Cleveland & Krashinsky, 1998).

Despite the partial success of social programs and welfare reform, poverty has continued to increase in North America. These increases may be due to several factors (Huston, McLoyd, & Garcia Coll, 1994). The loss of blue-collar jobs through recessions, the increased numbers of single mothers with children, and the decline in government benefits have all contributed. The latest statistics suggest that poverty affects approximately 22 percent of the population in the United States, and in Canada one in six families are poor (Larson, Goltz, & Hobart, 1994; Duncan, Brooks-Gunn, & Klebanov, 1994).

Political ideologies will affect the government's willingness to spend taxpayers' dollars on programs that help prevent or reduce poverty. The will to make changes to significantly reduce poverty seems to be lacking in our society (Ward, 1994; Freiler & Cerny, 1998). The danger is, however, that poverty tends to repeat itself in future generations. The cost of allowing poverty to continue is high, both in terms of human suffering and in purely economic terms. One recent Canadian study suggests that, in view of the consequences of leaving people in poverty, steps should be taken to alleviate poverty in the short term, and prevent it in the long term (Martin Spigleman Research Associates, 1998). Even though addressing poverty is costly, the alternative—simply to ignore poverty—poses a grave risk to society (Chafel, 1990).

In fact, there has recently been a plethora of policy changes that adversely affect children and families in Canada. For example, federal assistance for health, post-secondary education and social assistance has decreased; family allowances are almost non-existent; child tax benefits have been minimized (Ross, 1998).

The Role of Early Childhood Professionals

As we mentioned earlier in this chapter, our deep-seated attitudes and beliefs about the poor will affect the way in which we understand the problems of poverty and also the short- and long-term solutions that we promote to deal with these problems. As members of a helping profession, we have an ethical obligation to accept and respect people regardless of their social or economic standing. Sorting out one's personal beliefs about people who are poor is an important first step. Asking the questions listed in the "Examine Your Attitudes" box might help clarify your present attitudes and beliefs.

Understanding and Empathizing

Providing support to children and families in poverty requires the ability to empathize with their difficulties. Try to imagine what young children might feel like when

- they can never be sure where they will sleep from night to night;
- they go to a day care or nursery school, but don't know if they will be able to return the next day;
- they have no space or toys to call their own;
- they have no consistent routines, may not have clean clothes or the opportunity to bathe; and
- they sense the feelings of hopelessness, despair, and frustration felt by their parents, and feel helpless themselves.

Now try to imagine what it might be like for parents who may

- be embarrassed about being homeless;
- be unable to give their children even the most basic and simple provisions (snacks, a hot drink, or 25 cents for a hot dog for lunch);
- feel isolated and alone;
- have no links with or support from their community;
- fear having their children taken away from them;
- fear being perceived as neglectful or abusive parents;
- fear being perceived as vagrants or law breakers;
- know that many judge them and their children by their appearance;
- feel unprotected and vulnerable; and
- have no privacy for intimacy with their partner.

It is important not to stereotype homeless people or to make assumptions. The questions above may apply to many people in such a situation, but not to all. It is also wrong to assume that homeless families are dysfunctional families. They are enduring highly stressful circumstances, and extended periods of homelessness can indeed lead to family breakdown. We must be very careful not to "blame the victims," but rather, to understand the circumstances that lead to poverty and homelessness.

For many children who are homeless or poor, the child-care centre or other early childhood program can be a crucial source of stability and support. Recognizing the special needs of children and families in these circumstances can help staff meet their needs in a supportive and sensitive manner. Klein, Bittel, and Molnar (1993) point out that a quality centre can be an antidote for a stressful home environment if it is built around a "homelike nurturing environment." Cleveland and Krashinsky (1998) have emphasized repeatedly the absolute importance of quality child care in ensuring development for young children.

Scenario

Jimmy and His Toys

When Jimmy lay down for his afternoon nap, he insisted on taking his favourite toy, jacket, shoes, hat, and snack with him. On some days, there were so many belongings on his cot that there was no room for Jimmy. When the caregiver mentioned this to his mother, she learned that Jimmy's family had been evicted from their apartment and were staying with friends some nights, and some nights at shelters. No wonder Jimmy was clinging to his belongings.

It is important to remember that for children living in shelters, every hour can bring a new surprise and, therefore, change can be frightening. The routines at the centre, and special care in preparing children for transitions, can ease their stress. Mealtime can be difficult for children who are chronically hungry, and who may not be accustomed to eating at regular times (Klein, Bittel, & Molnar, 1993). Staff can help by reassuring children that there is more food available if they want it. It is also extremely important to remember (and this is true for all children) that food should never be used as a reward, punishment, or play item. Night-time at a shelter can be noisy and scary, and therefore some children may need extra support at nap time. Klein, Bittel, and Molnar (1993) stress the importance of a child's cot being in a consistent place and of staff being prepared to provide some children with extra attention to help them fall asleep.

Scenario

Sensitivity Pays Off

Staff at an inner-city day-care centre were well aware that most children were coming in hungry and that the day care provided for most of their nutritional needs. With some extra funding, they started a program in which extra food was prepared for lunch and snacks, and children were encouraged to take food home for a snack for themselves and to share with their siblings. Centre staff were sensitive to the needs of these families. The program was especially successful because poor children were not singled out. All the children enjoyed having the opportunity to take home things that they made or received at the centre.

Sometimes a centre can be too stimulating for children whose homeless environment may be either over- or under-stimulating. Like all children, poor or homeless children need to be able to make choices, but the amount of choice should be modulated according to their ability to cope. Sometimes children who have been deprived of toys and playthings will require help in choosing toys that are common to their age group. Open-ended materials are particularly important, as are materials that encourage self-expression and exploration. Children who are suffering from stressful home conditions may require more individual attention and small group, rather than large group, activities. Klein, Bittel, and Molnar (1993) recommend enlisting the help of volunteers to provide individual time, but remind us that too many adults coming and going in these children's lives may be an added source of stress.

A homelike environment with many private areas and personalized space with pictures, photographs, and personal cubbies is important to all children, but will be vital to children who lack this in their lives outside the centre. Most important is the development of a trusting relationship with a staff member who can anticipate some of the feelings associated with poverty and homelessness, and who is willing to find many small ways to make the child feel welcome, appreciated, and safe.

Supporting Parents of Poor and Homeless Children

Many parents who are poor will appreciate the support provided by early childhood professionals, provided that it is offered in a nonjudgmental and dignified manner. As one parent in these circumstances noted, "The last thing I need is to come to a parent meeting and have someone try to teach me how to be a better parent." Little gestures, such as having coffee, juice, and a quiet place to sit for a while can make all the difference. Practical supplies like some extra clothing, toys, books, or food for emergency use should also be on hand. Provision of snacks and meals might be a major factor in the selection of child care for families living in poverty.

Scenario

Low-Cost or No-Cost Activities

Several day-care centres working with disadvantaged children incorporated different ideas for involving and benefiting their families. One centre started a lending library of toys and books for children to take home to ensure that they had stimulating, educational materials there. Another centre organized an exchange of toys, clothing, and other belongings. Each family brought items they no longer used to trade for other items. Families were able to replenish toy, book, and clothing supplies while at the same time sharing resources with other families. Another centre accomplished the same by having a garage sale. This resulted in parents being able to purchase toys, clothing, and items for a token fee, and raised a few dollars for the centre to purchase art equipment. The common factor in all these activities was that families were involved at no extra cost in a manner that did not differentiate between families who were poor and families who were able to make a contribution in some manner.

It is important not to assume that poor or homeless parents do not want to or cannot be involved in the program. They can be asked, without placing pressure on them, if they want to accompany the children on a field trip or help with serving lunch. One problem is that parent meetings held during evening hours often require that parents pay for a babysitter. Meetings during afternoon hours, with child care and food provided, if this is possible, are more likely to be attended.

Sometimes the centre can be a focal point for meeting with other parents in similar circumstances, for providing information about services and resources, or simply to provide a place to go that is safe and where parents will be accepted and respected. This can be a most meaningful form of support. More importantly, these strategies may become coping devices for the families involved. One strategy often employed by families living in poverty is the sharing of resources. Clothing, food, money, and child care are commonly shared among households. This exchange pattern can turn friends into family and be a crucial social support system (Eshleman & Wilson, 1995).

In one important study, parents were asked what they wanted preschool personnel to know about their situation (McCormick & Holden, 1992). Below are the parents' responses.

Consider the Family's Feelings

Early childhood professionals should be aware that:

1. Children may be embarrassed about being homeless.

2. Parents may be dealing with many problems in addition to homelessness and child care (e.g., spousal abuse, depression, lack of support payments).

3. Even parents who may seem distracted really care about their children.

4. It can be very stressful, difficult, and time consuming to have to plan for and organize transportation every day.

5. Many questions asked by staff members make parents uncomfortable (because the reason for the question is not always clear).

6. Children (and parents) should not be asked about absences or length of time in other programs.

7. Requests for children to bring baked goods or other goodies and school supplies often constitute a great hardship for families who are poor. Consider other means of involvement.

8. Being homeless or poor does not necessarily mean that a family is dysfunctional.

Keeping these points in mind will enable early childhood professionals to provide support in a sensitive and unobtrusive manner.

Source: McCormick & Holden, 1992.

> **Tips for Providing a Sense of Security to Young Children**
>
> 1. Provide a "homelike" environment with private areas and personal space.
> 2. Provide consistent routines and preparation for transitions.
> 3. Assure children that there is plenty of food at mealtimes.
> 4. Never use food as a reward, punishment, or play item.
> 5. Provide a consistent place for each child's cot at nap time and extra attention when needed to help children settle.
> 6. Provide an appropriate number of toy choices and help children decide.
> 7. Provide open-ended materials.
> 8. Ensure that each child receives some individual attention and that all children participate in small group experiences.
> 9. Enlist volunteers (when appropriate) to provide more adult–child interaction.
> 10. Develop a relationship with the children by helping them to feel welcome, appreciated, and safe.

Beyond the Centre

At the beginning of this book, we described the family as a system that affects and is affected by other systems in society. The well-being of children is ultimately linked to the well-being of the family, and the well-being of families is inextricably connected to societal factors such as employment, housing, neighbourhoods, child care, and social assistance. Increasingly, experts in early childhood are pointing out the need to go beyond caring for children and families within the confines of the centre. In fact, Chafel (1990) suggests that the early childhood profession has a moral obligation to work actively for the eradication of poverty and offers a number of possible strategies, including learning the facts about poverty in your area and making childhood poverty a high-priority issue with professional organizations and at public forums. Writing letters to editors, seeking media coverage, and writing to legislators about the problems of poverty are among the more specific strategies mentioned. Early childhood professional organizations might try to network with other professions, for example social workers, to develop a broad-based coalition. Community and business leaders should be enlisted to support the cause. As with any kind of advocacy and activism, it is important to be well prepared, and to have accurate and up-to-date information at both the local and the national level. The other aspect of this is that early childhood professionals must begin to recognize and appreciate the critical role they play in the lives of young children—all children, but especially those children at risk because of the situations they live in. Along with awareness, caregivers must be confident of their abilities and the increasingly important role they play in the lives of children and families.

Conclusion

This chapter has explored the many dimensions of poverty and how each of these dimensions may affect families. Poverty has profound effects on family structure and parenting and puts every family member at risk. Families exist within a societal framework and are therefore affected by their neighbourhood, the available supports, and the quality of child care.

Early childhood professionals can play a major role in providing support to children living in poverty and to their families. Regardless of our own experiences with poverty, our beliefs about its causes, and our opinions about dealing with it, we must acknowledge the urgency of the problem and the need to find solutions for the children in our care and the children of future generations as well.

Exercises

1. Write one paragraph summarizing your feelings about each of the following:
   a) parents who bring their children to the centre poorly dressed and hungry,
   b) parents who spend social assistance money to smoke, drink, and play bingo,
   c) parents who are social assistance recipients.

   Now write a brief analysis of your own attitudes towards poor people.

2. Brainstorm ideas about how you could help a child feel safe and secure in your centre. Review the chapter and list all of the ideas suggested, then add your own.

3. Help a child create a personal space of his or her own by using a cardboard box big enough for the child to crawl into. The box can by made comfortable with a pillow or rug, have windows cut out, and possibly a "door" for privacy. Take some pictures of the child, family members, and friends, and let the child paste them to the walls. Provide a flashlight, books or tapes, or other objects that will help make the child feel comfortable.

4. Provide a "personal bag" for every child in the program to store his or her treasures.

5. Check your community for resources that may be available for families living in poverty. Be sure that you check the cost before recommending ideas (e.g., it may be better to recommend a babysitting co-op rather than paid babysitters).

6. Consider ideas for exchanges and sharing that the day-care centre could initiate or be a part of (e.g., clothing exchanges, buying bulk foods, and making meals).

7. Check your local library or bookstore for books that may be suitable for children or their parents.

8. Check on the Internet to find groups that advocate ending child poverty in Canada. What responsibility do early childhood professionals have in addressing the problem of poverty in Canada?

A Death in
the Family

chapter 10

Objectives

- To describe the impact that a death in the family has on family members.

- To explore how the grief process occurs for children and adults.

- To discuss the importance of helping children to cope with a death in the family.

- To highlight the role of early childhood professionals when a death occurs in the family.

Sylvia was a 4-year-old girl whose father was tragically killed in a car accident. He was a musician who performed in bands during evening hours and had played a major role in her care and nurture during the day. For several months, Sylvia would play "funeral" in the doll corner. It was a daily ritual, to which she would invite the children. One day Marie, the caregiver, said to her supervisor: "That child has a problem. She seems so morbid." The supervisor reflected for a moment. She had noticed that when Sylvia had first begun to enact the funeral, her face was tense and it was obvious that she was deeply distressed. As time passed, the funeral play became lighter, and Sylvia clearly enjoyed arranging flowers, singing, and telling the other children where to sit. In the end, the supervisor told Marie that Sylvia's play seemed a healthy and natural way of coping with her father's death.

When we think of a death in the family, we usually associate it with the passing away of an elderly relative. A glance at North American statistics tells us that most people can expect to live a long and healthy life. There are significantly fewer deaths of infants, children, and young adults today than in times that our grandparents can remember (Skolnick, 1992).

Discussing death often causes discomfort. In many parts of our modern world, deaths occur in hospitals, away from the family (Goodwin & Davidson, 1991). Although there has been a movement towards hospice care, in search of a "good death," some authors suggest that societal discomfort with death is still evident in the way dying people are often treated (Hart, Sainsbury & Short, 1998). Many people today have never witnessed the death of a person, and just thinking about that image can be stressful for many. Death today is considered an unnatural event or accident (Bernstein, 1977). Television provides confusing images of death. Cartoon characters die yet regularly rise again for the next blow. News shows flash endless images of death, so much so that we may have become desensitized or fail to understand the true meaning of what is perhaps the most traumatic event in the course of a family's lifespan.

Scenario

Is Death Forever?

A 6-year-old boy named Lucas watched a television drama where the main character, a 9-year-old boy, died of AIDS. Lucas was moved by the show and asked many questions of his parents about death and dying. Three weeks later, he was watching a weekly television serial in which the same actor appeared. Lucas could not understand how the boy could be dead and then alive again. Perhaps death did not really last forever as his mother had told him. Lucas's mother realized that he was confused and that she would have to explain death to him once again.

In spite of the long life expectancy of North Americans, many children in preschool programs do in fact experience the death of a loved one (Furman, 1982). It could be the loss of a grandparent or less commonly a parent or sibling; and the death could be the result of violence, accident, or illness. For many children, even the loss of a pet can be devastating. Responses to death are influenced, in part, by the nature of the relationship with the deceased. It would not be exaggerating to say that the experience of losing an intimate family member has a profound and pervasive effect on the entire family that often lasts for many years. Religion and cultural beliefs play a major role in people's conception of death (Braun & Nichols, 1997).

Perspectives

Glenna is an Aboriginal social work student at a community college. During a discussion of grief counselling, she described how death is explained to young children in the Stoney culture.

"In the old days, children were kept away from the person making his final journey. Children were not told about death. They were forbidden to attend the wake services and the burial grounds. They never looked at a deceased person.

"The purpose of not telling a child about death was to alleviate the disturbing emotions and to respect our traditions. It was said that a child's soul is sacred, and therefore they should not be near a dead person, for the dead may be in need of a holy soul to lean on. Once the soul has been dominated by the dead spirit, the child's spirit will be possessed through eternity. The only way to bring the child's spirit back into the body is for a very powerful medicine man to perform a very sacred ceremony, which our forefathers say is not easy; only some are successful. Therefore, children were kept away from the dead person during the two nights and three days of the wake service and right up until after the body was buried.

"Nowadays, since we are living in a new generation and shifting into a new style of life, this kind of tradition cannot be maintained. Some people who prefer to attend church services take their children with them. There a child learns about our Saviour, how He died and His promise of a new world, a paradise called Heaven where all the nations in this world will eventually meet. Children realize that the dead are not living in the ground permanently, but are merely awaiting His calling.

"But for some who still practice the traditions, some things have changed. Upon the loss of a loved one, the eldest member of a family—someone well respected—is the one who does the explaining to the children. It must be done before the children can look at the deceased, or even before they hear about it from someone else. If children hear from another person, they say, they will have ambivalent feelings, and it will take a long time before the children accept the loss or heal."

Social Aspects of Death

Death often has an impact on the family life that goes beyond the members' emotional responses. If a spouse dies, the family income often decreases significantly (Ward, 1994). Many widows slide into poverty on the death of their husbands. The loss of a spouse can also often result in the loss of identity and status (Schwartz & Scott, 1994). Men often experience more difficulties since they typically rely on their wives for emotional support. Feelings of loneliness and social isolation and a perceived need for major changes in lifestyle often accompany the loss of a spouse (Eshleman & Wilson, 1995). One young widow revealed that, within a year after her husband was killed in a car accident, her whole social network collapsed. Most of the friendships they had developed were through his place of employment and so were joint friends. A long illness before a death can deplete the family resources and take an emotional toll. The death of a grandparent can result in a number of changes in the family, particularly when the surviving grandparent cannot live on his or her own.

Unclear Norms Regarding Death

People sometimes don't know how to behave when there is a death in the family. In our society, there are few guidelines or rules concerning appropriate length of time for mourning, dress, behaviour, and remarriage (Schwartz & Scott, 1994). The lack of norms is even more noticeable for nontraditional families. The following example highlights the fact that whatever guidelines do exist have not kept pace with social changes.

Who Goes to the Funeral?

Leslie had been divorced from Norman for two years. They had two teenage children, Anna and Peter. Norman remarried a year after the divorce and had a child with his new wife, but he maintained regular contact with his teenage children. Shortly after the birth of this new child, Norman was in a tragic accident and died. His children, Anna and Peter, were devastated and wanted their mother, Norman's ex-wife, to accompany them to the funeral. Norman's widow did not want Leslie to attend. Leslie felt that, even though she was the ex-wife, she too had lost the father of her children and her ex-spouse. "There is no acceptable way for an ex-wife to mourn," claimed Leslie.

Cohabiting partners or same-sex couples may, like Leslie, feel that, although their grief is as intense as that of a traditional spouse, they lack the support of the community.

The death of an unborn child through miscarriage or stillbirth is another area where people are uncertain of how to respond. For the parents (sometimes only for the mother) the loss of a fetus may be as devastating as the death of any other close family member (Jaffe, 1991). The mother may experience extreme guilt along with many other emotions associated with grieving. The parents often feel isolated in their grief because family members and friends did not have a chance to know the baby, and therefore they do not feel the loss in the same way.

Adult Psychological Responses to Grief

Kübler-Ross (1974, 1969) identifies five stages in the grieving process as denial, anger, bargaining, depression, and acceptance. Her work has been widely accepted in the field and, although modified somewhat, it is also used to help understand what people go through when they experience the loss of a loved one (Quine & Pahl, 1987). The stages identified by Kübler-Ross have often been interpreted as distinct phases that succeed one another until the process of grieving is complete. But human beings rarely follow precise formulas, and this is especially true for people in acute emotional pain. Grief reactions are highly individual; they may occur in different sequences, and the components of the grief response can occur and reoccur in an unpredictable fashion (Brooks, 1987; Sprang, 1997). Certain events can evoke strong emotions and grief years after the death has occurred. Bearing in mind the reservations about categorizing into stages, it might be helpful to understand some of the most salient components of responses to grief.

Shock and Denial

Shock usually refers to the initial reaction following the death of somebody close. Some refer to this stage as denial. Essentially, this initial response to a death involves feeling numb, or not being able to believe that the death has occurred. One man said that as he was coming up the steps to his apartment after his wife's funeral, he was expecting her to be at the door so he could tell her who attended. This response can be likened to a physical response of those in shock. Often people do not feel physical pain at the moment the body is wounded. The feeling of pain occurs only when the shock subsides.

Anger and Protest

The second stage of grief is described as that of anger, protest, or guilt. The anger is often directed at the person who died ("Why did you leave me?"), the doctor or nurse who cared for the deceased ("They didn't do enough!"), or oneself ("Why didn't I make sure he kept to his diet?"). In this stage of grief the mourner may cry a lot, have a difficult time sleeping, and try to "bargain" to get the loved one back.

Bargaining

Bargaining is perhaps easier to understand before the death has occurred. Pleas directed at God, the dying person, or the doctor may include statements such as "Please just let him live to see his daughter graduate," or "Please let him live and we'll never fight again." These kinds of bargaining thoughts do occur more often before a death rather than after.

Depression and Despair

A period of despair or depression is common among those in mourning. This experience often involves feeling apathetic, being disorganized, and lacking purpose and direction. Behaviour sometimes regresses, and people in this stage of mourning may want to sleep excessively. Feelings of hopelessness and helplessness are common.

Adjustment and Acceptance

In the adjustment phase, people begin to feel some mastery over their lives again and a sense of hope. They begin to loosen the psychological ties with the deceased and to reorganize their lives. In this stage, people attempt to find ways to maintain the memories of their deceased loved ones while moving forward with their own lives. With this adjustment and time comes acceptance.

Children's Responses to Death

Children's grief responses may be different from those of the adult (Cuddy-Casey, Orvaschel & Sellers, 1997). Their different cognitive abilities and relative lack of experience limit their understanding of death and thus their response to it. In earlier generations, it was common for children to be present when a family member died, to participate in the funeral preparations, and to be involved in the funeral itself (Goodwin & Davidson, 1991).

The Naturalness of Death

An older student told the following story to a class of young early childhood students. "I grew up on a farm with my family and grandparents. When I was 3 and 4 years old, I always napped in the afternoons with Grandpa in the parlour. My grandfather died when I was 4, and, as was customary at the time, he was laid to rest in a coffin in the parlour for the three days prior to the funeral. On each of those three days, I crawled in with him to continue our tradition of napping together." The students were aghast at this tale, but the one who told it replied that at that time death was a very natural thing handled in a very natural way by all members of the family.

Children in modern society do not have much opportunity to experience death naturally, as part of the life cycle of families (Goodwin & Davidson, 1991). They often live away from older relatives, and when deaths do occur they are often in hospitals, where children are not allowed to be present (Weber & Fournier, 1986). Children miss out on what happens and subsequently miss many of the rituals associated with death. City children often are not exposed to the natural births and deaths of animals.

Don't Hide Death from Children

Marylea had a 4-year-old and a 2-year-old when the family dog began to suffer from the effects of old age. Marylea and her husband thought that the best course of action would be to put the dog to sleep before its suffering became unbearable. Unable to tell the children, they made the appointment, carried through, and then told the children that the dog had run away. For weeks, the two children frantically searched for the dog and were heartbroken. Marylea realized that she hadn't done anybody a favour and that taking the easy way out was not always the best way.

Many adults find it difficult to explain death to children, either because they think that children should not have to think about death or because their own conception of death is unclear. Children often talk about death in a much less inhibited fashion than do adults, *until* they learn that death is not a topic for discussion or that it is improper (Bernstein, 1977). Children are naturally curious about death (Wilken & Powell, 1998; Jaffe, 1991). They are fascinated by dead insects, they pretend to kill each other, and they may enjoy retelling morbid descriptions of worms eating the eyeballs of a corpse, for instance (Bernstein, 1977). This is the child's way of learning about what happens, and about the irreversibility and permanence of death (Bernstein, 1977). When children are denied these opportunities, or when the dead pet is immediately replaced, they are deprived of an opportunity that helps them to understand and cope with death.

Children's Developmental Understanding of Death

Babies and toddlers

The way children perceive death depends largely on their developmental level (Bernstein, 1977). Babies have no understanding of death per se, but from a very early age they will be disturbed by being separated from a family member to whom they had an attachment (Goodwin & Davidson, 1991). Toddlers seem to relate to a deceased member of a family more in terms of missing someone who is no longer around, rather than by attaching any particular meaning to death.

Preschoolers

Preschoolers typically think in what is referred to as "one-variable thinking." That is, they might take one factor out of what has been explained to them and identify it as the cause of death.

Scenario

One-Variable Thinking

The father of a preschooler was telling some friends that his mother-in-law, weakened by cancer, had contracted a viral infection, which he referred to as a "nasty bug." This, he said, ultimately led to her death. The young grandson was soon heard saying, "Gramma died because she ate a dirty bug."

Young children may, egocentrically, assume they are responsible—that their thoughts and feelings have caused this event. In addition, preschool children may also associate particular places with death. For example, they often think that hospitals cause death.

Scenario

A Child's Confusion

Jonathan's 5-year-old friend, David, died over the summer vacation. Jonathan was told that David got sick and was taken away in an ambulance. Two months after David died, Jonathan was injured at a soccer practice and an ambulance was called. He was very quiet, but as they were driving off, he turned to the attendant and said, "You killed my friend David." Everyone in the ambulance was stunned by his comment, but the ambulance attendant calmly responded that they always tried their best. Sometimes, he said, people do die in ambulances, but usually they get them to the hospital so they get better.

Many preschoolers understand death in specific concrete terms (Wilken & Powell, 1998), thinking it is similar to sleep (Goodwin & Davidson, 1991) or not being able to move (Hoch, 1989). They cannot understand the finality of death, and tend to believe that the dead person or animal will wake up and be able to move again. Preschoolers lack time concepts, and it has been suggested that the concept of death develops for children along with the concept of time (Bernstein, 1977). They do not understand "forever." They believe that death is reversible, and they talk about the deceased person as if he or she were still alive (Weber & Fournier, 1986; Greenberg, 1996). As mentioned before, television and cartoon shows in which the fictional characters "die" but are then alive in the following episodes can add to the confusion and misconceptions children may have about death. Another characteristic of preschoolers is their fascination with details, which is sometimes disconcerting for adults who view this as morbid curiosity. The following are examples of typical questions that children may ask: "How will Gramma be able to go to the bathroom?" "Will the worms eat her eyes?" "How will she stay warm?" Such questions reflect a young child's natural curiosity about all the concrete and practical aspects of death (Jaffe, 1991). Young children will and need to ask questions over and over again. It is through this repetition that they come to understand death.

Preschoolers, like Sylvia in the opening vignette of this chapter, often act out the funeral or dying in pretend play (Andrushko, 1989). Although this may seem morbid, it is a natural way of attempting to understand, to make sense of what has happened (Bernstein, 1977). Preschoolers may also exhibit what is referred to as the "short sadness span" (Bernstein, 1977). They may be extremely sad when they hear of the death, but then seem to forget about it shortly after, often while engaged in play. Then, hours, days, or even weeks later, the child will display signs of sadness again. These types of reactions are typical for this age group.

It is often thought that children do not grieve, that they forget and get over things quickly (Andrushko, 1989). While the typical grieving stages described previously are seen in children as well as adults (Weber & Fournier, 1986), children often have specific responses of which adults should be aware. The shock or denial typical of the adult grief response (Brooks, 1987) is complicated in children by their inability to comprehend finality. "It was just a bad dream; Mommy will come home" is something that would not be uncommon for a 5-year-old child to believe. As with other sources of anxiety for children, a death in the family may cause certain bodily reactions such as stomach aches, lack of appetite, headaches, or changes in sleeping habits (Bernstein, 1977; Andrushko, 1989). This loss may evoke a sense of loss of security. As a result, they may become clingy or more demanding (Wilken & Powell, 1998). Regression to earlier behaviour may also occur, for example, thumbsucking, bedwetting, or the need for a security item. A child's anger is often directed at the loved one who died, and comments such as "Mommy is bad for dying" may be heard, or felt but not expressed.

Because preschoolers are egocentric, they often believe that since they are alive so must everyone else they care for (Bernstein, 1977). Young children are also at risk of feeling responsibility or guilt (Jaffe, 1991), thinking, for example, "Daddy died because I was bad." Children who are beginning to understand the finality of death may be stricken with feelings of genuine panic, wondering who will love them and care for them. When faced with the death of a friend's parent, children often become fearful that their own parents will die (Bernstein, 1977).

Preschool children sometimes take on certain characteristics of a loved one whom they have lost (Brooks, 1987). The family member who has died may also be idealized by the child. For example, a child may remember his mother as being "perfect in every way." This, of course, makes it very difficult for someone else to attempt to fill the role of the deceased person.

Five- to ten-year-old children

Children between the ages of 5 and 10 begin to understand that death is final, but they think that it only happens to others (Goodwin & Davidson, 1991; Brooks, 1987). They see death as a mysterious force, and personify it as an angel or bogeyman (Bernstein, 1977).

Some children in this age group think that old people die because they cannot run fast enough when "Mr. Death" approaches (Hoch, 1989). Because death is a person, they think, it can be beaten and only takes away those too old or too weak to fight it off. Children will still have fears about death. In fact, some children this age are very afraid of being separated from loved ones, since the separation often kindles thoughts of death (Andrushko, 1989). Children at this age are often very curious about details.

Ten years old to adolescence

About the age of 10, children come to understand the finality, irreversibility, and inevitability of death (Goodwin & Davidson, 1991). They realize that death is a natural part of life (Bernstein, 1977). At this age, children are vulnerable to the effects of the loss and are also likely to understand the family problems that result from a death, such as the loss of income, a move to a new neighbourhood, and the effect of the death on other family members (Weber & Fournier, 1986). Yet children of this age, like younger children, rarely have the resources, abilities, or independence required to give them some sense of relief from their grief (Jaffe, 1991). They cannot simply decide that they want to spend time with a friend, for example, and make arrangements on their own to do so. Such arrangements would require involving family members who are often too busy to respond to the requests of the child.

Stages of Grieving in Children

Three additional stages of grieving may also be seen in young children (Brooks, 1987). In the first, the child tests reality until he or she comes to accept the reality that the person has died. For example, the child may continue to get Grandpa's fishing rod ready at the beginning of fishing season. In the second stage, children deal with memories. They may want to hear stories about the deceased and look at their pictures over and over. In the third stage, children may look for someone to replace the dead person. More than occasionally, a child might look for a family member or friend to take the place of the deceased. One mother related the story of how her 5-year-old asked the gardener if he could come and be the new daddy.

Goldman (1996) argues that information can help to reduce the amount of fear that children may experience, and that memorializing the deceased can help children understand death and create a foundation for the grief process.

The Family Dynamic of Grieving and Mourning

Many things change in the family system with the death of a family member, including the family roles. Often an older (but sometimes not old enough) son takes on some of the father's role. Sometimes a grandparent or other relative will step in temporarily or permanently. The death will sometimes fan the flames of hostility and rivalries within the family. We have all heard horror stories about siblings fighting over their inheritance, for example. For professionals involved with families who are grieving, however, the most significant factor to remember can be illustrated in the following anecdote told by a 30-year-old woman.

Can Those Who Mourn Comfort Each Other?

I always got along very well with my mother. She was always supportive of me, and as I got older, I was happy to provide her with a "shoulder to cry on" when she was in need. When my father died, I thought it made a lot of sense for us to spend time together, since we both loved him dearly. But as time went on, I felt that we were getting on each other's nerves, rather than providing comfort to each other. Then I realized—we were both so involved in our own grief, that we were not able to reach out and provide each other with the support we both expected to receive.

In other words, we must remember that a death in the family will likely affect each member deeply and that it may be very difficult for family members, even when the relationship between them is strong, to provide each other with the support they require (Jaffe, 1991; Eshleman & Wilson, 1995). This may have a negative effect on the parent–child relationship.

When children are reacting to the death of a loved one, it is likely that their close family members are also in mourning. They may not be emotionally available or may be too preoccupied with their own grief to provide the children with the support they need (Jaffe, 1991). Sometimes, parents may even feel that children should be protected from the harsh reality of death and the grief it brings (Weber & Fournier, 1986; Jaffe, 1991). Or they might believe that the child would not understand even if the situation was explained or that they may be asked to respond to the inevitable, difficult questions such as "Will I die?" or "Will you die?" (Furman, 1982). When children ask the same questions over and over, parents assume children do not understand. This reluctance to explain or to confront the issue squarely can contribute to the child's confusion. Although children feel the death of a loved one intensely, their grief spans are short (Brooks, 1987; Bernstein, 1977). While it is uncommon to see adults act lightheartedly soon after the death of a loved one, children do move in and out of mourning. They may be extremely sad, and then move quickly into a play situation. Parents often misinterpret this behaviour, which seems to confirm the belief that children are less capable of feeling and understanding the loss. Attention-seeking behaviour and withdrawal are similarly misinterpreted (Andrushko, 1989). Yet, the depth of the grief experienced by children should not be underestimated or ignored.

The Role of the Early Childhood Professional

When a death occurs in the family of one of the children in your care, there is much that you, as an early childhood professional, can do to help both the child and the family. In this instance, it is particularly important to understand how your own views and feelings about death can affect your ability to provide support (Greenberg, 1996).

The Fear of Showing Grief

A class of early childhood students volunteered for a play program for young disabled children. One of the children in the program was Arial, a 4-year-old girl with cerebral palsy. This little girl was often sick, and she died after the sixth week of the program. The students decided to go to the funeral together; however, the student who had worked most closely with Arial and had babysat for her family refused to attend the funeral because she felt she could not handle it. After the service, the parents graciously thanked each student for coming and noticed that Valerie was not there. When they asked about her, one of the students replied that she was afraid she'd find the funeral overwhelming so she didn't come. The parents looked surprised and replied, "What about us?"

Dealing with families who are grieving can often bring one's own grief issues to the surface. For example, one caregiver confessed that she had great difficulty dealing with a family who had lost a child. After counselling, this woman realized that she still had many unresolved feelings about her own miscarriage. Caregivers who possess this self-awareness will be better able to provide empathy and support to families, as well as concrete suggestions that will help parents deal with their children during this stressful and confusing time. Perhaps most importantly, parents will appreciate any extra efforts made by the caregiver to help their child at a time when their own grief has affected their ability to meet the challenges of parenting.

Examine Your Attitudes

The scenario about Sylvia at the beginning of this chapter indicates that some adults are uncomfortable discussing death. If this is the case with you, it could impede your ability to help others who are grieving. Early childhood professionals who are working with children and families should be aware of their own feelings about death and dying.

Answering the following questions might help to clarify your own thoughts and fears about death. If your answers indicate a high level of discomfort with the subject of death, you may wish to consider this in the context of professional development. Open and thoughtful discussions with counsellors, religious leaders, friends, and family members often help to alleviate much of the fear and discomfort people feel about death.

- Does the topic of death frighten you, or do you find it interesting to speculate about death and what it means?

- Have you ever experienced the death of a loved one? If so, did you attend the funeral or avoid it?

- Do you think children should be sheltered from the reality of death and kept from attending funerals?

- Are you disturbed by the physical degeneration of a lingering death and by the intellectual degeneration that often accompanies old age? Or do you think death could be an interesting experience?

Supporting Parents

Early childhood professionals, like everyone else, may feel uncomfortable in approaching the subject of death with a parent. Yet simply by offering condolences and expressions of empathy, they can help parents to feel supported. A simple exchange such as "Hello, Mrs. Dixon. I was sorry to hear of your mother's death. This must be a difficult time for you. Please let us know if there is anything we can do to help you" is much better than avoiding the issue as we are often tempted to do. Some parents may respond by talking about their feelings, while others may acknowledge this offer of sympathy with a simple thank-you or nod of the head.

Although early childhood professionals are not therapists and should not attempt grief counselling, they can listen with empathy. If parents seems to require more than this, or even if they seem to need extensive periods of time to talk, they should be referred to religious or counselling agencies. If a grief reaction seems too prolonged or too intense, it may be better to consult with a professional counsellor. Again, early childhood professionals need to be aware of their boundaries in working with parents.

Often caregivers can help by taking care of the technical details. They may ask another parent to drive the child home or prepare snacks for the day. Sometimes when people are in crisis situations, every small detail seems like a tremendous burden. Having an extra pair of hands may be just as welcome as the emotional support caregivers can provide.

Helping Parents Help Their Children

Early childhood professionals should understand how children may respond to a death in the family, and they should also understand how caring adults can help children to cope with death. Sharing this information with parents can be extremely important. Two points should be remembered, however. First, for many people death is a taboo subject or, at the very minimum, causes discomfort. Therefore, parents may not ask for information at a time when they need it most. Second, even if this information is shared with parents, their own grief responses may interfere with their ability to apply it. Therefore, the caregiver may need to communicate information in a variety of ways, for example, through modelling and discussions, or by providing books and pamphlets on the subject. At the same time, caregivers may need to understand and empathize with parents who may not be able to interact with their children optimally because of their grief. The two main areas about which parents may want information from early childhood professionals are (a) how to talk to children about death, and (b) what to do about children attending the funeral.

Talking to Children About Death

Open communication is the most effective way to deal with death (Nickman-Steven, Silverman & Normand, 1998). When children are included in the grieving process and participate in associated rituals, they gain a better understanding of death (Weber &

Fournier, 1986). Young children need rituals and tangible ways to express their grief (Wilken & Powell, 1998). A common mistake that adults make is assuming that children should not be exposed to discussions about death because it will upset them. However, when children are left out of these conversations, their imagination often takes over, and what they imagine may be more frightening than the truth. Therefore, when children are helped to understand how and why a person died, their fears may actually be alleviated (Andrushko, 1989).

Many adults are unsure of how they should talk about death with children (Jaffe, 1991). They will inevitably bring to their explanation their own thoughts and feelings about death. Cultural and religious factors also play an important role in determining how we perceive death. However, the following points may serve as useful guidelines in many cases.

Explain death as part of the life cycle

Children seem to appreciate the logic when death is explained as part of the life cycle of all creatures and as something that is therefore inevitable (Bernstein, 1977). Many children's stories about animals, plants, and people support this theme. This explanation may help to curb children's fears and guilt—they may stop feeling that someone, either themselves or the bogeyman, was directly responsible for the death. Children do, however, need some assurance that it is unlikely that they will die soon. It is truthful to tell children that usually people only die when they are very old, and that children (and their parents) will not be old for a long time.

Avoid euphemisms

Adults often speak about delicate or taboo subjects by using euphemisms. That is, they use vague and inoffensive terms to substitute for the actual word. These ambiguous responses may create confusion for the child. Death has been described to many children as "a long sleep" or "a long journey" (Bernstein, 1977). Young children think literally, however, and such terminology may lead to serious confusion and misconceptions (Goodwin & Davidson, 1991; Furman, 1982). If a grandmother's death was referred to as "a long journey," can you imagine how frightened a child might be the next time her mother goes on a business trip? Similarly, children have been known to fear going to sleep after hearing the death of a loved one referred to as "going to sleep forever" (Brooks, 1991). Children may become fearful of getting sick if they were told that Granny died because she was sick. It is difficult for children to sort out the difference between serious and common illnesses. Therefore, it is generally best to talk about death using accurate words (Essa & Young, 1994).

Encourage talking

In a discussion of death with children, one should bear in mind their curiosity and fascination with details, and establish an environment in which children feel free to ask any questions they may need answered (Jaffe, 1991). It is acceptable for adults to admit that they don't know all of the answers. Try to answer the child's questions as honestly as possible, even if the response is "I don't know" or "Some people believe that . . ." or "Let's ask your dad when he picks you up." Differences in religious or cultural beliefs may be handled in this way.

It is very important to maintain a dialogue with parents about what was said and what the child was told to prevent mixed messages. Children do not need to understand the answers fully; just talking to them and letting them know that people will respond may be sufficient (Goodwin & Davidson, 1991). Children need to know they can ask questions over and over again. Adults discussing death with children should bear in mind how much information a child is able to integrate. Young children may create misconceptions about death. It may be helpful to stress certain points:

- The doctors could not prevent death.
- The person loved the child.
- The child is not responsible.
- The child is loved and be cared for.
- All feelings are O.K.

While children need the opportunity to discuss death and their fears about it, at the same time they can be encouraged to focus on the living and on the pleasant memories of the person they have lost. Reading and talking about books that deal with death can be an additional way for children to cope. Jordan (1997) suggests that children's literature is a place where consolation can be sought and where children can gain a recognition that death is a part of life.

Attending the Funeral

Often parents will ask early childhood professionals whether they think the child should attend a funeral. Again, there will be differences of opinion based on culture, religion, and the particular circumstances of the families involved (Furman, 1982; Jaffe, 1991). We have noted earlier that children often have very vivid imaginations. Sometimes actually seeing a dead person, or a funeral, is much less frightening to a child than the images they may create in their imagination. Fantasies of reunions or of dead people coming back to life are often minimized with funeral attendance. A funeral is an event full of tradition and ritual in most cultures (Bernstein, 1977). It can be memorable and can help a child to understand the finality of death (Tramonte, 1996).

Scenario

Saying Goodbye

Jonathan was 5 years old when his grandmother died. Though he knew she was very sick and had seen her the day before at the hospital, it surprised him very much when his mother told him that Grandma had died. His first question was, "Are you sure she has stopped breathing and her heart isn't thumping?" His mother tried to assure him that the doctors had checked all of this. Jonathan still felt very unsure and cried that he needed to see for himself before she was buried. His mother brought him to the funeral home before the service and was amazed at the coolness he displayed while looking at his deceased grandmother. He touched her hand and face and placed his small hand over her heart to check if it was still thumping. He nodded his head and said a prayer. As he and his mother were leaving, Jonathan asked if he could just go back and say one more goodbye on his own. Upon arriving home, the first thing he told his father was that Grandma was okay because he had checked everything. He was quite pleased with himself and had experienced a meaningful closure.

Seeing the mourners express their emotions may help children to express their emotions as well. The funeral is a means of sharing memories among family and friends. Children can observe this and participate in the sharing of memories. Being part of this release may help children to realize that they are not alone in their feelings (Bernstein, 1977).

Attending the funeral may also help children to say their final "goodbye" to a loved one, since this is typically the culturally accepted way of saying farewell (Bernstein, 1977). This culturally accepted ritual can be very important for children to participate in.

Scenario

Not Attending the Funeral Can Be Painful

In a discussion of death in an early childhood classroom, students were asked if they remembered attending funerals when they were young. Many students recalled the funeral as a sad but memorable experience. Others claimed that their most vivid memories were of not being allowed to go to the funeral, and of the resentment they felt for not getting the opportunity to participate in the final goodbye. Many of these students reported that the anger, sadness, and fears that they felt about the person's death were heightened by not attending the funeral.

Preparing for the child's attendance at the funeral

Children attending funerals should be prepared in advance (Furman, 1982; Bernstein, 1977). They can be told what the funeral setting will look like, what the people there will be doing, and how the body of the deceased will be handled, that is, buried or cremated. Since the people who normally provide support for the child may be consumed by their own grief at the funeral, it may be appropriate for the child to be accompanied by an adult who is less directly and emotionally involved and who will be able to provide the child with support. Children are unlikely to be able to sit still throughout an entire service; they may need to leave to go to the bathroom, or to go outside to run around for a bit. Children need to know that it is okay for them to cry or to leave if they need to (Bernstein, 1977). If such arrangements can be made beforehand, the child is likely to benefit from the experience.

Alternatives to funeral attendance

When children decide they will not attend the funeral, they need to be supported in that decision. A caring adult can arrange a "special ceremony" for the child. For example, one child made a special scrapbook about his grandfather. Another made a bouquet to take to the grave. Children often have their own ideas of how they want to remember a loved one, and a caring adult can help them to implement those ideas.

Scenario

Another Way to Say Goodbye

Deborah's son Matthew was 6 years old when his best friend Robert died. Robert's parents did not inform his friends and classmates because they thought it was inappropriate for young children to attend a funeral. Matthew and his classmates were visibly upset by the death of their friend. Deborah suggested that they have their own farewell for Robert. Each child in the class was invited to attend, to share a memory, to talk about Robert, or to make a gift. All the children willingly took part, and the teacher was amazed at the amount of effort and care put into making each gift and to telling each story. She believed that it was a memorable occasion for all involved.

Helping the Children in the Centre

Most families will find comfort in the fact that their child's needs are being met by concerned and caring early childhood professionals. A child who is mourning may require some extra attention, a few moments longer in the caregiver's lap, or extra flexibility at naptime and at other transitions during the day. Early childhood professionals need to remember that the child may be reacting directly to the loss of a loved one, to a changed atmosphere at home, and to the parents' distress. The stability provided by the centre's routine and the warm interaction with caregivers are extremely important. In addition, several guidelines are listed below for caregivers to follow in helping children understand death and in working with children who are mourning the loss of a loved one.

Guidelines: Helping Children Cope with Death

1. Listen carefully to children as they talk about death. Try to understand their conceptions and misconceptions. When children do not talk, reassure them that you are available if they have questions or want to talk or just need a cuddle. We all avoid topics that we find uncomfortable, and a special effort needs to be made to ensure that we are not discouraging children, either through our body language or by avoidance of the subject altogether.

2. Try not to be overprotective of children. Whether it is seeing a dead bird or overhearing an adult conversation about someone who died, these experiences can be utilized to enhance the child's understanding of death.

3. Avoid euphemisms in explaining death such as "gone on a trip," "lost," or "sleeping." Children take such terms literally and may become fearful of sleeping or going on trips. It is best to use the terms "dead" or "died," and if necessary explain what that means in a physical sense to the young child. For example, "Grampa's heart is not beating any more; he can't breathe."

4. Support the attendance of children at funerals, unless there are religious or other factors that prohibit this. Ongoing discussion and collaboration with parents is necessary to clarify such a matter.

5. Be aware of children's short grief span, and ensure that this is not misinterpreted as denial. Ensure that parents also understand how children grieve, to prevent misinterpretation of a child's behaviour.

6. Be aware of hidden fears, such as Grandma dying in the hospital, which may cause the child to think he/she will die if hospitalized. Explain the circumstances of the death, such as a serious illness, old age, a car accident, etc. Also, children need information and reassurance about what would happen and who would care for them if their parents died.

7. While children should be encouraged to share their feelings, they should not be pressured to do so. Give the children permission to feel sad or confused, or to cry if that is what they want to do. We must take care not to interpret a child's feelings incorrectly. For instance, a little boy may be crying because another child took the ball away from him. We must not assume that those are tears of sadness due to his uncle's death.

8. Provide children with many opportunities to express themselves through play or creative expression such as art or music. Books and stories about death that are developmentally appropriate should be available to but not imposed on children (Goodwin & Davidson, 1991). Parents may also find such resources valuable in explaining concepts to their child. Let parents know about any good, age-appropriate resources.

9. When adults working with children have firm beliefs about death and the afterlife, they must be very cautious not to impose them on others. Children may come from families with very different belief systems, and all of their beliefs must be treated with the utmost respect. Collaboration with the child's parents will be necessary, and they should be encouraged to share their beliefs with their children (Goodwin & Davidson, 1991). If you are unfamiliar with the specific traditions of mourning in a different culture, be sure to ask about them. Most people would rather be asked what is appropriate in their culture, and they will probably appreciate your interest. Parents may not always realize that your customs and beliefs differ from their own.

10. Remember that there is no universally accepted way to grieve and mourn, and people vary widely in the time it takes to recover. In modern society, we have few built-in rituals to help with our mourning, and there often seems to be a rush to "get back to normal." Families and children may need more time than is formally allotted (compassionate leave at work, etc.) to recover from their loss. The patience and ongoing support of those who care about the bereaved family will be appreciated.

11. Perhaps most importantly, you should remember the tremendous impact that a death in the family can have on every family member. This may be one example of when early childhood professionals might want to "go that extra mile" for a bereaved family. For example, you could allow for extra flexibility in arrival and pickup times or agree to be flexible in the centre's rules in other ways that would make things easier for the grieving family.

Source: Includes material from Canadian Child Day Care Federation, n.d.

Conclusion

The death of a family member usually begins a period of crisis in the lives of the surviving family members. The time following a death will be a time of mourning for all family members. Children may understand death in ways different than do adults and may behave in different ways. It is important to put the child's reactions into a developmental context to better understand and help children to cope. Children need rituals so participating in ceremonies and traditions like funerals and memorial services can often help children to overcome their fears and misconceptions about death. The early childhood professional can play a valuable role not only in providing support to children, but also in assisting parents in their interaction with their young children.

Exercises

1. Discuss death and burial rituals with a number of different people from different cultural backgrounds. Compare their traditions and their beliefs with your own.

2. Discuss death and funeral attendance with a number of people. Do they have pleasant or unpleasant memories? Can they explain why? How has it affected their beliefs today?

3. Practise what you might say in response to a 3-year-old's questions about death. What if the same questions were asked by a 5-year-old? How would your answers differ?

4. If one child in your playroom experienced a death, what would your response be to the other children? Would you tell them? Would you talk about it? Would you let the parents know?

5. Check your local community for people who may be able to provide information or expertise in dealing with death (e.g., mental health agencies, funeral directors). Check whether the information is suitable to children under the age of 5 and whether the professionals working there have experience with young children. Many professionals specialize in grieving but may not have expertise in applying it to young children. Funeral directors also often have information specifically related to young children and families.

6. The resource sheet "Helping Children Understand Death," published by the Canadian Child Day Care Federation to aid parents, makes the following suggestion:

    Touring a neighbourhood funeral home and/or cemetery can be an excellent way to give your child accurate information about what happens to the body after death and the funeral process. Many funeral directors are experienced in answering children's questions, and often parents find such a tour extremely informative and interesting as well.

    Discuss this with your classmates and colleagues. Would you consider this? Why or why not?

Violence and Abuse in the Home

chapter 11

Objectives

- To examine different types of abuse and neglect of children.

- To examine the myths and characteristics associated with the perpetrators and the victims of abuse.

- To examine the role of the early childhood professional in monitoring and reporting abuse.

- To examine the role of the early childhood professional in preventing abuse.

- To describe strategies for supporting children who are neglected or abused.

- To examine the role of the early childhood professional in supporting families in which abuse and neglect occurs.

> The day after I saw the bruises on Johnny's buttocks, I thought I would faint when his father walked into the room. I wanted to scream at him, "How dare you hurt this innocent child!" Instead, I took a deep breath and approached him as calmly as I could. "Good morning, Mr. Smith," I said. "Would you please come with me to Mrs. Atari's [the director] office? There is something she would like to discuss with you." I accompanied him to the director's office door, then I left. But I couldn't do anything when I got back into the playroom. I was trembling so hard that I couldn't even speak.

The most difficult aspect of being a member of the early childhood profession consists of coming face to face with child abuse. Child abuse strikes at the very core of our professional commitment to the well-being of children. It is in polar opposition to all we believe about how children should be nurtured, respected, and protected. At the moment when we discover that parents have hurt one of their children, the idea of being accepting and nonjudgmental can seem like nothing more than a meaningless theory. In many cases, there is a long process in discovering abuse where the signs may be ambiguous.

Caregivers must be ever vigilant while deciding if it is the appropriate time to report. Although in many jurisdictions adults are legally compelled to report incidences of abuse, early childhood professionals must decide when it is appropriate to seek and provide families and children with additional support either from the centre or community resources and when child protection is required. This process and decision can be agonizing for the most seasoned professional.

Violence and abuse within the family are not new phenomena. In 1997, parents were the main perpetrators of assault against children and youth within families in Canada. Parents represented 65 percent of family members accused of physical assaults against children and youth, and 44 percent of those accused of sexual assaults (Statistics Canada). Both have existed throughout history and across cultures (Margolin, 1998; Ward, 1994; Drakich & Guberman, 1988; Couchman, 1988; Tower, 1989). Sometimes it seems as if violence within the home is more prevalent in today's society than in the past (Krishnan & Morrison, 1995; Wallach, 1995; Drakich & Guberman, 1988). However, the increase may not be in the number of people being abused but in the attention abuse has received, people's willingness to discuss it, and the availability of better reporting procedures.

Only recently has attention been drawn to the magnitude of violence and abuse in the home and also to the effect it has on family members, particularly the children (Krishnan & Morrison, 1995). Today, rather than keeping violence and abuse behind closed doors, women and children are more aware that services and supports are available. Victims of abuse, however, may still require support in taking the first step to change this aspect of their lives. Early childhood professionals are often in the best position to facilitate taking the first steps. Although this can be an unpleasant situation in which to be involved, protecting children from abuse stands as one of their ethical responsibilities.

In this chapter, we will examine both abuse and neglect of children in the home and discuss their effects on the adults and children involved. Though the focus will be on violence directed towards children, it must be recognized that any kind of violence and abuse within families (elder abuse, spousal abuse, sibling abuse) constitutes a serious problem with devastating and long-lasting effects on family members. It should also be clear that, even if children are not the direct victims, they are harmed as a consequence of any violent or abusive situation in a family. The chapter will close with a discussion of the role of the early childhood professional in relation to this very serious problem.

Defining Abuse and Violence

To begin, we shall try to arrive at a clear and practical definition of the terms "violence" and "abuse," since these words so often seem to be open to interpretation. What one person considers abuse (for example, corporal punishment), another may consider an appropriate response to bad behaviour (Health and Welfare Canada, n.d.). The circumstances may also vary—a child pushing an adult may not have the same consequences as when that adult pushes the child. *Violence* refers to an action that is intended to bring physical harm to another person (Ward, 1994). Violent acts include hitting, pushing, biting, or throwing objects. These acts involve the use of force and intimidation. Abuse is a more general term. It usually refers to a situation in which a more powerful person attempts to exert control over a less powerful person (Vanier Institute, 1994; Ward, 1994). Abusers employ threats and actions to keep control of their victims. Child abuse can include physical abuse, verbal abuse, sexual exploitation, emotional abuse, and neglect that results in physical or psychological harm to the child (Health and Welfare Canada, n.d.).

Understanding Abuse

Different types of abuse have been defined in a variety of ways. Prior to looking at specific definitions, we think it important to stress that one form of abuse seldom occurs in isolation. More often, two or more types of abuse occur simultaneously. Thus, although the categories of abuse can serve as guidelines, in certain cases they may need to be used in a flexible way.

Abuse can be divided into the following categories:

1. *Physical abuse* means that deliberate force has been used on the child to cause physical harm. Physical abuse can occur with or without verbal abuse.

2. *Emotional abuse* involves depriving the child of affection, love, and acceptance. Verbal abuse, a common form of emotional abuse, entails belittling and humiliation. Emotional abuse may also include intimidation, exploitation, or terrorization.

3. *Sexual abuse* involves the sexual exploitation of individuals against their will. It may include touching, forcing the child to touch, or forcing sexual acts such as intercourse upon the child.

4. *Neglect* describes a situation in which the child's needs are not taken care of by the adult to such an extent that it interferes with emotional or physical development (Health and Welfare Canada, n.d.). Physical neglect occurs when there is a failure to meet medical, dental, nutritional, sleep, or dress needs. Emotional neglect occurs when the child's needs to feel loved, worthy, and secure are not met. Neglect is the least likely of all forms of abuse to be reported (Health and Welfare Canada, n.d.; Vanier Institute of the Family, 1994).

Many documents that define and list indicators of abuse and neglect are available. The example below is from "Protocols for Handling Child Abuse and Neglect in Day-Care Services," published by Alberta Family and Social Services (1990). Indicators of abuse are given with descriptions of physical and emotional signs that may be detected in the child, and behaviours that you may see in the adult abuser are also listed. For instance, one of the most common signs of abuse or violence consists of the strained interaction between the abuser and the victim. A caregiver who knows a child well will usually notice if the child behaves strangely around certain adults, especially when the behaviour involves an obvious withdrawal from a person who is closely related to the child.

Child Abuse: What to Look For

<u>General Signs of Abuse or Neglect</u>
The child suffering from abuse or neglect may

- be anxious, depressed, unhappy.
- have poor relationships with peers.
- show extremes of behaviour—may be very passive or aggressive, outgoing or withdrawn, or swing between two opposite extremes.
- be absent frequently.
- be overanxious to please.

- show distrust of others.
- have low self-esteem.
- fear other people and avoid physical contact with them.

The adult who is abusing the child may

- suggest or indicate that he/she is lonely, isolated, or carrying a heavy burden of responsibility for the child.
- react with hostility, anger, or indifference when you discuss concerns regarding the child.
- have been abused as a child.
- misuse drugs or alcohol.

<u>Indicators of Physical Abuse</u>

Physical signs on the child might include

- bruises and welts where children do not typically bruise.
- bite marks.
- burns.
- lacerations and abrasions.
- dislocation of shoulders, hips, or other joints.
- head injuries.

Emotionally, the child may

- be wary of physical contact with adults.
- seem afraid of parents or other persons.
- be frightened in the face of adult disapproval.
- be apprehensive when others cry.
- show extremes of behaviour, acting in either an overly aggressive or withdrawn fashion.
- be overanxious to please.
- approach any adult, including strangers.

Emotionally, the adult may

- be angry and impatient, and frequently lose or come close to losing control.
- appear unconcerned about the child's condition.
- view child as bad or as the cause of life's problems.
- resist discussion of child's condition or family situation.
- view any questions with suspicion.
- use discipline inappropriate to child's age, condition, and situation.
- offer illogical, contradictory, unconvincing, or no explanation of injuries.
- show poor understanding of normal child development (for example, may expect adult-like mature behaviour from a young child).

Indicators of Emotional Abuse

The child's appearance may not indicate or suggest the extent of the difficulty. The child may appear clean, well groomed, and well nourished.

On the other hand, the child's facial expression and body carriage may indicate sadness, depression, timidity, or held-back anger.

The child may

- appear overly compliant, passive, or shy.
- show episodes of very aggressive, demanding, and angry behaviour.
- fear failure, have trouble concentrating or learning, and give up easily.
- be either boastful or negative about himself.
- constantly apologize.

The adult may

- blame or belittle the child in public and at home.
- withhold comfort when child is frightened or distressed.
- treat other children in family differently and better, showing them more acceptance and love and less criticism.
- tend to describe child in negative ways: "stupid," "bad," or "troublemaker."
- constantly predict failure or a poor future for the child.
- hold the child responsible for parents' difficulties and disappointments.
- identify the child with disliked relatives.

Indicators of Sexual Abuse

Physical evidence of sexual abuse is rare. Often with young children, abuse is not intercourse, but touching, which may leave no physical signs. Where physical evidence is present, it may consist of

- torn, stained, or bloody clothing.
- pain or itching in genital area or throat, difficulty going to the bathroom or swallowing.
- bruises, bleeding, or swelling of genital, rectal, or anal areas.
- vaginal odor or discharge.

The child may

- display unusual interest in sexual matters.
- use language and make drawings that are sexually explicit.
- fantasize excessively.
- show fear of closed spaces.
- resist undressing or diaper changes.
- masturbate excessively.
- exhibit seductive behaviour.

The adult may

- often be domineering but emotionally weak.
- suggest or indicate marital or relationship difficulties with adults.
- indicate own social isolation and loneliness, especially as a single parent.
- cling to child, both physically and emotionally, hold and touch the child in an inappropriate way.
- tend to blame others for life's problems and child's sexual behaviour—may even accuse child of causing sexual abuse.

Indicators of Neglect

The child may

- be underweight by more than 30 percent and gain weight when offered proper nutrition.
- show improvement of developmental delays following proper stimulation and care.
- demonstrate signs of deprivation: cradle cap, severe diaper rash, diarrhea, vomiting, anemia, recurring respiratory problems.
- be consistently dirty or dressed inappropriately for the weather, or wear worn clothing.
- often be hungry or thirsty.
- often be tired or listless.
- demand much physical contact and attention.
- assume role of parent or adult in the family.
- lack proper medical and dental care.

The adult may

- maintain a chaotic home life with little evidence of healthy routines.
- not supervise the child for long periods of time or when the child is involved in potentially dangerous activity.
- leave the child in the care of inappropriate persons.
- give the child inappropriate food, drink, or medicine.
- consistently bring the child in early and pick up late.
- be apathetic towards the child's progress, be hard to reach by phone, and fail to keep appointments to discuss concerns about the child.
- overwork or exploit the child.
- show evidence of apathy or feelings of futility.

Source: Alberta Family and Social Services, 1990.

Early childhood professionals should try to find a publication that provides written guidelines and other information for their own use and use by others in the day-care centre. These are often available from local child welfare offices, which provide specific information related to local legislation. In addition, national associations and clearinghouses that disseminate information exist in both Canada and the United States. Documents such as the one quoted above are intended to be used only as guides. Many of the indicators listed above characterize children who are experiencing problems yet are not abused or neglected. Therefore, it is important to be tentative about conclusions and open to new information. It is particularly important to consult with local child welfare agencies or other specialists in child abuse when suspicions of abuse arise.

Why Abuse Occurs

In this section, we will attempt to highlight some common characteristics associated with child abuse. Note that some of the characteristics focus on attributes of the abuser, while others focus on social conditions that make abuse more likely to happen.

Social Conditions Associated with Abuse

The societal view of abuse fits with the ecological model of the family, but it has been largely ignored in the study of abuse (Krishnan & Morrison, 1995). According to this view, child abuse is a community concern, one that is related to societal norms and values, to social and economic conditions. Changes in rates of reported abuse tend to be consistent with changes in family structure, unemployment rates, and the availability of support programs for families (Skolnick, 1992; Krishnan & Morrison, 1995). Statistics suggest that the majority of abuse occurs in low-income homes. However, this disproportionate representation may reflect the fact that low-income families are much more likely to be reported than middle- or high-income families (Health and Welfare Canada, n.d.). This situation may exist because low-income families are more likely to be involved with social service agencies, they may have fewer support systems to rely on, or people may simply be more willing to report such families (Vanier Institute, 1994).

Research also indicates that children in single-parent homes are at a higher risk (Krishnan & Morrison, 1995). There are two plausible and interrelated explanations for this phenomenon, both of them based on the ecological approach. First, the single parent experiences a high degree of stress in meeting the demands of childrearing alone. Second, stress levels are further aggravated because many single parents live in very deprived economic conditions. Poverty is a social condition that is most often associated with child abuse and neglect (Sedlak, 1997). This is but one example of how economic and social factors may interact to produce conditions in which the probability of abuse is high.

Other social factors associated with abuse are social values and norms of behaviour. Cultural traditions do exist that condone and even contribute to family violence (Eshleman & Wilson, 1995; Couchman, 1988). These traditions are strong in societies in which men are taught that they are in control and have the right to control others, especially their wives and children (Couchman, 1988; Fraad, 1996). Societies in which men are rewarded for using violence to solve problems and taught that women and children should be subservient are also more likely to experience high rates of child abuse (Eshleman & Wilson, 1995; Vanier Institute of the Family, 1994).

Norms and values related to the role of women in our society may also be a factor in abuse. A rather extreme explanation of abusive mothering has been posed by Margolin (1992), who connects women's lack of opportunity to child abuse. Many women's sole route to self-fulfillment is through their children; when the children do not measure up to her expectations, a mother's self-image and identity as a mother are threatened. This leads to more frustration; thus, the mother may be prone to use force or violence to punish.

A less dramatic explanation for why some mothers abuse their children or allow their children to be abused by their partners focuses on the expectations placed on women to be passive and the relative lack of power and control many women experience. Many women continue to live in situations in which they themselves are abused because they are financially dependent or have been socialized to believe that they cannot make it on their own (Eshleman & Wilson, 1995). Women are also often socialized to believe that their relationship with their spouse is the most important thing that can happen in their lives and that they are responsible for its success (Drakich & Guberman, 1988; Wallach, 1995). Although gender differences cannot adequately explain abuse, the socialization of men and women in our culture does need to be examined as a potential contributing factor to abuse.

Perspectives

Nita is a 32-year-old married woman with two preschool-age children. She shared this story in an early childhood class that she was taking in the evening.

"My parents emigrated from Lebanon and worked very hard to set up a business and raise a family in Canada. I have two older brothers and three younger sisters. We have always been a close family, keeping all of our religious and cultural heritage in this new country. Just like back home, my father was always the undisputed head of the house—he demanded respect and obedience, he set out all the rules according to tradition, and he dished out the discipline.

"I can't say when the abuse started; I can always remember being hit by my father when something went wrong or when I was bad. I know that my brothers and sisters were beat up too, but we never, never talked about it, because it was something that happened at home and stayed at home. I do remember that my father began to abuse me sexually when I was 12 years old. I never told anyone; it was his right as the head of the house, or so we were told. I think my mother knew, because she started to ignore me and was really distant. He came to my bed at night until I was 16 and couldn't stand it any more. I ran away from home and the small community we lived in to the big city. I worked the streets for a few years—what the heck, I had been doing it since I was twelve and now guys would pay me money and they were nice too.

"One day I was in the welfare office and met this really nice guy named Nick. He was in bad shape too and trying to start all over, so we tried together.

"That was five years ago. Now we're married, Nick works full time as a baker, and we have two children. Domenica is 19 months and Marguerite is 3 years old. I see my family, except for my father. Funny, everybody knew what Dad was doing, and he was doing the same thing to my sisters.

"I haven't talked about this much and haven't got any professional help. Maybe some day I will. But one thing I know for certain is that those things will never, never happen to my children. I will never let my children go through the hurt like I did, and I will do anything to make sure that it doesn't happen. My hurting will never go away, but it will always be a reminder of what kind of parent I should be."

Personal Attributes of the Abuser

Many myths surround abusers and victims of abuse. The two most common myths are that abusers fit one particular profile and that their victims somehow asked for or deserved the abusive acts. Both myths are untrue.

Abusive adults do, in fact, come from every walk of life—from every cultural group, socioeconomic level, and educational background. (Krishnan & Morrison, 1995; Corwin, 1995). There is no single description or profile that fits all abusers. However, there are some common characteristics that they share.

First, abusers who use physical force tend to be male, and their victims tend to be women and children (Drakich & Guberman, 1988; Vanier Institute, 1994; Margolin, 1992). This may be attributed to a number of factors. Fathers have always been perceived as more authoritarian than mothers (Margolin, 1992). When it becomes evident that the use of violence can be very effective in gaining and maintaining control of both women and children, its use is perpetuated. Again, there may be cultural sanctioning for the use of force in disciplining children (Krishnan & Morrison, 1995; Eshleman & Wilson, 1995).

The second common characteristic of abusers is that they frequently have difficulty dealing with their emotions. Men have been socialized to believe that displays of violence are normal and to be expected (Eshleman & Wilson, 1995; Margolin, 1992; Jacobs, 1995).

Third, abusers often blame other people or external situations for the violence they cause (Drakich & Guberman, 1988; Tower, 1989). For example, stress, alcohol, work, a messy house, or noisy children may trigger a violent reaction when they arrive home at the end of the day.

High stress levels and few coping mechanisms

Abusive adults, whether they are mothers or fathers, tend to be under a great deal of stress (Tower, 1989). One study found that this stress is often related to problems surrounding the attainment of adequate housing, and that families in which abuse occurs are more likely to move frequently or be homeless (Coohey, 1998). This stress may come from events at work, at home, or from any other source. In addition, abusive people tend to have few resources for coping with stress (Krishnan & Morrison, 1995). They often do not have access to good support systems, and even if they do they seem reluctant to use them (Margolin, 1992; Tower, 1989; Health and Welfare Canada, n.d.). Frequently, the only way that they know how to cope with or react to stress is by the use of violence. Lack of social support, inadequate means of coping with stress, and the perceived cultural support for the use of force in disciplining children can all contribute to the creation and perpetuation of abuse within families (Drakich & Guberman, 1988; Couchman, 1988).

The abuse cycle

Researchers have established that the majority of abusive adults were themselves abused as children (Kinnear, 1995; Couchman, 1988; Jacobs, 1995; Health and Welfare Canada, n.d.). A historical review suggests that this behaviour is indeed passed on from one generation to the next. It may be that children learn that violence is an apparently effective way to solve problems. Or they see that it is acceptable for men to hit women or for adults to hit children, and that there are no penalties to pay for the use of these violent acts within the home (Tower, 1989).

Another contributing factor may be that, as children, many abusive adults were made to feel unloved, unworthy, and unwanted (Health and Welfare Canada, n.d.). They perpetuate this perception of themselves when they become adults by abusing others, thus reinforcing that they are no good, but now as parents or husbands (Tower, 1989). This, however, must be seen only as a contributing factor, since not all abused children go on to abuse their own children or spouses (Tower, 1989).

Parenting skills

Abusive parents often think of parenting as stressful and have difficulty understanding the child's perception of the world (Ward, 1994; Tower, 1989; Dolz, Cerezo & Milner, 1997). They may believe that their children are out to get them and that they have little control over them. When the parent uses force or violence to control, there are immediate short-term effects (i.e., the problematic behaviour ceases), but the long-term negative effects are not considered. The child misbehaves again and the parent uses force to control the situation again. This often leads to the creation of more stress and less control in parenting, and before long, the cycle of abuse has become established within the home.

Abusive parents often have unrealistic expectations about their child's development and behaviour (Tower, 1989; Health and Welfare Canada, n.d.). They demand physical, social, and emotional abilities that are well beyond the child's developmental stage (e.g., demanding that the toddler not cry when Mommy leaves or expecting a baby to sleep through the night). When the child does not display these expected abilities, the parents may feel further frustration or they may look upon abuse as the discipline necessary to ensure obedience (Tower, 1989).

Relationship problems

Sexual abuse is more likely to occur with family members than it is with strangers (Corwin, 1995; Drakich & Guberman, 1988). In fact, it is far more common for children, especially girls, to be sexually abused by a person that they know and trust (Eshleman & Wilson, 1995; Vanier Institute of the Family, 1994). There are some common characteristics in families in which sexual abuse occurs. The adult is usually isolated and has difficulty in relationships in general, but predominantly in emotional and sexual relationships. As well, abuse is more likely to occur in families that are socially isolated and appear very close and traditional. They often have poor communication patterns and blurred boundaries between family subsystems, with role confusion or reversal. Parents in abusive homes tend to suffer from emotional deprivation and are therefore emotionally needy. Sexual abuse usually occurs in situations where there is some form of inequality; for instance, males typically abuse younger females.

Characteristics of Victims of Abuse

Vulnerability

Children who are subjected to abuse also display particular characteristics. They usually know their abuser and may have an emotional relationship with that person. In the case of sexual abuse, the abuser may be the only person to show the child affection, making the child more vulnerable to being taken advantage of. Children have been taught to obey and be polite to adults, not to question their actions or behaviour. In addition, children are generally unable to protect themselves from an adult, particularly one using physical force. Many abused children do not have well-developed social and emotional relationships with other people. This lack of support makes them feel isolated. All of these factors leave the child highly vulnerable to abuse.

Children with special needs

Recent research indicates that children who have special needs are more likely to be abused (Turnbull & Turnbull, 1990; Tower, 1989). This includes children who have developmental delays, physical disabilities, or chronic health problems, or whose temperaments make them difficult to raise (Margolin, 1992). For example, Harrington, Black, Starr & Dubovitz (1998) found that maternal reports of a more difficult child temperament often predict emotional neglect. Children living in foster or adoptive homes and those living with blended families or single parents (especially when the child was not wanted) are also at a higher risk for abuse (Tower, 1989; Health and Welfare Canada, n.d.; Ward, 1994).

Effects on children of witnessing violence

Children may be the victims of abuse or may be unintended victims in situations of domestic violence. More and more evidence is emerging that suggests there are immediate and long-term consequences of witnessing violence (Margolin, 1998). It should be noted that children who witness abuse are more likely to be the targets of abuse as well.

Children living with violence tend to live with several other notable stresses. Children have no ability to remove themselves from the situation. They are typically not cared for physically or psychologically. The home is no longer perceived as a safe refuge. Parents, experiencing their own struggles, may be less available to the child for support when the child is likely more in need of emotional support. Many parenting roles may be unavailable to the child when the parent is concerned with their basic safety. In addition, children witnessing abuse between parents may wonder who can be trusted or loved. Children may not understand why their lives are different from others' or why they have family secrets, can't bring friends home, or have no one to protect them.

Children living in domestic abuse often will experience physical health problems, such as weight, eating or sleeping problems, acting-out behaviours, low self-concept, anxiety, aggression, social isolation, difficulties interacting with other children (Margolin, 1998). Children who live in high-conflict homes tend to respond to conflict more readily and with more intensity. Whereas boys tend to react with higher levels of aggression and behavioural outbursts, girls tend to react with less empathy and more anxiety. It has been suggested that living with violence over extended periods of time causes the child to be constantly aroused or hypervigilant. Over a long period of time, the child may be irritable, distractible, nervous. The characteristics associated with this hypervigilance, in all situations, are similar to ADD and accordingly children may be labelled as ADD.

Developmental Effects of Child Abuse

Exposure to violence in the home may have long-term effects on development (Wallach, 1995; Osofsky, 1994; Wallach, 1997). Children's thinking about themselves and their world may be affected. They may feel that they are responsible for the beatings or the fights between their parents, and this will create in them a sense of guilt (Wallach, 1995; Vanier Institute of the Family, 1994). Children may feel that they are unloveable and worthless. They may feel shame and isolation and be unable to talk to anyone (Wallach, 1995). The abuser may have told them to be silent, that no one will believe them anyway, or may have threatened them (Health and Welfare Canada, n.d.). Children have demonstrated increased rates of negative and aggressive behaviour, withdrawal, depression, fearfulness, and disruptions in eating and sleeping patterns (Osofsky, 1994). They may experience nightmares, bedwetting, difficulties controlling emotions, insecurity, fears, or anxiety (Tower, 1989; Vanier Institute, 1994).

These children may also learn, by observation, that violence is the way to solve problems and is a normal behaviour (Tower, 1989). This has been set forth as one reason that abuse is perpetuated in families (Couchman, 1988). As children grow up watching violence, they come to assume that it is a normal part of their life.

Scenario

Stormy Monday

A new caregiver was starting in the day-care centre on a Monday morning. A young 5-year-old had just been dropped off by his mother and began acting out. He threw his backpack and coat to the floor, kicked the articles around, lay down, and began to kick the floor. Other violent behaviour followed. The staff appeared to be watching but not reacting to this display. When the new caregiver questioned what was going on, the child's caregiver replied, "It's Monday." Further probing indicated that the child's mother had been a victim of spousal abuse for a long period of time. This was a typical display of behaviour for this child after having been home for two full days on the weekend and witnessing the violence.

Disruptions in development occur when children are victims of abuse. Infants may have difficulty developing a sense of trust when their parents are unable to provide consistent, predictable care (Tower, 1989; Wallach, 1997). Parents who feel that they cannot protect themselves or their children may come to feel helpless or powerless and therefore grow passive (Osofsky & Jackson, 1994). Parents may grow insensitive and unresponsive to the needs of their children as they attempt to deal with their own lives, or they may become secretive and overprotective, never letting the child out of sight. Living in fear is not conducive to building a secure, trusting environment for children (Wallach, 1995). Continuous abuse produces chronic stress. Over the long term, children will have to deal with the loss of self-esteem, trust, and security in their family life and with the reinforcement of inappropriate means of dealing with stress and problems in their own lives.

The effects of abuse are far reaching and have serious consequences on the child's future development (Wallach, 1995; Ingrassia & McCormick, 1995). These effects may result in criminal activities, mental health problems, or developmental delays. We know that victims of abuse are at a higher risk of becoming abusers themselves (Drakich & Guberman, 1988; Health and Welfare Canada, n.d.), and that children growing up with violence risk becoming violent themselves (Wallach, 1995). And we must not forget that child abuse too often results in the death of children. For example, one study of children admitted to a pediatric intensive care unit found that child abuse cases represented 1.4 percent of admissions, but 17 percent of deaths, and the highest severity of illness and mortality rates (Irazuzta, McJunkin, Danadian, Arnold & Zhang, 1997). By understanding more about the abuser and the abused, the early childhood professional may be better able to assist the family through this crisis by not prejudging the abuser or blaming the victim. Understanding in a more objective way may help the early childhood professional provide support to the child and to the family.

Supporting Families

Throughout this book, we have attempted to highlight the interrelatedness of the well-being of the child with that of the family. Indeed, from the standpoint of the early childhood professional, support provided to families is based on the belief that it will directly or indirectly contribute to the well-being of the child. In the case of child abuse, however, the equation becomes more complex. Supporting a family in which child abuse is occurring often begins with reporting the family to the appropriate authorities. This step can lead to legal action against the abuser that culminates in a prison sentence or the removal of the child from his or her care. While many families who are helped by professional intervention may ultimately come to thank the person who first reported the abuse, it is unlikely that most perpetrators of abuse will be pleased initially. Regardless of how the parents view such intervention, though, when a child's psychological or physical safety is at risk, early childhood professionals have a moral and legal responsibility to intervene.

Scenario

Divided Loyalties

A young mother and her child's caregiver developed an excellent relationship over the two years that Jamie was in the day care. The mother had worked hard to overcome many of the difficulties associated with being a single working parent and was committed to taking excellent care of her daughter. One day, she told the caregiver that her boyfriend had hit Jamie and that she was worried he would do it again. She asked the caregiver to promise not to tell anyone, since this was the first serious relationship she had had in several years. She was sure that once her boyfriend got used to having a young child around, things would work out and her dreams of getting married would finally materialize.

Of course, the caregiver has an obligation to monitor and report if the abuse continues, but we cannot ignore how difficult this may be. It helps in this and similar situations to remind ourselves that protecting children must be our primary consideration, but also that reporting is often the first step in the long and painful process of helping, healing, and breaking the cycle of abuse.

Examine Your Attitudes

Do you agree or disagree with the following statements?

- Anyone who abuses children is a beast and should be locked away.
- A parent who knows that abuse is occurring but does nothing deserves to be punished.
- Victims of abuse deserve what they get.
- I would report child abuse only when I was absolutely certain that abuse was occurring.

With your instructor as moderator, organize a classroom debate on these questions and be prepared to defend your responses.

Dealing with the Caregiver's Emotional Response to Abuse

For people involved with early childhood care, abuse evokes many deep emotions. Some caregivers were themselves abused as children, or they witnessed the abuse of their parents or siblings. Coming into contact with an abusive parent, or a parent who allows abuse to occur, can trigger unresolved anger or feelings of helplessness. When this happens, it is very important to recognize and discuss these feelings with a counsellor or therapist. Even after successfully receiving treatment, people who have been abused often carry psychological wounds that require treatment at various times throughout their life.

For people who have not experienced abuse, it is sometimes difficult to understand or empathize with the abuser or the victim. Some people think, for example, "Why does she put up with that kind of treatment; why doesn't she just leave?" It is quite normal to have thoughts such as "Any person who would hurt his own child is a beast and should be removed from the face of the earth." We have, however, talked about acceptance, tolerance, and a nonjudgmental attitude as being the very essence of a helping profession. Accepting someone who abuses children is not easy for anyone to do, but it is especially difficult for those people who have chosen a career in early childhood education because of that strong commitment to children.

There is no easy solution to this dilemma. We maintain that it is important to remember several points. First, many people have the potential to become abusers. These include victims of abuse, people with limited coping and problem-solving skills, and people experiencing high levels of stress with few supports. Second, there are people who abuse, then feel deep sorrow, remorse, or feelings of failure (Tower, 1989). At the same time, however, they feel powerless to change their behaviour, and they often consider themselves to be victims of circumstance (Margolin, 1992). This is more common when women abuse or neglect their children (Tower, 1989). Accepting the perpetrator of abuse does not mean that we accept the abuse itself; it only means that we try to see him or her as someone in need of help, and who has the potential to be helped.

It is also sometimes very difficult not to blame an adult who is either a victim of abuse or does not actively prevent the abuse from happening. "How can she be so stupid?" we say. "Why doesn't she just leave?" "Doesn't she care about her children?" Again, while protecting the child has to remain our top priority, attempting to empathize with the victim or to understand the circumstances surrounding the situation is also important. Imagine what it would be like to live with such fear. Try to imagine how it would feel to have no safe place to run to. Try to imagine being raised in a situation where violence is considered normal. These and other considerations may help in developing empathy and may also help counter negative attitudes that we might hold against the adult.

Strong negative feelings towards the abuser, lack of sympathy for the victim, or even blaming the victim are common attitudes that interfere when working with families in which violence occurs. Once again, it is important to remind ourselves that developing empathy and understanding is a process that is an ongoing part of professional development.

Monitoring Potentially Abusive Situations

When an early childhood professional suspects that a child is being abused or neglected, it is crucial to monitor and document the situation consistently. Systematic monitoring will help establish patterns for symptoms of abuse or neglect that are not immediately obvious. For example, the appearance of a bruise may provoke further observation and monitoring but not necessarily a reporting of the incident.

We must also take care not to judge too hastily. For example, could the impression of neglect that we have formed be due to something as innocent as the child's desire for autonomy or the result of a simple lack of time on the parent's part? A boy may choose to wear summer clothing, such as shorts and a sleeveless top, in the middle of winter. We may misinterpret his quest for individuality here to mean that he does not have access to the appropriate clothing or that the parent is not paying sufficient attention to the child's well-being. Similarly, if a little girl arrives with her hair uncombed and face unwashed, this may be a result of nothing more than the parents' morning rush to work. When a child, however, is dressed in such a manner consistently or her hygiene is so neglected that it poses a risk to her health, this needs to be monitored closely. We must be careful to maintain our objectivity and ensure that we focus on behaviour or situations that pose a real risk to the child. A careful record of each sign of abuse, giving the date, time of observation, and an accurate description of the behaviour or symptom will be a crucial component of the assessment.

Bearing in mind that the well-being of the child is our primary concern, it is also crucial to note that often, if abusers suspect that they are being monitored, they may withdraw the child from the centre. This often prolongs the abusive situation, since it may then go undetected for some time before the next day-care centre observes a situation or pattern of behaviour. Therefore, it is often important not to let on that the child is being monitored or the abuse suspected until a plan of action has been determined. Being polite and acting as if all is well may not be easy, especially in light of the professional training that encourages open and honest relations with parents. Sometimes, however, this sort of conduct may be necessary and in the best interest of the child. During this time, seeking out and providing information or access to community supports may be crucial for this family.

Caregivers see young children every day. They see them in interaction with many different people, observe them as they engage in play, and often are involved in their personal care routines. From this vantage point, they can observe many things about the child. Caregivers need to document information on an ongoing basis in addition to making day-to-day observations. By doing this, the caregiver can make comparisons. For example, the caregiver is in a position to say whether the child is unusually passive or when the change of behaviour began. In addition, caregivers typically interact with a parent or parents on a regular basis. These interactions may also provide information regarding the relationship. Documentation will always be necessary if early childhood professionals plan to report their suspicions to the authorities.

Reporting

Child welfare legislation varies from province to province in Canada and is federally mandated in the United States. All states have mandatory reporting laws whereby professionals are required to report suspected cases of abuse to the child welfare authorities (Tower, 1989). In addition, legislation has been put in place that specifically protects individuals with disability at home or in care (e.g., Persons in Care Act in Alberta). Failure to do so can result in charges being laid against the child-care worker. In some places, complaints may be made on an anonymous basis. The authorities will then investigate and take further action if required. Some jurisdictions will require that the callers identify themselves, and in some cases caregivers are not legally bound to file a report. The intent of child welfare legislation also varies. In some areas, practices and procedures are in place to keep children within their families. The U.S. Adoption Assistance and Child Welfare Act of 1980, for example, is federal legislation that has the primary goal of keeping families together. Parents are given a period of time (e.g., eighteen months) to make efforts to get their lives in order or risk losing their children (Ingrassia & McCormick, 1995). Supports are provided to the family, and the child is only removed as a last resort.

In other areas, the legislation is written to protect children's immediate safety. In cases of suspected abuse, the child is removed from the home as soon as possible. When the courts deem that the family is ready, the child is returned to his or her parents. Laws and procedures vary from place to place. It is critical that early childhood professionals be aware of local policies in order to protect the children and themselves. In the United States, the National Centre on Child Abuse and Neglect, and in Canada, the National Clearinghouse on Family Violence coordinate and circulate information regarding child abuse. These organizations are good starting points for early childhood professionals to get more information.

The following box consists of an excerpt from the Alberta Social Services Protocols (1990), which provides one example of reporting practices in cases of suspected child abuse.

Reporting Protocol

When a person suspects a child is abused or neglected, the person must immediately report the situation to Child Welfare Services. Any person who fails to report is guilty of an offence and liable to a fine.

A person must report to Child Welfare Services regardless of how the information was obtained and regardless of advice or direction not to report.

Provide:

- name, age, birth date, sex, racial origin, and address of child concerned.
- names and addresses of parents or guardians.
- names and addresses of the alleged perpetrator (if known) and any other identifiable information about that person.
- full details of the incident or situation that precipitated your report. Try to be specific; include details, events, or behaviours that have caused concern. Include any previous dated documentation you may have collected.

No action will be taken against the person reporting unless the reporting is done maliciously or without reasonable or probable grounds for the belief.

Source: Alberta Family and Social Services, 1990.

It is not uncommon for staff to worry about repercussions after they report a case of suspected abuse. A report can lead nowhere or take a very long time until action results. Imagine what it feels like if you know that something is very wrong but, since it cannot be proven, nothing is done. Patience and careful observations can be most helpful in ensuring that this is not the case. In these situations, caregivers will require support from their peers and supervisors.

Responding to the Child's Disclosure of Abuse

It is probably a caregiver's worst nightmare when a child confides that a family member is doing mean things to him or her. How do you, as a caregiver, respond? We have seen what the professional response should be in regard to documenting and reporting, but how do you respond to the victim in your care? Early childhood professionals play an extremely important role in this regard. The child will have many needs at this time to which the caregiver will want or need to respond. At the same time, caregivers should be extremely careful when communicating with the child about abuse to ensure that the child does not receive the wrong message or that words are not put into the child's mouth. The box below provides several tips for the caregiver to use in this delicate balancing act.

Responding to a Child's Disclosure of Abuse

Remember these general guidelines:

1. Ensure that all children have the opportunity to form a meaningful relationship with a caring adult (Wallach, 1995). This can provide the opportunity for children to learn that there are people who care about them. Children may feel more comfortable about confiding in someone if this relationship is established.

2. If a child begins to tell you about an abusive incident, the first thing to do is to listen. It is very likely that the abuser will have told the child not to tell anyone because no one will believe the story anyway. By listening, you will let the child know that what he or she has to say is important. Listening may be enhanced by taking the child to a quiet place, away from the group, where you can listen without interruption.

3. Let the child tell you what has happened in his or her own words. Do not put words into the child's mouth by asking leading questions (e.g., "Did he hit you with his fist?"). If the incident is to be pursued by social workers or police, it will be questioned if the child uses an adult's vocabulary to describe events (Corwin, 1995).

4. Let the child know that you believe what he or she has said. Children rarely lie or make up details about abuse, particularly sexual abuse.

5. Reassure the child. Tell him or her that it was a good thing to tell somebody. Reassure the child that you will do something to help.

6. Do not make promises to the child. This may well be the hardest thing for the caregiver to do. Because caregivers feel a strong emotional bond and want to protect children from harm, their first reaction is to promise the child they will fix the situation. The professional must not promise the child that the abuse will not happen again or promise the child that they will not tell. Children will often begin their disclosure by saying that this is a secret and they will tell it only on that basis. The caregiver needs to let the child know that she will only tell to make sure that the child is helped and will only tell certain people (e.g., "I need to tell the director or the social worker, but I will not tell your mom"). Because this is so difficult for caregivers to do, it is important that they be aware of this potential hazard and of what their response might be. The consequence of making

---

and then breaking promises will be particularly devastating for the child who has already lost trust in adults closest to him or her. For the sake of the child, this must be avoided.

7. As difficult as this may be, it is important to remain calm and in control of your emotions. If you express disgust or horror, children may think that they cannot tell you all of the details or may interpret your reaction as your belief that the abuse was their fault (e.g., "How could this happen? How could someone do this to you?"). Acknowledge the information and the child's feelings without overreacting to the situation.

8. Involve the supervisor as soon as possible to determine what the next step will be. This may require that a report be filed or that the child welfare authorities be contacted. Knowing the local regulations before-hand and having documentation available will be helpful at this stage when emotions may be running high. Caregivers may also require support for themselves and shouldn't feel that they have to deal with this on their own. You can discuss your feelings with colleagues or friends without disclosing confidential information.

9. Document information on an ongoing basis.

10. If there are signs of severe abuse, call the police or child welfare authorities without delay.

Providing Ongoing Support to the Child

After the initial disclosure, early childhood professionals will have to be available to deal with the child for a long time to come. Sometimes disclosure is just the beginning of a long and stressful process for the child and the family. Caregivers must ensure that they provide care and support throughout this period. It is important that the environment remain as stable and consistent as possible, both in regard to the physical setting and in terms of routines and expectations. The child and family may be going through many changes, and a stable setting may be of the utmost benefit to the child at this time (Wallach, 1995).

It may be very important for children in this situation to be exposed to good role models so that they learn how to behave in nonviolent ways. Children will need to have contact with supportive adults who listen and allow them to express themselves. Having opportunities for self-expression in alternative ways such as art, music, and play will be beneficial as well. Again, in all of these strategies, early childhood professionals must be cautious and sensitive about how they approach and react to the child.

Working with Other Professionals

In situations of abuse, several professionals are usually involved, and it is vital to work effectively together. For example, doctors, social workers, psychologists, and counsellors may all be involved at some point. From the beginning, it is important to understand the role that each professional plays. Will the child welfare worker keep you informed? Does the therapist want observational data from you? How would the parent like you to be involved and in what ways? Early childhood professionals may be able to provide parents with resources and written materials either for their own use or for them to share with their child (e.g., books, stories, videos). The level and type of support expected from the early childhood professional should be clarified. The nature and degree of involvement required may change over time. Therefore, frequent communication between the different professionals may be necessary.

Ongoing Professional Development

All caregivers would certainly agree that abuse and violence in the home is the one issue that they hope they never encounter. Unfortunately, the statistics continue to rise and the likelihood of working with a child from an abusive or violent home is also increasing. Early childhood professionals can best assist if they are informed about local policies and practices and are prepared for such a situation. This may be accomplished through discussion within the agency, through workshops, or through guest presentations. When caregivers are trained and prepared, they will be more able to assist and to be supportive at a time when emotions are high and likely to interfere.

Accessing Expert Help

Adults who abuse children are in need of professional help that is beyond the scope of the early childhood professional. Caregivers must recognize, in any situation, when outside intervention is required and be prepared to refer families to qualified experts. Highly qualified therapists who have specialized in working with family violence have a good success rate in helping these families. However, it is important at the same time not to undervalue the role of the early childhood professional, who often has front-line contact with children and parents on a regular basis.

Preventing Abuse

One of the key roles of the early childhood professional is the prevention of abuse. This may happen in a number of different ways. Many programs are available to teach children to protect themselves from potential abusers. They provide advice on how to say no, how to report that they were approached, and how to avoid dangerous situations. These programs or kits have excited much controversy. Some say that they are necessary; others adamantly insist that the protection of children should remain the sole domain of their parents or guardians. The potential hazard with the kits currently in use is that they are not all developmentally appropriate.

Scenario

Stop, Danger!

A director in a day-care centre told how she reluctantly agreed to let an expert on preventing abuse speak to the children at her centre. The expert told the children that just like a red light means stop, danger, when someone touches you and it doesn't feel right, that is like a red light. The 4-year-olds listened intently. The next day, one of the caregivers came dressed in a red sweater. "Stop, danger!" exclaimed the children. They had understood that red means danger and the rest had gone over their heads.

Conclusion

Early childhood professionals can play a role in the prevention of abuse. Caregivers may act as role models for parents by demonstrating guidance, nonviolent discipline techniques, and ways of interacting with children. For example, they can demonstrate how to give the young child choices rather than expecting unquestioning compliance.

Early childhood professionals can also be of assistance by being aware of the child's family and of stressful events that might be occurring in their lives. Knowing, for example, that the father has recently lost his job can be the signal that there is the potential for additional stress within the family and that the family therefore needs more support. Developing and maintaining good parent–caregiver relationships before crises occur will be of the utmost importance in helping families feel comfortable in divulging such information.

As a caregiver, you may be able to create an atmosphere in which parents feel that they can confide in you when they are on the edge. Sometimes just being able to let off some steam may be sufficient, but there will also be times when families need extra help. Being familiar with community resources such as emergency shelters, relief homes, support groups, and telephone hotlines may be useful. If abuse is associated with other problems, other support groups and services may also be pertinent. These are the times when you may be called upon to go that extra mile to prevent a crisis (e.g., stay late, check out resources). When good relations exist, early childhood professionals can serve as an excellent support for children and their families.

Exercises

Based on the information from this chapter, review the following scenarios and discuss what a director of a day-care centre should do regarding reporting, responding to the child, and supporting the family.

Scenario

1

Bonnie (4 years old) came from a nice home. She attended the centre regularly, was well fed, and very well dressed. Her parents were reliable with their payments and followed up any of the centre staff's requests, but they had little involvement with the staff otherwise.

When Bonnie was at the centre, she was often apathetic and withdrawn. At other times, she would overreact or misbehave to get attention. One day, Bonnie confided in her caregiver that when she went home, she always ate, slept, and played in a closet so that she was out of Mommy and Daddy's way.

Scenario

2

Matt's mom, Mrs. Benning, was usually one of the last parents to pick up her child. She had to take a bus to the centre, pick up her son, and then take two more buses to get home. She was often very rushed and hurried to get Matt ready as soon as she got in the door.

One day, Matt wanted to show her what he had done at the art centre. Mrs. Benning stated that she had no time and told Matt to hurry up. Matt was deliberately moving very slowly towards his coat. Mrs. Benning became enraged and crossed the room yelling, "I'll show you what slow means!" and proceeded to spank him on his bottom five or six times. She then gave him a firm shaking, grabbed his coat, and dragged Matt from the room.

Scenario

3

The staff in the playroom for 3-year-olds have told you, the director, that Drew's mother has come to pick him up late three times this month. Each time, they could smell liquor on her breath. They ask you to stay in the playroom until she arrives this Friday after work. When she enters the room, it is obvious that she has been drinking, and she yells to Drew to hurry up because she's missing the party.

Scenario

4

Elaine is in the midst of a difficult separation from her husband. Her 5-year-old son, Shaun, has been unusually quiet and very reluctant to talk about what is happening at home. Late one afternoon, when most of the children have left, Shaun and the caregiver have just finished reading a story about a family of bears when Shaun remarks that he wishes his home was like that. When the caregiver asks him why, he explains that he wishes he could see his dad more and talk to his dad on the telephone and . . . At this point, his mother walks into the room and stares at Shaun. Shaun has a look of absolute terror on his face, covers his head with his arms, and then runs from the room in tears. Elaine states that the conversation is over and never to be brought up again and leaves.

Immigrant and Refugee Families

chapter 12

Objectives

- **To understand the demographic shifts in Canada as a result of migration.**

- **To understand the impact of war trauma and immigration on children and families.**

- **To understand the factors that influence adjustment and successful acculturation in Canada.**

- **To examine attitudes towards immigrants and refugees.**

- **To discuss ways in which the early childhood professional can support children and their families who are new Canadians.**

Ilana is the mother of a five-year-old girl who comes to a drop-in centre. Her husband was killed in the beginning of the war, and the family spent almost four years as refugees in another area of their country, sharing a small apartment with extended family members.

"It was a time of poverty, loneliness and sadness. Grief and loneliness seemed to be the only things I could feel. During our times as refugees, my daughter became extremely anxious when we were separated. She would cry at all times when I was out of sight. I wanted to look for work, or go to English classes, and tried to put my daughter in a day-care centre. Every morning, as we approached the centre, my daughter started to feel ill, cried and refused to stay. I was becoming so frustrated, and feeling a bit angry with my daughter.

"The staff at the centre helped me understand that my daughter had severe separation anxiety, as a result of the life we had led as refugees. My daughter really never had the opportunity to play, and we were always so tense. They helped me understand how important it was for me to let my daughter play, with me nearby. After a long time, she was O.K. if I left for a while. I can't believe that now I can leave for several hours, and my little girl lets me go. Sometimes she still fusses again, but I see other Canadian children behaving the same way. So I think that we are in a much better situation now. I am thankful for the help we received."

The cultural map of Canada has been changing considerably over the last few years. People immigrate to Canada for many reasons. For some, it is the opportunity to participate in, contribute to, and enjoy the economic and social opportunities that life in Canada affords. For others, coming to Canada is an opportunity to reunite with family and loved ones who have immigrated to Canada in the past. For others, Canada provides an escape and safe haven from war and other situations that are simply unimaginable to many Canadians. We will discuss in this chapter the demography of immigration, and the impact of immigration on children and families. Then we will consider the ways in which the early childhood professional can provide support to new Canadian families.

Immigrating to Canada

It is often difficult to imagine the experiences of New Canadians as they build their lives in Canada. Even under the best of circumstances, moving to a new location, communicating in a new language, and encountering a profusion of new sensations, experiences, and people can be simply overwhelming. Clark, Shimoni, Este, and Ksienski (1998) have described a number of risk factors faced by immigrant families. Some of these are the same risk factors that apply to many Canadian families, and some are unique to immigrants and refugees. However, as we have discussed in previous chapters, it is the intensity and number of risk factors facing a family at any particular time that we need to be concerned about. These risk factors include:

Underemployment or unemployment. Many immigrants to Canada arrive with education, experience, and professional qualifications from their home country. Due to a number of factors such as language barriers, different demand levels of occupations in various countries, and different criteria for qualifications, many immigrants do not find work in their own fields. For example, many of the immigrants who came from the former Yugoslavia during the past decade were highly trained engineers, technicians, or teachers. As one immigrant father told a staff member, "In Bosnia I wore a suit, carried a briefcase, earned a good salary, and came home from work feeling tired, but satisfied that I was doing important work, and providing well for my family. Here, I deliver pizza, but the truth is I am grateful to have any work at all." However, it is known that underemployment and unemployment can be quite devastating. The loss of the traditional role as breadwinner has been linked to ineffective or negative parenting and domestic abuse.

Role reversal. Often when new Canadians seek employment in Canada, women find jobs (often in child care or domestic realms) more easily than do their husbands. Therefore, in many immigrant families, the father becomes the primary caregiver of the children while the mother is at work. Some families find this "role reversal" very difficult, as fathers have not had the socialization or training to be the primary caregivers and nurturers of children.

Social isolation. Many immigrant Canadians left behind networks of family and friends. In their new country, feelings of isolation often intensify the social, psychological and economic pressures that they face. Immigrants are of diverse religious and cultural backgrounds. They often feel excluded from mainstream social events, and sometimes experience discrimination and exclusion. In addition, many refugees come from countries that were at war with each other, and, as a result, the clashes and hostilities that came with them to Canada further prevent community integration.

Barriers to helping services. There is a growing awareness of the barriers that prevent new Canadians from fully utilizing community and health services that offer support to individuals and families. An inability to communicate in English, lack of knowledge and information about services, perceptions that help is unavailable, or that professionals "won't be able to help them," fear of stigmatization and deportation, and lack of child care are seen as key barriers to accessing helping services. In addition, health professionals have suggested additional barriers such as fear of hospitals and clinics, lack of understanding on the part of professionals of immigrants' cultural background, and the inability of agencies to provide translators or workers who speak the first languages of the immigrants. While in recent years there have been many efforts made to improve the accessibility of services to diverse populations, barriers still exist.

English/French as a second language. Clearly, competence in the English or French language is necessary for success in Canada, and many efforts to help new Canadians focus on teaching and learning English. However, as pointed out by Chud and Fahlman (1995) people who required language training became labelled "ESL," much the same way that children were labelled "special needs." The skills, talents, and potential of the adult and child are often overlooked when the label "ESL" is applied.

Loss, grief, and depression. Espin (1992) has described the experience of uprootedness experienced by immigrants. This includes not only the obvious loss of country, way of life, and family, but also the more subtle pain caused by the absence of familiar smells, foods, and daily routines. The experience of uprootedness is inextricably linked with the realization that neither the old nor the new home is now fully home. Bylund (1992) has articulated the need to carefully examine the mental health status of people following migration. Depression has been noted as one of the most common problems among immigrants. This has a major impact on the childrearing capacity of immigrant parents who, for extended periods of time, may be emotionally unavailable to their children. In addition, studies on immigrants report that many cases of depression go undetected due to cultural barriers and inappropriate services.

Trauma induced by war or enforced refugee status. It is well known that families who have been affected by trauma events and refugees require special intervention and attention. Adults who have suffered these kinds of trauma appear to need to move through several stages as they seek to restore mental health after being uprooted and displaced. Overcoming the initial stigma of refugee status, acceptance of the refugee identity as self-identity, development of refugee pride, and then a transition from the refugee identity corresponding to the growth of a positive self-identity in the new country represent the primary stages refugees experience (Robertson, 1992). Immigrants and refugees need to deal with the impact of family separation and their concept of a family following their move to a new country. Gilan (1990) worked with several refugee families to identify characteristics common to different refugee situations. These characteristics included guilt caused by flights (this reaction is stronger in families that had to escape in secret), and trauma caused by the breaking apart and coming together as a family unit.

Effects of Refugee Experiences on Children

Young children who have experienced the trauma and horrors of war are often in need of extensive treatment and care. Imagine the impact of witnessing the torture or beating of a sibling, parent, or relative, of being moved from place to place to hide, and to go for days without shelter or food. These experiences, followed by a trying journey to a new and unfamiliar country, are overwhelming for children. Parents, who usually provide support for children in trying situations, may be so overwhelmed by their own reactions to trauma and grief that they are unable to provide the emotional support and security to their children. It is no wonder, then, that refugee children commonly display signs of chronic sadness. They may seem excessively fearful or shy, and many develop symptoms of school phobia. The opening scenario in this chapter portrayed a very common occurrence, that is, a heightened degree of separation anxiety that would under normal circumstances be seen as inappropriate for the age of the child. Regressive behaviour, learning disabilities, and poor school performance are often seen in refugee children. Hyper-alertness or hyper-aggressive behaviour is another common symptom.

Immigrant children who are not refugees will likely have experienced less severe trauma than what was described above. But they will have experienced the uncertainty, fear, and sadness associated with moving from their familiar setting to a new and strange country. As they grow up in their new country, many immigrant children experience conflict between the norms and values of their peers and their teachers, and those of their parents who maintain the beliefs and values of their country of origin. This is especially notable in the adolescent years.

Coping Strategies of Immigrant and Refugee Parents

The above description of the risk factors that apply to immigrant and refugee families may lead one to the mistaken conclusion that the odds are high against successful immigration. The truth, however, is just the opposite. After an almost inevitably difficult beginning, most immigrant families acculturate and become successful Canadian citizens. As with many of the issues facing families that have been described in this text, the appropriate support, at the appropriate time, when families have young children, can make a tremendous difference. For this reason, it is important to understand the risks facing immigrant families. It is equally important to understand differences in childrearing approaches and strategies so that we do not approach these families from an assumption of deficit. Effective support usually builds on the family's strengths.

Roer Strier (1999), after extensive work with immigrant and refugee families, has identified different frameworks that guide childrearing and coping strategies that evolve from these frameworks. If professionals who work with immigrant families and children understand these frameworks and strategies, they will be able to assess more effectively and less judgmentally the need for support, and be more effective in the provision of support.

Scenario

Different Strokes

Lee was doing his practicum in a family resource program in two locations in the city—one with predominantly young single mothers living in impoverished settings, the other with new immigrant families. One of his tasks was to plan play experiences for drop-in time, in both locations. For the young mother's group, he planned very open-ended activities that children typically worked on

> while their mothers interacted or attended support meetings. In the other location, the play experiences were totally different. Parents often stayed with their children and directed them in completing the tasks "right" for the "teachers." Parents often asked for models, sought clarification, and insisted children complete projects. They joined circle time to ensure their children paid attention and participated. Lee commented on the difference in his planning but how difficult this was for him since he really did not favour highly structured activities. However, he said that this was obviously important to those parents and that he would plan accordingly.

According to Roer-Strier (1999) each culture has an image of how children should be as adults. These images guide childrearing ideologies, perceptions, and values. For example, the image of a successful American adult may include being very independent, owning property, and having substantial wealth. This image guides childrearing practices in America. Gonzalez-Mena (1994) compared her own childrearing in America, and the way in which she raised her children, to childrearing in Mexico, where the image of a successful adult is more focused on family ties. Whereas American childrearing focuses on fostering independence, Mexican childrearing (as she concluded from observing her mother-in-law) was quite the opposite. Parents and grandparents constantly attempt to do things for the child, rather than encouraging the child to be independent (Gonzalez-Mena, 1994). As Gonzalez-Mena notes, this is not a matter of a right or wrong way of bringing up children. (In fact, she noted that the outcome of the Mexican-style upbringing on her husband produced a very independent adult.) It does illustrate, however, that the image (a very connected family vs. a very independent adult) correlated to different styles of upbringing.

When immigrants move from one culture to another, they can either preserve the image of a successful adult from their home country, or abandon it in favour of the image of the successful adult in their new country. In fact, it is never quite this clear cut. Many interrelated factors affect the image held by parents following immigration. But in each case, immigrant families have to find ways to cope with the different norms, expectations, and values regarding children that are prevalent in the new country, and that surface when they interact with professionals at preschool, school, and health and social services.

1. *The traditional unicultural style.* This has been referred to as the "kangaroo" style. It is seen as an attempt to protect children in a secure "pouch." Families who see themselves as their children's chief socializing agents, and who attempt to preserve the image of the successful adult from their home country, would fit this category. Outside influences would be seen as a threat to these families. Often, the confidence and consistency that these parents provide to their children provides a very secure base. Adherence to family roles, and family cohesion and support seem, in these families, to be related to less stress and less risk for parental mental health problems. However, this strategy taken to extreme does pose difficulties for children. If the children adhere to the family's standards, they may risk estrangement from their peers in their new country. On the other hand, if they choose to identify with the norms of the new country, they may feel that they are the object of disappointment.

2. *The rapid assimilation style.* The metaphor used for this strategy is the cuckoo-bird, whose offspring are cared for in the nests of other birds after the eggs hatch. Many immigrants will tell you that the prime reason they decided to immigrate to Canada

was to provide their children with the opportunity for a better life. Some of these immigrants believe that the faster their children adapt to Canadian norms, values, and behaviours, the easier it will be for them to succeed. In that case, they may see themselves as barriers to quick acculturation, and give up their role as the primary socializers of their children. Teachers and peers become the reference groups for their children. This approach in the extreme can result in a breakdown of family cohesion, and feelings of loss of control and helplessness. However, less extreme measures would result in fewer feelings of conflict in children as they adapt to a Canadian way of life, knowing that this is what their parents wanted for them.

3. *The bi-cultural style.* This strategy is represented by the chameleon metaphor, because of the chameleon's ability to change its colour to match the environment. Families characterized by this profile understand that there are major differences between the values and socialization practices of their former culture and the host society. They encourage the child to live peacefully with both cultures. The child is encouraged to behave, dress, eat, and talk like other children outside the home, while at home, the child is expected to behave, dress, eat, and talk according to the rules of "the old country." In these families, parents decide to share their role of socializer with the host culture's socializing agents, but do not give up their parental role. Families thus maintain their sense of control and family cohesion and are less at risk for anxiety and depression. Many children seem to navigate easily between the host and private cultures, and are protected from conflicting loyalties. Other children may find this "double life" difficult to manoeuvre.

The Meeting of Parental Styles with the Perceptions of Professionals

The attitude of professionals towards these different coping styles will impact their perception of the immigrant families and the kinds of relationships that will evolve. Roer-Strier (1999) found, not surprisingly, that many teachers seemed to prefer the "cuckoo-bird" strategy. This is not surprising because these parents would accept the authority of the teacher, and encourage the child to "fit in" with the expectations of the school, even if it is at the expense of his or her own culture. Social workers and educational psychologists were more concerned about this style, suggesting that it posed the greatest risk to the children's mental health. Pediatricians thought the "kangaroo" style proposed the most risk, as parents in these cases would rely more on their own beliefs about healing than on traditional medicine. Clearly, not only do countries have cultures, so do professions. In professions such as medicine, and perhaps education, the professional is considered the "expert." Therefore, the "cuckoo-bird" style fits well with that professional orientation. In fields such as early childhood and social work, where empowerment and self-actualization seem to be paramount, a socialization pattern that gives more power to the parents may be deemed more appropriate.

The "take-home" message from this description and analysis is this: Almost without exception, parents want their children to grow and develop to be successful adults. Parents who have immigrated to Canada may have very different ideas of what a successful adult is, and therefore will have different childrearing approaches and strategies. When they arrive in Canada and begin to interface with educational and other frameworks, they will develop strategies to cope with these differences. Some will hold dearly to the norms of their countries of origin, some will encourage the children to abandon these in favour of quickly becoming "Canadian," and others may attempt to help their children live successfully in both worlds. Usually these strategies are not seen in the extreme, but as general tendencies. There is no right or wrong way of making this adjustment to life in Canada. But if professionals understand these differences they will be better able to understand parents. The mother who doesn't come to parent meetings because she feels she has little to offer, and the teacher knows best anyway, is not acting out of lack of concern for her child. She may well believe that her non-involvement is in the very best interest of her child. Similarly, the parent who adamantly insists that his child should maintain customs and appearances that belong to the culture of their home country is generally doing this in the belief that it is in the best interest of his or her child. Therefore, rather than judging the behaviour of the parents and their approach to childrearing, it is vital to appreciate that there are differences that need to be respected and understood.

Scenario

Bridging the Gap

Shibana's parents immigrated to Canada before she was born. In some ways, they adapted to Canadian customs, but still held onto their cultural beliefs in other ways. When Shibana finished ECCE at college, her parents felt it was time that she marry and they began the search for a husband. Shibana felt caught but did agree to meet the many eligible suitors. After several years she decided to marry a man chosen by her parents who lived in the same city. Prior to her marriage, her colleagues at the child-care centre threw a very "traditional" bridal shower/stagette where many "marital aid" items were given as gifts. Shibana received all of the gifts good-naturedly but remarked that she was unsure what to do with all the gifts since they would be living with his parents, as expected.

The Role of Early Childhood Professionals

Working effectively with people from cultures very different from our own requires a willingness to examine our own values and biases. Much has been written about diversity education, and the importance of increasing the awareness and competence of Early Childhood Professionals in multiculturalism. While we can only touch on some of the principles in this chapter, we highly recommend that readers refer to the work of Chud and Fahlman (1995) on "honouring diversity." There are also many articles on multiculturalism in early childhood education in the professional journals. Answering the questions listed below in "Examine Your Attitudes" might help you clarify some of the areas that need further exploration.

- Is respecting parents more important than getting along with peers?
- Is it better to educate children in settings where boys and girls are together, or separate?
- Is it more important to adapt to "Canadian Ways" or to preserve your culture of origin?

There are no right or wrong answers to the above questions, although there would certainly be strong opinions that support one view or the other. If you do feel strongly about any of the above questions, it may be helpful to examine how your own cultural background influenced your opinion, and how and why a person from a different cultural background may have a different opinion.

Understanding and Empathizing

Providing support to children and families who are immigrants or refugees requires the ability to empathize with their difficulties. Try to imagine what young children who are refugees might feel like when

- They witness the torture or killing of a loved one.
- They live in fear and hiding.
- They see the fear and horror on their parents' faces, and don't understand why.
- They need to be "on the move" for days and weeks.
- They are hungry, exhausted, and confused.

Try to imagine the experiences of an immigrant child who

- Experiences strange smells, new sounds, and a very different home.
- Hears a strange language everywhere he goes.
- Meets new strange people.
- Doesn't see familiar people anymore, and doesn't understand why.
- Watches children behaving in very different ways from what she is used to.
- Sees and hears other children making fun of her because of the way she dresses or speaks.

Understanding the experiences of people who are victims of war is very difficult. You might want to watch a movie such as *Schindler's List* or *After the Rain*, and try to picture yourself in a similar situation.

Try to "feel" what a new Canadian might feel when

- People treat you as if you are stupid, because your English isn't perfect.
- You feel that you have no right to complain, because you will be told "if you don't like it, go back to your own country."
- You cannot work in your own profession, even though you have the appropriate education and experience.

- You cannot help your children with their homework, because the subject matter or the language was different in your home country.
- You want your children to get along well in Canada, but see them forgetting about the things that were so important to your parents and grandparents.

Scenario

Teaching Tolerance

Sharon, the caregiver, noticed that Miyoko was sitting in the corner of the playroom, and a tear was beginning to form in the corner of her eye. As she approached Miyoko, a little boy interceded. "Sharon," he said, "why does Miyoko talk funny?" "Miyoko doesn't speak funny, she speaks differently than you do," responded Sharon. "You speak English like your mom and dad. It is okay to ask questions about what Miyoko is saying, but it is not okay to say that she sounds funny because that can hurt her feelings."

Source: Adapted from Teaching Young Children to Resist Bias, Louise Derman-Sparks, NAEYC, Washington, D.C.

Providing support to parents

There are a number of ways in which you can provide support to parents who are immigrants and refugees:

- Provide them with easily accessible information about relevant resources. This would include information on preschools, day care, health services, social support and recreational services.
- Provide information in first languages. Many immigrant-serving agencies translate brochures, posters, and handouts into a number of first languages. This is extremely helpful to parents who are struggling to learn English.
- Make extra efforts to include newcomers in programs. Don't assume that, because they don't speak English, their knowledge is limited. Provide opportunities for parents to participate and contribute to programs. Just because someone doesn't know English, it doesn't mean they can't play a musical instrument, design a cover for your newsletter on the computer, or contribute in a variety of other ways.
- Bring representatives of other agencies to the centre to meet with parents. The community nurse, or social worker, could make a short presentation at a parent evening. It may be easier for parents to make contact with new agencies after meeting these professionals at a familiar place.

Children who are new Canadians can be helped by caregivers in a number of ways as well:

- Provide opportunities for staged entry into the program. As many immigrant and refugee children may feel very insecure in a new setting, particularly if they do not speak English, they may need to spend a lot of time at the centre with their parents.
- Learn a few key words in the first language of the children. "Dolly," "lunch," "book," and a few phrases such as "Good Morning" may make a child feel at home.

- Find symbols that represent their home country and culture. Parents will be able to help you or perhaps bring something from home, that will make New Canadian Children feel that the centre is their home away from home.

- Ensure that you are familiar with, and respect, the dietary laws. If possible, provide food and snacks that the child might be familiar with. (This is educational for all the children at the centre.)

- Be patient, and work hard to develop a trusting relationship with the child. Children may be wary of new people in their lives, especially when they do not understand the language you speak. Try to be nearby, and watch for opportunities to provide support, or to show the child something interesting. Gradually, a relationship will form.

Conclusion

Working with children and families who are new to Canada involves many of the same considerations as with any child and family. Understanding, empathy, and some special efforts to understand their culture, and to assist them in learning about life in Canada, can have a lasting positive impact.

Exercises

1. Oftentimes playrooms are multicultural and include families from diverse cultural and religious backgrounds. How will you accommodate the different, and sometimes conflicting, perspectives and requests in your playroom (e.g., food requests, celebrations)?

2. Review the "messages" a visitor to your centre would receive about culture. Look at toys, books, equipment and decorations, and information brochures and pamphlets on display. What cultures are represented? What would you change?

3. Consider different strategies that you might use if children and/or their parents do not speak English or French?

4. What are some of the resources available to new Canadian families in your community? How will you communicate this information?

5. What resources are available in your community to help staff work more effectively with New Canadians (translation services, multicultural training, etc.)?

Families and chapter 13
Resilience

Objectives

- **To understand some of the challenges facing families who adopt children.**

- **To understand some of the issues and challenges facing families with same-sex parents.**

- **To develop an awareness of the concept of resilience.**

- **To understand the role of the early childhood professional in promoting resilience in children and in families.**

> A nursery school teacher was engaged in a circle time discussion with her group of four-year-old children. The topic of discussion was "family" and who the members of their families were. Millie offered, "I have two mommies—my mom and my new mom, Shelly, that came to live with us this summer." Ferez jumped up and said, "Hey, I have two moms, too—I have my real mom and I have the mom that I live with now. We are the same!" The teacher was pleased with the discussion but, at the same time, it led her to reflect on the diverse types of families that her children are part of.

The preceding chapters in this book have reviewed and discussed issues affecting large numbers of Canadian families. We attempted to provide information that will help caregivers understand the potential impact of various family situations on children and parents so that they can provide appropriate support. Feedback that we have received from students and instructors has requested that we cover additional topics relating to families. Although some of these topics may not be as widespread as those covered in previous chapters, they touch many Canadian children and families.

Okun (1996) has estimated that close to 50 percent of families today are nontraditional families. Many nontraditional families (such as same-sex parents and adoptive parents) face unique challenges (Okun, 1996). Some of these challenges relate to the discomfort of feeling different or devalued. We need to understand and appreciate the unique approaches to family life, and the ways in which individuals and families cope with the reactions and restrictions that society has placed on those that challenge traditional values and structures. As professionals, it is important to understand the social context of all families, in order to provide appropriate support, and to work towards changing societal views that may impact children negatively. This approach—one of support and change—is congruent with both the family-centred and ecological perspectives presented in this book.

This chapter will review issues facing families headed by same-sex couples, and families who have adopted their children. While these subjects may seem unrelated, they share common elements. First, many of these families deal with negative societal views, lack of understanding, or discrimination. Second, the particular issues facing these families can become stressors that, like all stress factors, can impede positive child-parent relations and healthy child development. Third, if we work towards increased understanding and the elimination of stigma and prejudice, and provide appropriate support when and if required, children in these families can thrive. Remember that the issues facing families are often interrelated: an immigrant family may also be a blended family; gay couples can also be adoptive parents. It is equally important to remember that not all families that are described in this (and previous) chapters necessarily require support. Many families survive and thrive in spite of the potential and actual stresses in their lives. The intent of this chapter is to raise awareness of issues that may affect some families and assist in developing our understanding so that we may develop resilience in families. The latter part of the chapter is devoted to a discussion of the concept of resilience. The notion of resilience has been gaining importance in understanding and caring for children and provides a conceptual framework or potential strategies that caregivers may use in their practices with young children.

Adoption

Scenario

Walking on Eggshells

Two-year-old Jonah's mother watched his temper tantrum with an exasperated look on her face. "Jonah, Mommy has to go to work now.... Sarah (the caregiver) will help you take off your coat when you have settled down." After she left, Sarah commented to her supervisor that she is very careful about what she says to Jonah's mom. "I worry that when I say anything that may seem critical to her, she may think that her parenting is being scrutinized more closely because Jonah is adopted."

Several questions arise from the above scenario. The first is whether Jonah's temper tantrum has anything at all to do with the relationship between him and his adoptive mother. The second question is whether or not the caregiver's perception is accurate and her well-intended caution is warranted, or whether the caregiver's assumption that Jonah's mother may be more defensive than other mothers is based on a stigma associated with adoption. Whatever the truth of the matter, the fact is that there was an unhappy child, an unhappy mother, and a caregiver whose communication with the mother may have been hampered by concerns relating to adoption.

There is a large body of research that has investigated the effect of adoption on children's development. Although some studies that have suggested that adopted children have a higher degree of difficulty than children who are raised with their biological parents, other studies do not support this view (Borders, Black & Pasley, 1998). The fact remains that children and parents in adoptive families still face stigma that may cause extra pressure or stress in their lives.

Adoption is a complex process and experience. There are three sets of participants in every adoption: the birth family, the adoptive family, and the adoptees. Members of this adoption triangle may share some feelings and experiences but they also differ in what and how they experience adoption. "Each individual brings a unique set of biological and psychological propensities and characteristics to the process" (Okun, 1996, p. 24).

The last two decades have seen changes in the number of adoptions, the dynamics of and process for adoption. During the 1980s, domestic adoptions decreased by 47 percent (Wilson, 1997). Today, waiting lists for adoptions in many places range from seven to twelve years. This situation results from several factors. Fewer infants are available for adoption because of the high rate of abortion, an increase in support services for young parents, along with decreased stigma associated with single or teen parenting. In conjunction, the reported incidences of infertility have increased, which in turn is correlated with the increased demand for adoption. Often, couples choose international adoptions due to the lack of domestic adoptions available. Thus, adoption is not a new phenomenon, but its dynamics have changed.

Myths About Adoption

Many myths exist about adoption. Ask yourself and others whether the statements below are true or false. This will give you an indication of some of the prevalent misconceptions about adoption:

- The majority of children are adopted at birth.
- Adopted children experience lifelong difficulties.
- Birth mothers will forget about the child and the adoption process.
- Adoptive parents never feel the same way about adopted children as natural children.

These myths come from a long-standing belief or assumption that adoption is the "second-best route to parenthood" (Okun, 1996, p. 26). Adoptive families are in a precarious situation because of this "second-best" idea. Many feel that they have failed due to their inability to conceive their own children, and then they fail again because their adoptive family is only "second best." Adoptive parents often must deal with complex feelings about their infertility which are complicated by the assumption that a biological tie is a prerequisite for bonding and attachment. To make matters worse, adoptive children were sometimes considered inferior because they have an uncertain or unknown genetic past. Because of these stereotypes, many adoptive families have never felt truly comfortable in seeking assistance and, for the most part, have dealt with issues on their own.

Preconceived notions can interfere with our understanding of the experiences that each individual may have or share. However, awareness of the myths and misconceptions that exist may help professionals empathize with adoptive families and support children whose lives may be affected by these myths.

Open and Closed Adoption

Until the 1970s, formal adoptions were typically closed. The basis of a closed adoption was secrecy. Typically, the birth mother had "made a mistake" that had brought shame to her family. She was instructed to give up the child because that was "best for the baby" and forget about the matter. It was thought that if a birth mother received no information about the child and the adoption, she would be better able to get on with her life and forget about this mistake. Birth mothers usually kept their pregnancy a secret. Adoptive parents were given little to no information about the child's history and records were often sealed. Looking back on those times, it seems that denial of the child's background was used as a strategy to encourage the development of a primary attachment between the child and the adoptive family. The adopted child was thus given a chance at a "normal" family. Adopted children were told that they were chosen and therefore special. Many were never told at all. They were thus expected to suffer no consequences. Social workers were in place to select the best-suited family for any given child. Many believed that this process was best for all involved. The birth mother was helped to relinquish her child, she could grieve for the loss of her child, and the bonding and attachment between the child and adoptive family would be secured.

In the past two decades, several factors have resulted in pressure to change adoption policies and procedures. One factor has been the decrease in availability of healthy babies for adoption. Advances in psychological theories, particularly those related to attachment, have led to questioning the total lack of involvement of the child's biological family. Further advances in the study of genetics and medicine have highlighted the importance of knowing one's family history. In addition, professionals have suggested that secrecy and anonymity actually created difficulties for all parties involved. For example, secrecy can disrupt the child's development of trust and capacity for intimate relationships.

The result has been a trend towards open adoptions. In an open adoption process, birth parents and adoptive parents meet, exchange information, and potentially, carry on a relationship. The extent of "openness" within the adoption can range from minimal to a continuous long-term relationship. Open adoption is relatively new, but it has been gaining popularity in Canada and the United States. To date, open adoptions have been the subject of many novels and movies, but we have little research data to inform us as to the advantages and the problems that may ensue.

Scenario

Adoption Adjustment

Susan and her husband had tried to get pregnant for many years. They had tried a variety of fertility treatments and lived through the emotional roller coaster of unsuccess for too long. Around this time, a church member, feeling overwhelmed by being a single parent to a 6-year-old boy and 4-year-old girl, decided to put them up for private adoption through the church. Susan and Mark were absolutely delighted by this possibility, yet frightened at the potential task that lay ahead. They went to the interview and were selected by the birth mother. Then the fun began. The children moved in and everyone began the process of transition. There were questions—what to call their birth mother? what was the role of the birth mother? Over time, routines were developed and transitions made, sometimes difficult, sometimes joyous, but there was always the feeling that they were treading softly on new territory.

Age of Placement

It has long been assumed that the age of placement plays a role in the success or failure of an adoption.

Infants

A major concern for younger infants is related to bonding and attachment. Many factors can impact the child's ability to form a healthy attachment. Stresses related to the pregnancy and relinquishment of the baby, the age the child was relinquished, and the child's temperament are all factors in the development of the bond between the child and the adoptive parents. The child's ability to trust may be disrupted if there are multiple placements. Clearly, the expectations of the adoptive parents, their understanding of the child, their parenting skills, and often their persistence and determination will all play an important role. Until quite recently, these issues of attachment and multiple placements or age of placement have not been considered. Nowadays, more attention is being paid to how all of these factors facilitate both the parents and the child's adjustment to the adoption.

Preschool-age children

The child's awareness and understanding of adoption changes with maturation. During the early years, young children are learning about themselves and their world. It is often during this time that they come to learn that they have been adopted. Children are curious and ask questions and search for information. Through this process, they may come to realize that adoption is not typical, that they are not like everyone else. Given the child's mode of pre-operational thinking, they may experience confusion. The manner in which children are told about their adoption, and reassured of their parents' love, assists in their developing understanding (Garanzini, 1995). Confusion may resurface in adolescence when the individual is struggling with issues of identity and origin.

Scenario

Who Am I?

Dariel was adopted into a loving family as an infant. She recalls her parents explaining to her and her brother that they were adopted—what that meant and that they were special because they were chosen. Her parents explained this when she was six years old and she recalls feeling special. However, when she became an adolescent she said she began to question this—if you chose me, someone else chose not to keep me. This led to questioning of her identity and to a firm resolution to search for her birth mother so she could feel reassured. She contemplated initiating a search but, always sensitive to the reaction of her parents, she put it off and put if off. Her birth mother initiated a search when Dariel was in college. Although excited about this, Dariel was also unsure about proceeding.

School-age children

Children who have been adopted past the preschool age typically have had more adjustment difficulties related to adoption than those adopted as infants (Okun, 1996). These children have often experienced several disruptions in foster placements or previous adoption attempts. This contributes to later adjustment difficulties. Difficulties in adoption placements are associated with increased age of the child; the number of previous foster placements or adoption attempts; history of abuse, neglect or severe illness (Okun, 1996). There has been insufficient attention to the special needs of older adoptive children and their families. It has been assumed that a nurturing home environment will be sufficient.

> *Thus, some children who have been damaged by their early experiences may not be the most suitable candidates for adoption. Yet, because of the pressures for permanent placement, they may be unwisely placed. At the same time, some agencies do not provide adequate preparation and support for the necessary transition between foster care and adoption; they may not disclose full information about the child's past experiences and difficulties. And, after adoption, necessary follow-up and support services are not in place. (Okun, 1996, p. 27)*

An Optimistic View of Adoption

A recent study (Borders, Black & Pasley, 1998) conducted with adoptive families presents a different perspective. The authors suggest that many research studies have been based on a deficit model or pathological view. This means that problems are assumed and then a group of participants is selected to determine if the assumption is valid or the problem exists. In an attempt to counteract this, the authors selected a nationally based sample including all types of adopted families, not just those presenting problems. They focused their research on family functioning, not dysfunction. Their results suggest more normal/typical patterns of parenting and children's behaviour. Adopted children were not found to be at risk, there were few differences between adopted and non-adopted children in behaviour, nor were there increased difficulties with parents.

These results have particular relevance for adoptive families and the professionals interacting with children and parents. However, there is an important message for caregivers and other professionals. It is critical to read research carefully—if a study has been commissioned to study a deficit or problem, the participants and method will be chosen accordingly. If the premise of the research is that a family is considered normal/typical, these types of families will be chosen and more normal/typical behaviours will likely be studied and be found. This holds true for practices as well—labelling families and searching for difficulties may focus our attentions or direct our practices in counterproductive ways. Caregivers need to be mindful of this in their beliefs, in reading the research, and in their practices.

Role of the Early Childhood Professional

Adoptive families face many challenges—many similar to those faced by other types of families, others that are unique. Prevalent societal views have led to enormous pressures on adoptive families and at the same time have made them reluctant to ask for help, as this would reinforce the "second best" notion. In conjunction with the lack of resources available, many families have repressed and denied any problems that might exist. Early childhood professionals can play a very important role in supporting adoptive families. We must first examine attitudes that we may have about children or families.

In order to support adoptive families, we must first learn to differentiate between facts and myths, and critically examine new information that will help us better understand adoptive families. We can support families by actively working to diffuse myths and stereotypes. Then we can apply our understanding of children and child development to help children understand their own situations, and to take pride in their families.

Same-Sex Families

Scenario

Assumptions

Sarah came to her preschool accompanied by an adult who was not familiar to the caregiver. "Hello," she said, "I'm Jordana, Sarah's new stepmom." "Pleased to meet you," said Madhu, Sarah's caregiver. "I didn't realize that Sarah's dad had remarried." "He hasn't," said Jordana, "I am Sarah's mother's partner." When Jordana saw how uncomfortable the situation was for Madhu, she smiled and said, "Don't worry, this happens all the time."

In North American society, same-sex relationships evoke more intense negative and controversial reactions than any other kind. Basically, heterosexual is considered normal while homosexual is considered abnormal or deviant. Accordingly, homosexuals as individuals and as families continually live with extraordinary pressures. Although there is great diversity among parents who are same-sex partners and their children, they often share the same trauma living with homophobia. Homophobia can be characterized as conscious or irrational values, and behaviours or fear and intolerance of homosexuals. Homophobia in our society has resulted in oppression and marginalization of homosexual people. While many gay people take pride in who they are, and advocate for societal change, the effects of oppression and marginalization on the identity and self-concept of those who do not conform can cause people to feel shame, alienation, or even self-hatred. Same-sex couples and their children are at risk of isolation, prejudice, discrimination and invisibility in relation to society as a whole.

In 1989, it was estimated that there were over 1.5 million lesbian mothers and 1.3 million gay fathers in the United States (Okun, 1996). The number of children raised in gay or lesbian homes was estimated at between 6 to 14 million. It has been suggested that there are close to 400,000 gay parents in Canada (Wilson, 1997). However, these are only estimates as many parents are not open about their sexual orientation due to fears of rejection and the risk of discrimination in their communities and workplace (Tasker & Golumbok, 1997). In the past, most parents kept their sexual orientation a secret because of real fear of losing their children. Custody battles were typically swayed by sexual orientation. In custody battles between heterosexual parents, the mother is most often awarded custody of the children. When the mother is lesbian, custody is commonly denied.

Typically, homosexual individuals do not have access to the same supports that many other groups take for granted. In many jurisdictions in Canada and the United States, homosexual couples are not entitled to marry. These relationships are viewed as temporary and the bond less stable than between heterosexuals. Without public policy and the law to protect relationships, partners are denied rights such as community property or inheritance. In the event of separation, there may be a denial of custody or parental rights (Erera & Fredriksen, 1999). There is a general absence of religious or societal bonds and rituals along with the absence of public policy or law. We are seeing positive changes in this regard. Some corporations now give "paternity leave" or parental leave to women who are co-rearing a child. While the title "paternity" for a woman parent still implies a heterosexual model, the recognition of same-sex families as families is encouraging.

Myths and Stereotypes

Generally speaking, gay and lesbian parents encounter all the same problems as other families. In addition, however, they may encounter barriers related to prevalent myths and stereotypes about homosexuals. Homophobic attitudes can lead to the suggestion that gay or lesbian parents may be inferior or dangerous parents. There may be irrational fears that the child will be sexually molested. More typical fears include the belief that the gender and sexual identity of the child will be affected or deviant, that the child will grow up to be homosexual and that the children will be subjected to harassment by peers and be ostracized. Further myths suggest that lesbian mothers may lack the maternal instinct to mother and that children are at a higher risk for AIDS.

Lack of Support

Scenario

Two Mommies

Leila left an abusive relationship with her two young children. Two years later she moved in with Patricia—a loyal friend who had been a support through her divorce. Their relationship grew and developed until they decided to be together and hoped some day to marry. Four-year-old Jenna and 3-year-old Parker were delighted—Patricia was fun, energetic, and had always been there for both children. The children felt this was very natural. However, they did not understand why Patricia couldn't go to Nana's and Papa's house or why Nana and Papa always said bad things about Patricia or said God wouldn't let Patricia or Mommy into heaven.

The lack of social supports and financial benefits for gay couples may cause strain, which can ultimately affect the family's cohesion and longevity (Okun, 1996). Extended family members may not be accepting of gay couples and this can result in a lack of support.

In custody disputes, the sexual orientation of the homosexual parent typically becomes the focus rather than the best interests of the child. On that basis, the courts are still likely to remove the child from homosexual or lesbian parents.

> *Lesbian families experience stigma, homophobic stereotypes, discrimination, and prejudice. . . . These are expressed in the legal system that denies lesbian mothers child custody and visitation rights. . . . and in persistent beliefs, contrary to empirical evidence, that being raised in a lesbian family may adversely affect the social, psychological, or sexual and gender role development of the child. (Erera & Fredriksen, 1999, p. 26)*

Debunking the Myths

The reality is very different from the myths described above. Same sex parents are often deeply committed to creating a strong family with love and security. Lesbian and gay parents who overcome society's barriers tend to be highly motivated and very committed parents. Because of their own struggles with marginalization, they are very sensitive to diversity and help to foster the development of tolerance in their children. Lesbian mothers have been characterized as being just as warm, responsive, nurturing and confident as heterosexual mothers. Lesbian mothers often develop extended family ties within the lesbian community that provide support. They more typically find male friends to act as role models for their children and generally maintain better relations with their ex-husbands (or the child's biological fathers) than do heterosexual mothers.

Studies commonly suggest that children of same-sex couples are healthy. Those children who report stress from homophobia often report a greater sense of well-being, feel more sensitive, loveable and emotionally responsive (Okun, 1996). The assumption that children will experience more emotional or behavioural difficulties, more psychiatric disturbances or less self-esteem have all been shown to be invalid (Tasker & Golumbok, 1997). Children with gay fathers or lesbian mothers, like all children, live in unique family situations that require the development of coping strategies and may need help sorting out feelings about homosexuality and resulting confusion or anxieties but, for the most part, are adjusting well.

There is a commonly held view that children of same-sex couples will be teased and ostracized by their peers. It is surmised that this will cause distress for the child and interfere with the child's ability to build or maintain friendships. Children may be impacted by the need for secrecy, the fear of exposure and social isolation. Certainly some children may experience this, but studies have suggested that no differences in friendships were evident or that the experience of being teased or ostracized was significant.

Different Is O.K.

Julia noticed that 5-year-old Benedict was not playing with the other children as much as he had been. This was a change since Benedict had always been involved with 3-4 boys in her playroom. One day, Julia approached him while he played alone with the Lego. "Can I play with you?" she asked. "I guess so," answered Benedict. They played together in silence for some time and Benedict offered, "They're mean to me you know. They say it's stupid to have two moms and no dad." Julia knew that the situation had occurred over the summer but had no idea of its impact in her playroom. Julia talked to Benedict about teasing and then decided to plan some activities around families and all the different kinds of families, with the message that different is O.K.

Again, there may be children who experience some difficulties—some that may result from living in a home with same-sex parents and some that stem from other issues in the family. Some children are born into homes with same-sex parents but most have been born into a heterosexual marriage and may be experiencing the effects of separation and divorce (Tasker & Golumbok, 1997) in addition to adjusting to their new family.

The Role of the Caregiver

Early childhood professionals can play a vital role in the inclusion of same sex couples and their children. The same strategies that have been suggested in other chapters are relevant here as well. Make sure that pictures, books, and other materials reflect the diversity of the families in the centre—including gay families. An examination of our own attitudes is crucial here. In a society that has deemed homosexual people as deviant, or ill, for generations, it is understandable that fears and stereotypes persist.

Do you have strong beliefs about
- homosexuals or lesbians?
- homosexuals or lesbians
  - marrying?
  - having children?
  - having custody of children?
  - adopting or fostering?

If you hold beliefs about any of these issues, you need to consider how this may affect your behaviour, in particular, your interactions with parents and children in your care.

If you are uncomfortable with the notion of same-sex parents, take the time to educate yourself, both in terms of knowledge and attitudes. As with many minority groups, people often prefer to be asked direct questions respectfully, rather than to feel that people are uncomfortable in their presence. So ask, if appropriate, "What does Sarah call her mother's new partner? How are the parenting responsibilities shared? What help/support can we offer? Corbett (*Young Children,* March, 1993) summarizes the role of Early Childhood Professionals quite clearly:

> *If we treat all parents with respect and remember that anyone we meet may be homosexual, we could go a long way toward alleviating suspicion, bigotry, and the enormous pain deposited upon the gay community by the straight world. . . . As early childhood professionals, we weave the fabric of tomorrow. . . . Let us be brave enough to confront this great knot of prejudice. Homosexuals. . . . [are] deserving of all rights and courtesies we accord to others. We owe it to gay educators. We owe it to gay parents. We owe it to tomorrow's gay adults. And we owe it to ourselves.*

Resilience

We have reviewed some of the factors important in developing an understanding of how the child may comprehend their world and particular situations in their lives. Our role in interaction with the child is the dimension we will now consider.

The concept of resilience (Drummond, Kysela, McDonald, Alexander & Fleming, 1998) provides a useful starting point in conceptualizing the role of the caregiver in situations like the ones described in this chapter. Have you ever wondered how two siblings— in exactly the same situation—interpret and deal with the same life event in totally different ways? Part of the answer may be resilience—the ability to bounce back in the face of adversity. Drummond et al. (1998) define resilience as the "capability of individuals, families, groups, and communities to adapt successfully in the face of risk" (Steinhauer, 1996, p. 3). Researchers have identified several key factors associated with resilience:

- Availability of someone special in a trusting relationship
- Temperamental or personality characteristics of the child
- Ability of the child to seek out someone to help
- Warm, secure family relationships
- Supportive, predictable environments
- Development of coping strategies
- Individuals who listen
- Children who have a sense of control over their own life and are provided some degree of control

Resilience involves the balancing of two factors (Drummond et al., 1998). Firstly, it involves a reduction of risk factors. This means that it is important for early childhood professionals to understand the risks that exist with a particular child or family and attempting to assist in reducing these. This may be as simple as helping parents to find child care after hours or may involve accessing community support services for parents and families. The other factor in resilience is enhancing protective factors (Drummond et al., 1998). Protective factors may be within the individual (e.g., promoting health, self-esteem, self-efficacy, a feeling of control, social competence), within families (e.g., developing communication, effective parenting, providing supports or coping strategies), and within communities (e.g., developing a sense of community, increasing access to services). Resilience can be enhanced by assisting in the development of protective factors while attempting to control or decrease risk factors that exist.

Recently, the role of good quality child care has been discussed as one potential solution to serving children at risk. Cleveland and Krashinsky (1998) suggest that a myriad of changing societal factors (e.g., dissolution of family, increasing number of women in the work force) has left an increasing number of children at risk. Their literature demonstrated that quality child care has developmental benefits for "ordinary" children, compensatory benefits for children at risk and developmental benefits for all.

Cleveland and Krashinsky (1998) conclude by stating that good child care may outweigh costs by a two-to-one ratio. The benefits are not purely economic—they are seen in the healthy children and healthy families. This new trend toward the role of child care in healthy development must be taken seriously by caregivers. The responsibility of providing good quality child care will have lasting benefits to children and families.

Perspectives

Maureen was completing a diploma in Early Childhood Education and Care when she related this story about her life to us.

Maureen lived with two younger brothers in a home characterized by poverty, alcoholism and abuse. She remembers not having enough to eat at home—she would go to school and help the lunchroom supervisor to clean up but what she really wanted was to eat the leftover food. She recounted incidents of absolute terror and abuse in her home. Some of these incidents were directed at her, but many were directed at her brothers as well. She talked about how she would try to rescue her brothers and then would become the target of abuse herself.

Maureen told of how she tried to tell her teachers what was happening at home. Teachers in her elementary years ignored her disclosures, suggesting that she had an overactive imagination. In high school, she began to experience serious academic and social problems. She was sent to a counsellor and again told him what had been happening at home. He, too, suggested that she was exaggerating for attention and told her that if it was really that bad, she should call Child Welfare. Maureen said that she had never known that there were people out there who believed children and so she called. Child Welfare investigated and removed her from the home, although they found insufficient evidence to remove her brothers. She claims that her brothers were so terrified of their father, they would not even tell the child welfare authorities.

After this, Maureen was moved to foster care and group homes, and went through a period of rebellion including drugs, sex, and anything with a dangerous element. I asked her when all this changed and she offered the following:

"At one point, I was living in a house with a bunch of people. One of the ladies there had a three-year-old daughter, Sadie. She was so sweet and I began to wonder how this little girl would grow up with all these different people coming and going, being shipped off to the local day care every day from seven o'clock in the morning to six at night. Because I wasn't working at the time, I offered to pick her up and drop her off. Then I began to spend more time with her there. Sadie's caregiver, Margaret, was a young single mother who was just finishing off high school and hoping to go to college. We began to talk about how difficult her life was with two young boys and how she had had to struggle and work so hard to get where she was. She was so proud of what she had done and how she had done it. I looked at myself and thought, 'What a loser,' but then I looked at Sadie and Sadie's caregiver and thought, 'I can do this too.' I asked Margaret where she was finishing off high school and about her plans for college. Not only did she bring in reams of information for me, she took me along to the college when she went to register and helped me register for the English and Math courses that I needed. She gave me so much support in those first few months. It was the first time that I ever felt like somebody because Margaret cared about me. I did eventually finish high school and did enrol in the child care program at the college. I have remained friends with Margaret and I try to help her out sometimes, too. I don't even want to think of where I might be if Margaret had not taken those few extra minutes to make me feel like I mattered."

Caregivers are in a unique position to promote resilience. The following guidelines may be helpful in fostering resiliency.

- *Learn to identify risk factors and protective factors.* Caregivers may become aware of and attempt to alleviate risk factors in children or families and promote protective factors, for example, by focusing on and enhancing social competence of children, by noticing and listening to children, by acknowledging their feelings, by structuring activities for cooperation rather than competition.

- *Model coping behaviours.* Caregivers may model how to cope in positive, healthy ways.

- *Help children differentiate between reality and fantasy as they become developmentally ready to understand.* Use short but accurate explanations. Art, stories and books, and dramatic play can be used to promote discussion with children about complex and emotionally laden issues.

- *Become a special, caring person in the life of a young child.* Non-family members, such as teachers, coaches and counsellors, can often cushion a child from the adverse effects of a disturbing family situation. The presence of an adult who provides sensitive caregiving has been linked with adaptive functioning later in life (Heller, Larrieu, D'Imperio & Boris, 1999).

- *Practise responsive care-giving.* Provide opportunities for the child to develop confidence in the support others provide, to develop confidence in themselves, to view themselves as worthy, and to experience a sense of mastery of their world. The importance of this position cannot be overstated.

- *Be a good source of information for the child.* Caregivers may be in a unique situation to provide information in a clear and less emotional way (e.g., why some mommies give their children up for adoption) and provide support to the child (e.g., providing a better way to dealing with the hurt than hitting or acting out).

- *Support parents.* Caregivers can be instrumental in supporting parents in understanding the child's view and providing support at home (e.g., helping the parent to understand that the preschool will ask over and over in their attempt to understand, not because they don't understand or because they are trying to drive the parent crazy). Caregivers will need to work together with parents as situations arise to ensure that the child comes to understand and learns to cope.

- *Engage in professional development.* By broadening your own understanding and knowledge, you will be better prepared to deal with difficult situations, such as substance abuse in the family, or your possible discomfort with homosexual parents. Be prepared to work with the child, to provide ways for the child to cope and to come to understand the situation facing them.

- *Get support from friends, family, and professionals.* Dealing with difficult situations that may be encountered, or witnessing children in distress, takes an emotional toll on caregivers. It is very important that you protect yourself from over-involvement and/or burnout, by getting support for yourself.

Conclusion

This chapter has reviewed issues facing two kinds of traditional families. Although these families, like other families that we have examined in previous chapters, may live with stresses and pressures due their unique features, they may be just like most families in many other ways. It is important to be aware of the risks or the potential for stress or marginalization. Understanding children's perceptions and reactions from a developmental perspective may be helpful for adults interacting with children in times of stress or confusion. However, it is crucial to maintain a balanced perspective. There are many nontraditional families where such concerns may not arise. We must make very sure that we don't "pathologize" families simply because they are nontraditional. When caregivers are knowledgeable and prepared, they may be better able to promote resilience within children, parents or families if and when the circumstances arise. Caregivers are in the unique position of potentially being a special person in the life of a child and providing supports to families. Caregivers need to understand the risks and be prepared to enhance protective factors wherever and whenever they may be required.

Exercises

1. Discuss adoption and fostering within a group of colleagues. What are the different views expressed? How might these views affect the way a particular caregiver interacts with an adopted child? the parents?

2. What impact do you think adopting a child with special needs may have on the family?

3. Think about what you might say if a child says that he or she is adopted. How will you respond to other children in your group?

4. Think about what you might say if a child or parent tells you that they live in a gay or lesbian relationship. What will you say to other children in your group? What will you say to other parents?

5. Plan a series of experiences for young children around "different families." What will your message be? What types of activities will you incorporate into the children's day?

6. Check out different books and resources available for families with adopted children or same-sex parents. What are the prevalent messages?

7. Consider the topic of resilience. How does this pertain to your role with young children or their parents? What might you do in an attempt to build or increase resilience for young children?

Working with Families

part

3

Early childhood professionals have long recognized the importance and relevance of working with parents. The need to maintain positive parent-caregiver relationships has been studied and well documented in the literature. This section provides theoretical and practical knowledge focused specifically on collaborating with parents.

Chapter 14 examines different perspectives on parent involvement in the context of a family-centred approach. This examination provides a conceptual framework that will help early childhood professionals reflect on their own beliefs and practices.

Chapter 15 examines the potential sources of conflict and tension that can exist between parents and early childhood professionals. Guidelines for preventing and solving conflicts are presented, showing that the recognition of tension and its source should be the first step in resolution.

Chapter 16 provides practical suggestions for collaborating with parents, determining which activities are likely to be most meaningful to a particular group of parents.

Chapter 17 provides guidelines for evaluating the success of parent-staff collaboration.

Understanding Parent Involvement

chapter 14

Objectives

- To clarify the meaning of parent involvement.
- To discuss the concept of parent education.
- To discuss the issues related to parental influence and control.
- To examine the importance of continuity of care.
- To consider the importance of supporting and empowering parents.
- To view parent involvement in the context of the family-systems and ecological models.

> I was a caregiver and a director in a day-care centre for several years, and thought that I was quite an expert on parent involvement. Then I had my first baby and joined the ranks of all the struggling parents who juggle work, child care, and family. Parent involvement took on a very different meaning for me after I became a parent myself.
>
> (Janet, an instructor in an early childhood education program.)

Working with families, especially with parents, is widely accepted among caregivers as "an integral aspect of the early childhood teacher's job" (Galinsky, 1990: 2). The National Association for the Education of Young Children includes in its code of ethics the need to "bring about collaboration between home and school" (Feeney & Kipnis, 1989: 26). Most training programs for early childhood professionals, and most early childhood textbooks, contain a unit on working with parents; indeed, the ability to work in partnership with parents is considered a basic requirement of developmentally appropriate practice in early childhood programs (Bredekamp, 1987; Canadian Child Day Care Federation, 1991).

"Family-centred approach," "partnership with parents," "collaboration with parents," and "parent involvement" are but a few of the terms we see repeatedly in the professional literature. Yet many early childhood professionals admit that working with parents is frequently the most frustrating part of their work (Galinsky, 1990; Kontos & Wells, 1986; Powell, 1989).

Perhaps one reason for this frustration is that there are so many different expectations concerning the meaning and implementation of these terms. One caregiver in a day-care centre said, "They say I'm supposed to be a partner with parents, but parents treat me as if I am their private nanny. That doesn't exactly feel like a partnership to me." On the other hand, parents sometimes feel as though they have very little influence and control over what happens to their children on a day-to-day basis in day care or nursery school (Shimoni, 1992).

We cannot ignore the fact that, while the early childhood profession recognizes the importance of working with parents, difficulties in this area often do exist (Galinsky, 1990; Kontos and Wells, 1986; Powell, 1989). Kontos (1987: 94) claims that early childhood professionals "suffer from the . . . disease known as role ambiguity" when it comes to working with parents. When caregivers are not clear about how their role is defined, the result is often increased stress and discomfort—both for them and for the parents with whom they are expected to work. In 1980, Smith wrote that parent involvement is a "dustbin term" meaning different things to the different people that use it. As we enter the 21st century, we are still "hampered by imprecise definitions and lack of consensus" (Powell, 1989) regarding the work of early childhood professionals with parents.

As early childhood professionals, it is essential that we fully understand concepts before we try to implement them. Before we accept that we should work towards partnerships with parents, we should be able to answer three basic questions:

- What specifically are we attempting to achieve in our work with parents?
- Why is it important to achieve these particular goals?
- How can we ensure that we will achieve these goals?

A historical perspective can reveal to us where many of today's assumptions come from. Sometimes we accept models that worked in the past but that may not be appropriate under today's social conditions. For example, a common strategy for working with parents in the 1960s was home visits. Many well-researched programs (Ramey et al., 1977; Weber, Foster, & Weikart, 1978; Bromwich, 1981; Lombard, 1988, 1994) have demonstrated the effectiveness of early childhood professionals providing education and support to parents through regular home visits. Most of these programs, though, were designed to serve families whose children were at risk of school failure because of environmental factors or handicapping conditions. Although past and present interest in home-visiting programs indicates that they can be successful in some circumstances, they may not be appropriate for staff or parents in many day-care centres. Most parents with children in day care work during the day, and most of the children in day-care centres have not been identified as being "at risk."

In the same way, many model early childhood programs that were begun in the 1970s included a parent-involvement component in which parents would regularly participate in a preschool setting as volunteers or as paid aides (Beller, 1979; Katz, 1994). Although this strategy has many potential benefits, it may not be feasible for many working parents to attend a day-care setting regularly unless their work schedules are extremely flexible.

As responsible early childhood professionals, then, we need to evaluate carefully both the appropriateness and the effectiveness of different ways of working with families.

To do this properly, we have to examine the usefulness of each proposed strategy from the perspective of staff, children, and parents.

Defining Parent Involvement

Most of the literature on parent involvement relates to four main goals: (1) to educate parents, (2) to provide parents with the opportunity to influence or control the programs in which their children are involved, (3) to provide for the greatest possible continuity of care between home and centre, (4) to *empower* parents, a goal which has recently gained attention in the early childhood literature (Powell, 1989).

Underlying all the goals of parent involvement is the desire to support parents in their childrearing roles, not to parent. Although our review of parent involvement strategies, past and present, may seem critical, our intention is not to "throw the baby out with the bathwater." Rather, we want to encourage a continual clarification of our goals and strategies. Only in this way will we be able to ensure that parent involvement will benefit everyone in the early childhood programs—children, parents, and staff alike.

Perspectives

Professor Lillian Katz has been a dominant force in early childhood education for over two decades. She is the editor of ERIC Clearinghouse on Elementary and Early Childhood Education. She was interviewed about her views on parent involvement.

First, Professor Katz says that many educators pay lip service to the idea that all parents know their children best, while unfortunately, we too often see results of parenting that indicate otherwise.

Second, early childhood professionals have knowledge about what is best for children and should be using this knowledge in their interaction with parents. We must have confidence in our knowledge and understanding. Just as a teacher stands before a classroom because she knows more about the subject matter than the students, early childhood professionals should have some authority, based on their knowledge, that would come into play in their interaction with parents.

Third, Professor Katz feels that, although the relationship with parents is important, the primary consideration of the early childhood professional should be what is best for the client rather than what makes the client happy, and the two do not always coincide.

Professor Douglas Powell is acclaimed for his extensive research and writing on parent education and parent involvement in early childhood programs. He has been studying parent–child-care relations since the 1970s. In his 1989 book, *Families and Early Childhood Programs*, Professor Powell discusses differing views on parent involvement.

Professor Powell points out that widely varied views of the parental role in day care can be found both among early childhood professionals and among parents. The commonly used term "partnership" is itself open to interpretation.

One view of the parent-caregiver partnership, according to Professor Powell, is that parents are unable to provide the best possible environment for their child's development, due to lack of inner resources ("disposition") or physical resources (such as housing and income). In this view, the day-care program should "compensate for the deficiencies of the home."

An alternative view suggested by Professor Powell is that parents have parenting potential that should be supported by their child's caregivers. According to this view, "collaboration with parents is based on mutual respect and a desire to empower parents with information and roles that strengthen control of the environment" (Powell, 1989: 19-20).

Parent Education

Parent education is probably the oldest form of parent involvement. We can trace it back to the early 1900s, when day nurseries (the precursors of day-care centres) were first established to serve poor and needy families. Mothers were instructed about health and hygiene and about how to raise children in ways that would keep them from falling into lives of crime. In the 1920s, another form of parent education emerged as a spin-off from the nursery-school movement. As scientists were discovering just how important the early years of a child's life are for later development, middle-class mothers (many of whose children were in nursery schools) were meeting to discuss the latest research on child development and childrearing techniques.

Parent education became extremely popular during the 1960s and 1970s with the expansion of "head start" programs. During these years, it was widely believed that early childhood education could make a big difference in the lives of the poor. Education programs, it was thought, could help "close the gap" between children from advantaged and disadvantaged homes, but only if the parents were educated along with the children (Gordon, 1990). A number of different parent education formats evolved, including group meetings, home visits, and attendance by parents (usually mothers) at the preschool to learn from the teacher appropriate ways of interacting with children. The primary focus of many of these programs was teaching parents to interact with children in ways that would promote the children's intellectual development (Fein, 1980).

At the same time, many other kinds of parent education programs were being implemented. Nursery schools, churches, community centres, and other organizations were forming parent education groups. These groups were often inspired by the works of psychologists such as Dreikurs and Soltz (1964) and Ginnott (1965). They generally focused on communicating effectively with children, discipline, and related topics, and most of the parents attending were from the middle class.

Historians have recorded some interesting observations about parent education that we should keep in mind. First, throughout its history, parent education has been assumed to have a profound impact on the lives of children (Brim, 1965; Fein, 1980; Gordon, 1990). This impact presumably extends to the children's families and to society at large (Auerbach, 1968; Brim, 1965; Clarke-Stewart, 1988; Meyerhoff & White, 1990). Sometimes, however, the goals of parent education have been criticized for having a hidden agenda. Some writers attack them for "imposing white middle-class values on immigrants and the poor," and for "keeping middle-class women intellectually stimulated, but at home" (Fein, 1980). More recently, parent education goals have usually been articulated in terms of helping parents promote their children's development.

It has also been noted that two main streams of parent education have been active throughout its history: one for the poor and another for the affluent. It is a fact that parent education *has* often been imposed upon poor people and immigrants. In other words, receiving welfare benefits or a space in day care has been conditional upon parents' attendance at parent education programs. These programs have largely provided "instruction" to parents. On the other hand, middle-class parent education has been voluntary, rather than enforced, and based on "discussion" rather than instruction. To some extent, this dichotomy still exists today. An interview with the executive director of the Calgary Immigrant Aid Society revealed that many of the parent education programs designed for immigrants focus on teaching parents about health, safety, and nutrition (Ksienski, 1994). Programs that hope to attract middle-class parents, however, revolve around discussions of sibling rivalry or techniques for guidance and discipline.

Today, many early childhood professionals believe that educating parents is an ongoing process that best occurs through regular communication rather in than formal education programs. However, both caregivers and parents have cited problems that can occur with attempts to educate parents in this manner (Shimoni, 1992). First, as we shall see later in this chapter, opportunities for communication are often restricted to times when both staff and parents are busy and rushed; these are hardly optimum times for learning. Second, some parents may not think that caregivers have the necessary knowledge or expertise to provide them with advice and guidance (Shimoni, 1992). Third, although the caregiver's intention may be to educate the parent about the child's developmental needs, rushed communication can lead to misunderstandings and negative feelings. Kontos (1987) relates an anecdote about a caregiver who intervened when she saw a mother putting her toddler's coat on her. The caregiver explained that at the centre they let the toddlers dress themselves. She thought the mother would understand that this practice allows the children to practise their motor skills and become more autonomous. Instead the mother thought the caregivers were simply too busy to dress the children.

Since the concept of parent education has been so widely questioned in recent years, we will consider some of the points raised in these critiques in the following sections.

Does Parent Education Work?

While many parent education programs have undergone rigorous evaluation, we must be careful not to assume that all parent education programs have demonstrated their effectiveness. In fact, there is some evidence to suggest that parents who have very severe and specific problems with their children tend to drop out of conventional parent education programs (Anchor & Thomason, 1977). Although many studies have shown that parent education classes have influenced parents' attitudes or knowledge about childrearing, there is much less evidence to support the claim that real changes occur in families as a result of parent education programs (Dembo, Sweitzer, & Lauritzen, 1985; Van Wyk, Eloff, & Heyns, 1983).

Powell's review (1989) of the evaluative research on parent education programs cites some studies that have established short-term positive effects on the intellectual functioning of children, but it often happens that these gains are no longer evident a year after the program has ended. Some long-term positive results have been noted for parent education programs (Jester & Guinagh, cited in Powell, 1989), such as reduced rates of juvenile delinquency and a reduced likelihood of being involved in special education classes (Lally, Mangione, & Honig, cited in Powell, 1989). However, other large-scale evaluations of prominent parent education programs have failed to show any positive effects (McCartney & Scarr, cited in Powell, 1989). It is, therefore, very difficult to understand just what kind of parent education is effective, but there is some consensus that successful programs share the following characteristics (Stevens, 1978; Powell, 1989):

- They are intensive and extensive. That is, successful programs usually extend beyond one year and involve frequent contact between early childhood professionals and parents in a variety of formats.

- They are substantially funded. It is difficult to avoid the simple formula that quality programs are costly. All the parent education programs that have proven to be successful have received massive funding, usually from state (or provincial) and federal governments.

- They are conceptualized and implemented under highly qualified professionals in the field of early childhood development.

The conclusion that must be drawn from this review of the evaluative literature is that we have to proceed with caution and humility, since most of the parent education components of early childhood programs do not meet the above criteria. If we choose to take the time and meet the expenses of hiring professionals to organize and implement parent education programs, we must ensure that we also make the effort to evaluate what we are doing. We cannot proceed, as many people do, on the assumption that just any kind of parent education will automatically make a difference in the lives of children and parents.

Can Parent Education Undermine a Parent's Confidence?

After performing in-depth interviews with many mothers of young children, Barlow (1992) concludes that the involvement of so-called experts in childrearing has undermined mothers' belief in their own ability to raise their children. Fein (1980) has alleged that parent education is so rooted in middle-class North American values that parents from different classes and different cultures may well feel "inferior" or devalued. One mother said, after attending a parent education class, "If I see one more 'how to do it' video that shows me how everything I do is wrong, I'm going to surrender my children for adoption." Parent education does not have to undermine parents' confidence. The intention is just the opposite, to help parents gain confidence in themselves and thereby become better parents. Awareness of the potential impact on parents' self-image, and a sensitivity to and appreciation of different parenting styles, will help early childhood professionals ensure that parent education meets its goal.

Who Should Offer Parent Education?

Almost all the helping professions today engage in parent education. Nurses, psychologists, teachers, early childhood professionals, social workers, clergy, and even people with no related professional background now offer parent education. In some ways, this is a good thing, since families and family relations are the focus of many professions, and the different disciplines can enrich each other's perspective. However, a concern has been raised that parent education is hampered by "charlatanism in the field, and the lack of consensus concerning who should be a parent educator" (Morrison, 1978). One study found this uncertainty to be prevalent in day-care centres (Shimoni, 1992).

Who Is Qualified?

Marsha, a recent graduate of an early childhood education training program, expressed the view that she did not consider herself qualified to be an educator of parents. "In my training I learned a lot about child development and about how to care for children in a group. But I am not a parent; I have not brought up my own children. I can't teach parents how to do their job."

The sort of discomfort Marsha felt over being asked to provide parents with guidance and advice when she was not a parent herself is not uncommon among inexperienced professionals in a variety of fields. It is not unusual, for instance, for clients to ask their therapists if they have ever personally experienced abuse, addictions, or marital breakdown. The truth is that many professionals do, over time, become successful in helping people in a variety of situations, whether or not they have had similar experiences. With increased knowledge and experience in working with children, and by making a deliberate effort to empathize with both children and adults, early childhood professionals can also develop the confidence they need to think of themselves as a useful resource for parents.

Some parents do readily look to early childhood professionals for guidance about parenting. For instance, one mother said, "They are trained to deal with certain situations with children, and if they know a way that is better than the way I have been using to deal with a problem, I would want them to teach me" (Shimoni, 1992). One caregiver related an incident where a parent sought her advice and characterized their relationship as co-parents of the child (Baxter, 1998). The professional felt a heightened respect and regard in this statement.

Other parents have a different view, however. As one mother noted, "Oh, I might ask a caregiver to recommend a good book for a present, and I may or may not take their advice. But if they wanted to tell me how to be a better mother, I would make it clear to them that they should take their advice elsewhere" (Shimoni, 1992). The question, then, of whether early childhood professionals should engage in parent education cannot be answered simply.

The concept of parent education has been criticized because it implies a sharing of information that is "one way"—the "experts" provide the required information to the parents without ever asking for their opinion. Parents do, however, have a wealth of information about their children, and this knowledge is every bit as valid and important as the contents of child development textbooks. Therefore, many early childhood professionals have come to prefer the term "sharing information" to "parent education" (Shimoni, 1992) because "sharing" implies a two-way communication process. Therefore, in our next chapter, we usually refer to sharing information rather than parent education.

Parent Influence and Control

The second goal of many parent involvement strategies is to acknowledge the rights of parents to control, or at least to influence, policies and programs that affect their children (Greenblatt, 1977). The growing consumer movement has encouraged parents to exercise this sort of control over education programs to ensure that the values endorsed in them agree with individual family and cultural values, and to guarantee that programs become more sensitive to the needs of the populations they serve.

This is a very sensitive issue for many early childhood professionals. Through education and training, they have acquired values, beliefs, and a considerable degree of knowledge about what is good for the children in their care. They spend much time and effort developing programs for the children based on those beliefs. Letting parents share in decisions about the program is not always easy to do. For example, the following incident occurred not long ago in a day-care centre.

Scenario

Who Knows Best?

Marcy, the centre director, regularly scheduled large blocks of time for free play because she firmly believed it to be the most important learning opportunity for children. A group of parents expressed the concern that the children were not learning enough, and they pressed the centre to purchase computers and teach the children learning skills through computer use. The parents were not convinced by Marcy's argument that play is the most appropriate way for very young children to acquire knowledge and skills. The staff members were upset that parents ignored their expertise, and parents felt that their views were not being respected.

In Chapter 15, "Resolving Conflicts and Tensions," we will provide some suggestions for resolving issues similar to the one described above. This scenario illustrates one of the difficulties that might arise in regard to parents' influence on centre programs. Early childhood professionals have to be very careful to articulate clearly which areas of programming cannot be compromised. Literature published by the professional associations—such as the National Association for the Education of Young Children (NAEYC), the Canadian Association for Young Children, and the Canadian Child Day Care Federation—are vital resources for staff whose beliefs and practices are being questioned. When staff members are clear about the aspects of their program over which they will not surrender control, they can look carefully at parents' requests and respond positively to any that do not compromise their professional standards. By sharing their concerns with parents, and by showing their willingness to respond to parents' requests, caregivers can usually establish acceptable boundaries for parent influence on curricular decisions.

One common strategy for increasing parent influence and control is to establish parent boards or to encourage parent participation on the boards of early childhood programs. To be truly effective, parent participation on governing boards requires the knowledge and the commitment of both parents and staff. Boards can act as "rubber stamps," or they can form the lifeline of the program. Staff members need to learn how to utilize the board effectively, and often board members require some training before they can carry out their tasks effectively.

The majority of day-care centres do not have mandated parent boards or any other means of allowing parents to participate in decision making. Some parents have indicated a wish for more opportunities to influence programs than are presently afforded (Shimoni, Carnat, & Creighton, 1989). It has been suggested (Fein, 1980; Bradbard & Endsley, 1980) that one way parents could exert more control over early childhood programs is simply to be more selective about which day-care centre they choose. If early childhood programs depended entirely on parent satisfaction to continue to operate, parents would exert a tremendous amount of control. However, the truth is more complex than that. In North America, there is an insufficient number of high-quality day-care programs in most provinces and states, and many parents do put up with less than optimal programs because they have no choice. In addition, many parents feel that if they criticize the centre or the staff, their child might bear the brunt of staff resentment (Canadian Child Day Care Federation, 1991).

The involvement of parents in the decision-making process is very complex, and professionals need to consider very carefully which aspects of their program should be open to parental influence or control and how they can encourage parent participation in a way that will benefit everyone involved.

Continuity of Care or "Creating Bridges"

With rapidly increasing numbers of very young children being away from home for many hours a day, one important concern for early childhood professionals in their relations with parents is the difficulty children face in making the daily transitions between two environments that may be quite different. "Continuity between home and centre" is a concept that has received much attention in the early childhood literature. Bredekamp (1987: 12), for instance, states that "communication between families and teachers . . . provides greater consistency for children." The younger the children, the more vital this continuity or consistency is considered to be (Weiser, 1991).

Recently researchers in early childhood education have highlighted the need to clarify this assumption (Peters & Kontos, 1987). Some children seem to move in and out of different situations with very little difficulty, while others find such transitions upsetting. As early childhood professionals, we need to know more about which children are likely to find continuity helpful, rather than simply to assume that continuity is beneficial per se and in all circumstances. In spite of these hesitations, however, common sense tells us that most children need some assistance in these daily transitions, and that one way to "bridge" home and centre is to ensure that there is ongoing communication between parents and program staff.

In early childhood education, the concept of continuity has often been used as a way of ensuring that skills learned at preschool are reinforced at home. One caregiver called this the "multiplier effect." For example, in helping the child learn the concepts "big" and "little," we talk about big things and little things at preschool; if parents do the same at home, it helps the child integrate this concept more easily.

Wendy, who worked for years as an early childhood educator before she became an instructor of early childhood students at a community college, made the following observation about continuity of care.

Scenario

One Definition of Continuity

When people talk about the importance of continuity of care, they refer to grand notions of home and centre doing things in a similar fashion or responding to the child in similar ways. Educators like big phrases like "continuity of care." This is unrealistic. My job is to make the child feel welcome in the day care. Often he will talk about something relating to his home—his sick goldfish, or his brother's new shoes. If I know a little bit about those things (from talking with his parents), it is easier for me to talk with him about them and make him feel a bit more comfortable at the centre. It is that simple. That is what I mean by "continuity."

Continuity for this caregiver meant nothing more complicated than ensuring that she knew enough about the child's home life that she could help him make sense of his experiences throughout the day and feel more comfortable at the centre.

Sometimes when we talk about continuity, we really mean the opposite. If for some reason a child is experiencing stress at home, we actually want him or her to have the opposite experience at the day-care centre. This is reflected in the following remarks by Elizabeth, an early childhood professional.

Scenario

What You Need to Know

You need to know things that happen in the children's homes. If Mom and Dad have suddenly split up, I think it's important that we know that. We don't want to know who or why, but it is important to know that maybe Daddy left or Mommy has gone for a while. That is important because it is going to affect the child's behaviour, and we need to know what kind of support the child will require.

If continuity of care, or "bridging home and centre," is to happen at all, it presupposes that information about the centre will be taken home to the parents, and that information about the child's home life and family will be made available to the centre. Such disclosure requires a level of trust and openness that may not always be present. Some parents feel very strongly that their private life is not a concern of the early childhood professional. The following remarks made by one mother are typical.

Scenario

One Parent's View

Of course I will inform the caregiver of any sudden change in our family life, but only the bare details. All families have ups and downs, and I don't want to feel pressured to discuss these with my child's caregiver. It's not that I don't trust her; it's just that I didn't choose her, as I would a counsellor or psychologist. So if my husband walked out on me, I would mention that John was no longer living with us, but I would leave it at that.

Other parents, though, do look on the early childhood professional as a prime source of support, as someone with whom they can discuss family concerns. Sometimes this kind of support leads to very important actions, as the following scenario illustrates.

Some Timely Advice

A caregiver asked to speak to a mother whose child seemed to be under a lot of stress. The mother tearfully related that she was indeed having difficulty with the child just then. The little girl had just turned 4, an age that the mother associated with excruciating memories of the abuse she experienced as a child. The caregiver listened attentively and encouraged the mother to go to counselling at a nearby centre for adult victims of child abuse. Several years later, the mother recalled how it was the caring early childhood professional who facilitated the beginning of a healing process for herself and her family.

It is easy to see by reading through all the above scenarios that there are different opinions about the meaning and importance of continuity of care. Much of the debate seems to centre on the question of whether the day-care staff have a right to know about the home lives of the children in their care. For the concept to work, each side must be sensitive to the rights and values of the other. For this reason, we have listed some cautions that should be observed in the planning for continuity of care.

Bridging Between Centre and Home: A Two-Way Street

1. For some families, privacy is a highly esteemed value. Deciding what is absolutely necessary to know about the family's life, and what is not essential, will help you to respect the privacy of the family.

2. Early childhood professionals are not trained to be counsellors or therapists. Parents will often disclose highly personal information to the early childhood professional, who will then feel a strong desire to be helpful. However, knowing your professional limits is extremely important. Being able to refer parents to appropriate sources of support is part of the professional role.

3. Unfortunately, educators who believe in continuity of care often translate it to mean: "This is the way we do it at the centre, and therefore parents should do it this way at home as well." Bridging between home and centre has to be a two-way street. It may mean incorporating new ideas into the centre to bring it more into line with the way things are done at home, rather than the other way around.

Acknowledging Cultural Diversity

Continuity of care should also involve acknowledging the cultural values, practices, and traditions of the children and families in our care: "Children from minority backgrounds thrive best when their racial identity, culture and/or home language is supported and included in a respectful and meaningful way in their early childhood education experiences" (Fahlman, 1992). In recent years, the early childhood profession has become increasingly aware of the need to examine the ways in which families' cultural diversity can be incorporated into programs (King, Chipman, & Cruz-Jansen, 1994; Hall & Rhomberg, 1995). Measures you can take to reflect cultural diversity include:

- ensuring that classroom materials (dolls, posters, books, and toys) show people of different races and cultures;
- ensuring that children's home languages are used and represented in the centre; and
- ensuring that discussions with children and their parents relate to the children's home experiences, including festivities and traditions.

Early childhood professionals should utilize the many written resources available to assist them in supporting diversity in their programs. Perhaps the most important resource, however, will be the parents and families themselves, who along with co-workers, friends, and neighbors can inform and advise day-care staff on how to enhance the continuity of care by incorporating diversity into the classroom (Short & Johnston, 1994).

Empowering Parents

Scenario

Mother May Know Best

When I had my first child, I was a young single parent. I thought I knew nothing about children and I just waited for the caregivers to answer my questions and tell me what to do.

When my little girl "graduated" into the toddler room, I met Elcira, her caregiver, and continued to ask her questions. Elcira would listen to my questions but then would say things like "What have you been doing about that up to now? That seems to have worked well." Sometimes she would ask me what I thought would be the best way. Other times she would recommend a book to read.

At first I was annoyed with her. "Can't she just answer my questions?" I thought to myself. Gradually, I came to understand that she was giving me the message that I really do know what is best for my child and that I could rely more on my own knowledge and intuition. That was an important thing for me to learn.

Empowerment is a term that is used with increasing frequency in the helping professions (Pizzo, 1993). It denotes a move away from the traditional way of working with people, where an "expert" was assumed to know what was best for her or his clients. This change should result in a process by which families and communities increase their influence and control over their own circumstances (Barker, 1991). In an early childhood setting, empowerment means that parents are recognized to be in the best position to determine goals for their children. It follows that staff should utilize their knowledge and skills to help parents realize these goals by facilitating activities that are jointly planned by the centre staff and the parents of the children (Cochran, 1987). In this way, the model de-emphasizes the expert role, and "empowers" parents to make and implement decisions that will be in the best interest of their children.

All the goals of parent involvement already discussed in this chapter can be pursued in a way that empowers parents. First, parent education can empower parents if it is done in a manner that goes beyond just delivering reams of advice and information to parents. As part of the educating process, parents can also be encouraged to reflect on all the valuable information they already possess. This information can come from their own experiences with their children, from their own upbringing, and from their friends and relatives. In this way, parents will feel empowered to trust their own feelings and responses to their children.

Second, parents can be empowered by actively participating in the early childhood programs, at both the planning and implementation stages. This can only happen, though, in those centres where there is a genuine openness to parent influence. Third, parents can be empowered by many of the strategies that encourage bridging or continuity of care. Again, though, both parents and caregivers must work together to ensure that what they construct is a "two-way" bridge. Neither side will feel empowered if one side exerts complete control.

Goals of Parent Involvement

- To provide parents with information about their child's development and needs.
- To provide parents with opportunities to influence their children's programs.
- To foster continuity of care between the home and centre.
- To help parents to be aware of what their own goals for their children are and to empower parents to realize these goals.

The Family-Centred Approach

More recently, the term "family-centred" has been utilized in early childhood care settings. This represents a "movement away" from the traditional approaches where the "expert" designs and implements interactions without input from family members. It has grown from respecting the rights of families and consumers and the ecological perspective which recognizes the multiplicity of factors that influence development. In addition, evidence suggests that involving families more respectfully and fully is beneficial to families and children (McBride, 1999).

> *Family-centered practice is based on beliefs and values that (a) acknowledge the importance of the family system on child development, (b) respect families as decision makers for their children and themselves, and (c) support families in their role of raising and educating their children. (McBride, 1999, p. 62)*

The family-centred approach is grounded in values of respect and willingness to collaborate with families. The key guiding principles include the following:

1. *Make the family the focus of service.* This epitomizes the family systems approach in that the impact that the child may have on the family is recognized.

2. *Respect and support decisions families make.* This provision has been legally mandated in the United States for children with special needs and in some Canadian jurisdictions, with varying degrees of success. However, families will develop abilities when provided opportunities and when supported in their attempts to make decisions about their child's care and development.

3. *Provide comprehensive, responsive services to families.* A large part of providing flexible services and supports rests in honouring the diversity of children and families. Caregivers need to develop an understanding of cultural values and convey a feeling of respect. More and more, early childhood professionals are being requested to become aware of and work with a range of community resources to assists particular children and their families. Early childhood programs that link with family resource or community resource centres promote caring communities for children and families.

Family-centred approaches are more inclusive and may be faced with many challenges in development. Defining and refining family-centred practice will be an evolving process. Early childhood professionals will be faced with the challenge of communicating with and supporting adults as well as children in diverse settings. Awareness of and access to community resources will be increasingly important in an attempt to find flexible services to meet the unique needs of children and families. Early childhood professionals have a solid foundation and rich traditions of working with families from which to continue to grow and develop more family-centred practices. Family-centred approaches are not a new fad or phenomenon—they represent the best practices of early childhood professionals and a new perspective on families.

Partnerships

Quality child care serves the best interests of children and families in a partnership of parents, professionally trained care providers, all levels of governments, training institutions, and provincial and territorial and national organizations who carry out complementary responsibilities.

Quality child care . . .

- recognizes the role of the parent as the primary caregiver, and the role of the trained care provider as one which is supportive and enhancing to child and family.
- utilizes parent boards, advisory committees, cooperatives, etc., to maintain a philosophy consistent with the needs of the families served.
- ensures parents/boards have access to ongoing board development and training to ensure effective management of the program.
- has a developed program philosophy and posted policies for behaviour management, safety/emergency procedures, and the reporting of suspected child abuse.
- shares resources among parents and care providers within a supportive and complementary environment.
- adheres to all applicable provincial/territorial legislation with commitment to exceed legislation where possible.
- ensures that ongoing and annual program reviews/evaluations are conducted, both internal and external, to ensure delivery of quality service.
- initiates and maintains positive liaison/networking with community resources such as schools, religious institutions, Native band offices, community boards and agencies, and professional associations.
- provides for an administrative office for use by the director, where confidential records of children and staff are kept.

Source: Canadian Child Care Federation, 1991: 14.

Conclusion

In order to work with parents in a way that supports and empowers them, early childhood professionals should clarify their own goals for parent involvement, learn and understand what the parents' goals are, and work with the parents to develop strategies that will foster those goals. You should be familiar with the entire family system, and with the other informal and formal systems with which the family interacts. You should also be aware of the potential areas of misunderstanding, conflict, and tension that may arise between you and the parents of the children in your care. Finally, you should be able to provide an honest evaluation of the work you do with parents. We hope that the preceding pages will provide some background to help you sort out and formulate your goals. The following chapters will look at the practical application.

Exercises

1. In your own words, write a definition of the term "parent involvement."

2. Ask two caregivers to give you their definitions of the term "parent involvement." Summarize their responses in writing.

3. Ask two parents what they feel the term "parent involvement" means. Summarize their responses in writing.

4. Compare the responses of the caregivers and the parents you interviewed with your own definition. What are the similarities, and what are the differences? What do you think accounts for the similarities and the differences?

5. Brainstorm a list of reasons you might have for making a home visit. What are some things you could do in advance to ensure a successful home visit? Discuss the ethical considerations involved in home visiting.

Resolving Conflicts and Tensions

chapter 15

Objectives

- **To understand that conflicts and tensions may exist in some relationships with parents.**

- **To examine the sources of some of these conflicts.**

- **To discuss strategies that may help prevent or resolve situations where conflicts or tensions arise.**

One of the leaders in the field of early childhood education tells a wonderful story about how misconceptions develop between staff and parents. It was a bad day at the day-care centre: two staff members were off sick and no relief staff were available. In order to maintain the approved adult/child ratios, Andrea worked a shift and a half without so much as a coffee break. Just five minutes before closing time, when only one tired little girl remained at the centre, the telephone rang. The girl's mother was calling to say that she would be tied up in a board meeting for another 30 minutes. The exhausted caregiver put down the phone and went to tell the child that her mother would be late. As the long 30 minutes drew to an end, the child curled up in Andrea's lap to look at a picture book. The mother walked into the play-room, glanced at Andrea and remarked, "Boy, would I ever like to have an easy job like yours, where you can sit and relax in a rocking chair."

(Adapted from Stranger and Beatty, 1984.)

Almost all parents want what is best for their children. Early childhood professionals working with children are also committed to their well-being. This common goal should provide a sound basis for developing a positive relationship between caregivers and parents. Yet, over and over again, studies have substantiated what our conversations with caregivers over the years have suggested: that working with parents is often the most stressful component of the early childhood professional's role (Galinsky, 1990, 1988; Powell, 1989; Shimoni, 1992).

Many caregivers do describe parents as helpful, understanding, and cooperative, and they feel that their collaborative relationships provide each other with a major source of support. Sometimes, however, relationships between parents and early childhood professionals are badly strained, and both parties go out of their way to avoid each other. It can be frustrating when neither side really understands what is causing the discomfort or is willing to deal with it, which in turn can create further tension for both.

Although these conflicts are verbalized at times, most frequently they are not, making them even more difficult to understand or resolve. In this chapter, we will concentrate on identifying the sources of conflict between early childhood professionals and parents. We will also emphasize the importance of good communication with parents in preventing and resolving conflicts.

Sources of Tension

A number of studies have shed light on conflicts between parents and caregivers. Many caregivers have negative views of parents. Galinsky (1990) found that some caregivers characterized mothers as always rushing, pushing, and overindulging their children. In another study, caregivers described parents with terms such as "uncooperative," "illiterate," and "negative" (Boutte et al., 1992). Socioeconomic and ethnic factors seem to play a role in these views; parents held in low regard tend to be single, from an ethnic minority group, or from a lower income bracket (Kontos & Wells, 1986; Boutte et al., 1992).

However, caregivers are often not valued or appreciated by parents either. Galinsky (1988) found that some parents subtly communicate the message that child-care workers play a secondary role in society; that is, parents leave their children at the centre so that they can be freed to do "real work."

Researchers have tried to explain why the relationship between parents and caregivers is less than ideal. Powell (1989) suggests that parents and caregivers are "natural enemies" because their responsibilities towards and relationships with children *should* be qualitatively different but are not always so. Many parents fear being replaced in their child's esteem by an outsider, and caregivers seem to pose this threat. Caregivers' perception of the need for and desired scope of parent–staff communication differs from that of parents. Caregivers tend to see such communication as more important than parents do, and they expect to share information about the child's family life. The conflict between a caregiver's desire for better communication and the parents' desire to keep a certain distance between the child and the caregiver could be at the root of some feelings of tension.

Many of the problems between parents and caregivers, however, may stem from simple logistics. Busy parents and busy caregivers are often not able to find suitable times for communicating, and thus misunderstandings arise. Galinsky (1990) put forth the idea of the "arsenic hour" to portray the futility of attempting to engage in meaningful communication at pick-up time—the time when the highest frequency of parent–caregiver communication occurs (Powell, 1989). The end of the day tends to be a time when both parents and caregivers are stressed and tired. Parents try to avoid problems (Ghazvini & Readdick, 1994), causing frustration for the caregivers, who wish for more meaningful interaction with the parents (Galinsky, 1988, 1990; Powell, 1989).

Caregivers who are better educated and more experienced tend to be more positive about parents (Galinsky, 1988), suggesting that training for caregivers should include a focus on understanding and working with parents. When early childhood professionals deepen their understanding of the sources of tension and conflict, they can then take steps towards ameliorating their relationship with parents. Let us now examine in more detail some of the common sources of conflict between parents and staff.

Perspectives

Mercy and her family immigrated to Canada seven years ago. As a young woman, she had completed her teacher training at a college and worked as a teacher in an elementary school. At present, she is employed as a caregiver in a day-care centre and has one of her own children in another room at the same centre. Below are some of Mercy's comments about potential areas of conflict between parents and staff at day-care centres.

"As a parent and a teacher, I was rather disappointed in the lack of awareness of some of the staff about cultural differences. Several children at the centre are from countries where the diet is very different from here. My children, for example, were used to very spicy food and found some of the meals here literally hard to swallow. I was very disappointed to learn that my child had been punished for not finishing his main course. His dessert was taken away from him.

"Some children at the centre had never seen a child with dark skin before. I was pleased with the way staff in the playroom talked to the children in a matter-of-fact way about how some people have light skin and some have dark skin. I would have liked, however, to see more toys and dolls and books that had pictures of visible minorities. On the other hand, I would not want my child to be singled out in every possible discussion as a representative of a minority group. Staff need to stress the similarities among all children and not just the differences.

"Sometimes I have felt that people assume that I am less educated than they are because of my skin colour and my accent. I sometimes get tired of having things explained to me two or three times, or in 'easy English.' The truth is that I probably have more education than many of the people I work with and than many other parents of children in the centre.

"There were no day-care centres where I lived in India. Grandparents often take care of the children while parents go to work, and often parents take the babies with them to work, if they own their own business. I do remember, however, that there were excellent relations between the nursery school teachers and the parents. Most parents believe that teachers deserve a lot of respect and that, if they treat the teachers well, their children in turn will be treated well by the teachers.

"I wear two hats, that of a parent of a child in day care and that of a caregiver in a day-care centre. Of all the strategies for enhancing relationships between parents and staff, I believe the most important one is mutual respect. As a parent, I want my children's teachers to treat me as an enlightened and caring parent who may have different ways of doing things. As a staff member, I want parents to know that I am committed to high professional standards and the well-being of their children. I am open to their ideas and want to listen to them, but they need to understand that I am not their personal nanny but an early childhood professional."

Preconceived Ideas

Parents often have preconceived ideas about early childhood professionals, who in turn hold preconceived ideas about parents (Galinsky, 1990, 1988; Coleman, 1991; Pizzo, 1993). These ideas or prejudices may interfere with establishing or maintaining a good relationship. Following are examples of common misconceptions that parents and caregivers may hold.

Parents: Caregivers have an easy job

As the scenario at the beginning of the chapter shows, parents sometimes believe that caregivers have an easy job, thinking that all they do is play all day with children. They have little understanding of the factors underlying the caregiver's "easy" job—the planning, organizing, and preparation required in a group care setting. Parents who think this way have no qualms about asking for small extras (e.g., "Could you braid her hair?" "Please try to find his blue snow pants."). Nor do they realize that on a particularly busy day clothing sometimes will not get changed or toys will go missing. Especially parents who have never spent extended periods of time with groups of young children may truly not comprehend the nature of the job and may make such mistaken assumptions about the caregiver's role.

Caregivers: Children are not the parents' priority

Early childhood students and professionals often question the legitimacy of parents leaving their children in day care while they take the day, or part of it, off. Many of the younger students are shocked when they hear tales of parents who use day care so they can spend their leisure time without their child. Students who are parents, usually single parents, represent the other point of view. They point out, for instance, that this may be the only 20 minutes alone they have all day or night, that it is more efficient to grocery shop without their 2-year-old in tow, and that it is better to spend quality time with the children at home than to drag them through the store. Sometimes the day off is better spent cleaning, studying, and organizing home lives so that the parent is free to concentrate on her or his children when they are at home.

A family-systems approach reminds us that the well-being of family members is relational and that the happiness of one ultimately benefits all members of the family. For example, the mother or father who is more relaxed after a short break can have more positive interaction with the whole family.

Caregivers: Parents treat the day-care centre as a dumping ground

Some caregivers also believe that parents treat the day-care centre as a "dumping ground." Parents, they reason, are free to drop off a sick child, to control the payment of fees, or to dictate the child's pick-up time (Pizzo, 1993). Even though many centres have policies or guidelines stating that children should be in care for no more than 10 hours per day, parents choose the length of the day based on their needs. Caregivers believe that the "dumping-ground" syndrome may be more common with parents who are not very involved with the program.

From the parents' perspective, their hurried comings and goings may seem entirely reasonable. Parents are frequently rushed in the mornings; if they are to be on time for work, they have little time to linger at the day care's front door. The end of the day poses the same problem because the parent is often in a hurry to pick up other children or to get home and start supper. The parents may feel quite content with the level of care and the day-care centre itself, and thus feel that they really have nothing to report upon or query at each arrival or departure. This lack of communication may be their silent message that all is well (for now, at least). Caregivers, however, see staff–parent communication as being very important and are frustrated when parents do not (Ghazvini & Readdick, 1994; Shimoni, 1992).

Different Values and Beliefs

Parents and caregivers may have different values and beliefs about children and parenting. These may be based on their own experience, on how they were raised as children, or on cultural or religious beliefs. Sometimes, we are not even aware that we have these ingrained beliefs until we are confronted with a belief that is contrary to our own.

For example, if a caregiver truly believes that mothers should stay at home with their babies and toddlers, this idea may filter through in interactions with parents (Galinsky, 1990). Parents may be judged neglectful when their preschool-aged child arrives with her hair uncombed, face unwashed, and wearing a strange assortment of clothing. These aspects, however, may actually reflect nothing more sinister than the rush of the morning, the parent's inability to engage in just one more battle to clean the child up, or the child's own quest for autonomy in the choice of clothing.

Prejudgments may also be a result of cultural or religious differences (Boutte et al., 1992; Kontos & Wells, 1986). For example, parents who expect their child to be strong and independent may not spend a lot of time easing the child through the daily separation. Caregivers may judge these parents as cold and unloving, while the parents see themselves as teaching their children important cultural values. Likewise, the parents who indulge and overprotect their children may be doing so according to their cultural norms. Judgments may be made about these parents without attempting to understand their actions in light of these other considerations.

Cultural differences may also be relevant in relation to parent–staff relations. For example, the majority of parent education programs in North America have focused on the traditional family. Since in this system mothers are primarily responsible for child care, they tend to be the targets of most programs. This may cause conflicts in families where child-care responsibility falls on another family member or where extended families are an integral part of parenting (Short & Johnston, 1994).

Differences in Power and Status

Differences in perception of the professional status of child-care workers can be a source of tension. Parents often treat (or caregivers think they treat) child-care workers as nothing more than babysitters (Daniel, 1990; Galinsky, 1988). In fact, some parents' actions and statements may support this belief. When this happens, caregivers can feel intimidated by parents or think that parents are uninterested in their observations or views, particularly in the area of developmental concerns.

Furthermore, some parents may never come to view the day-care staff as a resource (Kontos & Wells, 1986). Often, caregivers actually have more training and applied education in development than many parents with careers in law, commerce, engineering, arts, and sciences. Parents' knowledge comes predominantly from family, friends, books, media, the popular press, and their own experience. Nevertheless, parents often consider that their sources of childrearing information carry more authority than early childhood professional resources. This attitude can lead them to feel that two-way communication with caregivers is unnecessary, and caregivers can interpret this lack of sharing as a reflection of their lower status in the mind of the parent.

Scenario

A Parent's Perception of Status

Elaine had two children who attended a day-care centre attached to the college where she worked as an instructor. When interviewed regarding her view of differences in status and power of day-care workers and parents, she said the following: "I am going to be very honest with you. When I want something to happen for my children at the day-care centre, I wear my business suit, walk in holding my briefcase and looking very professional, and make it very clear that I expect to have my own way. But you know, even though I think that my status as a professional exceeds that of the day-care worker, in the long run, the caregiver really holds the most power. At the back of my mind, I always know that if they don't like me, the staff might, probably not even consciously, take it out on my child."

Ironically, just as caregivers feel that the parent has the upper hand, it is not uncommon for parents to feel that early childhood professionals do. Who knows what really happens, a parent might think, when I'm not there? This thought is frightening, especially for the parent who is used to being in control. The following scenario vividly illustrates this fear.

Scenario

Who Really Has the Most Power?

One father, who himself was a university professor specializing in early childhood education, published a letter to his daughter's teacher, saying all of the things he couldn't say to her directly. He forwarded the letter with the comment that, in all our professional wisdom, we haven't made it safe for parents to communicate honestly.

"It has been a humbling experience, and a frightening one, for me to discover how little the accumulated wisdom in our professional literature really speaks to the circumstances of parents like me, parents who have discovered that the stakes are too high to open this particular conversation with this particular teacher. When I actually meet with her, I will temper my points, modulate my voice, tread so very carefully. Much will remain unspoken because I am so acutely aware of just how vulnerable my child is in this affair. My first agenda is the agenda of every parent: I must not make the situation worse. So where will parents' voices really be heard by teachers? Can parents' voices be heard in the professional literature without being encapsulated in someone else's study, framed by someone else's commentary; can parents be heard speaking on their own behalf? Sometimes they can, but still, not often." (Nuttall, 1993: 6)

Both parents and early childhood professionals expect to be heard and to have their views respected, since both feel they need to have some degree of control over the lives of the children (Pizzo, 1993). When parents interact with high-status professionals such as doctors or psychologists, it is rare for them to challenge openly the professional's views and opinions (Seligman, 1991). This will not stop the parents, however, from resenting the professional's level of control in their lives and, correspondingly, their own loss of control.

Parents who are unsure of the professional role and status of the caregiver may also be unsure of how to deal with control issues at the day-care centre. At times, they may demand control. At other times, these same parents may be content to leave the decision making up to the caregiver and not become involved. Part of this vacillation is a result of the increasing reliance on professionals in our society and part comes from the parents' changing perception of who should actually exert more control over the children (Seligman, 1991).

Uncertainty About the Caregiver's Role

Lillian Katz, a leader in the field of early childhood education, has described the relationship between parents and caregivers as one of "endemic ambiguity" (Shimoni, 1992). Uncertainty about the roles, rules, and the boundaries between the parent and the caregiver is inevitable (Katz, 1980). In the same vein, Kontos and Wells (1986) have stated that caregivers suffer from a sociological disease called "role ambiguity." Are they really respected professionals, or could they be referred to as maids and nannies? Some parents seem to think that the latter alternative is more accurate.

Scenario

Respected Professional or Hired Help?

A parent had been complaining regularly to her daughter's caregiver about issues such as soiled clothing, missing items, and reports of being hit and bitten by the other children. These allegations were for the most part untrue, and the caregiver attempted to explain the situation and reassure the parent that all was well. One morning, the parent arrived upset about yet another minor incident the preceding day. When the caregiver attempted to explain, the parent silenced her by stating that she was paying for service and she wanted things to change. Her expectations, at that point, were very clear. She expected to be treated like the consumer who was purchasing a service, and she believed she had hired the staff to provide that service. What would be the response of the staff, though, to such a demand?

Lack of clarity or agreement about roles can also lead to feelings of jealousy on the part of the parents. They naturally feel possessive about their children, but caregivers can also become attached to and possessive about the children in their care. This phenomenon is so common that it has been given a name; specialists refer to it as the "six week syndrome" (Galinsky, 1990). It can cause bitter rivalries (Powell, 1988).

Scenario

Transference at an Early Age

A young caregiver was caring for a group of children who ranged in age from a few weeks to 12 months old. A toddler had just begun to talk and very loudly and clearly called the caregiver "Mom" several times one day. When the child's mother arrived, the caregiver told her what had happened and was surprised when the parent responded with tears instead of laughter.

Parents may have serious reservations about placing their child in care in the first place, and these feelings will be heightened if they feel they are missing any of their baby's firsts, or that their child is transferring its natural affection for the parents to the day-care workers. This then increases any feelings of guilt or inadequacy they may have as parents, and feelings of jealousy or anger may result (Galinsky, 1988). Again, these negative emotions can usually be traced back to the original ambiguity about roles and responsibilities.

Discrepancy in Goals and Approaches to Learning

Parents and early childhood professionals may also have different goals for children. The most common discrepancy exists in terms of educational or developmental goals (Galinsky, 1990). The traditional difference occurs when parents want to see their preschool children "educated," that is, learning numbers and letters, while the caregivers' goals focus on education through play, discovery, and exploration.

These methods are not mutually exclusive, but rather represent different means of attaining the same goal of education or development. This distinction may not always be apparent, however. Thus, the parent complains that the child "plays all day" rather than spending time learning. This discrepancy in goals or in perceptions of how children learn may lead to tensions if the parent does not believe that the caregiver is fulfilling his or her duty to teach the child.

Different Perspectives

The last set of differences revolves around the different world views or perspectives held by parents and early childhood professionals. Katz (1980) discusses several distinctions between parenting and caregiving. Seligman (1991) discusses world views, focusing particularly on interaction between caregivers and parents of children with special needs. The differences in world views may be more broadly applied to all parents who interact with caregivers and desire the best possible experiences for their children. The different views may lead to very different ways of interacting with children and hence cause tensions that are difficult to resolve.

Ascribed or achieved status

The first perspective involves whether one comes to care for children through an achieved or ascribed status (Seligman, 1991). Early childhood professionals have chosen this career and have achieved their status by hard work and study. They then expect to enjoy the freedom and authority to practise in ways that they choose. Parents, on the other hand, have what is known as an ascribed role, that is, one that is assigned to them by society rather than one they achieve solely through their own efforts. Also, parents cannot choose what their children will be like—they have no control over their sex, temperament, abilities, or disabilities. In addition, there is no training—no guidelines or diplomas for good parents—as there is for professionals.

The discrepancy between an ascribed and an achieved role may be the cause of tension and conflict between the caregiver and the parent. For example, the caregiver may have more success in dealing with the child who presents behavioural problems because she has chosen to work with this type of child, she has personal skills related to this type of work, and she can go home after eight hours of work and leave the child with someone else. The parent, on the other hand, may not have chosen this child, may not have the specific personal skills needed to control the child, nor be able to leave the child after several exhausting hours of interaction.

Scope of function

Katz (1980) refers to a similar distinction as differences in scope of function. On the one hand, parents have all-encompassing responsibilities in the family; everything is their business, and they are never off duty. Caregivers, on the other hand, have fixed hours, and their functions are more specific and limited in scope. These differences mean that the two sides look at their child-care responsibilities from completely different perspectives, and this can cause conflicts.

The individual or the group

A third perspective is called "universalism versus particularism" by Seligman (1991), while others refer to the difference in perspective between the parents who focus on the individual child and the caregivers who focus on the group (Katz, 1980). For better or worse, parents are concerned exclusively with their own child and therefore have quite particular concerns. Parents may make demands for their child that inadvertently put other children at risk (Katz, 1980). For example, parents may choose to bring in a snack to which other children have allergies.

The early childhood professional, on the other hand, is concerned with all children under his or her care and must balance the needs of the individual within that group with the needs of the group as a whole. Sometimes this can be accomplished on an individual basis (e.g., each child is changed when wet or dirty), and sometimes this is best accomplished as a group (e.g., in drawing up snack and lunch schedules). When the focused perspective of the parent clashes with the broader outlook of the caregiver, there may be conflicts surrounding care.

Scenario

Why Should One Child Enjoy Special Privileges?

A day-care centre opened at 7:00 a.m. each morning, and children arrived steadily through to 9:00 a.m. One mother worked a late shift in a grocery store; this meant that she went to work later and arrived home later in the evening. She would let her son stay up until 10:00 or 11:00 p.m. so that she would have time to be with him. She would then let him sleep in until whenever he woke up and take him into the day-care centre between 10:00 a.m. and noon. The caregivers found this extremely difficult to plan around, since they did not know when he would arrive and felt that they could not leave the playroom until he did so. The child, in turn, found the arrangement trying because he often had to search to find his group in the morning and join them partway through an activity. He felt that he was missing out on the fun, and the other children had difficulty making room for him midway through their play. The parent's perspective was that she wanted to spend time with her son and fit care into her schedule, while the caregivers felt that the child should conform to the schedule that everyone else followed, in order to ease the child's transition and interaction in the group.

Children Insist on Being Treated Equally

One parent consistently brought her 3-year-old child in after the scheduled breakfast time. The child did not eat beforehand, so the parent and caregivers agreed that she could bring breakfast from home because it would be impossible for the centre to prepare it for him. This seemed to be a satisfactory solution until all of the other children began asking for the same treatment. It became obvious then that the arrangement created more problems than it solved.

In both these scenarios, the caregivers' view of group care has come into conflict with the parents' perspective of what is best for their child. When parents have not been involved in group-care settings themselves, the difficulties they are creating may not even be apparent to them. They only understand that they wish to ensure that their child's needs are met, and they view the caregiver as negligent if this does not occur. The potential for conflict here is obvious. While caregivers may find it difficult to accommodate the wishes of all parents, they should keep in mind that all children need a parent who cares about them more than anyone else.

In relation to this, Katz (1980) discusses the concept of *partiality*. Because parents have an emotional attachment to their child, they tend to treat their child as a special person. In group settings, this can lead parents to be partial to their own child, at the expense of all the other children in the group. The caregiver, however, needs to be equally available to all children. If she acts differently with one child, the other parents interpret this as favouritism.

Specific or diffuse functions

A fourth perspective centres around the context in which the child is viewed (Seligman, 1991). Caregivers usually see the child in only one setting, where they interact with peers and adults. Parents see the child in other settings, in interaction with a range of different people—especially extended family members and siblings. Sometimes the parent may not see the child function much within the peer group (i.e., with other children of the same age), but this is how the caregiver sees the child on a daily basis.

Thus, for example, when the parent reports certain behaviour, skills, or abilities of the child, the caregivers may find it difficult to believe because they have never seen the child act that way. Likewise, the parents often cannot understand the caregivers' concerns about the child's interaction with other children. In both of these examples, the perspective from which each individual views the child provides the framework for the way they know the child. The lack of opportunity to view the child in other contexts makes it difficult to understand the other person's view.

It's All a Matter of Perspective

Judy's caregiver and mother were in the middle of an unpleasant conflict. Her mother did not want Judy to nap for more than half an hour, so that she would not be up late at night. Her mother needed the time after 8:30 to devote to Judy's older sibling, who often required help with homework. The caregiver, however, found that with such a short nap, Judy was fussy and cranky for the rest of the afternoon. The mother's observations were quite different. On weekends, when Judy did not nap at all, she was fine until the early bedtime. It could very well be that, in the quieter home setting, Judy did not need a nap to cope with afternoon activities, whereas in the noisier, busier day-care centre, a nap was required. However, neither adult had the opportunity to observe Judy in both settings.

Intensity of affection

One of the cornerstones of traditional views of professionalism is objectivity and a lack of emotional involvement with clients (Katz, 1980). Recently this view of professionalism has been criticized, however, because it does not take into account the mostly female-dominated professions such as nursing, rehabilitation therapy, and early childhood education, in which warmth and caring are paramount (Baxter, 1998; Noddings, 1990; Shimoni, 1992; Griffin, 1989). However, the fact remains that many early childhood professionals do feel discomfort at the emotional bond that often forms between themselves and the children. Parents are expected to show affection to their children, but professionals are not. Whereas attachment is optimal for parents, detachment is considered optimal for professional practice (Katz, 1980). Attachment by caregivers can too often be interpreted as favouritism.

Professionals are trained not to become emotionally involved because it will affect their professional objectivity. Many human service professionals find themselves in conflicts because of this expectation. How does the nurse working with terminal patients not become emotionally involved with them? How does the professional working with children with special needs in a home setting not become emotionally involved? How does the day-care worker who interacts with young children all day, caring for their most intimate and personal needs, not become involved? The fact is that professionals *do* become involved because of the very nature of their work. The crux of the dilemma is this: it is difficult to give a child proper care without actually *caring for* that child. Parents who expect caregivers to be objective and detached and not become emotionally involved may find themselves in conflict when the child hugs the caregiver at the start of the day or expresses distress at having to leave the caregiver at the end of the day. These demonstrations of affection between the child and caregiver may be misunderstood by the parent, and it may be difficult for the caregiver to understand this reaction.

Scenario

Role Jealousy

A parent had her 4-year-old daughter in a family day home operated by her sister, the child's aunt. The child would call the caregiver "Auntie Debbie" during the day and would often call her mother "Auntie Mom" in the evenings. The parent initially thought this was cute but then began to question their relationship.

Katz (1980) discusses two other differences in relation to affection. The first is rationality. Society forgives parents a certain degree of irrationality when it comes to their children: they are expected to be "crazy" about their kids. As a consequence, parents become "ego involved" in parenting. When there is failure, of whatever sort, the parent might experience low self-esteem and guilt. Caregivers, on the other hand, are expected to be completely rational in their planning, observations, and interaction with the children in their care. Not being as emotionally involved, they can deal with failure in a more rational way.

The second difference is in spontaneity. Because of the nature of the relationship, parents can and should be spontaneous with their children. In fact, extensive training for parents has been questioned because it may make them behave in less spontaneous or more calculated ways (Katz, 1980). Professionals, on the other hand, are expected to set goals and act in deliberate ways at all times. This can cause some confusion for caregivers. Knowing that structured, formal learning approaches are inappropriate for young children, they wait for suitable moments. As they wait for these spontaneous moments to occur, they may feel that parents think they are not working or not being effective.

These are the perspectives or world views around which parents and early childhood professionals may experience tension and conflict. In most cases, it is not clearly understood that a difference in perspective exists, and this makes understanding the inevitable conflicts that much more difficult. Both sides may then attempt to rationalize their feelings (e.g., "She doesn't like me" or "She doesn't like my child"). We believe that an awareness and recognition of these perspectives can facilitate the development of more positive relations. It doesn't mean that the "problem" is solved but perhaps the caregiver may consider the parent's request from another perspective. For example, when caregivers recognize that it is natural for parents to advocate for their own children, it will be easier to think about complementary functions and about how caregivers and parents can work together in the best interests of the child without misinterpreting the parent's request.

Unclear Policies

Most day-care centres attempt to provide parents with as much information as possible, both during their initial orientation and on a daily basis. Nevertheless, conflicts still arise when parents claim that they were never informed about one thing or another. Parents may receive pages of policies and procedure information but not read it, or they may read it and not remember it. It is also possible that they will be given details at the end of the day when the only thing on their mind is getting home. This apparent lack of communication is quite common and can result in conflicts between caregivers and parents, either on a short-term or long-term basis (Powell, 1989; Galinsky, 1990; Ghazvini & Readdick, 1994).

In addition to the obvious difficulties that can result, the caregiver may begin to question the parents' level of interest in their child or their level of respect for the caregiver. Parents, for their part, may look to other places for support and not consider the exchange of information with caregivers as significant (Ghazvini & Readdick, 1994). The conflict then expands or continues to grow. As we mentioned earlier, the transition from home to day-care centre can be a stressful time for parents; therefore, it is probably not the best time to ask them to remember various details about centre policies.

Summary: Typical Sources of Stress and Tension in the Parent/Caregiver Relationship

1. Preconceived ideas:
    - Some parents believe that caregivers have an easy job.
    - Some caregivers believe that children are not really the parent's priority.
    - Some caregivers believe that parents consider the day care to be little more than a dumping ground for their children.

---

2. Different values and beliefs.
3. Differences in power and status:
   - Some parents find it difficult to view caregivers as professionals.
   - Both parents and caregivers can be uncertain of the early childhood professional's role.
4. Discrepancy in goals and approaches to learning.
5. Different world views:
   - Parents have an "ascribed" role with children, while caregivers have an "achieved" role.
   - Parents and caregivers have a different "scope of function" in relation to childrearing.
   - Parents will be chiefly concerned with their own child, while caregivers have to think about what is best for the children as a group.
   - Caregivers see the child functioning almost exclusively within the peer group (a "specific function"), while parents see their child functioning in a variety of situations—with siblings, with the extended family, and in other social circumstances (a "diffuse function").
   - Because of the ties of natural affection, parents are thought to interact with their children in a way that is primarily emotional. Early childhood professionals, on the other hand, are expected to react with the children in their care in a cool and rational manner.
6. Unclear policies:
   - Policies that are in any way unclear or ambiguous are a potential source of conflict.

Strategies for Dealing with Conflict

Techniques for Conflict Resolution

- Understand that there may be differences in values and beliefs between the caregiver and parents.
- Provide parents with up-to-date written policies and guidelines.
- Keep parents informed and provide them with opportunities to become involved in the centre's program.
- Attempt to resolve conflicts in a way that makes it a win-win situation for the parent and the caregiver.
- Respect and learn about families' cultural and religious traditions.
- Realize that each family is unique and develop strategies that allow you to empathize with different families.
- Acknowledge resource limitations.

We have examined many ways that conflicts and tensions can arise between parents and caregivers. While understanding the roots and sources of conflicts is an important first step in resolving them, this understanding needs to be followed by action. The following strategies may be helpful to caregivers in their continuing interaction with parents, and they may prove especially useful in preventing conflicts or dealing with tensions or conflicts when they appear.

Examine Your Attitudes

Ask yourself the following questions, and write out your reply to each one.

- What do you think are the qualities of a good parent?
- What values and attitudes do you have regarding children and their needs?
- Being as honest as you can, try to define your attitude towards parents in general. Do you judge them harshly or leniently?
- What is your attitude towards discipline and punishment within the family? Have you known parents who were harsh disciplinarians and favoured the use of corporal punishment like spanking? How did you feel about them?
- Does your attitude towards parents change based on any of the following factors: ethnic background, religious affiliation, income, or marital status?
- What behaviour do you associate with a caring attitude towards children?
- List all the characteristics of the type of family with which you would have the most difficulty working. Beside each characteristic, list the reason why you would find it troublesome. When you are finished, write a brief analysis of what this list tells you about yourself.

Examining the answers to these questions may help you to recognize how you feel about parents and parenting. Once caregivers are aware of their own beliefs, they may take the first step in understanding and improving their relations with parents (Galinsky, 1988). Your beliefs or values will not necessarily be altered, but perhaps you will understand why your relationship with Harry's mother is not like your relationship with the other mothers. This examination may also make caregivers more effective by ensuring that the parents who require assistance the most are actually getting it.

Understanding

Early childhood professionals need to be aware of their own beliefs, values, and attitudes and of how these may affect their interaction with parents. They may then have to determine how they will continue to show respect for some parents despite the differences of opinions and backgrounds that may exist between those parents and themselves.

Scenario

Achieving a Compromise

A young mother and a caregiver were at odds about toilet training practices. The mother believed that children should be trained by the time they were 1 year old. Everyone in her family had been successfully trained by that age. The caregiver believed that children should be trained when they are developmentally ready, when they show interest, and at their own pace. The caregiver had difficulty understanding the mother's position until they discussed their beliefs and attitudes. Their differences remained, but a compromise was achieved.

Scenario

Unspoken Attitudes

An older caregiver in a baby room believed that mothers should really stay at home with their babies. That was the way that she had been raised, and that was the way she had raised her own children. Although she never expressed her views verbally, they were clear in her approach with the babies and the mothers. She was often curt and cold to the parents, nonverbally communicating her lack of support for their actions. On the other hand, she was very cuddly and warm with the babies and viewed herself as the mother's replacement. Several of the parents complained to the director, claiming that the caregiver's need to be "a good mother" made her insensitive to the needs of the babies' real mothers. The real difference was in beliefs, and her behaviour clearly portrayed her underlying attitudes about babies in day care.

Once caregivers become aware of their own beliefs in relation to parenting and families, they may also come to realize that the source of the conflict lies in themselves, that is, within these basic values and beliefs. This understanding will be the first step in helping to ease strained relations (Coleman, 1991) and in developing more family-centred practices (McBride, 1999). They will then need to make some decisions about the next step. This decision may result in the use of strategies to change the situation (e.g., providing developmental information regarding toilet training), or it may result in a recognition that the situation will likely remain unchanged because of religious or cultural differences in childrearing (Katz, 1980), but a sense of respect for parents' opinions will prevail (McBride, 1999). Once caregivers recognize the diverse nature of families, they may acquire more appreciation of different cultures (Coleman, 1991). They may also realize that not all families will desire or choose to become involved in the same ways (Coleman, 1991; Galinsky, 1988).

Humility

Early childhood professionals must also recognize that there are limitations to their own knowledge (Galinsky, 1988). Caregivers do frequently have a solid foundation of child development knowledge. We have to act to the best of our ability, recognizing that this body of knowledge changes and develops over time. Childrearing practices, for example, have changed substantially over the years and continue to change today. We cannot assume that the way it is done in our culture, nor the way we learned it, is necessarily the best way in all circumstances. In addition, caregivers must acknowledge the centrality of family in the child's development and, accordingly, respect and support families (McBride, 1999). This dimension of practice may be new (e.g., for special education professionals) and continue to create challenges for early childhood professionals.

Policies

As we noted above, it is important for a centre's policies to be phrased in clear language and to be communicated to the parents in a way they will understand. Here are a few guidelines to follow in implementing this idea.

First, it is important to have a thorough orientation meeting at which the centre's philosophy, policies, and procedures are reviewed and explained to each parent (Essa & Young, 1994; Bundy, 1991). In this way, the parents will become aware not only of the policies but also of the rationale for each of them. They will also get to know the important people in the day-care centre, such as the director.

Second, a policy manual for parents can be developed and given to them for their own reference. Updating and adaptation will be required from time to time; when this occurs, parents should be kept up to date as well. Providing parents with this sort of information should reduce the potential for conflict at the centre. For example, parents will know beforehand that only certain snacks are allowed in the day-care centre, and they will understand procedures regarding clothing, lost items, and pick-up times. Providing opportunities for parents to have input in developing and adapting policies may also serve to increase their willingness to work with caregivers and centres.

Inform and Involve Parents

In Chapter 14, we considered the importance of two-way communication between parents and the centre and of the need to grant parents some measure of influence or control over centre policies. The more ongoing communication that occurs with parents, and the more parents are involved in the programs, the less likely it is that conflicts and tensions will arise. Chapter 16 will provide a number of strategies for enhancing communication and collaboration with parents on an ongoing basis.

Work Towards a "Win-Win" Solution

Resolving conflicts usually involves creating a situation where both parties win (Barker & Barker, 1993). It is up to you, as an early childhood professional, to see the conflict in that light. Ask yourself the following question: "What needs to happen so that the parent can walk out of here with her dignity intact and so can I?" If only one person wins, the other usually feels humiliated or victimized. Even though winning may feel good at the moment, it is rarely satisfying in the long run, if only because the conflict usually resurfaces in some other form. Caregivers need to act gracefully rather than defensively and to develop relationships with parents based on professional rather than personal issues (Katz, 1992).

When a conflict develops, try to remain calm and focused on the situation. Do not get defensive and escalate the problem. When parents feel respected and in control, they are more likely to respond in a similar unemotional fashion. Your calmness of tone and mannerism may precipitate a change in theirs. Remember that parents genuinely care about their children and attempt to do what is best for them. Attempting to work with the parents towards this common goal will be more effective than working against them. Again, recognizing the absolute importance of family, and working in respectful and supportive ways form the foundation of family-centred practice.

This does not mean that early childhood professionals must act in subservient ways or apologize every time something goes missing. If an apology is warranted, give it. If it is not, provide a clear explanation of what happened. The parent may have to go home to cool off and think about the situation, but your manner of handling it without reacting emotionally or being defensive will help the process.

Respect Cultural or Religious Differences

When conflicts or tensions result from cultural or religious differences, caregivers can do several things to bridge the gap for children and parents. First, don't make assumptions. For example, all families may not be able to participate in centre activities in the same ways (Coleman, 1991). Second, ask questions. Having factual information about traditions, beliefs, and their significance may lead to increased understanding. For example, appreciating why the child may be dressed in a particular way, eat certain foods, or demonstrate certain behaviour will enhance your acceptance of difference. Most parents are very willing to share their cultural heritage if they know that you care and desire the information. It is estimated that, by the year 2020, one in three families in the United States will be Black, Hispanic, or Asian. This growing trend across North America makes the acquisition of cross-cultural information by child-care workers more and more of a necessity. There is a need to develop varied strategies for families with different linguistic or cultural backgrounds; at present there is a distinct lack of parent education information in these areas (Powell, 1989). For example, some centres will find it necessary to locate people who can communicate in different languages, to help families adapt to Canadian or American cultural practices, and to find supports beyond the classroom, such as clothing or social services (Coleman, 1991; Short & Johnston, 1994; McBride, 1999).

Third, ask parents to share information with staff, children, and other families. When children observe tolerance in their daily lives and have opportunities to view differences among cultures as interesting instead of as something to be feared or criticized, they too will grow in tolerance.

Empathy Training

One of the most important reasons for writing this book was our desire to enhance the caregiver's understanding of the challenges faced by families today, so that the caregiver will be better able to empathize with families. It takes practice and commitment to develop empathy, but it is well worth the effort. There are several ways that it can be done.

The first way to develop empathy is fairly simple. Use the knowledge that you already possess and try to imagine what it would be like if you were in the same situation as the parent. What would it be like, for example, to go to work every morning having had no sleep because of a crying baby? What would it be like having to worry about where money for the next meal was coming from? What would it be like to lose an entire social network with the ending of a marriage?

Sometimes it is easier to empathize with people who are in the midst of a serious crisis or in very unfortunate circumstances than it is with people who seem to be successful. Therefore, try to imagine also what it would be like for a mother of young children who has invested heavily in her career, and is now struggling to juggle the demands of a job and family. Imagine the stress such a mother will feel when she has to be at work to negotiate a major contract she has spent months preparing and finds that her child has come down with chicken pox. Even if you think that a career should be secondary, try to imagine her frustration and fear in such a situation.

A second way to develop empathy is to listen to and talk with people who are in similar situations. Talk to single mothers about the stresses in their lives; listen to fathers who are trying to be nurturing parents but have had no one in their own lives to act as a model.

A third and more sophisticated way of developing empathy is to find parallels in your own life that can help you identify with the feelings of parents. Suppose, for example, that you are having trouble understanding what it would be like for a new immigrant to North America. Perhaps you can remember changing schools when you were little, or moving houses, or travelling in a foreign country where people did not speak the same language as you. In these and other ways, you may learn to sympathize with parents rather than to blame or judge them.

Know Your Limits

All human service professionals want to provide the best and most inclusive services possible. In keeping with this desire, it is important that early childhood professionals recognize the limits within which they work. Caregivers need to know when to say yes, when to say no, and when to refer (Galinsky, 1988). Further, caregivers need to feel confident in saying no or in sharing information with parents. Early childhood professionals also need to recognize the stress of their chosen career and ensure that they have supports in place for themselves.

Conclusion

The early childhood profession has made great strides in the last decade in articulating the professional role of caregivers and teachers. Collaboration with parents is part of the definition of quality care. NAEYC states that "teachers are responsible for establishing and maintaining frequent contacts with families" (Bredekamp, 1987: 12). However, the conflicts and tensions described in this chapter often present obstacles to successful fulfilment of the caregiver's role. Understanding the sources of conflict and developing strategies to prevent and overcome them will ultimately enhance the relationship between early childhood professionals and parents and benefit the children in their care.

Exercises

1. Check your attitudes by completing the following checklist regarding your feelings towards working with parents.

   As a caregiver, I . . .   YES   NO
   a) feel that parents are more work than help.
   b) feel stress when parents enter my playroom.
   c) prefer to work alone.
   d) compare siblings from the same family.
   e) feel threatened by parents.
   f) view parents as a great resource.
   g) enjoy having outside persons in the room.
   h) hold certain beliefs about certain groups of people.

i)   feel parents use television to babysit their children.

j)   feel that parents are not interested in their children.

k)   work better with a social distance between myself and parents.

l)   believe parents are irresponsible for letting children come to day care in inappropriate clothing.

m)   feel that a close working relationship with parents is necessary.

n)   feel that developing this relationship is part of my job.

o)   am pleased when all the parents leave.

p)   anticipate parent conferences with pleasure.

q)   use written communication to avoid face to face contact.

r)   feel that parents have resigned from their parental role.

s)   feel parents have their children overinvolved in activities.

t)   enjoy working with parents.

Source: Adapted from a class exercise used at Grande Prairie Regional College in Alberta.

2.   Reread the scenarios on pages 255, 256, and 257 and brainstorm some possible solutions to the conflicts.

3.   Identify your own areas of stress when working with families. List some of the factors outlined in this chapter that may help you or your colleagues to work through some of these difficulties.

4.   Read the following family situations, then

   a)   determine your attitude towards the parents described in each situation;

   b)   brainstorm ways to offering support to these families.

      i)   Mr. and Mrs. Ban own their own small business and find it necessary to put in long days. It is difficult for them to spend time in their children's centre because of their business.

      ii)   Mrs. Smith has not been seen at the centre for some time, and rumour has it that she has had a nervous breakdown. Her husband finally confirms that this is true. She is still interested in what happens to her daughter at the centre, but she is not ready yet for large groups or for attending meetings.

      iii)   Wanda Green is a single parent and has expressed interest in attending parent meetings. She has no car, however, and would have difficulty affording the extra expense of a babysitter to attend.

      iv)   Mr. and Mrs. Gupta are new to this country and have just enrolled their son in your centre. They have told him that he cannot participate in Halloween or Thanksgiving activities.

      v)   Jack Reed would like to meet more parents of the other children. He has approached the caregiver but has been ignored each time he suggests a get-together.

      vi)   Mona Perth is a very busy woman with three children and a full-time career. She feels that whatever happens during the day in the centre is the centre's problem and that the caregivers should handle it without bothering her.

      vii)   The day care uses a variety of food such as macaroni, flour, dried vegetables, and fruits for craft activities. One parent, Mrs. Earl, has a lot of difficulty with this since she is trying to teach her children to value what they have and is very involved in international relief. She believes that using food as toys is in conflict with her values.

5. Empathy exercise: For each of the following remarks, write down what feelings you think the parent may be experiencing:

   a) I'm not sure what I'm supposed to do when I come to the centre for the day.

   b) All my child does here is play. He never brings home worksheets or drawings.

   c) My son teaches every song he learns here to everybody in our family.

   d) The children are going on another field trip?

   e) My child's soiled pants were sent home, and I'd just like to know why you didn't get him to the bathroom on time.

6. Who can you talk openly with when you are feeling upset about a parent? How does talking to this person help you?

7. How do you feel when parents are present in the room? How do you think the parents are feeling? List some ideas of what you could do to help parents and caregivers feel more comfortable and welcome.

8. Ask people from different cultural backgrounds what their approach to conflict and conflict resolution is. How will this information assist you in your work with parents?

Enhancing Parent— Staff Collaboration

chapter 16

Objectives

- **To provide guidelines for planning activities with parents.**

- **To suggest activities that are congruent with the goals of parent involvement.**

- **To highlight special considerations in planning collaborative strategies.**

> Cathy, a recent graduate of an early childhood education program, sighed in desperation after a parent meeting that she had organized was poorly attended. "I don't know why I even bother," she said. "Parents just aren't interested in coming." At the same time Adele, a parent who did not attend the meeting, was having the following thoughts. "I wish they [staff] would give me more notice about parent meetings. Three days is not enough time for me to get child care arranged. They probably think I don't care."

The above situation is all too common. It shows why working with parents can be a frustrating experience—both for the day-care staff and for the parents themselves. If properly organized and carried out, however, collaborative ventures can be fun, they can communicate important information in both directions, and they can result in parents and caregivers working together for common goals. Several factors will influence the success of parent involvement activities. These include having a clear understanding of goals, having a repertoire of strategies and activities, considering the practical aspects beforehand, and having in place some way of evaluating the success of the parent involvement program on an ongoing basis. We refer to these considerations as the why, what, and how of working with parents and families. In Chapter 14, we discussed why parent involvement is an important component of early childhood programs. This chapter will focus on strategies to enhance parent involvement and to maximize family-centred practices.

The "What" of Parent Involvement: Clarifying the Goals

It seems appropriate that the discussion of strategies should begin with the process of clarifying goals. How we will work with parents will vary greatly depending on our own beliefs and goals as early childhood professionals. It is important to understand where we wish to go before we determine how we will get there. Clarifying the goals involves an awareness of both our knowledge and our feelings, which will both influence how we work with parents. For example, in the following scenario, a mature staff member admits that in the beginning of her career, her feelings influenced her more than her knowledge.

Scenario

Fear of Parents

In the beginning, I couldn't bring myself to initiate a discussion with parents. I would quickly say hello and then busy myself with the children to avoid further contact. I knew that I should be telling them about Johnny's artwork or about a new book that we had in the centre, and asking them about his trip to his grandmother's over the holiday. But every time I tried, I was overwhelmed by the fear that they would not really want to hear what I had to say.

Clearly, in this example, the inexperienced caregiver knew what she should have done, and probably could have easily explained why it was important. As she gained experience and confidence, she was more able to act in accordance with her professional knowledge. Understanding the goals of parent involvement is part of that knowledge.

It may be helpful to consider goals from the different perspectives of the child, the parent, the family, and the caregiver. Although it is common to think of goals in terms of one dimension only, the benefits of parent–staff collaboration often overlap. For example, if a parent accompanies a class on a field trip, it may benefit the children to have exposure to a new and interesting adult, and it will probably make the child of that parent feel very special indeed. Also, some staff value the assistance that a parent can provide on a field trip. However, sometimes staff feel that the time and planning required to accommodate parent participation is overwhelming.

The goals of parent–staff collaboration may be seen quite differently by different participants. One mother made the following remarks.

Scenario

Just Showing Interest Is Important

I always go to parent-teacher nights at school. I don't ever expect to learn very much, because it is always so busy there and the teachers have so many parents to deal with. I go just so that the teachers will know that I care about Jimmy's education. Then I make a separate appointment to discuss any concerns with the teacher.

One might assume that the teacher's goal in holding a parent–teacher evening is to provide parents with information or an opportunity to discuss concerns. However, the parent's goal in this case was quite different: she simply wanted to show the teacher that she cared.

In Chapter 14 we presented an overview of the most prevalent goals of parent involvement: parent education, parent influence or control, and continuity of care. It is important to realize that any one activity can meet a number of goals.

Scenario

Multiple Goals Covered by One Activity

When planning an "open house" evening for parents, siblings, and grandparents, staff members found they had different ideas of what goals could be accomplished by such an event. "This will provide us with the opportunity to informally discuss the importance of free play with parents," said one (i.e., parent education). "It will give parents an opportunity to see all the new pamphlets about community resources that we have on our bulletin board," said a second staff member (i.e., working within the ecological model). "My biggest concern is that parents feel welcome and able to make suggestions regarding the room arrangement," said a third staff member (i.e., parent influence and control). "It will be nice when parents see the new playground and can talk to the children at home about it," said another (i.e., continuity of care). Janet, a parent who had come in late and overheard the conversation, smiled and remarked: "The goal for me will be to come to a place where I will be served a free cup of coffee while the children are busy playing." (family-centred)

It is probably true that if an activity is designed to incorporate more than one goal, it is more likely to be well attended and well received than if the goals are too narrowly defined.

Input from Parents

Formulating the goals of parent–staff collaboration should always be done in conjunction with the parents. Caregivers need to provide opportunities to promote parents' choices and decision making (McBride, 1999). It is very disempowering to have others decide what is best for you (Pizzo, 1993). In addition, there is little point in planning an activity if parents do not feel that it would be a valuable use of their time. Information from parents on what they want from the centre or school can be gleaned from informal discussions or through a prearranged meeting to discuss the goals of collaboration. Seek parents' opinions and work with them to generate options. Another avenue may be to develop a questionnaire for parents so that they can, at their leisure and in privacy, provide information regarding their expectations and interests (Riepe, 1990; Essa & Young, 1994). If parents' responses are taken into account in the planning of activities, they may well be willing to increase their involvement. If a questionnaire *is* used to collect feedback on potential activities, it is important to bear in mind that, in responding, most people will choose to support only those activities with which they are familiar; they will not have the benefit of discussion or of hearing about others' experiences before they fill out the questionnaire.

Communicating Effectively with Parents

Effective communication is the framework for establishing and maintaining any kind of collaboration with parents (Essa & Young, 1994; Coleman, 1991). Although it seems logical that early childhood professionals should be able to communicate easily with parents and adults, this is not always the case. In fact, little training in early childhood education programs is directed at working with adults (Galinsky, 1988). Caregivers have been known to break out in a cold sweat at the very thought of interacting with parents. As we say in the chapter on conflicts and tensions, messages can be interpreted in unexpected ways. For example, when the caregiver remarks, "He's been so good all day," the parent might interpret that to mean, "My care is better than yours," leaving the parent feeling undervalued (Galinsky, 1988). Communication skills, however, can be learned and they can be improved, and caregivers should be willing to admit it if they need further training in this area.

As we have repeatedly emphasized, good communication begins with self-knowledge, that is, with an awareness of one's own beliefs and values (Adler & Towne, 1990). Our beliefs and values often lead us to make assumptions about other people the first time we meet them. These assumptions may or may not be accurate. A good communicator thinks about the initial assumptions he or she has made, but is careful not to pass judgment and is open to receiving new information (Galinsky, 1988). The ability to build effective communication with parents requires a rapport with them and a sense of trust. This serves as a foundation for all work with parents.

In addition to self-awareness and a nonjudgmental attitude, good communicators acquire a repertoire of verbal and nonverbal behaviours that facilitate good communication. Among these are the ability to listen, that is, to show by body language and spoken language that the speaker has your full attention. You can indicate your interest by paraphrasing what the speaker has said and by asking questions about points you may not have understood perfectly. Good communicators also learn to ask questions that provide direction for the conversation and solicit more information from the speaker. They do this with sensitivity and without prying.

Since communication skills are so essential for effective work with families, it is recommended that early childhood professionals continually assess and improve their skill in this area. Many continuing education programs hold courses and seminars in communication.

Communicating a Welcoming Attitude

In relation to communication, it is important for caregivers to ensure that parents feel welcome and know that their involvement is valued (Coleman, 1991). Even small things, such as how the room is set up and the way parents are greeted or spoken to, can convey this message.

Scenario

Make the Centre Inviting

After hearing about a variety of different centres in a class on parent involvement strategies, a student realized that the parents of her children never came into her playroom. When she asked several of the parents why, they all agreed

> that they never felt welcome in the playroom. The lockers and sign-up sheets were in the main entrance, and the parents perceived the door to the playroom as the cut-off point. After the caregiver moved the sign-up sheet inside the door and made an effort to greet each parent and invite them into the play-room, many of them were happy to visit.

Communication between staff and parents, and parent involvement, will occur more readily if parents feel welcome and think that their efforts are recognized. Providing opportunities for parents to participate, to share opinions, and to be involved in multiple ways will all serve to promote a welcoming partnership. Providing a space and acknowledging parents' presence will lay a strong foundation for designing fruitful parent involvement activities.

Ideas for Collaboration with Parents

Direct Communication

Once staff members have reflected on their attitudes towards parents and their goals for working with them (and once they have the necessary communication skills), the stage is set for the development of a broad range of plans to implement parent–staff collaboration. We must stress at the beginning, though, that there will always be a tremendous diversity in the interests and availability of parents (Coleman, 1991; Powell, 1989). Caregivers should consider the spectrum of needs evident in parents from various linguistic and cultural backgrounds and in parents with different levels of education. Therefore, we cannot provide any sure-fire "recipes" for parent involvement with ingredients that never vary. Instead, we present several ideas that are intended to be starting points and to stimulate creative thought. Rather than putting a lot of energy into one approach, consider as many options as possible, then allow parents to choose or "listen" to their feedback for future planning. It is not important to have perfect attendance for all approaches, rather to have each parent involved in one of the many types of strategies during the year. We begin with the kinds of activities that should be ongoing and almost automatic, and then consider strategies for collaboration that require additional thought and planning.

Daily conversations

All caregivers attempt to greet children and parents each morning and at the end of each day (Bundy, 1991). Children, especially young children, usually require assistance during these transition times. Caregivers often try to build this short conversation into their daily routine. This is the most common and frequent type of parent involvement activity (Powell, 1989; Galinsky, 1988; Ghazvini & Readdick, 1994; Gestwicki, 1992). These informal contacts and exchanges are perhaps also the single most important aspect of parent involvement (Essa & Young, 1994). However, the intention to speak to each parent each day is not always as easy to carry out as it seems. Parents often arrive all at the same time, and one small disaster (e.g., wet pants, lost shoes, a crying child) can inhibit even the best of intentions. Parents are sometimes tired or stressed at the end of the day, just as caregivers are. Rotating shifts often mean that the child's primary caregiver is unavailable for discussion. Caregivers may suddenly realize that they have said no more than "good morning" to some parents for days, if not weeks, at a time. Therefore, while the ongoing face-to-face interaction seems on the surface to be the best way to communicate, it often does not happen consistently, and there need to be safeguards to ensure that communication occurs regularly (Stipek, Rosenblatt, & DiRocco, 1994). It is important to keep a record of conversations with parents, and to review this record periodically, perhaps at the end of every week. If regular contact has not occurred at arrival and departure times, other arrangements should be made.

Phone calls

Telephone calls can be an effective way of communicating, provided that they occur at a time convenient for both parties (Essa & Young, 1994; Gestwicki, 1992). Staff should try to organize times when they are "covered" in the playroom and let parents know when it is convenient for them to take calls. Similarly, staff can inquire about convenient times to contact parents. Some parents enjoy receiving phone calls that are done simply to keep in touch and relate information about the child (Bundy, 1991) rather than just the bad news. One mother said that it made her day when she got a phone call from the centre with a funny story about her toddler's new accomplishment. Other parents may wish to communicate by telephone only if there is a specific need, as in a request for extra clothing, or an emergency.

Written Communication

Not all communication with parents is done face to face. Written communication can meet some of the objectives of parent–staff collaboration and can be used to reach either individual parents (e.g., through communication books) or groups of parents (e.g., through newsletters). The ideas below can serve as one- or two-way communication vehicles to (a) share information with parents, (b) provide a mechanism for parent input, or (c) help parents gain access to wider community networks. In this last case, the communication strategy leads to three-way communication.

Bulletin boards

Bulletin boards can be an excellent way of making available for parents a wide variety of information (Essa & Young, 1994). Pamphlets from community agencies, book reviews, community events, and excerpts from magazines can all be posted on the board for parents to peruse. Another part of the bulletin board can be more focused on centre activities, such as samples of children's artwork, photographs, information about daily activities, menus, and lost-and-found notices.

We must remember that bulletin boards will be useful only if they are read by the parents (Bundy, 1991). The information should be presented in an organized and appealing manner (Essa & Young, 1994). Sometimes, pictures of the children are effective in attracting parents' attention. The information on the bulletin board should also be updated consistently. If the information is out of date, parents will stop reading it. Parents may also have information that they want to share on the bulletin board and should be welcome to make use of it for this purpose. Whenever possible, have translations available for parents who do not read English.

Ideas for Bulletin Boards

1. Provide a bright, colourful background, that is, cover the board with an eye-catching background colour or design. Trim the board with a contrast colour.

2. Choose a spot where parents will see the board every day, near an entrance area or parent corner.

3. Provide some type of sign so that parents know the information is specifically for them, for example, PARENTS or INFORMATION.

4. Keep information current by treating topics that have a direct effect on the children or families: tips on time changes or summer safety. Be sure that parents know when information has been updated or changed by using a new sign or change of colour.

5. Provide information regarding upcoming family events in your community, especially if they are free.

6. Provide take-away information (e.g., pamphlets, articles, recipes) or a sign-up sheet so that you can make copies for those interested in the information.

7. Provide some humour in the use of pictures, cartoons, special messages, or thoughts for the day that would appeal to parents and bring a smile to their faces at the end of a long day.

8. Provide space for parents to post and exchange information with each other (e.g., child-care needs, interesting articles).

9. Attach a pen and paper to the board in case parents wish to jot down information.

10. Change information on a frequent and regular basis.

11. Avoid posting information that would more appropriately be delivered individually (e.g., overdue fees).

Parent corners

As an extension of the bulletin board, many centres set up a parent corner with a bulletin board and a table for displaying information. A few comfortable chairs and a coffee pot can be a sign to parents that they are welcome to stay for a few minutes to look through the material. Even though the times parents are in the centre (usually for dropping off and picking up their children) seem rushed, sometimes they are introduced to valuable sources of information during those few minutes. This may provide caregivers the vehicle to provide information in sensitive areas without pointing fingers at a particular family, parent or child.

Scenario

Unforeseen Consequences

A parent dropped off her two preschool-age children at the day-care centre. On her way out, she noticed an advertisement on the bulletin board for a meeting of Alcoholics Anonymous that was being held in the same building during the evening. This small, innocuous posting prompted her to attend the meeting. Twelve years later, when her new baby began at the same centre, she recalled fondly that the bulletin board played a significant role in changing her life.

Parent corners may also provide sufficient space for parents to advertise (e.g., for lost items, for a babysitter exchange, for articles they want to sell, etc.). Offering space for this purpose may also encourage parents to share information and resources with other parents. In fact, it is probably best to vary the kind of material in the parent corner. Some of the material can relate to children and child development, other material can relate to other interests parents may have (Bundy, 1991).

Scenario

An Exchange of Information

Students enrolled in an early childhood course on the family and the community were required to copy and read a number of journal articles on a wide range of topics. When one student had completed a module of readings, she decided to take them into her day-care centre and leave them on a table by the coat racks. She was amazed to see how quickly the articles were taken by the parents, and even more amazed to see parents bringing in other articles of interest to add to the collection. This exchange of articles provided the perfect opportunity for caregivers to share with parents and also for parents to share with other parents.

Considerations for a Parent Corner

1. Provide a special room, section, or corner for parents to call their own. This space should be well defined, easily accessible, and inviting to parents.

2. The area should include the parent bulletin board, comfortable adult-sized chairs or a sofa, a table, and coffee, if possible, so that parents are encouraged to stop and relax for a moment.

3. Start a parent information library in this area. Include books that may be borrowed and copies of articles or pamphlets that may be taken home or copied for personal use.

4. Provide a picture album of happenings in the day-care centre for parents to look at. Add new photographs or children's art regularly so that parents can keep up to date on daily activities. Be sure to represent all the playrooms and all the children.

Daily notes

In many cases brief notes sent home with the children can provide the parents with very important information (Bundy, 1991). Many parents of infants and toddlers will want to know how much they ate and slept, and whether or not a bowel movement occurred. Small, prepared, fill-in-the-blank notepads can facilitate this communication process. As the children get older, notes can contain other kinds of information, and the child may also wish to add a message with a picture or scribble, again to enhance the communication.

When using daily notes, as with all other forms of written communication, staff should take into account whether the parents will be able to read English. In some cases, it may be possible to have a daily communication form in a bilingual checklist format. Then staff could check off the relevant entries in English and the parents would be able to read them in their own language.

Communication books

Communication books are a useful resource for parents and staff, especially when they do not have the opportunity to speak together regularly. This situation occurs frequently when children are bused to their school or centre. A notebook that goes back and forth with the child provides the opportunity for the caregiver to write pertinent information to parents or to ask parents questions (Bundy, 1991). Parents can then respond and ask staff any questions that they may have. Topics may include eating, sleeping, a new accomplishment, and information about upcoming events. One drawback is that communication books can become a one-way vehicle for communication going from the centre to home but with no information returning. Caregivers can enhance the two-way nature by asking questions, by seeking information or clarification on a matter of concern, or by asking parents to share details of the child's life at home (e.g., "Ken says that you went to the farm this weekend. What did he enjoy the most?").

Sometimes, the information in the notebook can assist the staff and parents in helping children make themselves understood.

Scenario

A Communication Aid

Two-year-old Miguel came home from the centre one day, looked at his mother, and said "boat." "Did you read a story about a boat today?" asked his mother. Miguel shook his head no. His mother tried several more guesses, but each time her guess was wrong, Miguel seemed more frustrated, so she tried to distract him. That evening she wrote in the communication book that Miguel had been saying "boat" and she wondered if the staff knew what he was trying to tell her.

The caregiver wrote back that they had gone to the swimming pool and had watched the canoe practices there. The next evening Miguel's mother asked him about the canoes, and both Miguel and his mother seemed highly satisfied with the conversation.

Communication books can be delightful for parents and staff, but they can also become a burden if not done with sensitivity. Parents will vary in the enthusiasm of their responses, and they should not be judged if they do not write back. One mother was asked why she did not write in the communication book and responded as follows.

Scenario

Who Has the Time?

After work I rush to the centre to pick up Kaitlyn, then to the after-school program to pick up the boys. Supper, playtime, dishes, baths, teeth brushing, and a bedtime story for each child leave me pretty exhausted by the time they have gone to bed. If I don't have the energy to do both, I would rather communicate with my child than with the teacher.

Some parents do not write in the communication book because they are concerned about the impression they will give by using poor grammar and spelling. New Canadians or Americans may be particularly touchy about this, and staff must demonstrate sensitivity in this area. When a parent does write in the communication book, it is vital for the staff to continue to respond.

Considerations for Communication Books

1. Provide children with a small notebook that will easily fit in their diaper bag or backpack.
2. Write legibly about the children's day, what they did, and how they responded to routines such as naps, meals, or toileting. Include information about what parents will want or need to know, especially for younger children who may not be able to communicate this information. Remember, however, that older children may forget or answer every question from the parent with an "I don't know," so passing along information will still be considered useful. Include information about development or play.
3. Include questions for parents so that they know you want them to respond. Try not to ask too many questions, and phrase the questions in such a way that they require more than "yes" or "no" in reply.
4. Ask parents for information about what they have done as a family, to help you talk to the child about various matters.
5. Respect the parents' varying need or ability to write in the book.
6. Maintain confidentiality at all times.
7. Date and sign each entry.

Newsletters

Newsletters are a common means of sharing information with parents (Stipek, Rosenblatt, & DiRocco, 1994). A newsletter provides a different format for sharing much of the same kind of information that can be available on bulletin boards in parent corners. The advantage, of course, is that it is taken home and read at the parents' convenience. Newsletters are usually more effective when they have a personal touch and include entries from the centre director, board members, staff, and parents. They should have a good mixture of different kinds of information (Bundy, 1991). Some parents will be interested in reading about child development, some may want ideas for birthdays or recipes, and others may be more interested in learning about the resources in their community (Harms & Cryer, 1978). The best way to find out what parents want to read about is to ask them! It is also a good idea to find out whether the parents themselves would be willing to take over, or help, in the production of the newsletter.

Having places where children can be involved in the production may enhance parents' interest and serve to improve communication between parents and children. All parents have been faced with a typical conversation: "What did you do today?" "Nothing." "What did you have for lunch?" "Nothing." A small piece of information about the day or a special event may lead to more interactive communication. One day-care centre's newsletter always left one blank page where children could draw a picture of something special that happened to them that week or on that day. When the newsletter arrived home, the child could describe the picture and event in more detail to the parent. Because the picture arrived as part of the newsletter, it was considered very important by everyone.

Considerations for Newsletters

1. Newsletters should be published and sent home on a regular basis.

2. One page or section can include general information about the day-care centre, while another section or page can be more specific to a particular playroom or age group.

3. Include a title—something catchy or more personal than "A Monthly Newsletter." Ask parents for suggestions.

4. Use coloured paper if possible.

5. Try to have the information typed or keyboarded so that it is easier to read. Be sure to proofread it for spelling and grammatical errors.

6. Try to match the reading level or language to that of the parents. If language differences exist, try to enlist the assistance of an interpreter for the newsletter.

7. Get everyone involved in contributing information. Include the director, caregivers, cook, parents, and children.

8. Have a section where the children can draw a picture.

9. Have spaces for parents and community groups to add information as well.

Although bulletin boards, parent corners, and newsletters are usually considered strategies for sharing information with parents, other goals can be met at the same time. Parent participation in these activities furthers their influence at the centre. The information contained may help parents form their own networks of support and access wider-reaching community resources. This strategy is congruent with the model for working with families referred to as the ecological model, and is a key element of family-centred practices (McBride, 1999). Sharing information by these methods may very well assist parents in helping the child bridge the day-care experience with his home experience. Reading about a field trip in the newsletter, or learning about a new book or toy in the playroom, helps parents communicate better with their children about daily experiences.

Travelling goodie bags

Most children derive great pleasure from being able to share their experiences with their parents. A "goodie bag" that contains prized possessions from the day care that may be taken home for an evening may be a way of bringing a little piece of the centre home. For example, the children in one class each brought home a stuffed animal for a weekend and then drew pictures or wrote in a journal what they did on the weekend. The pictures and writing were then shared in class. Family theme bags (Helm, 1994) involve more comprehensive planning of activities, songs, crafts, and stories around a particular idea, but they also afford families the opportunity to spend some quality time together. Such take-home items help bridge the two environments in which the child spends time, allow the parent to see in what type of activities the child may be involved, and invite discussion between parents and their children (Stipek, Rosenblatt, & DiRocco, 1994), which can then be shared in the centre. Goodie bags and family theme bags may have special merit for low-income families where toys and books can be shared. Some items could be kept by the families (such as play-dough and craft supplies).

Newsletter—One Suggestion

Page One

[CATCHY TITLE]   *[DATE]*
"Small Town Crier"   *March 2000*

A Note from the Director
- review of policy
- staff changes
- room changes
- welcome to new families

Calendar of Upcoming Events
- meetings
- pot-luck suppers
- field trips

Cook's Corner
- new recipes
- menu changes

Parent Contributions
- ask parents to share informa-tion, ideas, concerns that would be pertinent to other parents
- thank-yous

Classifieds

Page Two

[Room Specific]
"Toddler Tattler"

Primary Caregiver's Contribution
- update about what is going on in the room
- requests for donations

Children's Contributions
- pictures
- stories
- jokes
- dictated "stories"

Parent Information *(related to parents with children in this age group)*
- courses / workshops (for parents and children)
- book reviews
- child development information
- ideas for "to dos" with children
- coping strategies

The goodie bag can be assembled by the child, and the caregiver can add to it according to her professional judgment. It is important to be cautious. If, for example, a family is in the throes of the divorce process, they might appreciate a book that explains divorce in language a child can understand. However, such a gesture may also be viewed as a criticism or an intrusion into family life. Sometimes day-care staff are concerned that the contents of the goodie bag will not be cared for or returned to the centre. It has been our experience, however, that families and children usually value this sharing and return the contents in good condition.

Just as bringing a piece of the centre home can be enjoyed by children and their families, the reverse is just as important. Children often enjoy it when a "piece of home" is brought to the centre, in the form of picture albums of family members (photographs or children's drawings), as well as toys and objects. It is easy to avoid these activities by rationalizing that things from home may be lost or damaged, or that health and safety concerns do not allow for toys from home. Commitment to the idea of closer links between home and centre will help staff find ways around these obstacles.

The strategies suggested above to enhance continuing communication with families relate primarily to the goal of bridging the home and day-care experiences for the child, or to establishing continuity of care. The ongoing communication often results in the sharing of information with parents and in parents' being able to bring their suggestions and knowledge of their own child to the centre staff. Through ongoing communication, support can be offered to the entire family system, and the family can be assisted in accessing wider community networks.

Parents as Volunteers in the Day Care

In the 1970s, there were a large number of centres and preschools that relied on parent "volunteers" to participate and assist on a regular basis (Katz, 1994). The benefits of such active participation were varied. Parents learned about their own children in a group setting, and saw their children interact with peers and teachers often in a very different way than at home (Katz, 1994). Parents and teachers really got to know one another. Children were usually very proud of their parents when it was their turn to be present. And teachers often appreciated having an extra pair of hands.

Today the realities of work and family mean that it is much more difficult for parents to be involved in this fashion (Coleman, 1991; Powell, 1989; Ghazvini & Readdick, 1994). However, with advance planning, parents may still be available to attend the centre. For example, many parents enjoy celebrating their children's birthday with their friends in the centre. Also, parents can play a number of roles within the playroom—as a special helper, an extra guide for a field trip, or a guest speaker to talk about their job or a hobby (police officers and firefighters seem to be among the most popular).

Parents need to feel welcome, and they may require sufficient notice to plan for such a day. When caregivers provide the opportunity and demonstrate appreciation, parents may be more willing to come. Parents can benefit from seeing and participating in their children's lives at the centre and from meeting their friends. This experience may also heighten the parents' understanding of the complexity of the caregiver's role and the demands of the job.

Caregivers can often learn much about the children by observing their interaction with their parents. It is important, though, to remember not to make hasty judgments based on a single observation of child–parent interaction. A parent might not feel comfortable enough to act naturally at first; therefore, the behaviour you see may not be at all typical. Because of the many demands on parents today, those who are not able to participate in this way must not be judged negatively. Instead, the caregiver needs to find other opportunities or activities for involvement that are more suited to that parent.

Considerations for Parents Visiting the Room

1. Welcome parents and thank them for coming.

2. Provide parents with an information sheet that welcomes them and gives some directions about what they can do in the room.

3. Invite parents to hang up their coat with their child's then to feel free to observe or follow their child to the activity of their choice.

4. If parents want to be assigned tasks, they may assist in the art area by making sure that children's names are on their work, by observing, and by listening to comments made by the children.

5. Invite parents to join in any games, dramatic activities, or play that may develop, since the children will enjoy their participation.

6. Make sure that parents are enjoying their time in your playroom, and check regularly that they feel comfortable and at home.

7. Try to have a variety of tasks available for parents to do. Some parents may feel more comfortable completing tasks such as hanging up artwork, cutting out pictures, or cleaning up an area, whereas other parents will want to spend their time with the children. A survey or questionnaire beforehand and regular checking during the visit will help ensure that parents always feel comfortable.

8. Try to thank parents for their involvement as they leave, reinforcing how valuable their contribution was to the playroom and to their child.

Evening Activities

For those parents who are unable to come to the centre during daytime hours, activities during the evening may provide the only opportunity they have to be actively involved in the centre. It is important to bear in mind that working parents have very little time to spare, and therefore any evening activities must be very worth their while (Bundy, 1991) and be convenient. Evening hours are often precious to staff as well, and their sacrifices to ensure successful evening events must be recognized. Evening activities can relate to a number of parent involvement goals: education, socializing, fund-raising, linking with the wider community, or simply having parent input and spending time together (Stipek, Rosenblatt, & DiRocco, 1994). These activities may include speakers, celebrations, or social activities. Any of these events present an opportunity for fund-raising. A family picnic or carnival presents the opportunity for socializing, and often parents who can afford it won't be averse to paying a nominal fee if they know that the money will be put to good use within the day-care centre. Parents may actually be more willing to contribute and be involved in an event like this than other fund-raising activities (e.g., selling merchandise or tickets). Caregivers should always consider families' ability to pay and choose other means of raising funds if this presents concerns for some children or families.

Speakers

Engaging a speaker to discuss a topic of interest to a group of parents is one activity that is often well received. The speaker may be from another profession, such as a doctor, nurse, psychologist, or social worker, or may be one of the staff. Sometimes early childhood professionals do not give their own expertise enough credit, and a gentle reminder might be in order that the parents might very well prefer listening to the caregiver who has daily contact with their children discuss topics like discipline or development. In addition, it is important to remember that parents themselves have a wealth of knowledge and information and may be invaluable as "guest" speakers. These events require considerable planning and input from parents to ensure that there is sufficient interest and ability to attend. Attendance may be improved by providing child care during the parent education activity.

Sample Parent Meeting Agenda

5:00–6:00   Supper with the children in the out-of-school care room (chili and toast—vegetarian substitute available).

6:00   Parents adjourn to the lounge for the meeting. Child care provided in the 3-4-year-old room.

Agenda

1. Welcome from the Director
2. Guest speaker—Mary Adams
   Topic: Guiding Your Child's Behaviour
3. Centre update
   • playground
   • fees
   • licensing inspection
4. Questions and feedback

7:30   Adjournment.

Celebrations and social activities

Social activities may include informal gatherings such as afternoon or evening tea or coffee parties, pot-luck suppers, or fund-raising dinners (such as spaghetti nights, pancake breakfasts, or barbecues). Sometimes parents enjoy evenings planned around children's activities at the centre, such as art shows or, if the children are old enough, performances of songs or plays. Even though some caregivers may have concerns about children performing, parents and grandparents treasure these moments.

A Creative Idea

The director of a day-care centre was getting tired of constantly having to dispose of children's artwork and of cubbies filled to the brim. She decided to stage an "art show." All pieces of artwork were labelled and displayed. Families were invited to view the children's accomplishments. The children took great pride in showing off their artwork. The evening ended with each child leaving with his or her pieces of art—this alone fulfilled the director's goal for the evening, but the enjoyment experienced by the children and their families was a pleasant bonus.

One centre regularly held an evening where the daily program was simulated, so that parents could actually experience "a day in the life of a child at the centre." Special people were invited to attend for an evening and, even though fathers were the most commonly invited guests, special people also included siblings, grandparents, cousins, and friends.

Holidays and special occasions are often good motivators for get-togethers between families and the centre. Halloween parties, Mother's and Father's Day celebrations, and cultural awareness evenings are often popular. Fund-raising events such as games nights, cakewalks, or carnivals can provide families with a fun night out and at the same time give them an opportunity to support the centre.

Scenario

Fathers, Too

One caregiver explained that Mother's Day was always so easy to plan for—a tea party, a fashion show—and these events were always well attended. She confessed to being stumped for Father's Day when another caregiver suggested a beer (root beer) and pretzel party that dads could attend on their way home from work. It was a hit.

Activities need to be arranged to fit parents' schedules and needs. For example, parents who need child care in the evening will be more likely to attend family events or activities that begin at pick-up time or have child care built in. However, parents with other young children at home will likely find these arrangements more difficult. Parent input will help guarantee a higher attendance rate. Caregivers should be careful to include diverse families in all events. A Father's Day event or craft may serve to alienate children who come from divorced families or single-parent homes. Ensure that children know that they have the option of inviting a special person or of making the craft for that special person.

Home Visits

Home visits have traditionally been used as a form of parent–caregiver involvement (Johnston & Mermin, 1994; Gestwicki, 1992). The advantages of home visits are seen in terms of allowing the caregiver to learn about children in their "natural setting," and providing the opportunity for parents and staff to become acquainted in the comfort of the parents' home. Children can feel very special when their teacher visits their home. However, home visits can be problematic at times. Some parents feel that they are intrusive. Many families value the privacy of their home and are uncomfortable at the thought of a visit by a caregiver. Children may not understand the reason for the visit and misinterpret the intent. Staff also have observed that the time involved in visiting the parents of all their children is unrealistic given the demands of their work. For all these reasons, home visits have waned in popularity and are seldom implemented these days, except in the case of children with special needs (Powell, 1989).

If home visits seem like a worthwhile strategy, it is essential that the goals of the visit are clear to both staff and parents, and that both parties are comfortable with the visit. Sometimes home visits can provide staff with important information, but it is dangerous to assume that you will have a complete understanding of the family from one home visit. Extreme sensitivity and professional finesse are required for this strategy of parent–staff collaboration (Johnston & Mermin, 1994). Some discomfort on both sides seems inevitable, as the following scenario illustrates.

Scenario

Tension During Home Visits

One day our daughter's preschool teacher came to our home for a visit. We lived in the same community and had been friends for some time before she became my daughter's teacher, so we were expecting a pleasant visit. My daughter felt strange calling her "Mrs. Smith" instead of "Sandy" and taking her on a "tour" of her room. At the end of the visit, her teacher said, "You know, the next time I come here it will be just as a friend, not as your teacher." My daughter sighed with relief (so did I) and said, "Oh good, then we can really visit."

This anecdote highlights the boundary issues involved in home visits. Usually people who visit are friends, and the home visit by a caregiver can sometimes be stressful. The problem can be partially resolved by both sides having a very clear idea of the purpose of the visit.

Parent Meetings and Conferences

Parent–teacher meetings tend to be more formal and are a way of ensuring that regular communication occurs. Just as the school system schedules regular meetings or interviews with parents, so do some day-care centres. Meetings can be called for a special purpose (e.g., to discuss a concern, or to develop a joint plan for toilet training), or they can serve to update the parents on the children's experiences at the centre. These meetings have tended to focus on child-related topics (e.g., the child's day, activities, accomplishments) rather than family or centre issues (Powell, 1989).

Parent meetings can be stressful for caregivers. Some staff actually freeze at the idea of having to discuss problem behaviour with parents. Parents too can view the meeting with trepidation ("What bad news am I going to hear this time?") because of previous bad experiences that ended in misunderstandings (Riepe, 1990).

Good rapport and effective planning are essential ingredients for successful parent–teacher conferences. Conferences should always begin and end on a positive note (Essa & Young, 1994; Riepe, 1990). Other suggestions for effective planning include gathering documentation from other staff members, organizing the material to be shared with parents, and being prepared for questions from parents. It is just as important to listen to the parents' perspective as it is to make the points you want to convey.

Scenario

A Successful Conference

Jennifer, a caregiver, decided to ask Norman's parents to come in for a meeting. Norman had been so restless at nap time that the caregivers had had trouble settling him down for a sleep. When Jennifer discussed this with his parents, they said that bedtime at home had been difficult too. Norman's parents thought that he was having strange fears at night, which is quite usual for children around the age of 3. His parents had found that a nightly "ritual" of looking under the bed and placing a stuffed animal "on guard duty" seemed to alleviate his fears. The staff suggested that the parents bring the stuffed animal to the centre, so it could guard Norman at nap time as well. This input from the parents was most helpful.

Planning effective conferences with parents requires considering who should come (mother, father, step-parent, grandparent), when they will come, what will be discussed, and how the discussion will be organized. This may be particularly important with parents from diverse cultural or linguistic backgrounds (Coleman, 1991) or when children present special concerns. After a parent–teacher conference, there is sometimes a tendency to feel that the issue has been dealt with, and a lapse in communication occurs. It is often a good idea to follow up a conference with a phone call to report any progress or changes, or simply to thank parents for their collaboration. Parent conferences can meet several goals of parent involvement: they are an opportunity for sharing information with parents, for providing a format for parent influence, and for "bridging the gap between home and centre" (Coleman, 1991).

Considerations for Parent-Caregiver Conferences

1. Be prepared.
   - Consider who the most appropriate staff members are to be involved in the conference. Most likely, these will be the primary caregivers.
   - Familiarize yourself with the child and parent by reviewing records and previous observations.
   - Have a clear idea about why you are holding the conference and what you hope to achieve.

2. Set the stage.
   - Choose a time that is mutually convenient for both parents and staff. Try to ensure that no one is rushed, either getting there or during the meeting itself. Allow at least half an hour.
   - Let the parents know what you are going to be discussing ahead of time so it is not a surprise and so they also have the opportunity to organize their thoughts and ideas.

- When the parents arrive, make them feel comfortable, provide adult-sized chairs in a quiet area, and offer refreshments if possible.
- Have all the necessary information with you so that you will not have to disrupt the meeting.
- Attempt to start every conference on a positive note.
- Begin with something personal about the child—an anecdote or a picture.

3. Lead the way.
   - Inform the parents about the child's life at the centre by sharing, throughout the conference, observations, anecdotes, and specific examples of what the child is doing.
   - Speak in plain, clear English. Avoid the use of jargon and terms with which parents may not be familiar.
   - Listen to the parents and try to understand their perspective, their concerns, and their interpretation of what you are telling them. Be open to learning more about the child from the people who know him or her best.
   - Present child behavioural problems as challenges requiring joint problem solving.
   - Be prepared to offer parents ideas, resources, or referrals.
   - Work out a plan of action with parents that will be in the best interest of the child, planning subsequent meetings or forms of communication if necessary.
   - Close the conference on a positive note. Summarize what has been discussed and the plan of action, if there is one. Set a time to review progress, if necessary.
   - Thank the parents for coming and for their input.
   - Follow up after a few days with a note of thanks, a summary of the meeting, or a progress review.

Parent Boards

Many nonprofit day-care centres and nursery schools are run by a volunteer board of directors. The director of the centre is accountable to the board of directors and reports to it regularly on all aspects of the centre, including finances, personnel issues, and programs. Often the board of directors consists of members of the community with knowledge and talents in particular areas, such as accounting, fund-raising, law, health, or human resources. When parents volunteer to be on the board of directors, their involvement gives them the opportunity to influence, and even control, the policies that govern the centre and its staff (Essa & Young, 1994). In some centres, the board of directors consists of volunteers who are members of the community at large, rather than parents of children at the centre, and the board may ask one parent to be the "parent representative" on the board.

It is often difficult for early childhood professionals to accept that they are account-able to people who are not trained in their discipline. They may feel that decisions, particularly decisions about the daily occurrences at the centre, should be made by people who have appropriate training. However, the strong impetus for parent involve-ment on boards came from increased concerns that early childhood professionals need to be more sensitive to the diverse needs of parents and children in the centre (Coleman, 1991). This feeling can be particularly strong when the parents belong to a minority. Sometimes, staff and parents have negotiated "territories" of control. In this system, the parent board is responsible for areas other than the curriculum, and staff maintain control of the day-to-day activities of the centre. Although this may be easier for the caregivers, it may not necessarily be in the best interest of the children and their fami-lies. Caregivers who are comfortable with parent influence and control are usually those who are experienced and knowledgeable in their field and confident in their ability to advocate on behalf of the children whenever a disagreement may occur between them and the parents (Stevens, 1991).

Parent Advisory Committees

Advisory committees have less power than boards of directors. In fact, sometimes it seems that the term "advisory committee" is a misnomer. That is, they usually do more helping than advising. For example, the Early Childhood Services program in Alberta had established parent advisory committees for each program that it operated. Parent func-tions, which were determined by the staff at the very beginning of the program, include helping with daily set-up and snack time, with social events, or with hands-on assistance with the children in the classroom. All parents had the opportunity to be involved, but the type of involvement has been predetermined by the staff and is therefore usually very helpful indeed to the caregivers. It is unclear, however, whether these types of advisory boards have been effective in meeting parents' needs for influence and control.

Although parent boards and advisory committees obviously relate to the goal of providing parents with influence or control over the centres that their children attend, these groups may also aid other goals. In the 1970s, when many women did not work during their children's preschool years, participation in the management of the centre gave them the confidence and experience that was often a stepping stone to their career development. We have seen many parents grow in self-confidence as they take on more responsibility on boards and advisory committees. These parents have also remarked that they have acquired an increased understanding of the needs of children through their participation. This kind of parent involvement, then, can be very educational for parents, as well as enlightening and helpful to the centre staff (Essa & Young, 1994).

Beyond the Centre:
Working with Wider Systems
Working with Community Resources

Sometimes families require assistance and support that goes beyond the time limitations or professional boundaries of the early childhood professional. Many families have adequate support networks and can access required assistance without the help of the centre. However, for others, assistance provided by the centre in accessing community support networks can be invaluable (Coleman, 1991; Stevens, 1991).

It is not uncommon for families who have successfully overcome pressing problems to recall that "taking that first step" to getting help was the most difficult part of the process. The early childhood professional who has established rapport with the parents through daily interaction can often be instrumental in advising the family on the best way of getting the help that they need.

Knowledge of community resources

Early childhood professionals should be aware of the different types of resources that exist in their community. This knowledge will help them provide accurate information to parents about resources that can meet their particular needs. However, parents' ability to make choices on their own must be respected, and sometimes the role of the caregiver is simply to provide information about existing resources so that the parents can independently decide what to do.

There are a number of services in each community that provide support for a wide range of family or individual problems. An annual update of services will help keep caregivers abreast of agencies that may be helpful. When investigating community services, centre staff should gather specific and detailed information to ensure that their recommendations are appropriate. Considerations may include the following:

- *Is the agency a self-help group run by people with similar problems, or is there professional support?* For some parents, self-help groups are invaluable, but for others, professional counselling and guidance will be their first choice.

- *Is there a cost for the services, and can the costs be claimed (e.g., through insurance policies or deducted from income tax)?* Does the agency have a sliding fee scale where clients are charged according to their income? It will not be helpful or in the best interest of the family to recommend a service that they cannot afford. Providing alternatives may prevent the awkward situation of parents having to admit that they cannot pay for such a service.

- *Does the agency have entrance criteria?* Often agencies have to limit the number of people they deal with by imposing criteria based on age, disability, or type of problem. For example, some organizations that pair boys from father-absent homes with volunteers will only consider children above the age of 8. Many organizations do not have the resources to assist children with special needs. Sometimes, the agency will openly state their criteria, but in some cases, guidelines will be vague and the early childhood professional will need to clarify them for the parents.

- *Does the agency staff have expertise in working with preschool children?* Because most caregivers reading this book will be working with preschool children, a good question to ask is whether the agency has past experience working in this area. Frequently agencies state that they work with children, but upon being questioned they will admit that the children are usually school age.

- *Will the agency allow the involvement of the early childhood professional?* Some agencies work very closely with early childhood staff and invite observations and opinions from the caregivers who are with the children on a day-to-day basis. Other agencies will not choose to work in active collaboration with the centre or even to keep staff informed of what is happening. Depending on the organization, its structure and purpose, the nature of the problem, and the wishes of the family, the desirability of centre involvement will vary. For example, one family may be reassured to know that there will be a link with the early childhood professional. Other parents would be much more comfortable knowing that the problems they discuss in another agency are separate and apart from the child's day care or preschool.

- *How does one access the agency?* Some agencies require a referral from a family physician, child welfare worker, or social worker. Other agencies are based on self-referral. A family in stress does not need to make extra phone calls. Finding out the appropriate way to access services is important.

- *Is there a waiting list?* Some agencies have a waiting list of six months or more, while others will see people in crisis immediately. This information is vital to have.

- *What kind of support does the agency offer?* Some agencies provide group structures for people with problems, some work with families together, and some do individual counselling. Some offer "crisis intervention," that is, short-term intensive support, while others may offer less intense support over a longer period of time. Many agencies offer a variety of formats.

Once the information is available, thought needs to be given to the question of how best to pass that information to parents and help them, if so required, to "take that first step." Sometimes, a display of pamphlets from different agencies in the parent corner or on the bulletin board is sufficient. Sometimes, a short article in a newsletter can help parents learn about a possible source of support. Often, however, it is through the personal relationship between the early childhood professional and a parent that the parent is encouraged to seek outside assistance.

Parent Advocacy

In describing the ecological approach to understanding families and children, we mentioned how social policies and societal attitudes in general can affect the well-being of children and families. Sometimes government policies do not appear to be in the best interest of families and children, and individuals often feel powerless to change any aspect of these large and impersonal systems. Early childhood professionals can assist parents in exerting influence and control over the lives of their children by encouraging and facilitating their efforts to advocate. Meetings can be held at the centre to inform and plan strategies for advocating. Parents of children with special needs have, in the past, achieved significant gains in their struggle for appropriate services for their children and for the integration of children with special needs into regular community frameworks (Turnbull & Turnbull, 1990).

Scenario

Political Advocacy

In Alberta, a new government threatened to diminish funding for early childhood services, specifically for Kindergarten classes. Many parents voiced their concern by writing letters to officials, contacting the media, and drumming up support among friends and acquaintances. When a group of early childhood teachers invited the parents to hold meetings at their schools, the turnout was impressive. All the teachers had to do was to offer the use of the building. The parents did all the rest, and a significant message of protest was sent to the government.

Effective advocacy takes time, planning, and organization. Many parents will already have these skills, and the role of the early childhood professional may be simply to offer technical advice or moral support. Sometimes a caregiver can provide resources and information on how to advocate effectively. This is not only sharing information with parents, but empowering them to exert influence and control on the systems that directly affect their children.

Making Collaboration Work

Even with the best intentions, early childhood professionals who overlook certain considerations can hamper effective collaborative strategies, and sometimes this can result in negative feelings towards the centre by parents. Following are some considerations that should apply to the planning of all attempts to collaborate with parents.

Cultural Sensitivity and Inclusion

Sometimes, even though it may happen inadvertently, certain people are made to feel left out. The anecdote below provides an example.

Scenario

Be Sensitive to Multicultural Concerns

Staff at a day-care centre put up a poster in the parent corner that advertised a new indoor park in the downtown area of the city. The poster had a picture of a number of people sitting on benches in a lovely area that was full of plants and flowers. The writing on the poster said, "Relax together in your garden." One staff member who had attended a workshop on multicultural awareness took a good look at the poster and commented that there were no people of colour in the picture, no people in wheelchairs, and no elderly people. All the people in the picture were well dressed, White, middle-aged, and fairly well off financially. The staff member felt that the poster subtly excluded many people from feeling that they had been invited to "relax in your garden."

There is an increasing awareness that the words and pictures we use carry strong messages, and early childhood professionals should be sensitive to this issue. Do the pictures and posters that invite parents to participate reflect the ethnic and economic diversity of parents in the centre? Do they reflect the different family structures, such as single-parent and step-parent families? Do they include parents and children with disabilities?

The level of language used can also be inclusive or exclusive. Early childhood professionals have been blamed for using difficult language and jargon that sets them apart from other people (Coleman, 1991). Certainly in the education and training process they become accustomed to using jargon. But use of phrases like "developmentally appropriate" or "hand-eye coordination" can create distance between parents and caregivers. If we are confident in our professional knowledge, we should be able to communicate ideas without relying on jargon.

Some centres have made the effort to have their written material translated for parents who have difficulty with English. This is time consuming and sometimes expensive, but when there is a commitment to the principle of inclusion, it is possible to find a way. Sometimes parents who are fluent in a second language are happy to help out.

Perspectives

Dianna is a 45-year-old mother of seven children. She was born and raised on a Blackfoot reserve and married into the Tsuu T'ina Nation.

"I come from a large family, five sisters and four brothers. My native language is Blackfoot. I attended boarding school from Grade 1 to Grade 10, and came to the city to finish high school. I have recently completed a diploma in social work and am working in child welfare on the reserve. From my experience as an Aboriginal person, and as a parent, I see much that caregivers can do to enhance the relationship between us. What I am saying is undoubtedly influenced by my own experiences of racism and discrimination, my sense that mainstream culture is sometimes very apathetic concerning what has happened to Native people, and my feelings that I and my children have not always been free to express our opinions about our values and beliefs.

"The caregiver should be aware of the children's ethnic and cultural origin, including their history, extended family, and community. Caregivers should not just read books, which are often written by Whites, but should actually talk to tribal members. First, I would educate caregivers a bit about my culture, in order for them to better understand the Aboriginal lifestyle.

"Some of the customs that we watch for are these:

- We do not let children go outside after dark, because of the night spirits.
- We teach them patience and respect for elders.
- We teach them to respect and never abuse nature, for it has a life form in itself.
- We believe that children should never, ever be shamed, for shaming a human being is not acceptable in our culture.

"The caregiver should also be made aware of the communication patterns of the native child. When native children are asked questions, they often take time to respond. People sometimes think our children are dumb because they do not answer quickly. They do not answer quickly because we teach them to think carefully and formulate a precise answer before responding.

"Caregivers should know that, for many of us, grandparents and aunts and uncles have much responsibility for the children. In many cases, these extended family members take on lots of roles that you would assume belong to the parents.

"I would have been very happy to participate in activities in my children's day care, as I do in the schools today. Some of the activities I think suitable are story-telling by elders, organizing cultural days, taking children on nature walks, and demonstrating Aboriginal arts and crafts. I would also suggest that Aboriginal parents help the day-care staff design and decorate the day-care centre so that it reflects Native culture as well as the cultures of other children in the centre."

Timing the Activities

Imagine what it would be like to be invited to a parent–teacher conference at 5:00 p.m. on Christmas Eve, a time when your family has a traditional get-together every year. This happens all too often to families who celebrate their festivals and holy days at different times throughout the year. Several multicultural calendars are now available, and it is important to ensure that parent activities do not conflict with special days from any of the religions and cultures that are represented at the centre. If in doubt, it is always better to ask than to plan without consulting parents.

Timing activities also entails finding out parents' schedules, child-care arrangements, and other details that may prevent them from attending. While it is probably unlikely that an event can be timed to please all parents, efforts to take their schedules into consideration will be appreciated. Parents who lead busy lives need advance warning so that they can plan to attend functions after work or during work hours. It is disrespectful to send a note home "summoning" parents to attend a meeting the next day!

Cost

Bringing food to a pot-luck dinner may be a luxury that some families cannot afford. Attending a picnic with little to put in a picnic hamper may be so humiliating for some families that they may choose not to attend. Child-care arrangements may make evening activities too expensive for some parents to attend. Even extra bus fare to attend an evening session may not be available. There are solutions to some of these obstacles, such as providing child care on site, or fund-raising to purchase food for the picnic. Awareness of the cost implications of parent activities is very important.

Location

One mother related the following incident.

Scenario

Be Considerate

Last Wednesday I was invited to a parent discussion evening at the centre. I worked behind the cash counter until 5:00 p.m., rode home on a crowded bus, and quickly went through the children's supper, bath, and bedtime routine. Then I jumped into the shower, dressed, and ran out the door to catch the bus to the centre. When I got there I almost broke into tears. The little chairs that the children sit on were arranged in a circle, and we (the parents) were expected to sit on them and listen to an expert tell us about reading stories to children.

The physical arrangements of the space in which parent activities are held should be given careful consideration. The arrangement of chairs can appear formal (in rows, as in a lecture), or the space can be arranged comfortably and informally. It is a matter of common courtesy to take into account how the physical setting will influence the feelings of the participants.

Other Issues

Early childhood professionals often want to initiate collaborative efforts with parents but do not know where to begin. A survey of parents' interests, ideas, and concerns may be a logical starting point. Parents using the day care for the first time may not understand what parent collaboration involves, and a survey may act as an introduction for them. Staff can also survey the type, length, and scheduling of activities. For example, if child care is a concern, perhaps parents would prefer having family events or child care available. Parents may be more willing to engage in social activities as fund-raisers rather than having to commit to fund-raising events through the year. When parents feel that they have some input into activities, they will likely be more committed to them. This may also help the staff to feel that they are part of the process and have some input.

Take Care of Yourselves

One final and crucial consideration in planning collaboration with parents is the staff's time. Many early childhood professionals volunteer time, after working for eight hours a day with children, in order to organize and attend meetings with parents. While their commitment to working with parents is honourable, it should not be taken advantage of. Even if the centre is under severe financial restraints, caregivers need to be paid for their work or given time off in lieu. Centre directors and staff need to balance the demands of the program with the physical and emotional well-being of the staff.

Conclusion

This chapter has made a number of suggestions for enhancing collaboration with and involvement of parents. The ideas in the box below can serve as a reminder. Staff and parents will have their own suggestions to add to this list.

Methods of Parent-Caregiver Collaboration

Direct Communication:
- daily conversations
- phone calls

Written Communication:
- bulletin boards
- daily notes
- newsletters
- parent corners
- communication books
- travelling goodie bags

Volunteering or Visiting at the Centre

Evening Activities:
- speakers
- fund-raisers
- family or social events
- discussion groups

Home Visits

Parent-Caregiver Conferences

Parent Boards

Parent Advisory Committees

Beyond the Centre:
- referrals to community resources
- parent advocacy

The first step in planning successful parent–staff collaboration consists of understanding your own attitudes towards it and then making a commitment to its success. The next step consists of developing good communication skills and a repertoire of strategies that can be adapted to individual situations. With careful planning, sensitivity to parents' needs and concerns, and the assistance and input of parents, many positive results can be attained. In order to ensure that parent–staff collaboration is maintained over time, staff must continually evaluate their efforts. The next chapter highlights some of the questions that might be addressed in this ongoing evaluation of parent–staff collaboration.

Exercises

1. Interview three parents about what types of communication they find to be the most effective and why.

2. Role-play the following scenario. It may be a good idea for the "players" to switch roles after their first performance to get the benefit of the other perspective.

   Perspective A

   You are Ms. Renaud, director of the South East Day-Care Centre.

   Billy Blake, aged 4, has been in your centre about six weeks. He has adjusted well and appears to be an active, happy child. He participates in most activities, asks interesting questions, and particularly enjoys the block area and water play. He is less interested in the story corner, but seems really to enjoy playing with the other children.

   This morning when Mr. and Mrs. Blake dropped Billy at the centre, Mrs. Blake asked for an appointment to speak with you this evening. You do not know the Blakes well, but they seem very pleasant and genuinely interested in hearing about what Billy does at the centre every day. Mrs. Blake is a lawyer, and her husband is a co-owner of a small construction firm.

   Draw up a plan for the best way of preparing for this appointment.

   Perspective B

   You are Mrs. Blake, a lawyer with a large Edmonton firm. Your husband is co-owner of a construction company. Your son, Billy, aged 4, has been in the day-care centre for about six weeks.

   Although the day-care director, Ms. Renaud, and the staff seem very pleasant and friendly, and although Billy seems to enjoy his time at the centre, you and Mr. Blake have serious reservations about it. You do not think that Billy is learning anything. He is a bright child, and should be learning to read and write—not just playing with blocks or at the water table all day. This is a competitive world; if Billy is to get into a good university, he must have a good start. These years, when he is so eager to learn, are being wasted.

   You have decided to talk to Ms. Renaud, the director, and this morning you made an appointment with her for when you pick Billy up this evening.

   (Forget everything you know about the value of play, and do not make this easy for Ms. Renaud.)

3. Interview a family agency using the format suggested in this chapter (pp. 288–89). Present the information in a pamphlet form that would be practical for families to use.

Assessing Parent– Staff Collaboration

chapter 17

Objectives

- **To emphasize the importance of an ongoing assessment of parent–staff collaboration in early childhood centres.**

- **To provide guidelines for evaluation and assessment.**

- **To discuss ethical issues involved in evaluation and assessment.**

> The director of an early childhood centre announced at a staff meeting that the focus of program evaluation for the coming month would be on parent–staff relations. Jana, a new staff member, seemed quite distressed. She had just begun to work at the centre two months before and felt that just remembering all the parents' names was quite an achievement at this stage. When she expressed her concern to her co-worker, she was relieved to find out that evaluation meant something quite different from what she had expected.

Many people feel uneasy at the thought of being evaluated (Shimoni, Baxter, & Kugelmass, 1992). We often associate evaluations with tension-producing experiences such as driving tests, examinations, or skill tests for job placements. However, in the context of early childhood programs, evaluations should be seen as an ongoing tool for improving the quality of the centre. In fact, what has come to be called "developmentally appropriate practice" requires that all programs be regularly evaluated (Bredekamp, 1987). Parent–staff collaboration is an essential ingredient of a quality program and should be evaluated just as the other program components are.

Evaluation need not, and should not, be considered a "test," but rather a means of gathering information and promoting discussion that will help staff and parents clarify their goals. It will also help them to implement strategies that can lead to an enrichment of staff–parent relations and to successful collaboration between parents and staff.

What Is Evaluation?

Evaluation has been defined as a systematic, objective way of acquiring information. "Systematic" means that evaluation needs to be done according to a formulated method or plan. "Objective" means that effective evaluation should be viewed as an inquiry that is not influenced by personal feelings, judgments, or prejudice. However, social scientists have recently acknowledged that personal feelings and judgments are important and valid to consider in evaluative research (Lincoln & Guba, 1985). Therefore, rather than struggling to keep personal feelings out of the process, it is important that the evaluation reflects the subjective feelings of all those involved in the program—parents, staff, children, and any others who may be affected. These interested parties, or people who have some "stake" in the program, are commonly referred to as "stakeholders."

In addition to being systematic and objective, effective evaluation should also be an ongoing process. We evaluate to identify the strengths and weakness of a program, then we use the evaluation to make improvements, and finally we re-evaluate to see what progress has been made (Shimoni, Baxter, & Kugelmass, 1992). This is particularly important in working with families, because sometimes staff efforts seem to go unappreciated. Consider, for example, the scenario at the beginning of Chapter 16 of a poorly attended parent evening. The caregiver will be tempted to conclude that parents don't care or are too busy to be involved, and she may then abandon any similar attempts in the future. However, an evaluation of this activity may well suggest that some of the caregiver's goals may have been achieved in spite of the poor attendance. In addition, the evaluation may provide information that will help her in planning a better attended event in the future.

Deciding What to Evaluate

As this book should have made evident, parent–staff relations, support for parents and families, and collaboration with parents are all multifaceted, subtle, but important aspects of a program. It may not be possible (or desirable) to carry out a comprehensive evaluation of all these aspects simultaneously. Therefore, clear priorities have to be established when the evaluation questions are first formulated.

What to Evaluate

1. Consider the philosophies or beliefs of parents and staff.
2. Consider the different goals of parents, staff, and the centre.
3. Consider which aspects of collaboration should be evaluated, such as
   - timing (e.g., evenings, Saturdays, after work)
   - location (e.g., will parents have to travel back?)
   - child-care arrangements
   - parent versus family events
   - other considerations (e.g., length, time of year)
4. Consider who the stakeholders are.

Following are some questions that might help clarify points to consider in an evaluation.

What Are the Beliefs Underlying Parent-Staff Collaboration?

Often people are not really aware of how their beliefs influence their day-to-day lives and work. Some early childhood professionals believe deeply in the value of strong social relations and networks among the parents of children in the centre. Others may think the centre's primary value is in caring for the children and passing on information to parents.

Scenario

Social Relations

In a research study on parent involvement, parents were asked to respond to a question about the value of a certain activity that had been designed for their benefit. One parent felt that the activity was extremely valuable, but another parent responded that parent activities in general were of no particular interest to her. Further questioning established that the first parent valued the social aspect of the activities, the opportunity to meet other parents, while the second parent felt that her social life and the day-care centre were two separate aspects of her life.

As we have discussed previously, there will be differences in attitudes and beliefs among individual staff members and among parents. When evaluating parent–staff collaboration, these differences should be articulated and understood.

Examine Your Attitudes

To give yourself a clearer idea of what you feel your role is in collaborating with parents, complete the checklist below. Answer each question by using the following scale:

4   essential

3   moderately important

2   sometimes

1   never

As a caregiver, I believe I should. . .

1.   Listen to what parents are saying.
2.   Encourage parents to drop in.
3.   Give parents an opportunity to contribute to my program.
4.   Send newsletters home to parents.
5.   Contact parents before a child begins my program.
6.   Contact parents when a child does well.
7.   Accept parents' views on childrearing even if they differ significantly from my own.

8. Learn what objectives parents have for their children.

9. Learn about interests and special abilities of children.

10. Visit children at home.

11. Show parents examples of the children's activities.

12. Enlist parent volunteers for my program.

13. Encourage both mother and father to attend conferences.

14. Make parents feel comfortable when they visit the centre.

15. Include parents in plans for their children.

16. Try to be open and honest with parents.

17. Send notes home with children.

18. Keep both parents informed if parents are separated.

19. Consider parents as partners with the centre staff in the caregiving responsibilities.

Comparing scores with other caregivers will highlight differences in attitudes, comfort level, and skills in working with parents so that goals can be set for professional development and differences can be discussed.

What Are the Goals Underlying Parent-Staff Collaboration?

Goals refer to an end result, that is, what the expected outcome will be of a strategy or activity. As we have seen, different people often have different perceptions of what the goal of an activity should be, and any single activity may be congruent with a number of different goals. Caregivers may wish to consider the positive value of goals for themselves as professionals, for parents and for the child. When benefits are seen from multiple perspectives, goals may be seen as more worthwhile.

Scenario

One Activity, Two Different Goals

A day-care centre hosted a guest speaker for the evening. Parents arrived throughout the informal discussions and asked few questions, but after the meeting there was a lively debate over coffee and donuts. One caregiver was quite upset at the low turnout and thought the late arrivals showed a lack of interest in the speaker. Another caregiver was pleased with the event since a significant number of parents did in fact attend (albeit not on time) and engaged in animated debate and socializing after the lecture. The first caregiver thought the goal of the evening was to provide information to the parents through the guest speaker. The second caregiver's goal for the meeting was to provide parents with the opportunity to socialize with and support each other.

Evaluation, then, should consider not only the underlying beliefs of the parties involved, but also the goals of the strategy that is being evaluated. These should be clear to all the stakeholders.

What Are the Collaboration Strategies?

Aside from a clarification of beliefs and goals, other worthwhile considerations for an evaluation can be found in most of the suggestions offered in the previous chapter as strategies for encouraging parent–staff collaboration. For instance, an evaluation can address the issue of inclusion and multicultural sensitivity, with input from several stakeholders, such as parents, staff, children, and leaders from religious and ethnic communities. Evaluation can focus on the structure and timing of activities as well as their appropriateness. The parents' perspective should also be addressed in any comprehensive assessment. The example below illustrates how a very simple evaluative strategy led to the planning of a successful parent activity.

Scenario

Father Participation

One day-care centre monitored the participation of parents in the scheduled activities for a period of several months. They noticed with concern that very few fathers attended. One staff member commented that perhaps parent activities are more geared to mothers than fathers. For example, every Mother's Day, children and staff host a tea party. This simple observation of participation provided the impetus for staff to plan an activity geared specifically for fathers. An activity (e.g., soccer, hockey, video) for fathers once a month right after work was programmed. The activities were flexible enough that fathers could come and go according to their own schedule and the children loved this special time with someone special.

Other aspects to consider might include parent and staff interests. For example, are parents interested in parent education and speakers or would they prefer discussion groups? Will this group of parents have child-care concerns that prevent their involvement? Can this problem be solved either by having family events rather than just parent events or by having simultaneous activities for children while their parents are occupied?

Will the time or the place pose difficulties? For example, if the centre is located at the parents' work site, scheduling events for the end of the day may be easier than asking parents to come back to the centre in the evening. On the other hand, for parents with other children, having events in the evening after everyone is home and settled may be more advantageous.

There may be other considerations particular to each and every centre. The bottom line is that staff members need to evaluate parent collaboration activities in a multifaceted manner, asking a variety of questions to ensure that attempts will be successful. Asking parents for input through a questionnaire and following up each event with feedback should produce the intended results.

Who Are the Stakeholders?

In our discussion of goals in the previous chapter, we mentioned that goals can be viewed from the perspective of staff, parents, and children. Likewise, benefits can be considered from all three perspectives.

Benefits for the Child

- Children whose parents support the program are better motivated and enjoy the program more.
- Children may feel more secure knowing that their parents are involved with and like the centre.
- Parent involvement increases the children's self-confidence and makes them pleased and proud that their parents are interested in what is happening in their lives.
- Collaboration provides information and knowledge of cultural or religious influences that may allow for a better understanding of the children and their families.

Benefits for the Parents

- Collaboration strengthens families by helping them to have shared interests and goals.
- It can give parents something to talk about with their children.
- Collaboration increases parents' self-esteem by making them feel more confident of their parenting skills.
- Parents form new friendships.
- Parents have the opportunity to observe new or different parenting techniques.
- Parents can see other children of the same age as theirs, and they can also see their children in the developmental context of their peer group.

Benefits for the Caregiver

- Collaboration provides another opportunity to find out more about the children they are working with.
- Caregivers have more time when a parent takes responsibility for certain jobs (e.g., snack preparation, fund-raising, field trip supervision).

As the following scenario illustrates, there may be other stakeholders whose views need to be considered as well.

Scenario

Who Are the Stakeholders?

A parent meeting was held at a day-care centre to discuss city council plans to build a new mall in the neighbourhood. Many parents were concerned that the increased traffic that would result would be a danger to the children. The parents organized a campaign and were effective in influencing the city's plan. In this case, the stakeholders were not only the parents who attended the meeting, but all of the families with young children in that community.

When evaluating parent–staff collaboration, it is important to ask who is likely to be affected and then to ensure that there is representative input from all stakeholder groups. An open house for parents during regular centre hours can be the most exciting day of the year for the children, but it may be difficult for parents to arrange work schedules in order to attend. Also, some staff might view the open house as more bother than it is worth. Sometimes, the different perspectives of stakeholders reveal a conflict in goals.

Scenario

How Do You Measure Success?

A local association for children with special needs hosted a guest speaker who discussed sleeping disorders. The parents who regularly attended were not impressed by the talk since their children, for the most part, were older and past this developmental period. However, one new parent came to the meeting precisely because her 18-month-old child with special needs was experiencing major difficulties in sleeping. This parent was extremely grateful for the information and support that resulted from this evening. She left feeling confident that her severely handicapped son would be able to learn to fall asleep on his own.

It was difficult for the staff to view this event as successful, since many of the parents did not feel positive about this session. However, the value achieved by one parent (and indirectly her child) was likely not included in their assessment of the evening's success. Clarifying criteria for success is an important part of evaluation. Early childhood professionals need to bear in mind the vast differences in the parents' interest level, their available time, and the ways in which they want to become involved. "Success" may not always be determined in terms of the number of parents involved in a particular event, but rather, the number of different ways that parents can participate.

Community Relations

In the context of the ecological model, the centre's relations with the larger community need to be considered. A well-functioning day-care centre provides support for children, families, and the community at large. In turn, a community can support the operation of a day-care centre. This reciprocal relationship may be very useful in times of need. At present, this is often a hit-or-miss effort, and staff often do not seriously consider themselves part of the community at large or utilize community resources except when necessary. Early childhood professionals can be so focused on the child, the program, and collaboration with parents, that the more global involvement in the community can be easily overlooked or forgotten. It is true, though, that when caregivers do consider community involvement, the families they serve will benefit.

Community Relations

A small day-care centre hosted a multicultural pot-luck supper on an annual basis. The first year approximately 40 people attended, mostly families of the children. The next year, the number doubled, and by the third year, more than 150 people attended. It was no longer just an event for families; it had become a community event.

When parent involvement activities are intended to build social networks, support may be *informational* (e.g., advice), *instrumental* (e.g., clothing, food), or *emotional* (e.g., expressions of confidence) (Stevens, 1991). Establishing links with support systems in the community will ensure that appropriate assistance will be available to families when the need arises. Another consequence may be that the day-care centre itself will be seen as a community resource. For example, in jurisdictions where child welfare legislation focuses on the family and attempts to keep families together, one of the first support systems recommended for families in crisis is that the children be placed in day care. Not only does this allow parents the respite they may need to put their lives in order, but the child welfare worker can also be confident that children are being cared for in developmentally appropriate ways.

Day-care centres can become part of the community not only by actively utilizing the resources available but also by making themselves known as a community resource. Since this is the case, early childhood professionals may need to evaluate their community involvement and relations.

How Will Information for the Evaluation Be Gathered?

How Information Can Be Gathered

1. Through simple observations.
2. By keeping written notes and records.
3. By formulating questionnaires.
4. Through conversations with parents and staff.
   - randomly select participants
   - purposefully sample a representative group
5. Through group discussions.

Depending on the time and resources available to the centre, a variety of methods can be used to gather information that will help in the evaluation of programs. We will briefly discuss observations, recording, questionnaires, and dialoguing with parents and staff individually and in groups.

Sometimes simple observations can provide much useful information. One staff member can be actively involved in an activity with parents, and another can be more of an observer, watching for signs of interest and participation.

Keeping records of attendance at events and of different kinds of contact with parents can provide a good overview for analysis and discussions. These are some of the questions that can be resolved by keeping regular records:

- Are there parents who consistently do not attend functions?

- Are certain types of events better attended than others?

- Does the timing of events seem to have an impact on participation?

Records accumulated over a period of time can produce useful information.

We sometimes forget that the simplest way to receive information is to ask people for it. Questionnaires can be a very useful way of getting information from staff and from parents. It is important, however, to word a questionnaire carefully and avoid "leading" questions. Someone experienced in the social sciences can provide useful assistance in constructing a questionnaire.

Formulating a Questionnaire

Before developing a questionnaire, you may want to consider the following questions:

- What information do I want?
- Is a questionnaire the best way to get this information?
- Should it be followed up with an interview or discussion?
- What format should I use?
  - Checklist
  - Yes/no questions
  - Open-ended questions
- When will I distribute the questionnaires?
- How will I collect them?
- How will I use the information?
- How will I provide feedback?

Example of a questionnaire for parent profiles

1. Provide spaces for parents to list their name, address, telephone numbers, composition of family, occupation, and hours of work.

2. Next, formulate a question asking whether they want to participate in centre activities.

3. Then list ways that they may be involved, with a box beside each item so they can check which activities interest them. You can list a variety of options and leave room at the bottom of the list in case they have a suggestion that had not been considered. Be sure to list here any committees of which they could become members.

Conversations with parents and staff can be the most important source of information. While it is often not feasible to interview each and every stakeholder during an evaluation process, two techniques are worth considering. The first is "random sampling." This means choosing a set number of participants in a random fashion and obtaining information from them. The second technique is referred to as "purposeful sampling." In purposeful sampling, the evaluators try to ensure that specific groups of people are represented in the sample. For example, the evaluator would attempt to obtain information from a two-parent family, a lone parent, a young parent, an older parent, and parents from different ethnic backgrounds. When deciding from whom to obtain information, we are more concerned about having the opinions and responses from the different stakeholders than we are about being scientific and objective.

Group discussions, or focus groups, are another commonly used method of obtaining evaluative information. A centre staff member could, for example, ask a group of parents to spend an evening reflecting on the events of the past year. The main points of the discussion should be recorded and discussed by the staff. It is important to have a skilled facilitator at focus group discussions to ensure that all the participants have the opportunity to express their opinions.

Ethical Issues in Evaluation

If the evaluation process is to become an effective way of monitoring and improving programs, certain ethical issues have to be considered. First, information that is deemed "confidential" must be treated as such. Sometimes parents will hesitate to provide constructive criticism because they feel that the caregiver might take it as personal criticism. Questionnaires provide an opportunity to respond anonymously, and the confidentiality must be protected. On the other hand, participants in an evaluative process have a right to be informed of the results. This information needs to be disseminated in a way that protects confidentiality. If a questionnaire had been distributed to parents asking about the accessibility and availability of the caregivers, the results could be reported back to parents in terms of percentages of parents who complained and of caregivers about whom there were complaints, without revealing the names of either.

Second, if people take the time to participate in an evaluation, there must be a commitment on the part of the staff to put the information to use if possible, or at least to consider it very carefully. Staff should plan in advance how the information will be disseminated, how it will be used, and who has the responsibility for implementing changes based on the evaluation.

Finally, the purpose of an evaluation must always be clarified at the very beginning of the process, and the information obtained should not be used for any additional purposes. For example, a staff member reluctantly agreed to invite the director to attend a parent meeting that she was facilitating. The director said that the reason she wanted to sit in was to evaluate the parents' level of participation. When the staff's performance appraisal was done at the end of the month, however, the caregiver was quite distressed to find that the director had been observing her interaction with the parents and had used that information in the performance appraisal. Trust is a paramount consideration in the evaluation process.

Conclusion

Evaluation need not be too time consuming, nor should it be very complex. If staff members are committed to an ongoing process of asking for, processing, and acting on the feedback they receive from families, their success at planning collaborative activities will very likely increase. In addition, obtaining feedback through ongoing dialogue with parents may well serve as the basis for each side getting to know each other better and thereby strengthening the relations between staff and parents.

Exercises

1. Design a poster, brochure, or short video that explains the benefits that parent–staff collaboration offers for

   - the child
   - parents or families
   - caregivers

2. Interview parents and staff about a particular event or issue affecting them in the day-care centre. Gather the information first by using a random sampling and then by using a purposeful sampling. Compare the results. How are they similar and how are they different? Which type gave the most pertinent or useful information in this situation?

3. Describe a situation where you have worked with parents, sharing information and coordinating plans. How did you feel? How do you think parents felt? What happened for the child?

4. The following information was taken from questionnaires that evaluated staff–parent involvement strategies. Based on this information, formulate some strategies and goals for your own program for the upcoming year.

   All seven staff responded. Of forty parents surveyed, thirty-eight parents responded as follows:

   - Twenty-eight parents felt they did not know the staff very well.
   - Fourteen parents disliked evening meetings.
   - Thirty-five parents appreciated their children going on field trips.

- Most staff felt that field trips were not supervised well enough.
- Thirty-seven parents needed care earlier than 7:00 a.m., and two needed care later than 6:00 p.m.
- Seven parents enjoyed coming to the centre for lunch.
- Nineteen parents were willing to contribute to snacks or lunch.
- Some staff did not know what to do when parents were in the room.
- Some parents did not know what they were supposed to do in the room.

References

Abbott, C.F., and S. Gold. 1991. Conferring with parents when you're concerned that their child needs special services. *Young Children* 46 (4): 10–14.

Adler, R.B., and N. Towne. 1990. *Looking out, looking in.* 6th ed. Fort Worth: Holt, Rinehart and Winston.

Ahrons, C.R., and R.H. Rodgers. 1987. *Divorced families: A multidisciplinary developmental view.* New York: Norton.

Ahrons, C.R., and L. Wallisch. 1987. The relationship between former spouses. In *Intimate relationships.* Edited by D. Pulman and S. Duck. Newbury Park: Sage.

Ainsworth, M.D., and B.A. Witting. 1969. Attachment and exploratory behavior in one-year-olds in a strange situation. In *Determinants of infant behavior.* Vol. 4, pp. 111–136. Edited by B. Foss. London: Methuen.

Alberta Family and Social Services. 1990. *Protocols for handling child abuse and neglect in day care services.* Alberta Family and Social Services.

Aldous, J. 1995. New views of grandparents in intergenerational context. *Journal of Family Issues* 16 (1): 104–22.

Aldous, J., and D.M. Klein. 1988. The linkages between family development and family stress. In Klein and Aldous, 1988.

Amato, R. 1993. Children's adjustment to divorce: Theories, hypotheses, and empirical support. *Journal of Marriage and the Family* 55 (1): 23–38.

Ambert, A. 1990. Marriage dissolution: Structural and ideological changes. In *Families: changing trends in Canada.* Edited by M. Baker. Toronto: McGraw-Hill Ryerson.

Anchor, K.N., and T.C. Thomason. 1977. A comparison of two parent training models with educated parents. *Journal of Community Psychology* 5: 134–43.

Anderson, K.L., et al. 1988. *Family matters: Sociology and contemporary Canadian families.* Scarborough, ON: Nelson.

Andrushko, B. 1989. The caregiver's role: Helping children cope with loss. *Interaction* (winter): 23–24.

Arnup, K. 1993. *Education for motherhood: Advice for mothers in twentieth-century Canada.* Toronto: University of Toronto Press.

Austinn, E.W., C. Knaus, and A. Meneguelli. 1997. Who talks to their kids about TV: A clarification of demographic correlates of parental mediation patterns. *Communication Research Reports* 14 (4): 418–430.

Auerbach, A.B. 1968. *Parents learn through discussion: Principles and practices of parent group education.* New York: Wiley.

Baker, M. 1997. Between breadwinning or caregiving. Fathers and Canadian divorce laws. *Lien-Social-et-Politique—RIAC* 37 (7): 63–74.

Bank, L., M.S. Forgatch, G.R. Patterson, and R.A. Fetrow. 1993. Parenting practices of single mothers: Mediators of negative contextual factors. *Journal of Marriage and the Family* 55: 371–84.

Barker, L.L., and D.A. Barker. 1993. *Communication.* 6th ed. Englewood Cliffs, NJ: Prentice Hall.

Barker, R.L. 1991. *The social work dictionary.* 2d ed. Washington: National Association of Social Workers.

Barlow, C. 1992. Doctoral dissertation. Department of Educational Psychology, University of Calgary.

Barnett, D. 1997. "Parenting" teenage parents: A clinician's notes. *Family Relations* 46 (2): 186–189.

Barrett, K.C., K.D. Kallio, R.M. McBride, C.M. Moore, and M.A. Wilson. 1995. *Child development.* New York: Glencoe.

Baxter, J. 1998. A Qualitative Study of Caregivers. Ph.D. Dissertation, University of Calgary.

Baydar, N., and J. Brooks-Gunn. 1995. Does a mother's job have a negative effect on children: Yes. In DelCampo and DelCampo, 1995.

Beiser, M. 1998. *Growing up Canadian: A study of new immigrant children.* Working Papers/Canada Human Resources Department. Hull, PQ: Human Resources Development Canada, Strategic Policy, Applied Research Branch, vi, 43 pp.

Beller, E.K. 1979. Early intervention programs. In Osofsky, 1979.

Belsky, J., M.E. Lang, and M. Rovine. 1985. Stability and change across the transition to parenthood: A second study. *Journal of Marriage and the Family* 45: 855–65.

Bennett, T., D.A. DeLuca, and R. Allen. 1996. Families of children with disabilities: Positive adaptation across the life cycle. *Social Work in Education* 18 (1): 31–44.

Benokraitis, N.V. 1993. *Marriages and families: Changes, choices and constraints*. Englewood Cliffs, NJ: Prentice Hall.

Benzeval, M. 1998. The self-reported health status of lone parents. *Social Science and Medicine* 46 (10): 1337–1353.

Berns, R.M. 1993. *Child, family, community: Socialization and support*. 3d ed. Orlando: Harcourt Brace.

Bernstein, J.E. 1977. Helping young children cope with death. In Katz, 1977.

Bernstein, L. 1993. Sex, love and teddy bears. In Pocs, 1993.

Bird, G.W., and M.J. Sporakowski. 1994. *Taking sides: Clashing views on controversial issues in family and personal relationships*. 2d ed. Guilford, CT: Dushkin.

Blickstead, M. 1996. Parents of children with special needs benefit from mutual aid. Child & Family Canada [On-line]. Available: www.cfc-efc.ca

Bogert, C. 1995. White ghetto? In Gilbert, 1995.

Borders, L.D., L.K. Black, and B.K. Pasley. 1998. Are adopted children and their parents at greater risk for negative outcomes? *Family Relations* 1998 (47): 237–241.

Bourianova, I. 1996. *Housing of female single-parent families with special reference to Point St. Charles (Quebec)*, McGill University, Montreal, 136p.

Boutte, G.S., D.L. Keepler, V.S. Tyler, and B.Z. Terry. 1992. Effective techniques for involving "difficult" parents. *Young Children* 47 (3): 19–22.

Bowlby, J. 1969. *Attachment—Attachment and loss: Volume I*. London: Hogarth Press.

Bowlby, J. 1951. *Maternal care and mental health*. Geneva, Switzerland: World Health Organization.

Bradbard, M., and R. Endsley. 1980. The importance of educating parents to be discriminating day care consumers. In *Advances in early education and day care*. Vol. 2. Edited by S. Kilmer. Greenwich, CT: Jai Press.

Brammer, L.M. 1988. *The helping relationship: Process and skills*. 4th ed. Toronto: Allyn and Bacon.

Braun, K.L. and R. Nichols. 1997. Death & dying in four Asian cultures: A descriptive study. *Death Studies* 21: 37–359.

Bredekamp, S., ed. 1987. *Developmentally appropriate practice in early childhood programs serving children from birth through age 8*. Expanded ed. Washington: National Association for the Education of Young Children.

Brillhart, B. 1988. Family support for the disabled. *Rehabilitation Nursing* 13 (6): 316–19.

Brim, O.G. 1965. *Education for child rearing*. New York: Free Press.

Bromwich, R. 1981. *Working with parents and infants: An interactional approach*. Baltimore: University Park Press.

Bronfenbrenner, U. 1979. *The ecology of human development: Experiments by nature and design*. Cambridge: Harvard University Press.

———. 1986. Ecology of the family as a context for human development. *Developmental Psychology* 22 (6): 723–42.

Brooks, J.B. 1987. *The process of parenting*. 2d ed. Palo Alto, CA: Mayfield.

———. 1991. *The process of parenting*. 3d ed. Mountain View, CA: Mayfield.

Bundy, B.F. 1991. Fostering communication between parents and preschools. *Young Children* 46 (2): 12–17.

Burke, S. 1996. Perceptions of childhood family of origin well-being, self-esteem, and attitudes towards the divorced single mother. *Early Child Development and Care* 26: 83–99.

Bylund, M. 1992. Women in exile and their children. *Women and Therapy* 13 (12). Special issue: 54–63.

Byrd, B., A.P. DeRosa, and S.S. Craig. 1995. The adult who is an only child: Achieving separation or individuation. In DelCampo and DelCampo, 1995.

Canadian Child Care Federation. 1991. *National statement on quality child care*. Edited by S. Fanjoy. Ottawa: Canadian Child Care Federation.

Canadian Child Day Care Federation. N.d. Helping children understand death. By G. Garvie. Resource Sheet No. 10. Ottawa: Canadian Child Day Care Federation.

Caplan, P.J., and I. Hall-McCorquodale. 1985. Mother blaming in major clinical journals. *American Journal of Orthopsychiatry* 55 (3): 345–53.

Card, D., and P.K. Robins. 1996. *Do financial incentives encourage welfare recipients to work? Initial 18 month findings from the self-sufficiency project.* Research Papers Series/Canada. Human Resources Development Canada. Vancouver, BC: Social Research & Demonstration Corporation. Hull, PQ: Human Resources Development Canada, Strategic Policy, Applied Research Branch, July 27, 1999, viii, 55 pp.

Carter, B. and M. McGoldrick, eds. 1989. *The changing family life cycle.* 2d ed. Needham Heights, MA: Simon & Schuster.

Carter, E.A., and M. McGoldrick. 1980. *The family life cycle: A framework for family therapy.* New York: Gardner Press.

Chafel, J. 1990. Children in poverty: Policy perspectives on a national crisis. *Young Children* (July): 31–37.

Chekki, D.A. 1998. *How do Canadian cities cope with rising poverty?* Department of Sociology, University of Winnipeg, Manitoba, International Sociological Association.

Cheung, C., and E.S. Liu. 1997. Impacts of social pressure and social support on distress among single parents in China. *Journal of Divorce and Remarriage* 26 (3): 65–82.

Chud, G., and R. Fahlman. 1995. *Honouring Diversity within Early Childhood Care and Education.* British Columbia Ministry of Skills, Training and Labour and the Centre for Curriculum and Professional Development.

City of Calgary. 1985. A profile and needs assessment of Calgary's single parents. Calgary.

Clark, D., R. Shimoni, D. Este, and H. Ksienski. 1998. *The Mosaic Centre: A Family Resource Centre for Immigrants and Refugees.* Ottawa: Health Canada.

Clarke-Stewart, K.A. 1988. Evolving issues in early childhood education: A personal perspective. *Early Childhood Research Quarterly* 3: 139–49.

———. 1989. Single parent families: How bad for the children. In *Annual Editions: Early childhood education 89/90,* Article 26. Guilford, CT: Dushkin.

Clawson, M.A., and K. Bigsby. 1997. *Families of children with and without special needs: A comparison of family processes.* Paper presented at the Annual Meeting of the National Council on Family Relations (59th, Washington, DC).

Cleveland, G., & M. Krashinsky. 1998. *The Benefits and Costs of Good Child Care: A Policy Study.* Toronto: University of Toronto.

Clingempeel, W.G., E. Brand, and R. Levoli. 1984. Stepparent–stepchild relationships in stepmother and stepfather families. *Family Relations* 33: 465–73.

Cobia, D.C. 1996. Structure and characteristics of the stepfamily: Implications for counseling.

Cochran, M. 1987. The parental empowerment process: Building on family strength. *Equity and Choice* 4 (1): 9–22.

Coleman, M. 1991. Planning for the changing nature of family life in schools for young children. *Young Children* 46 (4): 15–20.

Coleman, M., and L.H. Ganong. 1991. Remarriage and step family research in the 1980s. In *Contemporary families: looking forward, looking back.* Edited by A. Booth. Minneapolis: National Council on Family Relations.

Coley, R.L., and L.P. Chase-Lansdale. 1998. Adolescent pregnancy and parenthood: Recent evidence and future directions. *American Psychologist* 53 (4): 152–166.

Collins, S. 1991. The transition from lone-parent family to step-family. In Hardey and Crow, 1991.

Conway, J.F. 1995, July 25. Canadian family under siege as neo-conservatism triumphs. *The Toronto Star.*

Coohey, C. 1998. Home alone and other inadequately supervised children. *Child Welfare* 77 (3): 291–310.

Cooksey, K. 1991. Love takes more than words. *Modern Maturity* (1991/92): 41–42.

Corbett, S. 1993. A Complicated Bias *Young Children* 48 (3) (March): 29–31.

Corwin, D.L. 1995. How to recognize and prevent child sexual abuse. In Junn and Boyatzis, 1995.

Couchman, R. 1988. Wife assault in Canada: Concern is not enough. *Transition* (September): 4–6.

————. 1994. From cloth to paper diapers and back: Reflections on fatherhood during two generations. *Transition* 24 (1).

Coughlin, C., and S. Vuchinich. 1996. Family experience in preadolescence and the development of male delinquency. *Journal of Marriage and the Family* 58: 491–501.

Cox, F.D. 1987. *Human intimacy: Marriage, the family, and its meaning*. 4th ed. St. Paul: West Publishing.

Cragg, M.I. 1996. The dynamics of welfare use in Canada. *Canadian Journal of Economics* 29: S25–S32.

Creighton, L.L. 1991. Silent saviors. In Pocs, 1993.

Crow, G., and M. Hardey. 1991. The housing strategies of lone parents. In Hardey and Crow, 1991.

Cuddy-Casey, M., H. Orvaschel, and A.H. Sellers. 1997. *A scale to measure the development of children's concepts of death*. Paper presented at the annual meeting of the American Psychological Association (105th, Chicago, IL, Aug. 15–19).

Dainton, M. 1995. The myths and misconceptions of the stepmother. In Gilbert, 1995.

Daniel, J. 1990. Child care: An endangered industry. *Young Children* 45 (4): 23–26.

De'Ath, E. 1996. Family Change—Stepfamilies in context. *Children & Society* 10 (1): 80–82.

DeAngelis, T. 1995. Homeless families: Stark reality of the 90s. In Junn and Boyatzis, 1995.

Debord, K. 1996. *Helping children cope with stress*. North Carolina State University: North Carolina Cooperative Extension Service.

Decoste, G. 1994. Talking about fatherhood. *Transition* 24 (1).

DelCampo, R.L., and D.S. DelCampo, eds. 1995. *Taking sides: Clashing views on controversial issues in childhood and society*. Guilford, CT: Dushkin.

Dembo, M.H., M. Sweitzer, and P. Lauritzen. 1985. An evaluation of group parent education: Behavioral, PET and Adlerian programs. *Review of Educational Research* 55: 155–201.

Dolny, C. 1996. A home economist speaks out: Need for a parenting course. *Canadian-Home-Journal of Economics* 46 (2): 82–84.

Dolz, L., A.M. Cwewzo, and J.S. Milner. 1997. Mother-child interactional patterns in high and low risk mothers. *Child Abuse & Neglect—The International Journal* 21 (12): 149–158.

Dooley, M.D. 1994. Women, children and poverty in Canada. *Canada Public Policy* 20 (4): 430–43.

Drakich, J., and C. Guberman. 1988. Violence in the family. In Anderson et al., 1988.

Dreikurs, R., and V. Soltz. 1964. *Children: The challenge*. New York: Knopf.

Drummond, J., G.M. Kysela, L. McDonald, J. Alexander, and D. Fleming. 1998. *Risk and resilience in two samples of Canadian families*. Funded by Health Canada: Children's Mental Health Unit, National Health Research Development Program and Alberta Heritage Foundation for Medical Research.

Duberman, L. 1977. *Marriage and other alternatives*. 2nd ed. New York: Praeger.

Duncan, G.J., J. Brooks-Gunn, and P.K. Klebanov. 1994. Economic deprivation and early childhood development. *Child Development* 65: 296–318.

Dunn, J. 1992. Siblings and development. In *Annual Editions: Child growth and development 94/95*. Article 36. Guilford, CT: Dushkin.

————. 1993. Birth order, age gap, gender and large families. In *Readings on the development of children*. Edited by M. Gauvain and M. Cole. New York: Scientific American.

Eby, L., and C.A. Donovan. 1995. Single parents and damaged children: The fruits of the sexual revolution. In Gilbert, 1995.

Egeland, B., and E.A. Farber. 1984. Infant-mother attachment: Factors related to its development and changes over time. *Child Development* 55: 753–771.

Erera, P.I. & Fredriksen, K. 1999. Lesbian stepfamilies: A unique family structure. *Families in Society: The Journal of Contemporary Human Services* (May–June): 263–271.

Erikson, E.H. 1963. *Childhood and society*. 2nd ed. New York: Norton.

Eshleman, J.R., and S.J. Wilson. 1995. *The family: Canadian edition*. Scarborough, ON: Allyn and Bacon.

Espin, O. 1992. Roots uprooted: The psychological impact: Historical and political dislocation. *Women and Therapy* 13 (12). Special Issue: 54–63.

Essa, E., and C. Murray. 1994. Young children's understanding and experience with death. *Young Children* 49 (1): 74–81.

Essa, E., and R. Young. 1994. *Introduction to early childhood education.* Scarborough, ON: Nelson.

Fahlman, R. 1992. Multicultural ECE: one step at a time. *Multiculturalism* 14 (2–3): 7–9.

Farrell, M. 1989. Separation and divorce: Implications for teachers of young children. *Canadian Child* 14 (1): 39–49.

Feeney, S., and K. Kipnis. 1989. A new code of ethics for early childhood educators! Code of ethical conduct and statement of commitment. *Young Children* 45 (1): 24–29.

Fein, G. 1980. The informed parent. *Advances in Early Education and Day Care* 1: 155–87.

Fine, M.A., L.H. Ganong, and M. Coleman. 1997. The relation between role construction and adjustment among stepfathers. *Journal of Family Issues* 18 (5): 503–525.

Fowler, N.A. 1993. Stages through which a step-mom passes in developing a mutually suitable relationship with her stepdaughter. Master's thesis, University of Alberta, Edmonton.

Fraad, 1996. At home with incest. *Rethinking Marxism* 9 (4): 16–39.

Fraser, I.H, T.A. Fish, and T.M. Mackenzie. 1995. Reactions to child custody decisions involving homosexual and heterosexual parents. *Canadian Journal of Behavioural Science* 27 (1): 52–63.

Freiner, C. & J. Cerner. 1998. *Benefiting Canada's children: Perspectives on gender and social responsibility.* Ottawa: Status of Women Canada, xiii, 101, xiii, 111p.

French, M. 1991. Becoming a lone parent. In Hardey and Crow, 1991.

Friedrich, W.N., D.H. Cohen, and L.S. Wilturner. 1987. Family relations and marital quality when a mentally handicapped child is present. *Psychological Reports* (61): 911–19.

Frieman, B.B. 1993. Separation and divorce: Children want their teachers to know—meeting the emotional needs of preschool and primary school children. *Young Children* 48 (6): 58–63.

Furman, E. 1982. Helping children cope with death. In *Curriculum planning for young children.* Edited by J.F. Brown. Washington: National Association for the Education of Young Children.

Furstenberg, F.F., and J.O. Teitler. 1994. Reconsidering the effects of marital disruption. *Journal of Family Issues* 15 (2): 173–90.

Galarneau, D. & J. Sturrock, 1997. Family income after separation. *Perspectives on labour and income* 9 (2): 18–28.

Galinsky, E. 1981. *Between generations: The six stages of parenthood.* New York: Times Books.

———. 1986. How do child care and maternal employment affect children? *Child Care Information Exchange* 48: 19–23.

———. 1988. Parents and teacher-caregivers: Sources of tension, sources of support. *Young Children* 43 (3): 4–12.

———. 1990. Why are some parent/teacher partnerships clouded with difficulties? *Young Children* 45 (5): 2–3, 38–39.

Gallagher, J.J. 1993. The future of professional/family relations in families with children with disabilities. In Paul and Simeonsson, 1993.

Ganong, L.H., and M. Coleman. 1989. Preparing for remarriage: Anticipating the issues, seeking solutions. *Family Relations* 38: 28–33.

Ganong, L.H., and M. Coleman. 1997. How society views stepfamilies. *Marriage-and-Family-Review* 26 (1–2): 85–106. *Family Journal: Counseling and Therapy for Couples and Families,* 4 (1): 37–43.

Garanzini, M.J. 1995. *Child-centered, family-sensitive schools: An educator's guide to family dynamics.* Washington, DC: National Catholic Educational Association.

Garbarino, J., et al. 1982. Who owns the children? An ecological perspective on public policy affecting children. *Child and Youth Services* 5 (1–2): 43–63.

Garret, O., N. Ng'andu, and J. Ferron. 1994. Poverty experiences of young children and the quality of their home environments. *Child Development* 65: 331–45.

Gavidia-Payne, S.,and Z. Stoneman. 1997. Family predictors of maternal and paternal involvement in programs for young children with disabilities. *Child Development* 68: 701–717.

Gestwicki, C. 1992. *Home, school and community relations.* 2d ed. New York: Delmar.

Ghazvini, A.S., and C.A. Readdick. 1994. Parent–caregiver communication and quality of care in diverse child care settings. *Early Childhood Research Quarterly* (9): 207–22.

Gilan, L. 1990. Refugees in Newfoundland: Families after flight. *Journal of Comparative Family Studies* 21 (3): 379–393.

Gilbert, K.R., ed. 1995. *Annual editions: Marriage and family 95/96.* Guilford, CT: Dushkin.

Giles-Sims, J., and M. Crosbie-Burnet. 1989. Adolescent power in stepfather families: A test of normative resource theory. *Journal of Marriage and the Family* 51: 165–78.

Gilligan, C. 1982. *In a different voice: Psychological theory and women's development.* Cambridge: Harvard University Press.

Gillis et al., eds. 1989. *Toward a science of family nursing.* California: Addison-Wesley.

Ginott, H.G. 1965. *Between parent and child.* New York: Macmillan.

Gleason, P., A. Rangarajan, and P. Schochet. 1998. The dynamics of receipt of aid to families with dependent children among teenage parents in inner cities. *Journal of Human Resources* 33 (4): 988–1002.

Glossop, R. 1992. Family definitions: What's it to me? *Transition* 22 (1): 5–9.

Glossop, R., and I. Theilheimer. 1994. Does society support involved fathering? *Transition* 24 (1).

Goetting, A. 1986. Parental satisfaction. *Journal of Family Issues* 7 (1): 83–109.

Goldenberg, I., and H. Goldenberg. 1985. *Family therapy: An overview.* 2d ed. Monterey: Brooks/Cole.

———. 1994. *Counseling today's families.* Pacific Grove, CA: Brooks/Cole.

Goldenberg, W.A., E. Greenberger, S. Hamill, and R. O'Neil. 1992. Role demands in the lives of employed single mothers with preschoolers. *Journal of Family Issues* 13 (3): 312–33.

Goldman, J.L. 1996. We can help children grieve: A child-oriented model for memorializing. *Young Children* 51 (6): 76–77.

Gonzalez-Mena, J. 1994. Learning to see across a cultural gap. *Child Care Information Exchange* 97: 65–68.

Goodwin, C., and P.M. Davidson. 1991. A child's cognitive perception of death. *Day Care and Early Education* 19 (1): 21–24.

Gordon, I.J. 1990. Parent education and parent involvement: Retrospect and prospect. In Jensen and Chevalier, 1990.

Gould, R.L. 1988. *Transformations: Growth and changes in adult life.* New York: Simon & Schuster.

Greenberg, J. 1996. Seeing children through tragedy: My mother died today—when is she coming back? *Young Children* 51 (6): 69–73.

Greenblatt, B. 1977. *Responsibility for child care.* San Francisco: Jossey-Bass.

Griffin, S. 1989. Early childhood education and care: In search of a profession. *Interaction* 3: 11–14.

———. 1993. Caring for a living in a world that just doesn't understand. *Interaction* 6: 25–28.

Gringlas, M., and M. Weintraub. 1995. The more things change... Single parenting revisited. *Journal of Family Issues* 16 (1): 29–52.

Group for the Advancement of Psychiatry (GAP). 1973. *The joys and sorrows of parenthood.* New York: Scribner.

Haberstroh, C., B. Hayslip, Jr., and P. Essandoh. 1998. The relationship between stepdaughter's self-esteem and perceived parenting behaviour. *Journal of Divorce and Remarriage* 28 (3–4): 161–175.

Hall, N.S., and V. Rhomberg. 1995. *The affective curriculum.* Scarborough, ON: Nelson.

Hallahan, D.P., and J.M. Kauffman. 1994. Toward a culture of disability in the aftermath of Deno and Dunn. *Journal of Special Education* 27 (4): 496–508.

Hardey, M., and G. Crow, eds. 1991. *Lone parenthood: Coping with constraints and making opportunities in single-parent families.* Toronto: University of Toronto Press.

Hardey, M., and J. Glover. 1991. Income, employment, daycare and lone parenthood. In Hardey and Crow, 1991.

Harms, T., and D. Cryer. 1978. Parent newsletter: A new format. *Young Children* 33 (5).

Harrigan, S. 1992. Places everyone. *Health* (Nov/Dec): 66–71.

Harrington, D., M.M. Black, R.H. Starr, Jr. and Dubowitz. 1998. Child neglect: Relation to child temperament and family context. *American Journal of Orthopsychiatry* 68 (10): 108–116.

Hart, B., P. Sainsbury, and S. Short. 1998. Whose Dying? A sociological critique of the "good death". *Mortality* 3 (1): 65–67.

Hashima, P.Y., and P.R. Amato. 1994. Poverty, social support and parental behavior. *Child Development* 65: 395–403.

Havinghurst, R.J. 1972. *Developmental tasks and education.* 3d ed. New York: McKay.

Health and Welfare Canada. N.d. Child abuse and neglect. Ottawa: National Clearinghouse on Family Violence.

Heath, H.E. 1994. Dealing with difficult behaviors: Teachers plan with parents. *Young Children* 49 (5): 20–27.

Heller, S.S., J.A. Larrieu, R. D'Imperio, and N.W. Boris. 1999. Research on resilience to child maltreatment: Empirical considerations. *Child Abuse and Neglect* 23 (4): 321–338.

Helm, J. 1994. Family theme bags: an innovative approach to family involvement in the school. *Young Children* 49 (4): 48–52.

Hendler, D.M. 1997. *Family therapy with families who have special needs children.* University of Manitoba, 127 pp.

Herrenkohl, E.C., R.C. Herrenkohl, and B.P. Egolf. 1998. The relationship between early maltreatment and teenage parenthood. *Journal of Adolescence* 21 (3): 291–303.

Hetherington, E.M., M. Cox, and R. Cox. 1982. Effects of divorce on parents and children. In *Nontraditional families: Parenting and child development.* Edited by M. Lamb. Hillsdale, NJ: Erlbaum.

Hetherington, M., M. Stanley-Hagan, and E.R. Anderson. 1995. Marital transition: A child's perspective. In Junn and Boyatzis, 1995.

Hoch, C. 1989. When scientists dissent. *Society* 26 (4): 8–11.

Hogan, D.P., D.J. Eggebeen, and C.C. Clogg. 1993. The structure of intergenerational exchanges in families. *American Journal of Sociology* 98: 1428–58.

Honig, A.S. 1984. Developmental effects on children of pregnant adolescents. *Day Care and Early Education* (fall): 20–26.

Hope Irwin, S. & Lero, D. N.d. Paid work and parenting kids with special needs [On-line]. Available: www.cbnet.ns.ca/~special link

Huston, A.C., V.C. McLoyd, and C. Garcia Coll. 1994. Children and poverty: Issues in contemporary research. *Child Development* 65: 275–82.

Ihinger-Tallman, M. & Pasley, K. 1997. Stepfamilies in 1984 and today. A scholarly perspective. *Marriage-and-Family-Review* 26 (1–2): 19–40.

Ingrassia, M., and J. McCormick. 1995. Why leave children with bad parents? In Junn and Boyatzis, 1995.

Irazuzta, J.E., J.E. McJunkin, K. Danadian, F. Arnold, and J. Zhang. 1997. Outcome and cost of child abuse. *Child Abuse and Neglect* 21 (8): 751–757.

Irwin, D.B., and J.A. Simons. 1994. *Lifespan developmental psychology.* Dubuque, IA: Brown & Benchmark.

Isolina, R. 1980. *Mom's house, Dad's house: Making shared custody work.* New York: MacMillan.

Jacobs, G. 1995. Where do we go from here? An interview with Ann Jones. In Gilbert, 1995.

Jaffe, M.L. 1991. *Understanding parenting.* Dubuque, IA: Brown & Benchmark.

Jendrek, M.P. 1993. Grandparents who parent their grandchildren: Effects on lifestyle. *Journal of Marriage and the Family* 55: 609–21.

Jensen, M.A., and Z.W. Chevalier, eds. 1990. *Issues and advocacy in early education.* Boston: Allyn and Bacon.

Johnston, L., and J. Mermin. 1994. Easing children's entry to school: Home visits help. *Young Children* 49 (5): 62–68.

Jordan, A.D. 1997. Separation, Part I: Death. *Teaching and Learning Literature with Children and Young Adults* 6 (5): 13–25.

Junn, E.N., and C.J. Boyatzis, eds. 1995. *Annual editions: Child growth and development 95/96.* Guilford, CT: Dushkin.

Kain, E.L. 1990. *The myth of family decline.* New York: Free Press.

Kaiser, J., and Rasminsky. 1993. Perceptions of well-being among child care teachers. *Early Childhood Developmental Care* 87: 15–28.

Kalmuss, D., and J.A. Seltzer. 1989. A framework for studying family socialization over the life cycle. *Journal of Family Issues* 10 (3): 339–58.

Kaplan, L., and C.B. Hennon. 1992. Remarriage education: The Personal Reflections Program. *Family Relations* 41 (2): 127–34.

Karen, R. 1994. *Becoming attached: Unfolding the mystery of the infant-mother bond and its impact on later life.* New York: Warner Books.

Katz, L.G. 1980. Mothering and teaching: Some significant distinctions. In *Current topics in early childhood education.* Vol. 3. Edited by L.G. Katz. Norwood, NJ: Ablex.

———. 1994. Parent involvement—co-op style. *Young Children* 49 (1): 2–3.

———, ed. 1977. *Current topics in early childhood education*. Norwood, NJ: Ablex.

Katzev, A.R., R.L. Warner, and A.C. Acoot. 1993. Girls or boys: Relationship of child gender to marital instability. *Journal of Marriage and the Family* 56: 89–100.

Kelly, R.F., and S.H. Ramsey. 1991. Poverty, children, and public policies: The need for diversity in programs and research. *Journal of Family Issues* 12 (4): 388–403.

Kheshgi-Genovese, Z. and T.A. Genovese. 1997. Developing the spousal relationship within stepfamilies. *Families-in-Society* 78, (3): 255–264.

King, E., M. Chipman, and M. Cruz-Janzen. 1994. *Educating young children in a diverse society*. Boston: Allyn and Bacon.

Kinnear, K. 1995. *Violent children*. Denver, CO: ABC-CLIO.

Kitson, G.C., K. Babri, M.J. Roach, and K.S. Placidi. 1989. Adjustment to widowhood and divorce: A review. *Journal of Family Issues* 10 (1): 5–32.

Kitzinger, S. 1978. *Women as mothers*. Glasgow: Fontana.

Klein, D.M., and J. Aldous, eds. 1988. *Social stress and family development*. New York: Guilford.

Klein, T., C. Bittel, and J. Molnar. 1993. No place to call home: Supporting the needs of homeless children in the early childhood classroom. *Young Children* 48 (Sept): 22–31.

Kontos, S. 1987. The additional context of family day care relationships. In Peters and Kontos, 1987.

Kontos, S., and W. Wells. 1986. Attitudes of caregivers and the day care experiences of families. *Early Childhood Research Quarterly* (1): 47–67.

Kostelnik, M.J., A.K. Soderman, and A.P. Whirin. 1993. *Developmentally appropriate programs in early childhood education*. New York: Macmillan.

Koulouras, K., M. Porter, and S. Senter. 1986. Making the most of parent conferences. *Day Care Exchange* (July).

Krishnan, V., and K.B. Morrison. 1995. An ecological model of child maltreatment in a Canadian province. *Child Abuse and Neglect* 19 (1): 101–13.

Ksienski, H. 1994. An unpublished discussion with the executive director of Calgary Immigrant Aid Society.

Kübler-Ross, E. 1969. *On death and dying*. New York: Macmillan.

———. 1974. *Questions and answers on death and dying*. New York: Macmillan.

Kurtz, L. 1994. Psychosocial coping resources in elementary school-age children of divorce. *American Journal of Orthopsychiatry* 64 (4): 554–63.

Kurtz, L., and J.L. Derevensky. 1994. Adolescent motherhood: An application of the stress and coping model to child-rearing attitudes and practices. *Canadian Journal of Community Mental Health* 13 (1): 5–25.

Lally, J.R., P.L. Mangione, and A.S. Honig. 1988. The Syracuse University Family Development Research Program: Long-range impact of an early intervention with low-income children and their families. In Powell, 1988.

Lamb, M.E. 1998. Non-parental childcare: Context, quality, correlates and consequences. In *Child psychology in practice*. Edited by I.E. Siegel and K.A. Renninger. New York: Wiley.

Larson, L.E., J.W. Golz, and C.W. Hobart. 1994. *Families in Canada: Social context, continuities, and changes*. Scarborough, ON: Prentice Hall.

Leder, J.M. 1993. Adult sibling rivalry. In *Annual editions: Personal growth and behavior 94/95*. Article 31. Guilford, CT: Dushkin.

LeFrancois, G.R. 1995. *Of children: An introduction to child development*. 8th ed. Belmont, CA: Wadsworth.

Levin, I., and J. Trost. 1992. Understanding the concept of a family. *Family Relations* 41 (3): 348–51.

Lewis, M. 1987. Social development in infancy and early childhood. In *Handbook of infant development*. Edited by J. Osofsky. New York: Wiley.

Lincoln, Y.S., and E.G. Guba. 1985. *Naturalistic inquiry*. Beverly Hills: Sage.

Lochead, C., and E.R. Shillington. 1996. *A statistical profile of urban poverty*. Ottawa: Canadian Council on Social Development, Centre for International Statistics, iv, 71pp.

Lombard, A. 1988. Home-based early childhood education programs. *International Journal of Early Childhood* 20 (2): 33–35.

———. 1994. *Success begins at home: The past, present and future of the home instruction program for preschool youngsters*. 2d ed. Guilford, CT: Dushkin.

Lowe-Vandell, D., and J. Ramanan. 1995. Does a mother's job have a negative effect on children: No. In DelCampo and DelCampo, 1995.

Luker, K. 1997. *Dubious conceptions: The politics of teenage pregnancy.* Cambridge, MA: Harvard University Press.

Lupri, E. 1991. Fathers in transition: The case of dual earner families in Canada. In Veevers, 1991.

Luster, T., H. Perlstadt, and M. McKinney. 1996. The effects of a family support program and other factors on the home environments provided by adolescent mothers. *Family Relations* 45: 255–264.

MacAuley, J. 1996. Self-help and support groups for parents of children with special needs in Canada. *Child & Family Canada* [On-line]. Available: www.cfc-efc.ca

Margolin, G. 1998. Effects of domestic violence on children. In *Violence against children in the family and community.* Edited by P.K. Trichett & C.J. Schellenbach. Washington, DC: American Psychological Association.

Margolin, L. 1992. Beyond maternal blame: physical child abuse as a phenomenon of gender. *Journal of Family Issues* 13 (3): 410–23.

Marion, M. 1973. Create a parent-space: A place to stop, look and read. *Young Children* (April).

Marks, J. 1993. "Will the kids ever adjust to our divorce?" In *Annual editions: Marriage and family 94/95.* Article 33. Guilford, CT: Dushkin.

Martin Spigleman Research Associates. 1998. *Unfulfilled expectations and missed opportunities: Poverty among immigrants and refugees in British Columbia.* Prepared for the working group on poverty. Victoria: Ministry Responsible for Multiculturalism & Immigration: Immigration, Policy, Planning & Research Division, 110 pp.

Marzollo, J. 1990. What birth order means. *Parents* (Dec).

Mattes, J. 1994. *Single mothers by choice: A guidebook for single women who are considering or have chosen motherhood.* New York: Times Books.

McBride, S.L. 1999. Family-Centered Practices. *Young Children* 54 (3): 62–69.

McCartney, K., and S. Scarr. 1989. Far from the point: A reply to Levenstein. *Child Development* 60: 517–18.

McCloskey, D., ed. 1997. Till Death Do Us Part? Divorce in Canada. *Transitions* 27 (4).

McCormick, L., and R. Holden. 1992. Homeless children: A special challenge. *Young Children* 47 (Sept): 61–67.

McDonald, W.L. & A. DeMaris. 1996. Parenting stepchildren and biological children. *Journal of Family Issues* 17 (1): 5–25.

McGoldrick, M. 1982. Overview. In *Ethnicity and family therapy.* Edited by M. McGoldrick, J.K. Pearce, and J. Giordano. New York: Guilford Press.

McKenzie, B. and I. Guberman. 1997. For the sake of the children: A program for separating and divorcing parents. *The Social Worker* 65 (3): 107–118.

Mellor, S. 1995. How do only children differ from other children? In DelCampo and DelCampo, 1995.

Meyerhoff, M.K., and B. White. 1990. New parents as teachers. In Jensen and Chevalier, 1990.

Montgomery, M.J., and E.R. Anderson. 1992. Patterns of courtship for remarriage: Implications for child adjustment and parent-child relations. *Journal of Marriage and the Family* 54: 686–98.

Morrison, G.S. 1978. *Parent involvement in the home, school, and community.* Columbus: Merrill.

National Indian Council on Aging. 1981. White House Conference on Aging: The Indian issues. *National Indian Council on Aging Quarterly* 4:1.

Needle, R.H., S.S. Su, and W.J. Doherty. 1990. Divorce, remarriage, and adolescent substance abuse: A prospective longitudinal study. *Journal of Marriage and the Family* 52 (1): 157–69.

Neisworth, J.T., and S.J. Bagnato. 1986. Curriculum-based developmental assessment: Congruence of testing and teaching. *School Psychology Review* 15 (2): 180–99.

Nickman-Steven, L., P.R. Silverman, and C. Normand. 1998. Children's construction of a deceased parent: The surviving parent's contribution. *American Journal of Orthopsychiatry* 68 (1): 126–134.

Nissivoccia, J.D. 1997. *The influence of parental separation and divorce on adolescent academic achievement: Developmental issues.* Research report, Nova Southeastern University.

Noddings, N. 1990. Feminist critiques in the professions. *Review of Research in Education* 16: 393–424.

Nuttall, D. 1993. Letters I never sent to my daughter's third grade teacher. *Young Children* 48 (6): 6.

Offord, D. 1991. Growing up poor in Ontario. *Transition* (June): 10–11.

Okun, B.F. 1996. *Understanding diverse families: What practitioners need to know.* New York: Guilford Press.

Olson, D.H., Y. Lavee, and H.I. McCubbin. 1988. Types of families. In Klein and Aldous, 1988.

Osofsky, J.D. 1994. Introduction to Caring for infants and toddlers in violent environments: Hurt, healing and hope. *Zero to Three* 14 (3): 3–7.

———, ed. 1979. *Handbook of infant development.* New York: Wiley.

Osofsky, J.D., and B.R. Jackson. 1994. Parenting in violent environments. Caring for infants and toddlers in violent environments: Hurt, healing and hope. *Zero to Three* 14 (3): 8–9.

Parke, R.D. 1981. *Fathers.* Cambridge: Harvard University Press.

Paul, J.L., P.B. Porter, and G.D. Falk. 1993. Families of children with disabling conditions. In Paul and Simeonsson, 1993.

Paul, J.L., and R.J. Simeonsson. 1993. *Children with special needs: Family, culture, and society.* 2d ed. Orlando: Harcourt Brace.

Peck, J.S., and J. Manocherian. 1989. Divorce in the changing family life cycle. In Carter and McGoldrick, 1989.

Peck, R.C. 1968. Psychological development in the second half of life. In *Middle age and aging.* Edited by B.L. Neugarten. Chicago: University of Chicago Press.

Pence, A., and H. Goelman. 1988. Parents of children in three types of day care: The Victoria Day Care Research Project. *Early Child Development and Care* 33 (1–4, April).

Peters, D.L., and S. Kontos, eds. 1987. *Continuity and discontinuity of experiences in child care.* Norwood, NJ: Ablex.

Phillips, D.A., M. Voran, E. Kisker, C. Howes, and M. Whitebook. 1994. Child care for children in poverty: Opportunity or inequity? *Child Development* 65: 472–92.

Piaget, J. 1972. Development and Learning. In *Readings in child behavior and development.* Edited by C.S. Lavetelli and F. Stendler. New York: Harcourt, Brace & Jovanovich.

Picot, G. & J. Myles. 1996. Social transfers, changing family structure and low income among children. *Canadian Public Policy* 22 (3): 244–267.

Pittman, J.F., C.A. Wright, and S.A. Lloyd. 1989. Predicting parenting difficulty. *Journal of Family Issues* 10 (2): 267–86.

Pizzo, P.D. 1993. Parent empowerment and child care regulation. *Young Children* 48 (6): 9–12.

Pocs, O., ed. 1993. *Annual editions: Marriage and family 93/94.* Guilford, CT: Dushkin.

R. Popham. 1992. Campaign 2000, Partnerships to end child poverty. *Canadian Women Studies* 12 (3).

Porter, P., D. Munn, V. Buysse, and S. Tyndall. 1996. *The effects of Smart Start on young children with disabilities & their families.* A final report. North Carolina University, Chapel Hill. Frank Porter Graham Center.

Powell, D.R. 1989. *Families and early childhood programs.* Washington: National Association for the Education of Young Children.

———, ed. 1988. *Parent education as early childhood intervention.* Norwood, NJ: Ablex.

Powell, T.H., and P. Ahrenhold Ogle. 1985. *Brothers and sisters: A special part of exceptional families.* Baltimore: P.H. Brookes.

Quine, L., and J. Pahl. 1987. First diagnosis of severe handicap: A study of parental reactions. *Developmental Medicine and Child Neurology* 29: 232–42.

Ramey, C., M. Holmberg, J. Sparling, and A. Collier. 1977. An introduction to the Carolina Abcedarian Project. In *Infant education: A guide to helping handicapped children in the first three years.* Edited by B. Calwell and D. Stedman. New York: Walker.

Rangarajan, A. and P. Gleason. 1998. Young unwed fathers of AFDC children: Do they provide support? *Demography* 35 (2): 175–186.

Read, K., P. Gardner, and B.C. Mahler. 1987. *Early childhood programs: Human relationships and learning.* 8th ed. New York: Holt, Rinehart and Winston.

Reed, S., and R. Sautter. 1991. Children of poverty: The status of 12 million young Americans. In *Annual Editions: Early childhood education 91/92.* Article 2. Guilford, CT: Dushkin.

Richardson, C.J. 1988. Children of divorce. In Anderson et al., 1988.

Riepe, L. 1990. For the benefit of all: Planning and conducting effective parent conferences. *Day Care Exchange* (74): 47–49.

Robertson, M. 1992. Birth, transformation and death of refugee identity: Women and girls of the Intifada. *Women and Therapy* 13 (12). Special Issue: 35–52.

Robinson, B., and R.L. Barret. 1986. *The developing father: Emerging roles in contemporary society*. New York: Guilford.

Robinson, B.E. 1998. Children of Workaholics: What practitioners need to know. *Journal of Child and Youth Care* 12 (4): 75–85.

Roer-Strier, D. 1999. Coping strategies of immigrant parents: Directions for family therapy. *Family Process* 35: 363–376.

Ross, D. 1998. Child Poverty in Canada: Recasting the Issue. Speaking notes, April 1998, Toronto [On-line]. Available: www://ccsd.ca/pubs/recastin.htm

Ross, D. 1996. Measuring social progress, starting with the well-being of Canada's children, youth and families. Speaking notes for Canada's Children . . . Canada's Future: A National Conference, November 25, 1996, Ottawa [On-line]. Available: www.ccsd.ca/sp_dross.htm

Ross, D.P., K. Scott, and M. Kelly, 1996. *Child poverty: What are the consequences?* Ottawa: Canadian Council on Social Development, Centre for International Statistics, iv, 30 pp.

Ruggles, S. 1997. The rise of divorce and separation in the United States, 1880–1990. *Demography 34* (4): 455–466.

Rutter, V. 1995. Lessons from stepfamilies. In Gilbert, 1995.

Ryerse, C. 1991. Poverty and child care in Canada. *Interaction* (fall): 12–14.

Sanders, J.L. and S.B. Morgan. 1997. Family stress and adjustment as perceived by parents of children with Autism or Down Syndrome: Implications for interventions. *Child and Family Behaviour Therapy* 19 (4): 15–32.

Scarr, S. 1984. *Mother care, other care*. New York: Basic.

Scarr, S., D. Phillips, and K. McCartney. 1995. Working mothers and their families. In Junn and Boyatzis, 1995.

Schorr, L.B., and D. Schorr. 1988. *Within our reach: Breaking the cycle of disadvantage*. New York: Doubleday.

Schneider, M. 1998. How divorce fuels your child's fears. *Parenting* 12 (2): 170–175.

Schwartz, M.A., and B.M Scott. 1994. *Marriages and families: Diversity and change*. Englewood Cliffs, NJ: Prentice Hall.

Sedlak, A.J. 1997. Risk factors for the occurrence of child abuse and neglect. *Journal of Aggression, Maltreatment & Trauma* 1 (1): 149–187.

Seligman, M., ed. 1991. *The family with a handicapped child*. Boston: Allyn and Bacon.

Shaw, S. 1991. The conflicting experiences of lone parenthood. In Hardey and Crow, 1991.

Shimoni, G. 1994. The relationship between father absence and juvenile delinquency. Unpublished paper, University of Calgary.

Shimoni, R. 1992. Parent involvement in early childhood education and day care. *Sociological Studies of Child Development* 5: 73–95.

Shimoni, R., and C. Barlow. 1993. Parent education and attitudes to mothers: Opposite sides of the same coin. Paper presented at the Learned Society Conference, University of Calgary.

Shimoni, R., J. Baxter, and J. Kugelmass. 1992. *Every child is special*. Don Mills, ON: Addison-Wesley.

Shimoni, R., M. Carnat, and T. Creighton. 1989. Parent involvement: An exploratory study. In *Seeds for tomorrow: Conference booklet 1989:* 25–42. Calgary: Alberta Association for Young Children.

Short, K.H., and C. Johnston. 1994. Ethnocultural parent education in Canada: Current status and directions. *Canadian Journal of Community Mental Health* 13 (1): 43–53.

Simeonsson, R.J., and N.E. Simeonsson. 1993. Children, families and disability: Psychological dimensions. In Paul and Simeonsson, 1993.

Simons, R.L. 1996. *Understanding differences between divorced and intact families: Stress, interaction and childhood outcomes*. Thousand Oaks, CA: Sage.

Skeen, P., and P.C. McKendry. 1980. The teacher's role in facilitating a child's adjustment to divorce. *Young Children* 35 (5): 3–12.

Skeen, P., B. Robinson, and C. Flake-Hobson. 1984. Blended families: Overcoming the Cinderella myth. *Young Children* 39 (Jan): 64–74.

Skolnick, A.S. 1992. *The intimate environment: Exploring marriage and the family*. 5th ed. New York: HarperCollins.

Skolnick, A.S., and J. Skolnick. 1992. *Family in transition*. 7th ed. New York: HarperCollins.

Smith, C. 1993. North American view on disability. In Paul and Simeonsson, 1993.

Smith, T. 1980. *Parents and preschool*. Ypsilanti, MI: High/Scope.

Sprang, G. 1997. PTSD in surviving family members of drunk driving episodes: Victim and crime-related factors. *Families in Society* 78 (6): 632–641.

Sprujit, E. and M.P.M. de Goede. 1997. Transitions in family structure and adolescent well-being. *Adolescence* 32: 897–911.

Standing Senate Committee on Social Affairs, Service and Technology. 1991. Children in poverty: Toward a better future. *Canadian Women Studies* 12 (4).

Starrels, M.E., S. Bould, and L.J. Nicholas. 1994. The feminization of poverty in the United States. *Journal of Family Issues* 15 (4): 590–607.

Statistics Canada, *The Daily,* Tuesday, October 14, 1997 [On-line]. Available: www.statcan.ca/daily/english/971014/a971014.htm

Steinhauer, P. 1996. *Methods for Developing Resiliency in Children from Disadvantaged Populations*. Adapted from: Summary of *Developing Resiliency in Children from Disadvantaged Populations*, by Paul D. Steinhauer. In *What Determines Health?: Summaries of a Series of Papers on the Determinants of Health*. Commissioned by the National Forum on Health, 1996.

Steinhauer, P.D. 1998. *How's a child's early experiences affect development*. Proceedings Report from *Linking Research to Practice: A Canadian Forum*. Ottawa: CCCF.

Stevens, J. 1978. Parent education programs: What determines effectiveness. *Young Children* 33: 59–65.

Stevens, J.H. 1991. Informal social support and parenting: understanding the mechanisms of support. In *Issues in early childhood curriculum*. Vol. 2. Edited by B. Spodek and O.N. Saracho. New York: Teachers College.

Stipek, D., L. Rosenblatt, and L. DiRocco. 1994. Making parents your allies. *Young Children* 49 (3): 4–9.

Stolberg, A.L., C. Camplair, K. Currier, and M.J. Wells. 1987. Individual, familial and environmental determinants of children's post divorce adjustment and maladjustment. *Journal of Divorce* 11 (1): 51–70.

Stranger, C., and T. Beatty. 1984. *Seeing infants through new eyes* (video). Washington: National Association for the Education of Young Children.

Suri, K.B. 1994. The problem of teenage pregnancy: An educational imperative. *Journal of Multicultural Social Work* 3 (3): 35–49.

Swanson, J. N.d. The ELP dictionary of social policy newspeak. Action Line social policy supplement. Vancouver: End Legislated Poverty.

Sweet, L. 1992. Stakes are high in the war over the family. *Transition* (March): 14.

Taitz, S. 1990. The new grandparents. In Pocs, 1993.

Tasker, F.L. & Golumbok, S. 1997. *Growing up in a Lesbian Family*. New York: Guilford Press.

Theilheimer, I. 1992. Are the kids alright? What's shaping the attitudes, values, and behaviours of our young people. *Transition* 22 (4).

Thomas, A., and S. Chess. 1977. *Temperament and development*. New York: Brunner/Mazel.

Tomlinson, P.S. 1986. Applying stress theory to nursing practice. *Nursing Practice* 11 (10): 76–81.

Tower, C.C. 1989. *Understanding child abuse and neglect*. Boston: Allyn and Bacon.

Tramonte, M.R. 1996. *Culturally diverse beliefs concerning dying, death and bereavement: A school psychologist's intervention*. Paper presented at the annual convention of the National Association of School Psychologists (28th, Atlanta, GA, March 14, 1996.

Trent, K., and S.L. Harlan. 1994. Teenage mothers in nuclear and extended households: Differences by marital status and race/ethnicity. *Journal of Family Issues* 15 (2): 309–37.

Turecki, S., and L. Tonner. 1989. *The difficult child*. New York: Bantam.

Turnbull, A., and H.R. Turnbull III. 1990. *Families, professionals, and exceptionality: A special partnership*. 2d ed. Columbus: Merrill.

Turner, D. 1998. Child Hunger in Canada. *Perception* 22 (Dec)(3): 5–7.

Umberson, D., and C.L. Williams. 1993. Divorced fathers: Parental role strain and psychological distress. *Journal of Family Issues* 14 (3): 378–400.

Van Wyk, J.D., M.E. Eloff, and P.M. Heyns. 1983. The evaluation of an integrated parent-training program. *Journal of Social Psychology* 121: 273–81.

Vanier Institute of the Family. 1994. *Profiling Canada's families*. Ottawa: Vanier Institute of the Family.

Veevers, J. ed. 1991. *Continuity and change in marriage and family*. Toronto: Holt, Rinehart and Winston.

Visher, E.B., and J.S. Visher. 1989. *Parenting coalition after remarriage: Dynamics and therapeutic guidelines*. New York: Norton.

Wald, E. 1981. *The remarried family: Challenge and promise*. New York: Family Service Association of America.

Wallach, L. 1997. *Violence and young children's development*. ERIC Digest. Champaign, IL: ERIC Clearinghouse on Elementary and Early Childhood Education.

Wallach, L.B. 1995. Helping children cope with violence. In Gilbert, 1995.

Wallerstein, J.S. 1991. The long-term effects of divorce on children: A review. *Journal of the American Academy of Child and Adolescent Psychiatry* 30: 349–60.

Ward, M. 1994. *The family dynamic: A Canadian perspective*. Scarborough, ON: Nelson.

Weber, C.U., P.W. Foster, and D.P. Weikart. 1978. *An economic analysis of the Ypsilanti Perry Preschool Project*. Monograph No. 5 of the Educational Resources Foundation. Ypsilanti, MI: High/Scope.

Weber, J.A., and D.G. Fournier. 1986. Death in the family: Children's cognitive understanding and sculptures of family relationship patterns. *Journal of Family Issues* 7 (3): 277–96.

Weibel-Orlando, J. 1990. Grandparenting styles: Native American perspectives. In *The cultural context of aging*. Edited by J. Sokolovsky. New York: Bergin and Garvey.

Weikart, D. 1989. *Quality preschool programs: A long-term social investment*. Occasional Paper No. 5. New York: Ford Foundation.

Weiser, M.G. 1991. *Infant/toddler care and education*. 2d ed. New York: Macmillan.

Welfare Canada. *Poverty Profile 1992*. A report by the National Council. Ottawa.

Wells, L.E., and J.H. Rankin. 1991. Families and delinquency: Meta-analysis of the impact of broken homes. *Social Problems* 31 (8): 71–93.

Whiteside-Mansell, L., S. Pope, and H. Bradley-Robert. 1996. Patterns of parenting behaviour in young mothers. *Family Relations* 45: 273–281.

Wilken, C.S. & J. Powell. 1998. Learning to live through loss: Helping children understand death. Reprinted with permission from the National Network for Child Care [On-line]. Available: www.exnet.iastate.edu/pages...ncc/Guidance/understand.death

Wilson, L. 1997. *Partnerships: Families and communities in Canadian early childhood education*. Toronto, ON: ITP Nelson.

Wolf, L., S. Fishman, & D. Ellison. 1998. Effects of sibling perception of differential parental treatment in sibling dyads with one disabled child. *Journal of the American Academy of Child and Adolescent Psychiatry* 37 (12): 1317–1325.

Wrigley, J. 1989. Do young children need intellectual stimulation? Experts' advice to parents. *History of Education Quarterly* 4: 173–79.

Wylie, B.J. 1992. What is a family? *Transition* 22 (1): 10–13.

Zastrow, C., and K. Kirst-Ashman. 1994. *Understanding human behavior and the social environment*. Chicago: Nelson-Hall.

Zinsser, C. 1990. The disgrace of child care salaries. In Jensen and Chevalier, 1990.

Index

chameleon metaphor, 211
child abuse
    accessing expert help, 203
    caregiver's emotional response to, 198
    characteristics of victims, 194–195
    defining, 186–191
    developmental effects of, 195–196
    disclosure by child, 201–202
    emotional abuse, 187, 189
    intervention, 197
    monitoring potentially abusive situations, 198–199
    negative attitudes, 198
    neglect, 187, 190, 199
    ongoing support to child, 202
    personal attributes of abuser, 193–194
    physical abuse, 187, 188
    preventions, 203
    professional development, 203
    repercussions of reporting, 200
    reporting, 186, 199–200
    sexual abuse, 187, 189–190, 194
    signs of, 187–190
    social conditions associated with, 191–192
    special needs children, 195
    statistics, 186
    understanding, 187–191
    vulnerability, 194
    witnessing violence, 195
    women and, 191–192
    working with other professionals, 202–203
childrearing issues, 94
children
    adolescent. *See* adolescent children
    adoption, effect of, 218
    attending funerals, 180–181
    benefits of parent-staff collaboration, 300
    birth of, 43–44
    blended families, 91–92
    and death, 168, 171–175, 178–180
    "difficult," 129
    disclosure of abuse, 201–202
    and divorce. *See* divorce
    equal treatment, 256
    older, 46
    poverty, 154, 157
    preschool. *See* preschool children
    refugee experiences, 208–209
    resilience, 226–229
    school-age. *See* school-age children
    and single-parent families, 103–104
    special needs. *See* special needs children
    stages of grieving, 175
    trauma of war, 208–209
    witnessing violence, 195
    young, 45
closed adoption process, 219
cognitive development
    attachment, 59–60
    brain, 60
    early years, 57–59
    emotional, 60
    infants, 57–58

    preschool children, 58
    school-age children, 59
cohabiting couples, 5
collaboration with parents. *See* parent involvement; parent-staff collaboration
communication, 270–271
    bulletin boards, 272–273
    communication books, 275–277
    daily conversations, 271–272
    daily notes, 274–275
    direct, 271–272
    "goodie bags," 278, 280
    newsletters, 277–278, 279
    parent corners, 273–274
    telephone, 272
    written, 272–280
communication books, 275–277
community relations, 301–302
community resources, 287–289
conflict resolution
    compromise, 261
    cultural differences, 263
    empathy training, 263–264
    humility, 262
    informing parents, 262
    limit recognition, 264
    parent involvement, 262
    policies, 262
    religious differences, 263
    techniques for, 259–260
    understanding, 261
    unspoken attitudes, 261
    "win-win" solutions, 262–263
consumer movement, 238
continuity of care, 240–243
costs, 292
"creating bridges," 240–243
cuckoo-bird metaphor, 210–211
cultural beliefs
    acknowledging diversity, 242–243
    divorce, 77
    family development theory, 48
    grandparent role, 39
    immigrant families, 210
    and parenting, 51
    prejudgments, 251
    respect for, 263
    sibling rivalry, 37
    special needs children, 132
cultural sensitivity, 290–291
custody arrangements, 72–73
custody disputes, 223, 224

D

daily conversations, 271–272
daily notes, 274–275
death
    acceptance, 171
    adjustment, 171
    adult psychological responses, 170–171
    anger, 171